BEST OF ARCHITECTS' WORKING DETAILS
Volume 1: EXTERNAL

BEST OF ARCHITECTS' WORKING DETAILS
Volume 1: EXTERNAL

Colin Boyne CBE HonFRIBA
Lance Wright RIBA

Butterworth Architecture

London   Boston   Sydney   Singapore   Toronto   Wellington

Butterworth Architecture
is an imprint of Butterworth Scientific

 PART OF REED INTERNATIONAL P.L.C.

All rights reserved. No part of this publication may be reproduced or transmitted in any form or by any means (including photocopying and recording) without the written permission of the copyright holder except in accordance with the provisions of the Copyright Act 1956 (as amended) or under the terms of a licence issued by the Copyright Licensing Agency, 33–34 Alfred Place, London, England WC1E 7DP. The written permission of the copyright holder must also be obtained before any part of this publication is stored in a retrieval system of any nature. Applications for the copyright holder's written permission to reproduce, transmit or store in a retrieval system any part of this publication should be addressed to the publisher.

Warning: The doing of an unauthorised act in relation to a copyright work may result in both a civil claim for damages and criminal prosecution.

This book is sold subject to the Standard Conditions of Sale of Net Books and may not be re-sold in the UK below the net price given by the Publishers in their current price list.

First published in 1982 by the Architecture Press Ltd. This reprint published by Butterworth Architecture 1988

© **Butterworth & Co. (Publishers) Ltd, 1982**

ISBN 085139 766 2

Library of Congress Cataloging in Publication Data

Boyne, Colin.
   Best of Architects' working details.

   Includes indexes.
   Contents: v. 1. External —v. 2. Internal.
   1. Architecture—Details. I. Wright, Lance. II. Title.
NA2840.B682 1982   729   82-10606
ISBN 0-89397-142-1

Printed in Great Britain by
Anchor Brendon Ltd., Tiptree, Essex

FOREWORD

The object of the original series of *Architects' Working Details*, published first in the weekly *Architects' Journal* and then as a set of 15 books by the Architectural Press, was to find the equivalent to the professional and scientific tradition of precedent in medicine and law, built up through the exchange of information. The working details were intended both to cover everyday design problems and to record the latest stage in the development of a design solution and so provide the architect with a starting point from which he could develop his own improvements.

This selection of some 100 details (there is a further set of 100 in the companion volume to this book), from over 1600 originally published between 1953 and 1971, is intended to reflect those original aims. Some are chosen as classic examples of good design of everyday architectural elements. Others have been selected because they represented, at the time of their design, the latest stage in the development of a design problem. Inevitably some of the details shown reflect the interests of their time, which are not necessarily those of today – for instance, the preoccupation with the curtain wall, and the abundance of canopies (now reduced to a few classic examples).

The popularity of the original series, year after year, shows how great a gap it filled. Similarly this selection should be an essential document for those who do not have the original series of *Architects' Working Details*.

The Publishers

CONTENTS

WALLS

Copper-faced wall: University of Durham. *J. S. Allen, architect; Oscar Faber and Partners (consulting engineers)*   2

Tile hung wall panels: Flats at Richmond. *Eric Lyons, architect*   4

Louvred cladding: Timber drying store, Aldenham, Herts. *Thomas Bilbow, architect; K. J. H. Seymour (architect-in-charge)*   6

Factory cladding: Factory at Hemel Hempstead, Herts. *Ove Arup and Partners, designers; Philip Dowson and Francis Pym (architects-in-charge)*   8

Wall panels: Police headquarters at Wellington, Salop. *C. H. Simmons, architect*   10

Cladding: Factory at Heidelberg, Germany. *Ernst Neufert, architect*   12

Slate facing: Hospital at Swindon. *Powell and Moya, architects*   14

Wall: Warehouse in Zurich, Switzerland. *Otto Glaus, architect*   16

Glazed wall: Technical school at Delft, Holland. *J. H. Van Den Broek and J. B. Bakema, architects*   18

Concrete wall: Church in Rotterdam, Holland. *J. H. Van Den Broek and J. B. Bakema, architects*   20

Glass curtain wall: Office building in New York, U.S.A. *Skidmore, Owings and Merrill, architects*   22

Glazed wall: Technological Institute, Chicago, U.S.A. *Mies Van Der Rohe, architect*   24

Glazed wall: Office block in Stockholm, Sweden. *Sven Markelius, architect*   26

Curtain wall: Office building in Copenhagen, Denmark. *Arne Jacobsen, architect*   28

Curtain wall: Office building in Sarnia, Ontario, Canada. *John B. Parkin Associates, architects*   30

Curtain wall: College at Slough, Bucks. *F. B. Pooley, architect*   32

Glazed wall: School in London, W.C.1. *Hubert Bennett, architect*   34

Curtain wall: Offices in New York, U.S.A. *Mies Van Der Rohe and Philip Johnson, architects*   36

Curtain wall: Department store in Denver, Colorado, U.S.A. *I. M. Pei, architect*   38

Curtain wall: Offices in Creve Coeur, Missouri, U.S.A. *Vincent J. Kling, architect*   40

Glazed wall: Offices in London, N.W.1. *Gollins, Melvin, Ward and Partners, architects*   42

Curtain wall: Deckel Building, Munich, Germany. *Walter Henn, architect*   44

Curtain wall: Embassy in Athens, Greece. *Walter Gropius, architect*   46

Glazed wall: Museum of Fine Arts, Expo, Osaka, Japan. *Kiyoshi Kawasaki, architect*   48

Façade: Time and Life Building, Chicago, U.S.A. *Harry Weese and Associates, architects*   50

Window wall: Coliseum Arena, Nimitz Freeway, Oakland, California, U.S.A. *Skidmore, Owings and Merrill, architects*   52

Glazed wall: Exhibition Hall in Rotterdam, Holland. *J. H. Van Den Broek and J. B. Bakema, architects*   54

Glass wall to boiler house: Factory at Hemel Hempstead, Herts. *Ove Arup and Partners, designers; Philip Dowson and Francis Pym (architects-in-charge)*   56

Screens: Office building in Don Mills, Ontario, Canada. *John B. Parkin Associates, architects*   58

External sun visor and platform: Metropolitan Water, Sewerage and Drainage Board, Sydney, Australia. *McConnel, Smith and Johnson, architects*   60

External wall: Metropolitan Water, Sewerage and Drainage Board, Sydney, Australia. *McConnel, Smith and Johnson, architects*   62

BALCONIES

Balcony and windows: House near Halland, Sussex. *Serge Chermayeff, architect*   64

Wall and balconies: Maisonettes in London, S.W.1. *Powell and Moya, architects*   66

CONTENTS

Balconies: Flats in London, S.W.1. *Powell and Moya, architects* — 68
Balcony: Cricket Pavilion at East Molesey. *Basil Ward, architect* — 70
Balustrade: School in London, E.5. *J. M. Austin-Smith and Partners, architects* — 72
Balconies: Flats in Helsinki, Finland. *Viljo Revell, architect* — 74
Balcony façade: Asker Town Hall, near Oslo, Norway. *Nils Slaatto and Kjell Lund, architects* — 76

STAIRCASES

Spiral staircase: Offices in Copenhagen, Denmark. *Eske Kristensen and E. Barfoed, architects* — 78
Fire-escape staircase: Tower in Geneva, Switzerland. *A. Bordigoni, J. Gros, A. de Saussure and R. Fleury, architects* — 80

ROOFS

Roof: Factory at Hemel Hempstead, Herts. *Ove Arup and Partners, designers; Philip Dowson and Francis Pym (architects-in-charge)* — 82
Roof truss: Chapel at Otaniemi, Finland. *Heikki Siren, architect* — 84
Roof: Factory in Dublin. *Ove Arup and Partners, designers* — 86
Roof: Factory at Poole, Dorset. *Farmer and Dark, architects* — 88
Monitor roof: Factory in London, E.8. *Walter Segal, architect* — 90
Monitor roof: Factory at Gotham, Notts. *Bartlett and Gray, architects* — 92
Timber roof: Farm near Sutton, Suffolk. *C. H. Smith and Partner, designers* — 94
Roof: Music bowl in Melbourne, Australia. *Yuncken, Freeman Brothers, Griffiths and Simpson, architects* — 96
Northlight roof: Factory in Gossau, Switzerland. *Danzeisen and Voser, architects* — 98
Timber roof: Snack bar near Athens, Greece. *P. A. Sakellarios, E. Vourekas, and P. Vasiliades, architects* — 100
Monitor roof: Library at St Austell, Cornwall. *F. Kenneth Hicklin, architect* — 102
Roof: Kindergarten, St Ives, Sydney, Australia. *Callard, Clarke and Jackson, architects* — 104
Roof: Factory at Vich, Barcelona, Spain. *Miguel Fisac, architect* — 106
Rooflight: Community hall at Hatfield. *Lionel Brett and Kenneth Boyd, architects* — 108
Monitor rooflight: Art gallery in Copenhagen, Denmark. *Jørgen Bo and Vilhelm Wohlert, architects* — 110
Laylight: Monastic church at Saunen, Obwalden, Switzerland. *Naef, Studer and Studer in association with G. Zimmerman, architects* — 112

WINDOWS

Window wall: Laboratory building in Illinois, U.S.A. *Holabird and Root, and Burgee and Associates, architects* — 114
Sliding windows: House at Kingston, Surrey (now Greater London). *E. Maxwell Fry, architect* — 116
Windows: Flats in London, S.W.1. *Powell and Moya, architects* — 118
Glazed wall: Surgery in doctor's house, Detroit, Michigan, U.S.A. *Leineweber, Yamasaki and Hellmuth, architects* — 120
Windows: School in London, W.C.1. *Hubert Bennett, architect* — 122
Display window: Sweden House, Stockholm, Sweden. *Sven Markelius, architect* — 124
Glazed wall: House at Dusseldorf, Germany. *B. M. Pfau, architect* — 126
Window wall: School at Oldbury, Worcester. *F. R. S. Yorke, E. Rosenberg and C. S. Mardall in association with F. W. B. Yorke and H. M. Barber, architects* — 128
Window: Hospital in Swindon. *Powell and Moya, architects* — 130
Sliding windows: House near Halland, Sussex. *Serge Chermayeff, architect* — 132
Bay window: Studio in Bristol. *R. Towning Hill and Partners, architects* — 134
Window: Offices in London, W.C.1. *David du R. Aberdeen and Partners, architects* — 136
Window in flat: College in Oxford. *Architects' Co-Partnership, architects* — 138
Window: College in Oxford. *Architects' Co-Partnership, architects* — 140
Glazed wall: Hospital in Swindon. *Powell and Moya, architects* — 142
Window: College in London, S.W.7. *Richard Sheppard, Robson and Partners, architects* — 144
Glazed wall: House at Uppsala, Sweden. *Hans Matell, Viking Göransson, Carl-Eric Nohldén and Ulla Hansen-Campbell, architects* — 146
Bay windows: House in London, N.W.3. *Architects' Co-Partnership, architects* — 148
Windows: Offices in London, N.W.9. *Walter Segal, architect* — 150

CONTENTS

Windows: Hospital in London, S.E.1. *W. G. Holford and L. G. Creed, architects* 152
Windows: Flats in London, S.W.1. *Walter Segal, architect* 154
Windows: Flats in London, S.W.3. *Walter Segal, architect* 156
Window: School at Amersham, Bucks. *Chief Architect's Department, M.O.E., in collaboration with the County Architect, Buckinghamshire C.C.; J. S. B. Coatman, Mary B. Crowley, David L. Medd and C. E. D. Wooster (architects-in-charge)* 158
Windows: Offices in Helsinki, Finland. *Alvar Aalto, architect* 160
External wall: Offices in Helsinki, Finland. *Alvar Aalto, architect* 162
Glazed wall: Offices in Athens, Greece. *Doxiades Associates, architects* 164
Window and door, Audiometry room: Hospital in London, W.C.1. *Easton and Robertson, architects* 166
Acoustic window: Concert hall in Copenhagen, Denmark. *Frits Schlegel and Hans Hansen, architects* 168

DOORS

Glazed entrance doors and screen: Society headquarters, London, N.W.1. *John and Elizabeth Eastwick-Field in collaboration with Hugh Pite, architects* 170
Entrance doors: Offices at Bristol. *Leonard Manasseh and Partners, architects* 172
Entrance door: Hospital in London, N.W.3. *John Lacey, architect* 174
Entrance door: Magistrates' Court at Slough, Bucks. *F. B. Pooley, architect* 176
Wrought iron gate: College in Oxford. *Architects' Co-Partnership, architects* 178
Entrance door to flat: College in Oxford. *Architects' Co-Partnership, architects* 180
Door and screen: College in Oxford. *Architects' Co-Partnership, architects* 182
Main entrance doors: Law Courts, Tel-Aviv, Israel. *Rechter and Zarchi, architects* 184
External doors: School at Hyvinkää, Finland. *Marjo and Keijo Petaja, architects* 186
Security doors: Summer house at Tisvilde, Denmark. *Vilhelm Wohlert, architect* 188
Revolving door: Massachusetts Institute of Technology, Cambridge, Massachusetts, U.S.A. *I. M. Pei and Partners, architects* 190
Glazed sliding doors: House in Florida, U.S.A. *Ralph S. Twitchell and Paul Rudolph, architects* 192
Sliding door: House in California, U.S.A. *Richard J. Neutra, architect* 194

COVERED WAYS AND CANOPIES

Orchestra canopy: Royal Festival Hall. *Robert H. Matthew and J. L. Martin, architects; Edwin Williams (senior architect-in-charge); Peter Moro (associated architect)* 196
Canopy: London Airport. *Frederick Gibberd, architect* 198
Canopy: Factory at Aalborg, Denmark. *Preben Hansen, architect* 200
Canopy over entrance: Town Hall at Rødovre, Denmark. *Arne Jacobsen, architect* 202
Canopy: Office block in Vevey, Switzerland. *J. Tschumi, architect* 204
Entrance canopy: Embassy in Athens, Greece. *Walter Gropius, architect* 206
Entrance canopy: Museum in Oslo, Norway. *Eliassen and Lambertz-Nilssen, architects* 208
Canopy: Tourist information pavilion, Oslo, Norway. *Odd Brochmanns, architect* 210
Connecting bridge: School at Great Missenden, Bucks. *Frederick B. Pooley, architect* 212
Light louvres: School in Fresno, California, U.S.A. *David H. Horn and Marshall D. Mortland, architects* 214

EXTERNAL FEATURES

Double-action gate: Cattle market at Gloucester. *J. V. Wall, architect* 216
Control gates: Coliseum Arena, Nimitz Freeway, Oakland, California, U.S.A. *Skidmore, Owings and Merrill, architects* 218
Garden wall: House in Berlin, Germany. *Eduard Ludwig, architect* 220
Chimeny stack and water tank: School at Oldbury, Worcester. *Yorke, Rosenberg and Mardall in association with F. W. B. Yorke and H. M. Barker, architects* 222
Tank cover and screen: School in London, W.1. *Drake and Lasdun, architects* 224
Street shelter: Stockholm, Sweden. *Stockholm Parks Department, designers* 226

GLOSSARY OF FOREIGN TERMS 228

CONVERSION TABLES 239

2 WALLS

COPPER-FACED WALL: EXTENSIONS TO UNIVERSITY OF DURHAM
DESIGNED BY J. S. ALLEN; OSCAR FABER AND PARTNERS (consulting engineers)

A copper-lined gutter behind the top of the plinth collects any rain water from the sheeting.

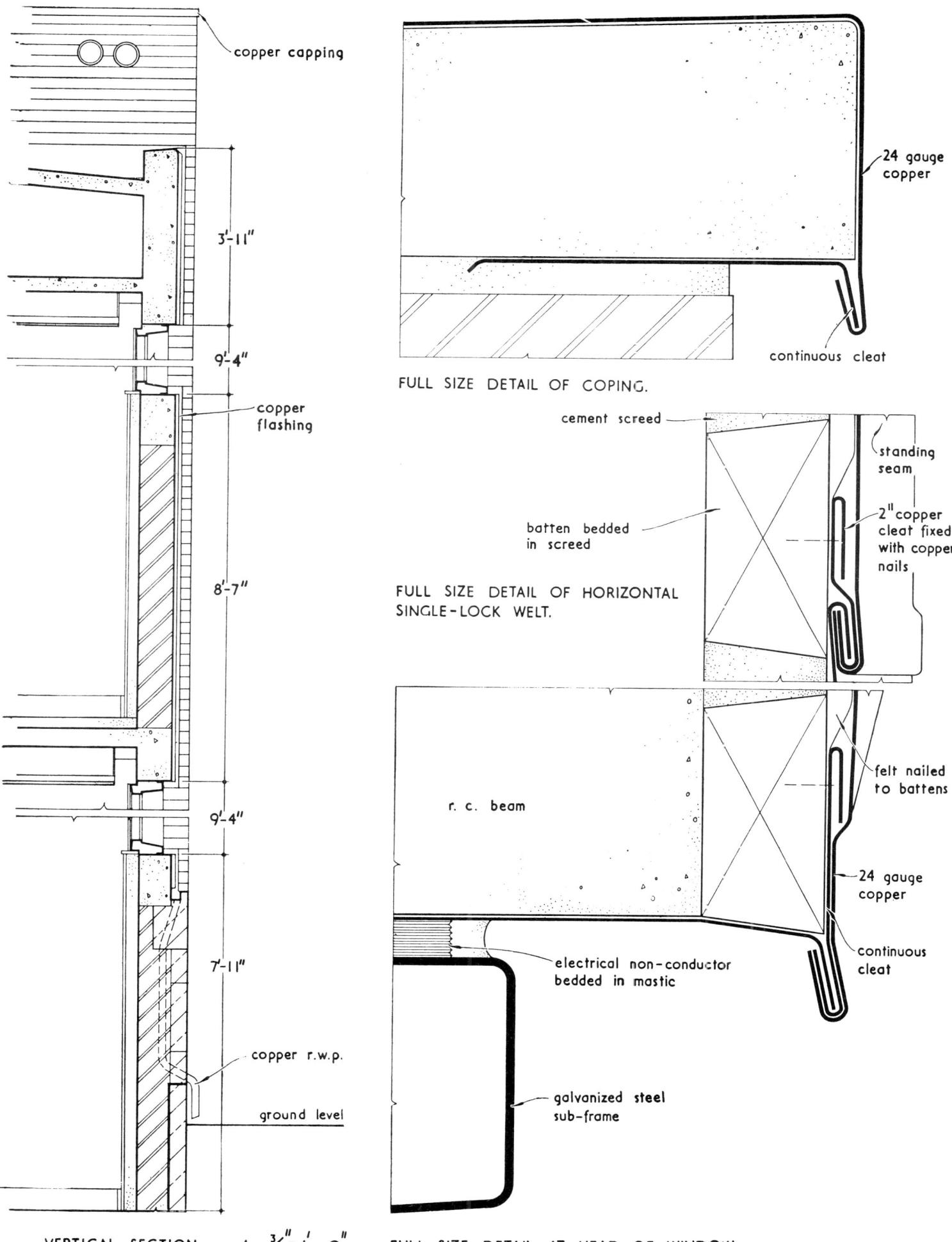

4 WALLS

TILE HUNG WALL PANELS : FLATS AT RICHMOND
DESIGNED BY ERIC LYONS

The panel wall behind the tile hanging is of timber framing with clinker block and woodwool infill. The picture-frame window is a standard heavy-section casement.

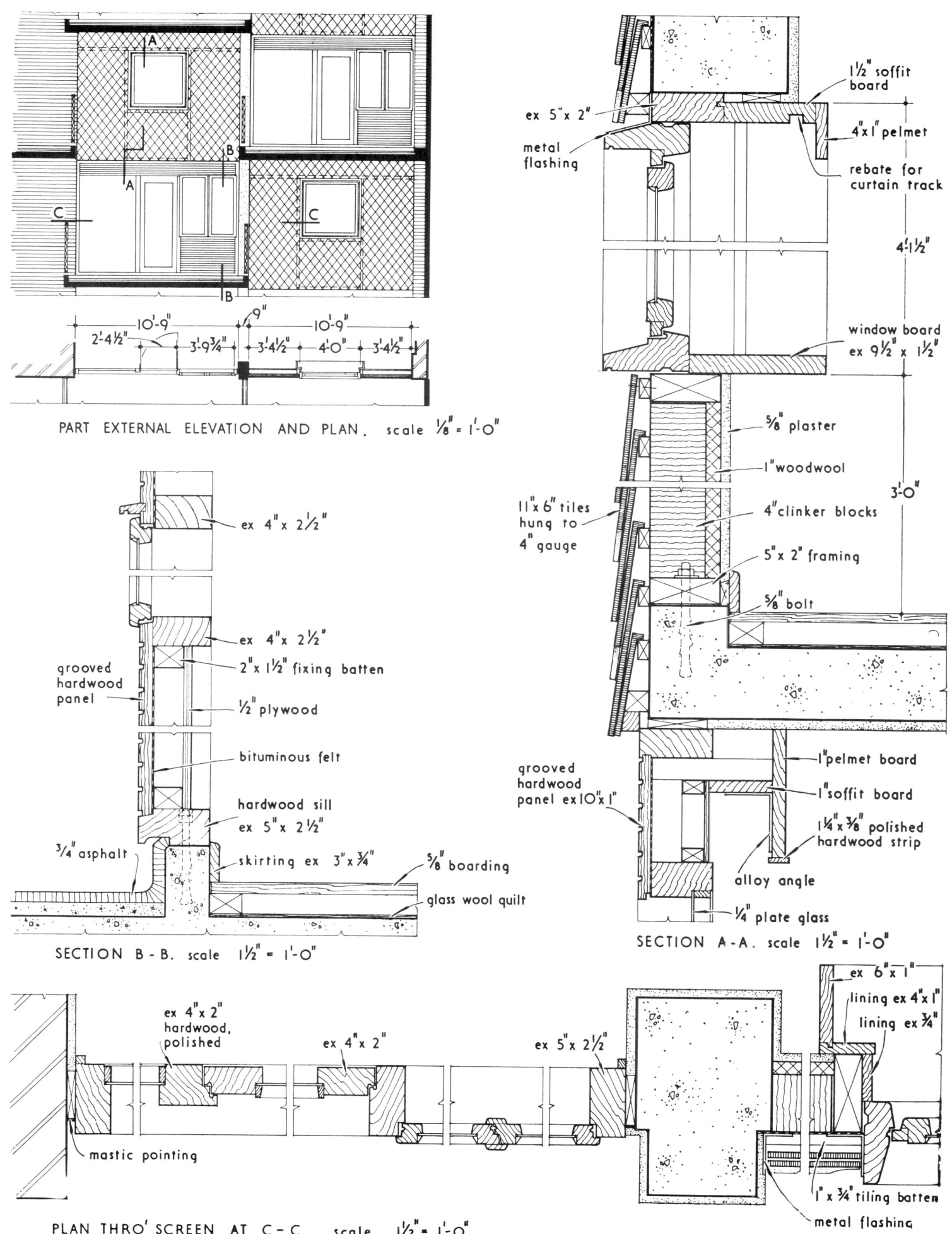

6 WALLS

LOUVRED CLADDING: TIMBER DRYING STORE, ALDENHAM, HERTS
DESIGNED BY THOMAS BILBOW (architect to the London Transport Executive); K. J. H. SEYMOUR (architect-in-charge)

Asbestos louvre blades have been used instead of wood to save maintenance and because there was no serious danger of shattering. The neat appearance is largely due to the fact that all fixing is concealed from the outside.

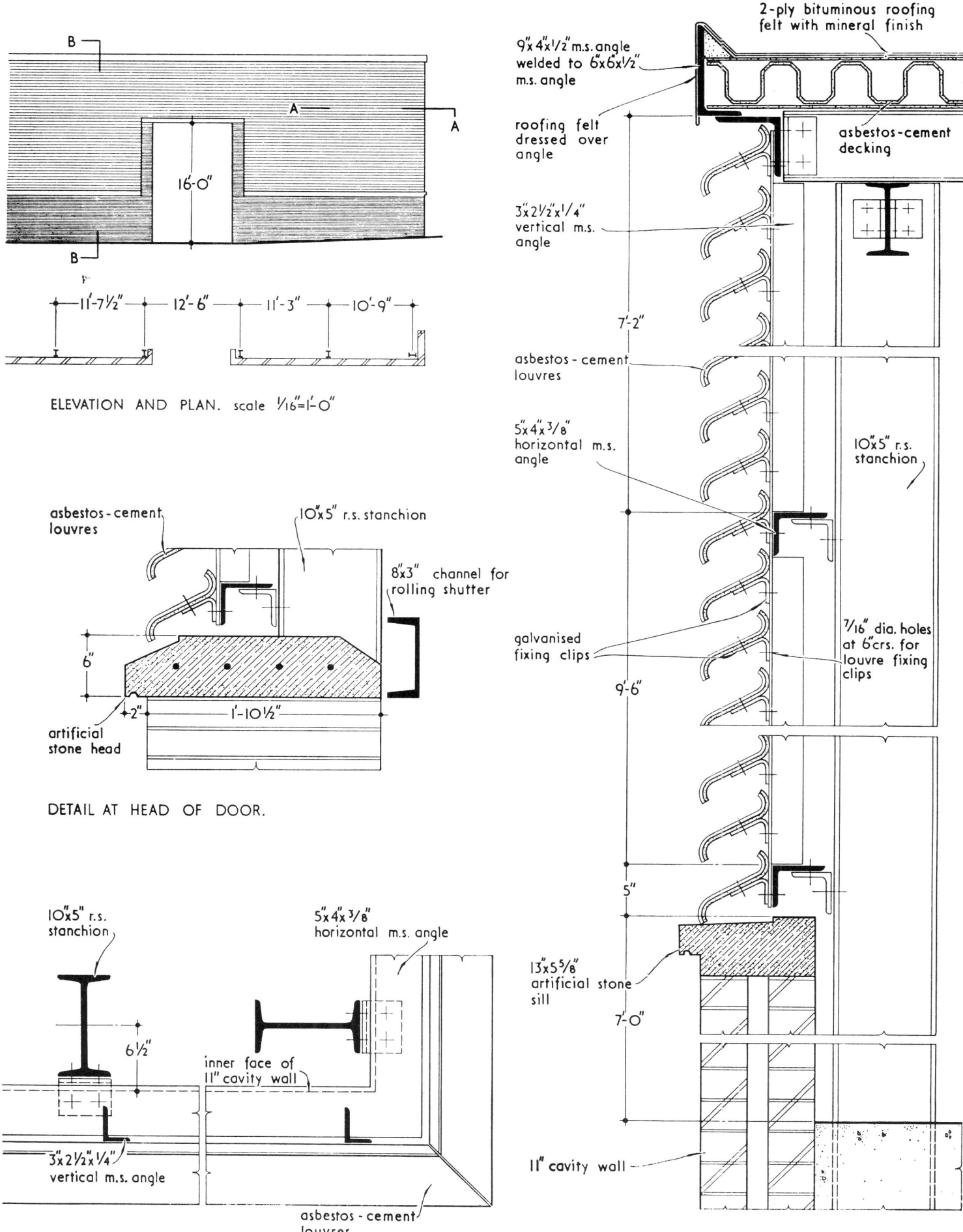

8 WALLS

FACTORY CLADDING: FACTORY AT HEMEL HEMPSTEAD, HERTS
DESIGNED BY OVE ARUP AND PARTNERS; PHILIP DOWSON AND FRANCIS PYM (architects-in-charge)

The steel trusses which provide the framing for the upper part of the wall are supported on brackets bolted to r.c. columns placed behind the inside face of the wall. The lower part of the wall is 9-in. brickwork built in two 4½-in. skins to give a fair face on both sides. The gap between the top of the wall and the bottom chord of the trusses is closed with a continuous strip of glazing held top and bottom in aluminium alloy sections, the 5-ft. long strips of glass being jointed with lead cames.

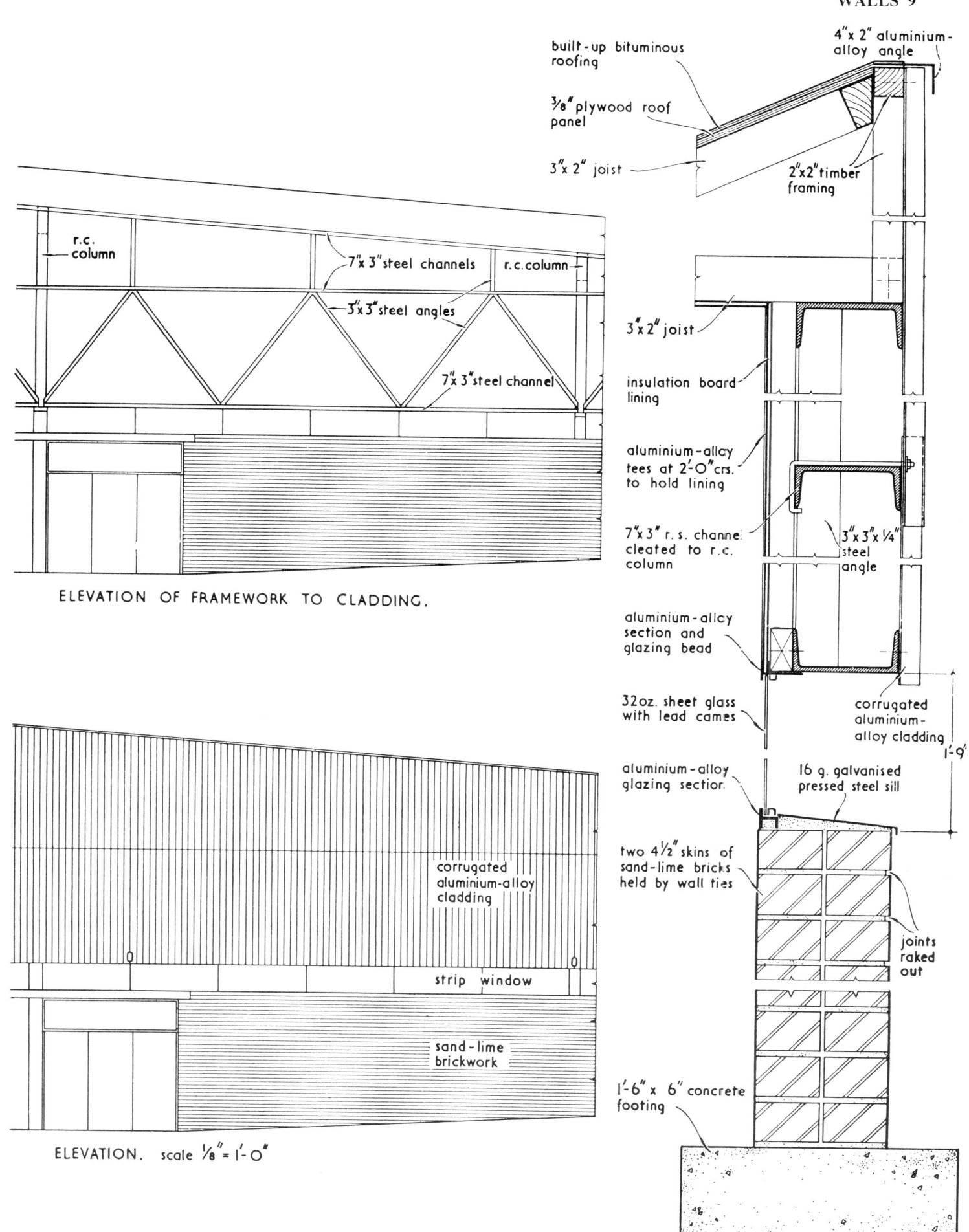

WALL PANELS: POLICE HEADQUARTERS AT WELLINGTON, SALOP
DESIGNED BY C. H. SIMMONS (architect to the Salop County Council)

The softwood frames enclosing these inset panels are fixed proud of the supporting beams and columns and are painted white so that they and not the in-situ concrete structure determine the character of the façade. A deep upstand beam is concealed behind the panel at first floor level.

WALLS 11

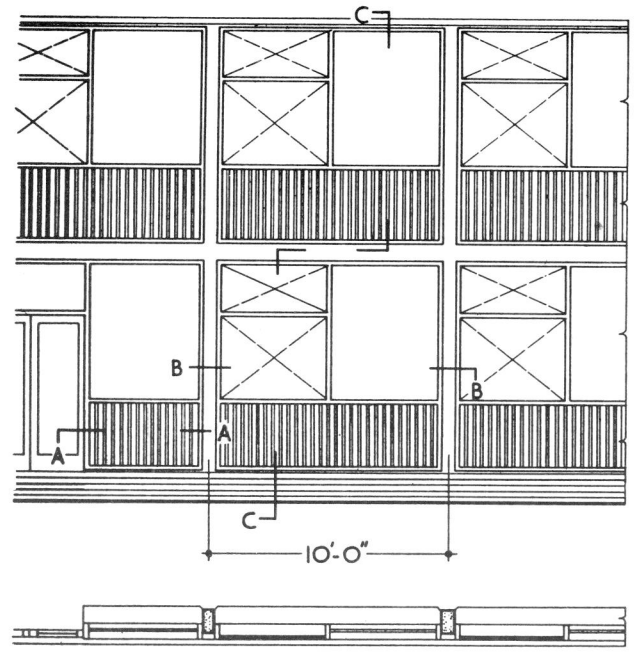

KEY ELEVATION AND PLAN. scale 1/8"=1'-0"

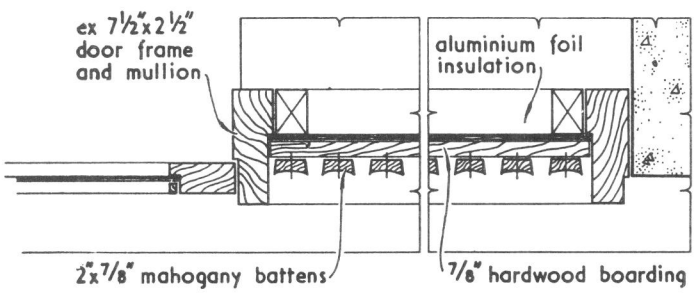

SECTION A - A.

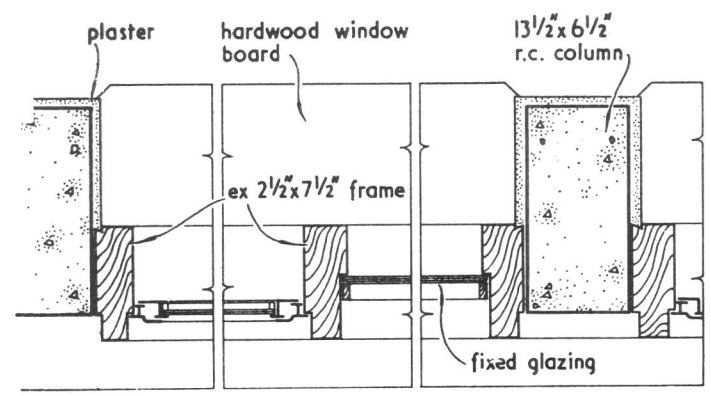

SECTION B - B.

SECTION C - C. scale 1"=1'-0"

12 WALLS

CLADDING: FACTORY AT HEIDELBERG, GERMANY
DESIGNED BY ERNST NEUFERT (*Material supplied by D. Parker*)

An interesting use of asbestos cement as cladding to an r.c. structure. This use, common in Germany, is encouraged by the well-thought-out asbestos-cement accessories obtainable there. Note the internal sill and ventilator. The gantry above the first floor is to assist maintenance and guard against breakage of the cladding.

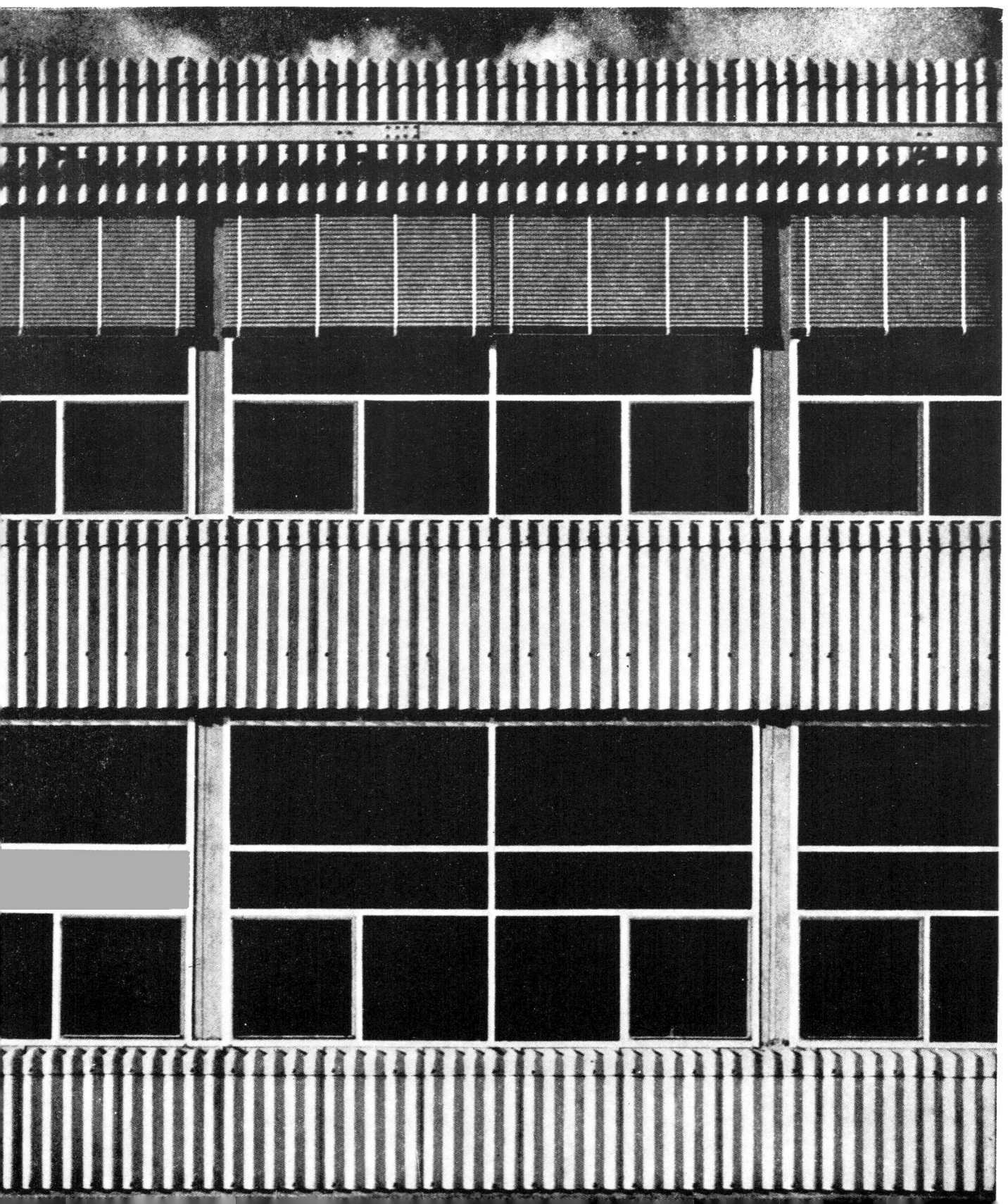

WALLS 13

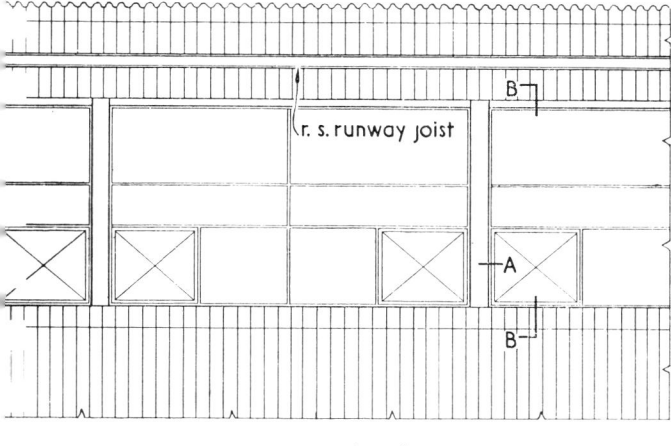

ELEVATION. scale 1/8" = 1'-0"

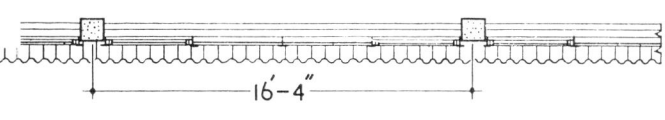

PLAN. scale 1/8" = 1'-0"

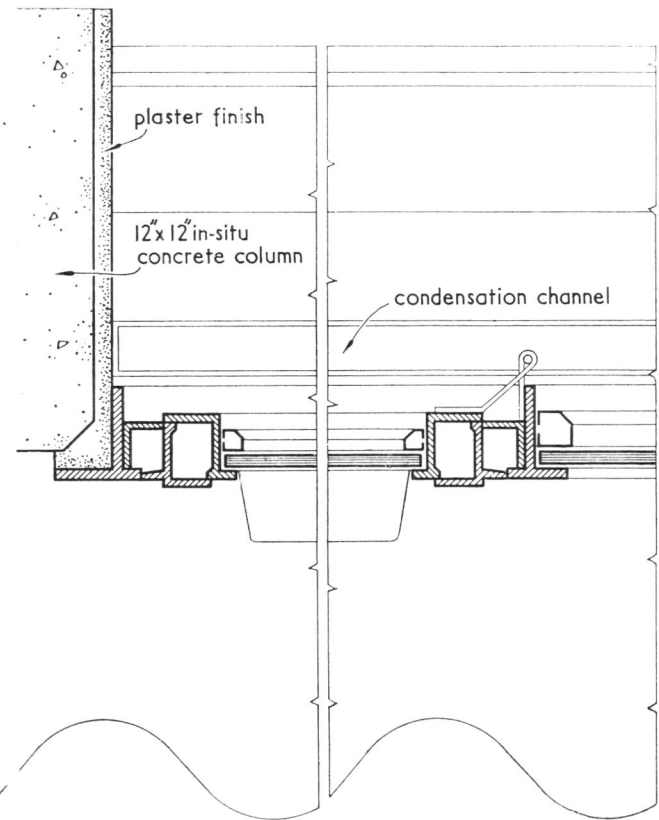

PLAN AT A. scale 1/4 full size

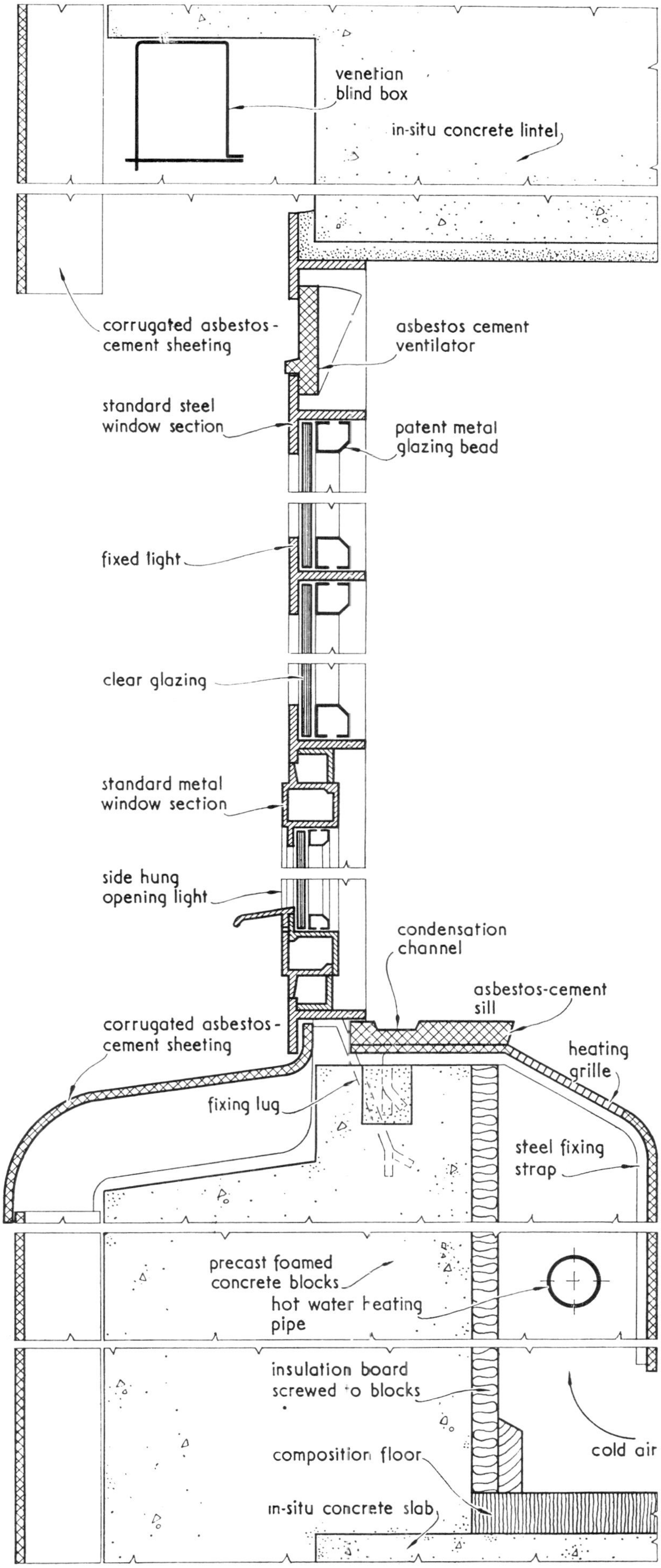

SECTION B-B. scale 1/4 full size

note. figured dimensions in feet and inches are approximate

14 WALLS

SLATE FACING: HOSPITAL AT SWINDON
DESIGNED BY POWELL AND MOYA

This example is concerned with the slate fascias and column cladding and the flashings. Note the recession to receive the flashing, a refinement made necessary by the smoothness and precision of the slate. The facing to the horizontal string at first floor level (B-B) is restrained by cramps similar to those used on the fascia (C-C).

WALLS 15

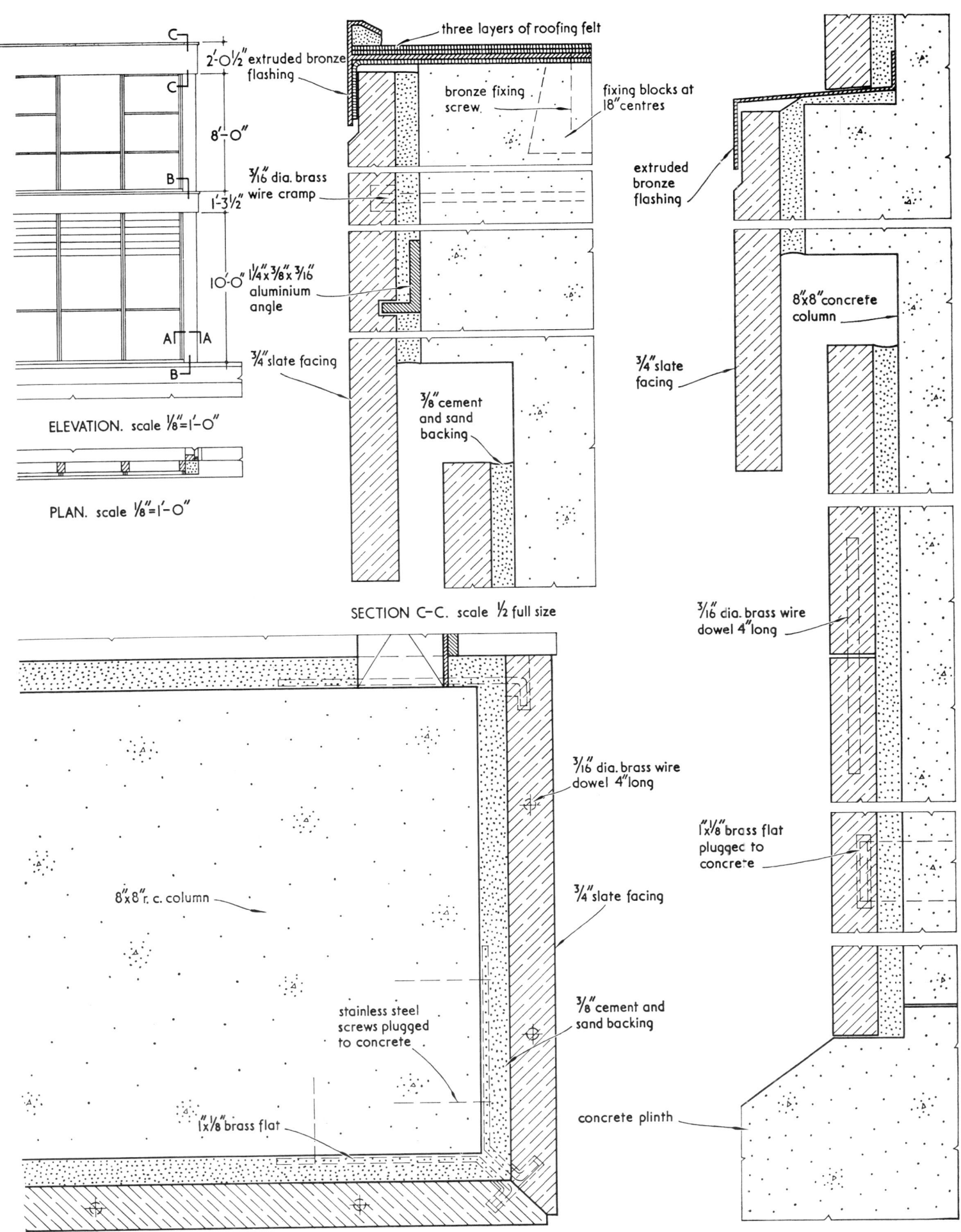

16 WALLS

WALL: WAREHOUSE IN ZURICH, SWITZERLAND
DESIGNED BY OTTO GLAUS

(Material supplied by Dariush Borbor)

The infill panels of this exceedingly interesting façade are timber framing clad with asbestos cement: flat sheets to cover the window surrounds and corrugated sheets for the sill-height cladding. These last are projected sufficiently proud of the framing to serve as a protection for the Italian-type roller blinds.

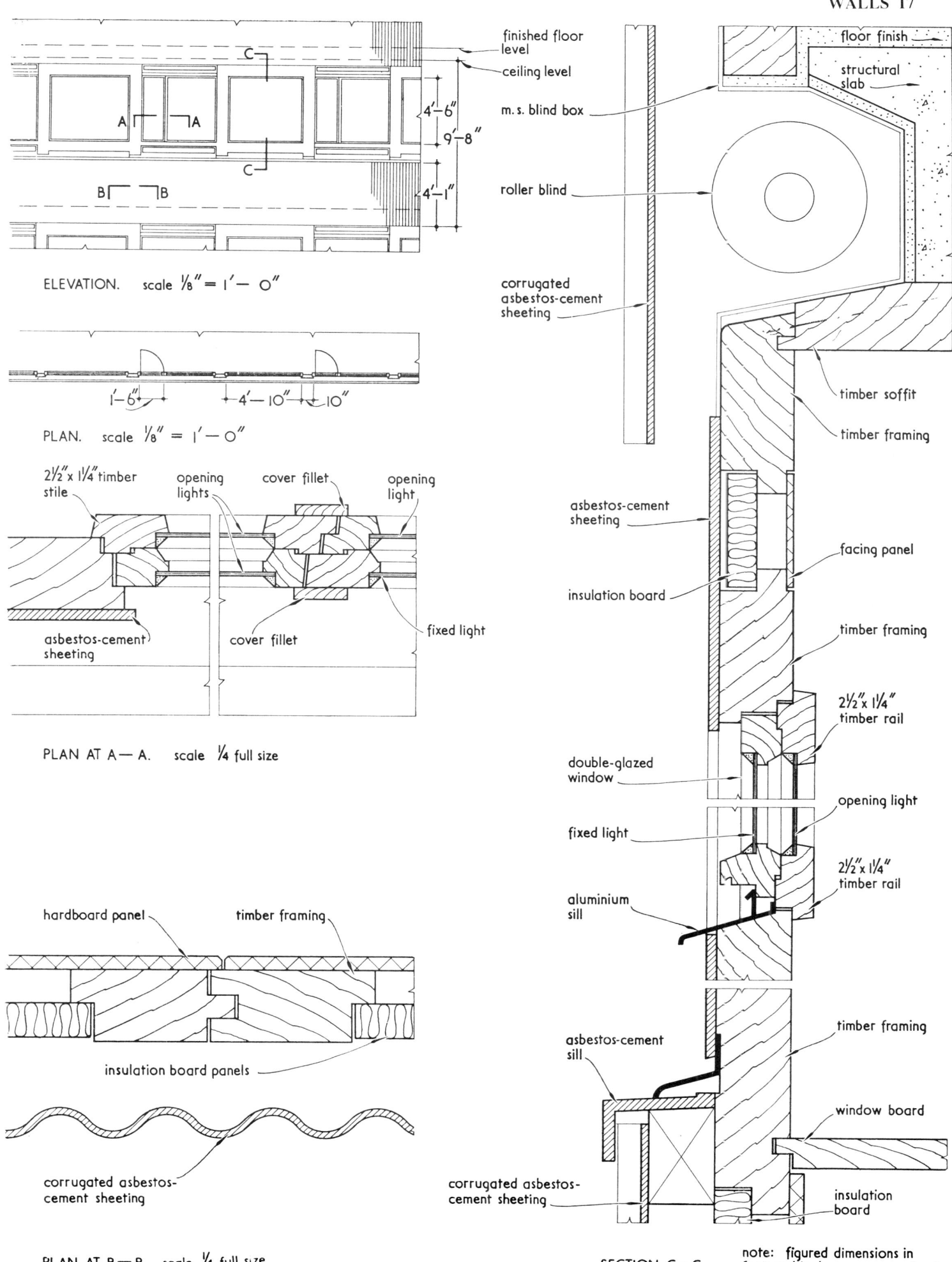

18 WALLS

GLAZED WALL: TECHNICAL SCHOOL AT DELFT, HOLLAND
DESIGNED BY J. H. VAN DEN BROEK AND J. B. BAKEMA *(Material supplied by Ranjit Sabikhi)*

This detail shows once more the excellent use Dutch architects made of precast concrete. Notice the use of chases in the transom sections to minimise the effect of the metal frames and the detail of the horizontal sash which opens by sliding outside the fixed sash.

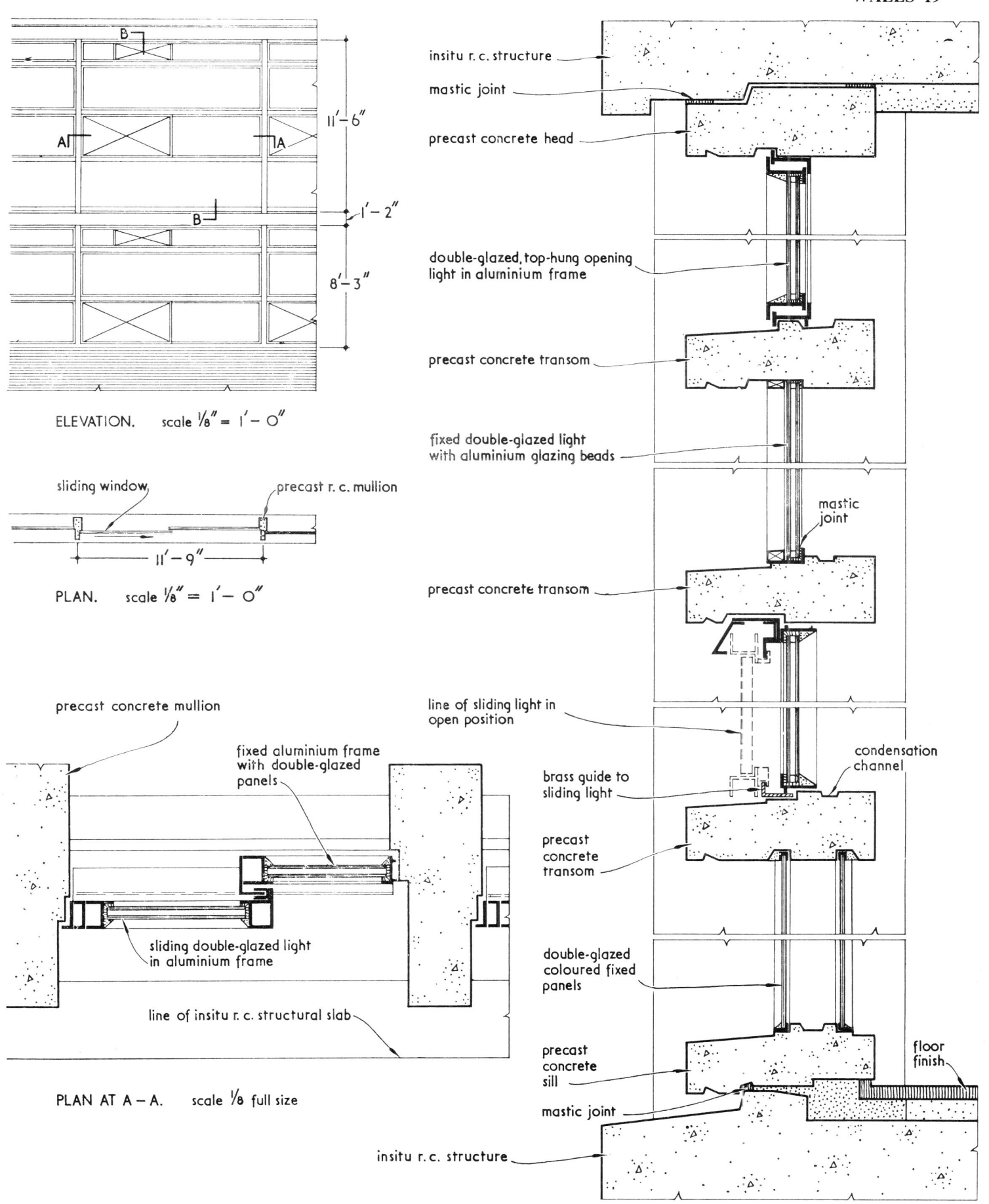

20 WALLS

CONCRETE WALL: CHURCH IN ROTTERDAM, HOLLAND
DESIGNED BY J. H. VAN DEN BROEK AND J. B. BAKEMA (*Material supplied by Martin Lawrence*)

This is a very accomplished example of the use of high-quality precast concrete in external panel walling. Note the section round window openings and the avoidance of a separate frame for fixed lights.

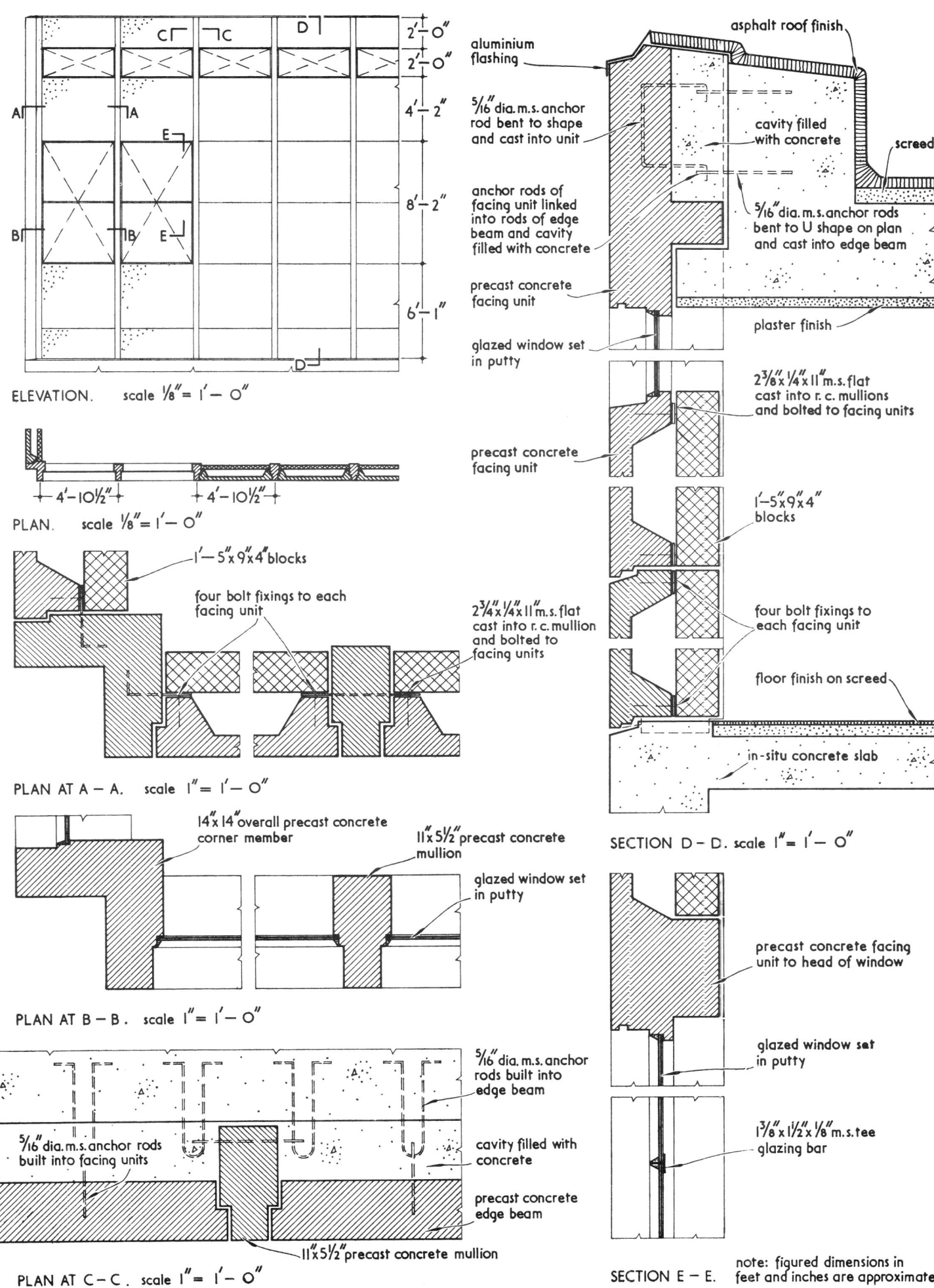

22 WALLS

GLASS CURTAIN WALL: OFFICE BUILDING IN NEW YORK
DESIGNED BY SKIDMORE OWINGS AND MERRILL

The mullions which are attached direct to the main supporting structure comprise two 5½ in. × 1½ in. × 3/16 in. steel channels which interlock but do not touch and thus serve as expansion joints. They are concealed on the outside by a coverstrip of 16 gauge stainless steel.

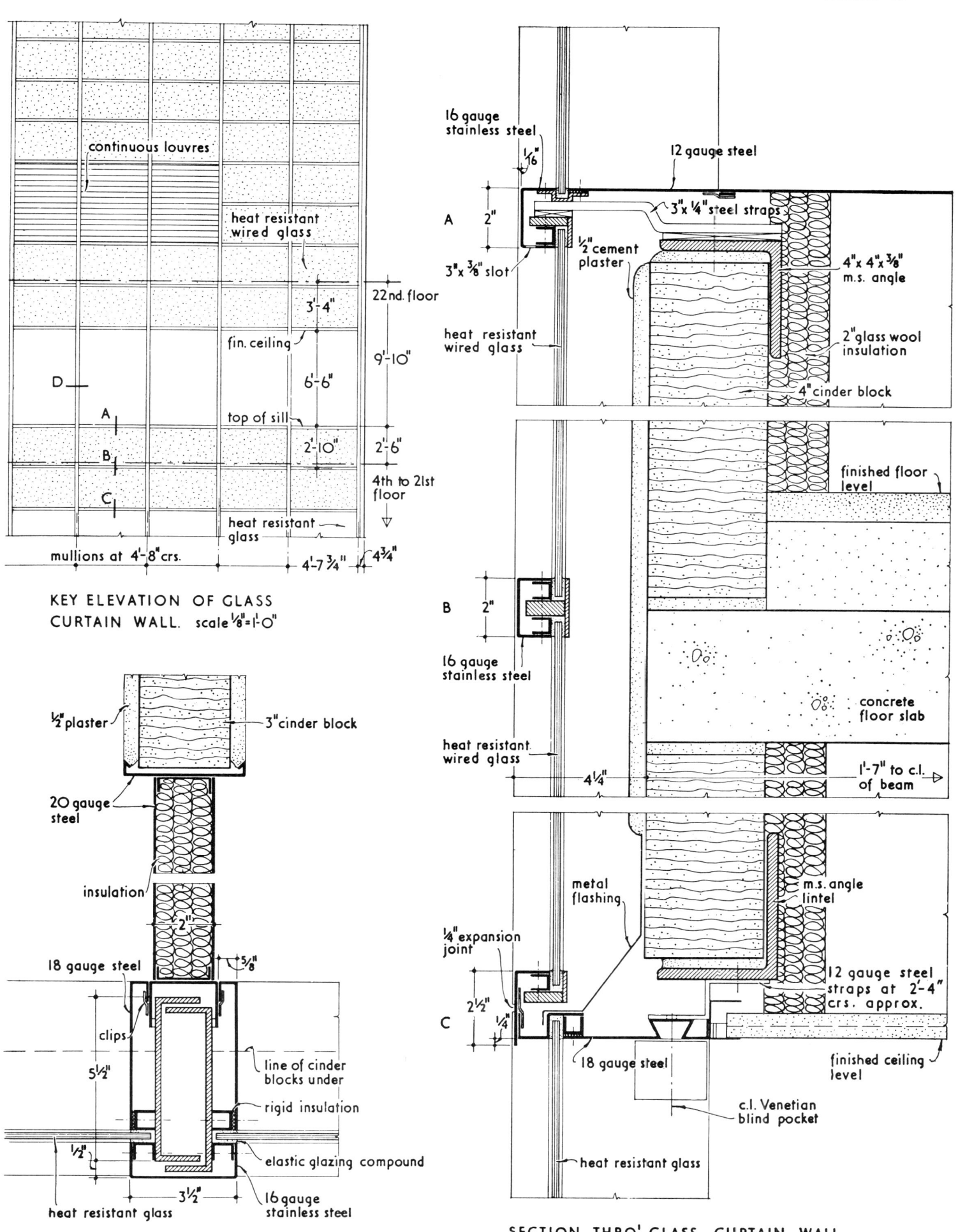

24 WALLS

**GLAZED WALL: TECHNOLOGICAL INSTITUTE IN CHICAGO, U.S.A.
DESIGNED BY MIES VAN DER ROHE** (*Material supplied by Tim Sturgis*)

An interesting example of an all-steel curtain wall with supporting columns in front of the window line. All framing (including the beads) is in solid m.s. rectangular sections screwed together. All ventilation is through the narrow louvre band immediately above the main floor level. The joints between all main structural members and the window framing are sealed with mastic tape.

Photograph: Bill Engdahl, Hedrich-Blessing

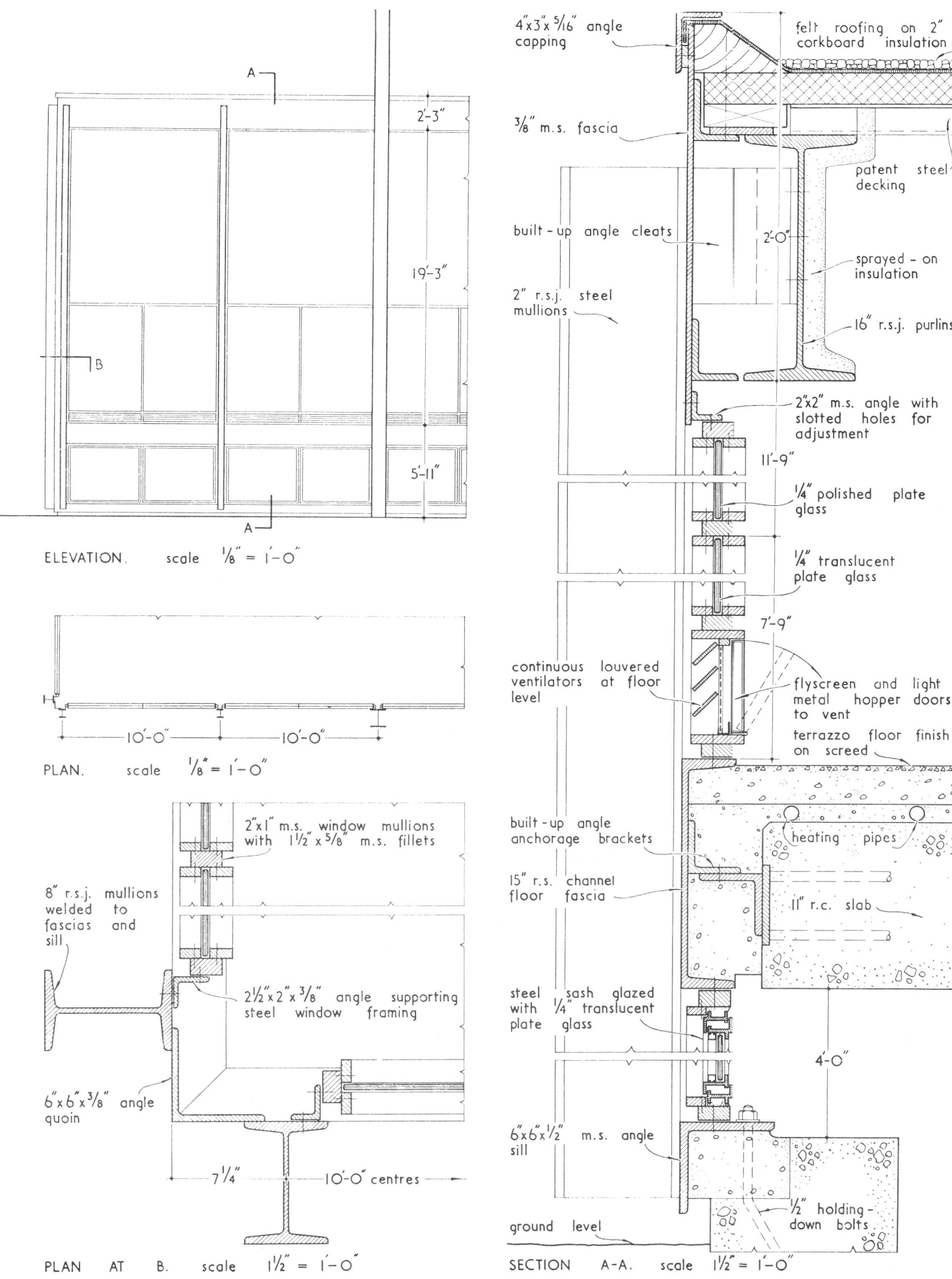

26 WALLS

GLAZED WALL: OFFICE BLOCK IN STOCKHOLM, SWEDEN
DESIGNED BY SVEN MARKELIUS (*Material supplied by John Whalley*)

This curtain wall shows an unusual solution to the problem of cleaning. Vertical sashes (aluminium outside with teak frame within) are hung proud of the line of the fixed glazing. These sashes are double-framed so that when they are in the 'closed' position they can be opened inwards. It is then a relatively easy matter to clean not only the windows themselves but the narrow fixed lights at the sides and the opaque panels below.

WALLS 27

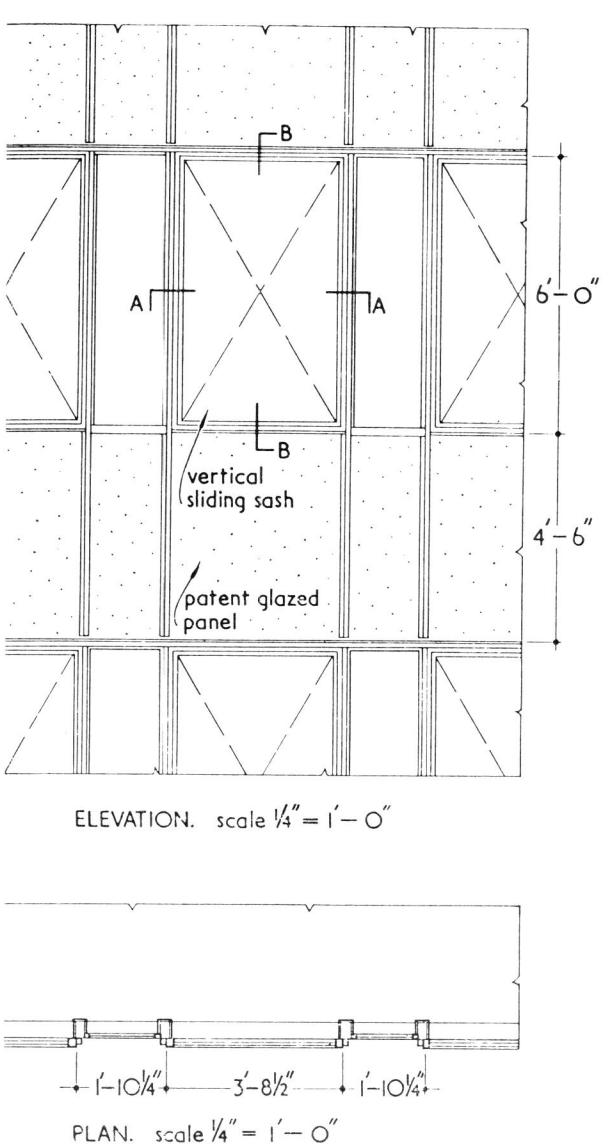
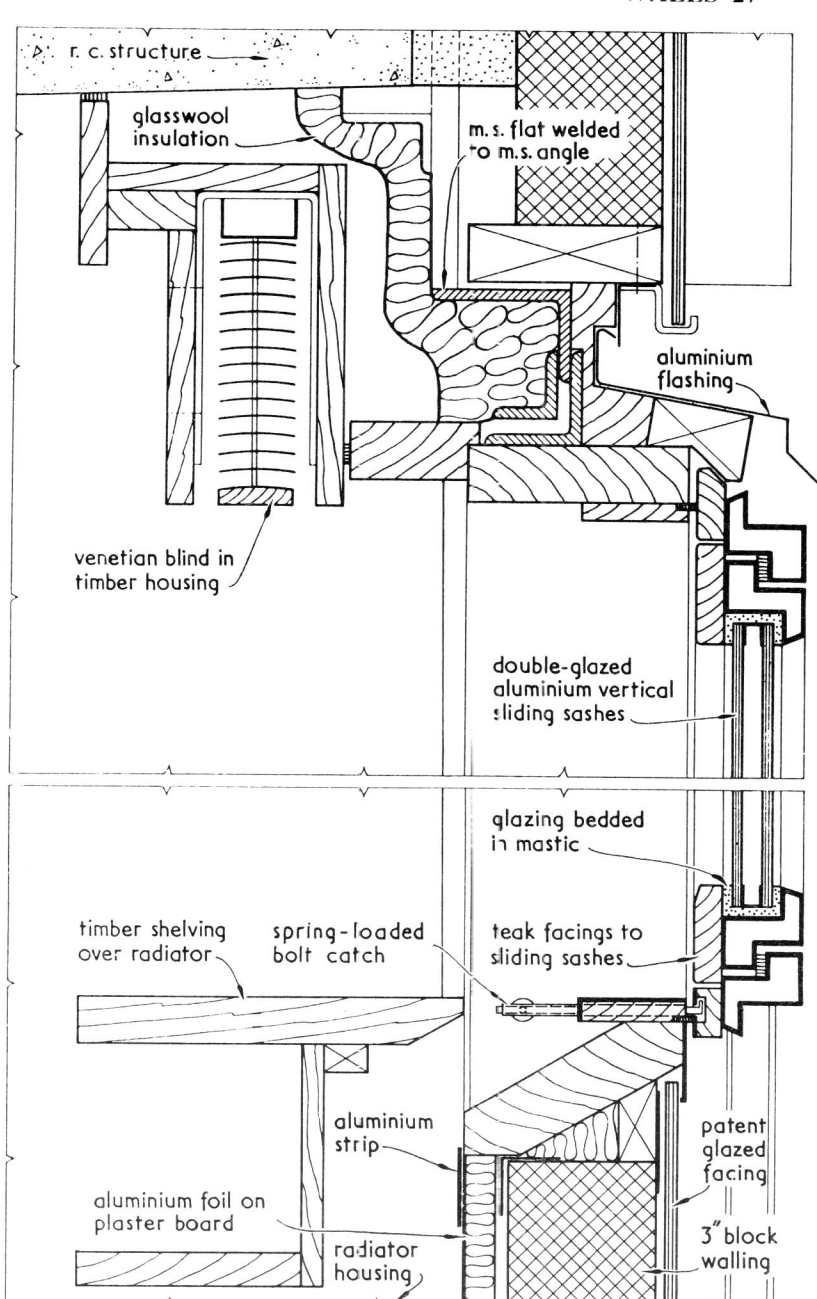
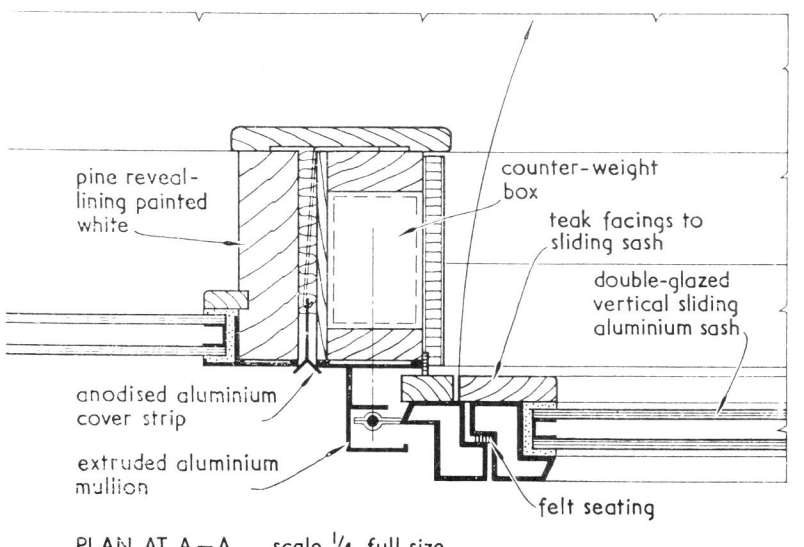
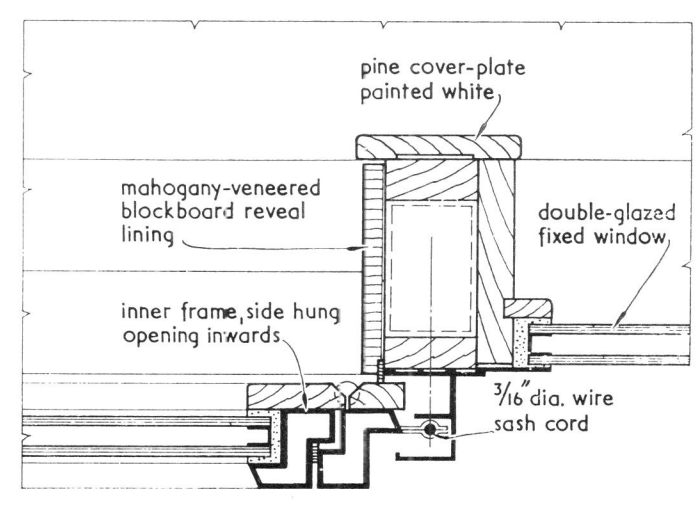

28 WALLS

CURTAIN WALL: OFFICE BUILDING IN COPENHAGEN, DENMARK
DESIGNED BY ARNE JACOBSEN *(Material supplied by D. J. Leadbetter)*

The curtain walling to this eight-storey building is supported by steel channels lugged to the edges of the cantilevered floors. After fixing the channel, the plates which support the mullions were welded on in-situ. The timber mullions, each consisting of four laminations bolted together in the joiners' shop, were then bolted into place. The transoms are housed into them with a simple carpenter's joint. The aluminium glazing beads clip over patent screw heads. The green coloured glazing (a German product) of the solid panels consists of two layers of thin glass with adhesive paint in between. Ventilation is by slots in the transom.

WALLS 29

ELEVATION. scale 1/8" = 1'-0"

PLAN AT C. scale 1½" = 1'-0"
- glazed partition
- 5"x3" built-up timber mullion
- double glazing
- aluminium sheathed nosing

PLAN AT B. scale 1½" = 1'-0"
- 5/16" bolt at 1'-7¾" crs.

note: figured dimensions in feet and inches are approximate

SECTION A-A. scale 1½" = 1'-0"
- 5/16" m.s. plates welded to channel nosing supporting vertical framing
- no. 4 5/8" bolts
- coloured glass panel in patent aluminium glazing beads
- ventilation tube
- double glazing in patent aluminium glazing beads
- aluminium sheet cladding to all external timber members
- 3"x 2½" head and sill members
- 1" sprayed asbestos and ¼" plywood facing
- 2¼" glass wool insulation between 3/8" plaster board
- p.v.c. floor tiles on hardboard and 1¼" battens
- r.c. slab 1'-2"
- ½" softboard lining with perforated hardboard soffit
- curtain track
- continuous built-up timber mullion
- window board
- duct for power supply
- panel for service outlets
- duct for electrical and telephone services
- 1" sprayed asbestos and ¼" plywood facing
- 5½" r.s. channel nosing lugged to r.c. structure
- plywood soffit lining

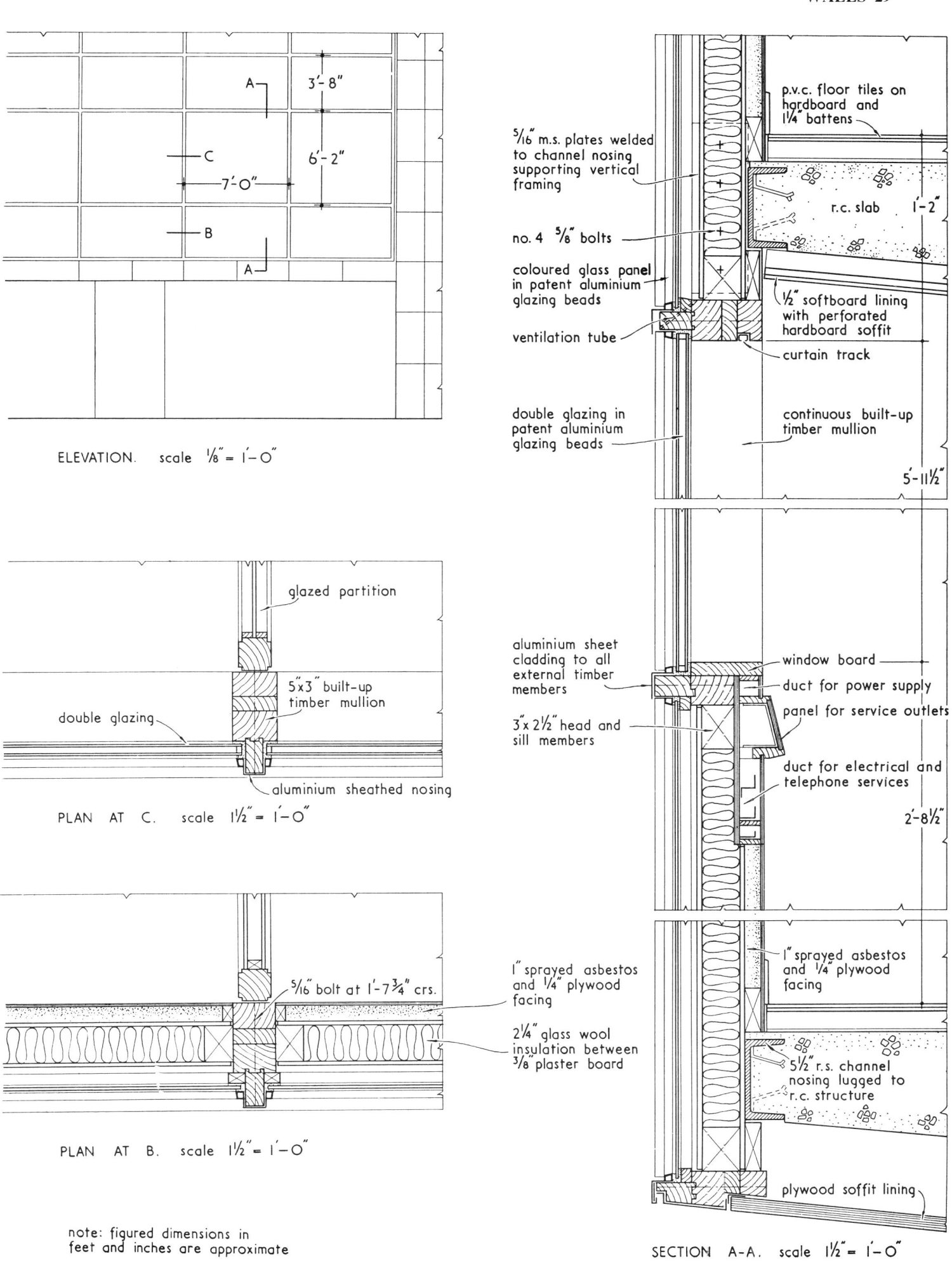

30 WALLS

CURTAIN WALL: OFFICE BUILDING IN SARNIA, ONTARIO, CANADA
DESIGNED BY JOHN B. PARKIN ASSOCIATES *(Material supplied by Felix Moore)*

In this very sophisticated version of the two-storey curtain wall, a steel structure supports precast concrete floors and lightweight precast concrete back-up walls, the curtain itself being of extruded aluminium. Note (on the drawing) the neat detailing at the eaves and at the foot of the cavity.

WALLS 31

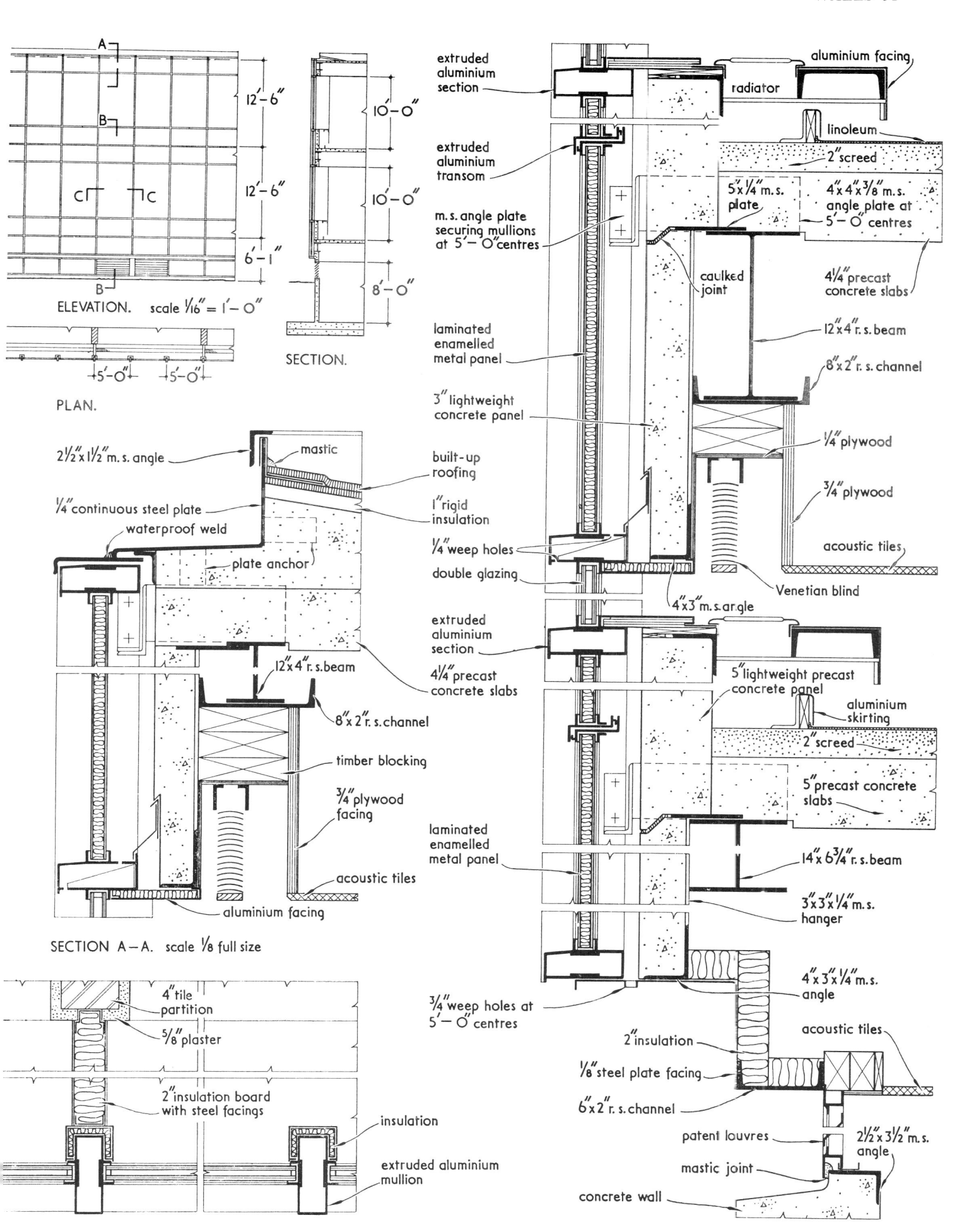

CURTAIN WALL: COLLEGE AT SLOUGH, BUCKS
DESIGNED BY F. B. POOLEY (architect to the Buckinghamshire County Council)

Architect-designed prefabricated timber curtain walls for multi-storey buildings are still comparatively uncommon. The frames are of storey height and 10 ft. wide, the joints between frames being masked by the channel sinking incised in main mullions, heads and sills. The deep zinc flashing at the foot shields the brickwork from water falling off the curtain. As the drawing shows, this design requires a back-up wall to meet fire protection needs.

WALLS 33

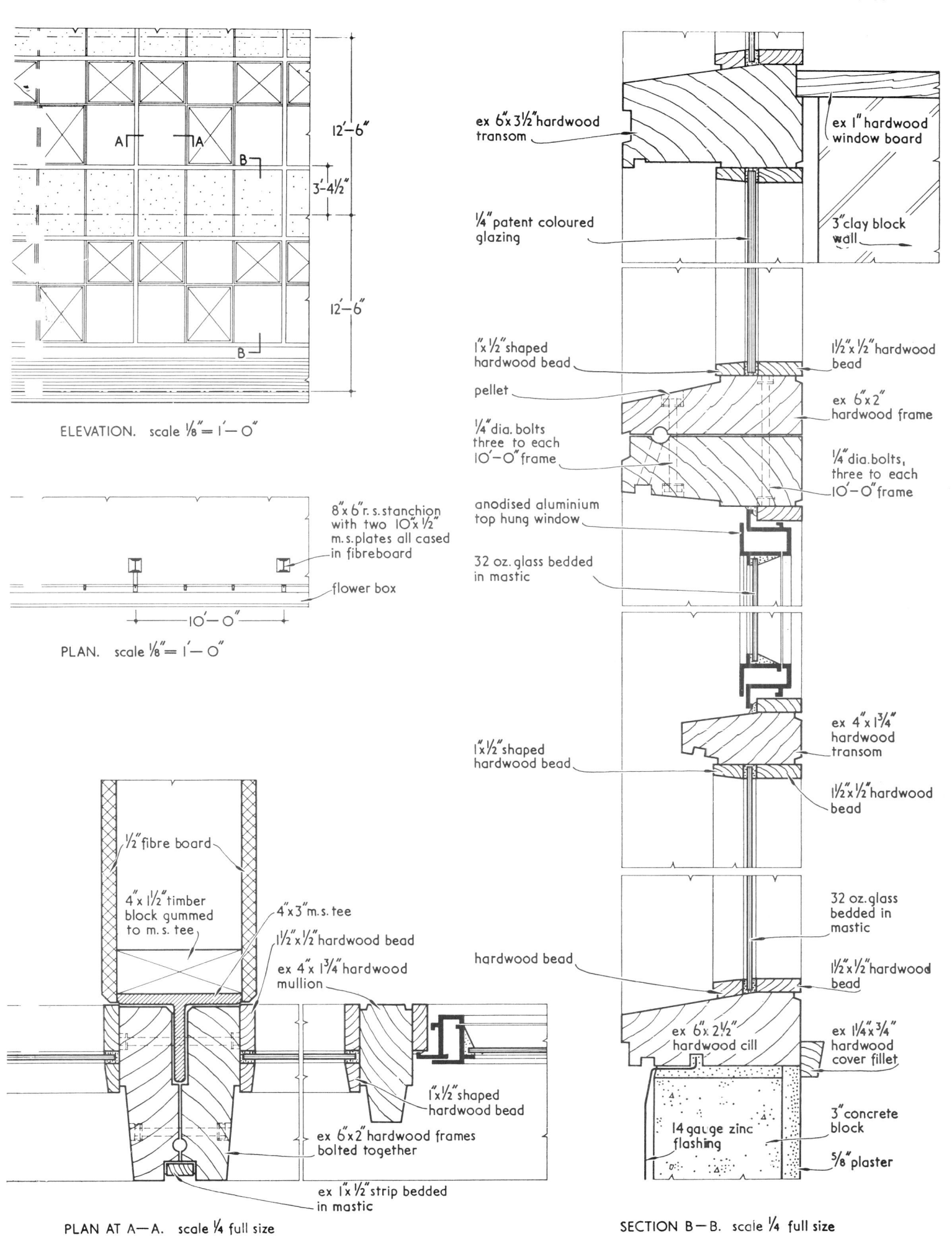

ELEVATION. scale ⅛"= 1'—0"

12'—6"
3'—4½"
12'—6"

PLAN. scale ⅛"= 1'—0"

10'—0"

8"x 6" r.s. stanchion with two 10"x ½" m.s. plates all cased in fibreboard

flower box

PLAN AT A—A. scale ¼ full size

½" fibre board
4"x 1½" timber block gummed to m.s. tee
4"x 3" m.s. tee
1½"x ½" hardwood bead
ex 4"x 1¾" hardwood mullion
1"x ½" shaped hardwood bead
ex 6"x 2" hardwood frames bolted together
ex 1"x ½" strip bedded in mastic

SECTION B—B. scale ¼ full size

ex 6"x 3½" hardwood transom
ex 1" hardwood window board
¼" patent coloured glazing
3" clay block wall
1"x ½" shaped hardwood bead
1½"x ½" hardwood bead
pellet
ex 6"x 2" hardwood frame
¼" dia. bolts three to each 10'—0" frame
¼" dia. bolts, three to each 10'—0" frame
anodised aluminium top hung window
32 oz. glass bedded in mastic
1"x ½" shaped hardwood bead
ex 4"x 1¾" hardwood transom
1½"x ½" hardwood bead
32 oz. glass bedded in mastic
hardwood bead
1½"x ½" hardwood bead
ex 6"x 2½" hardwood cill
ex 1¼"x ¾" hardwood cover fillet
14 gauge zinc flashing
3" concrete block
⅝" plaster

34 WALLS

GLAZED WALL: SCHOOL IN LONDON, W.C.1
DESIGNED BY HUBERT BENNETT (architect to the London County Council)

This detail is interesting for its use of timber as an engineering material. Note the laminated timber mullions and beam above. Note also (particularly on the drawing) the exceptionally neat framing to the window.

WALLS 35

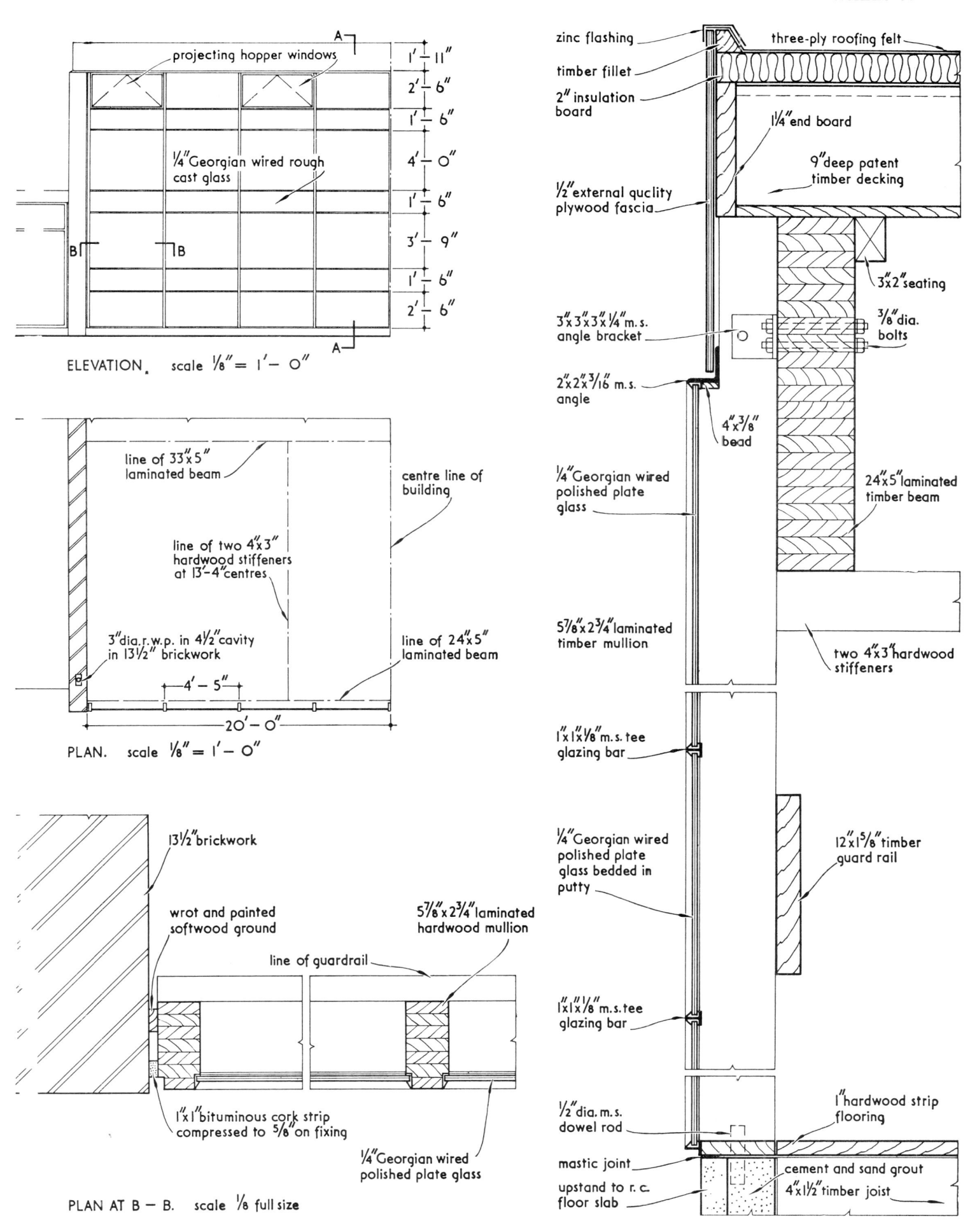

36 WALLS

CURTAIN WALL: OFFICES IN NEW YORK, U.S.A.
DESIGNED BY MIES VAN DER ROHE AND PHILIP JOHNSON ASSOCIATES   *(Material supplied by Felix Moore)*

This characteristic American curtain wall for very tall buildings employs an external 6 in. by 4½ in. steel mullion with a clamping box backing on to the inside flange. This box covers the brackets connecting the mullion to the steel edge beam and holds the prefabricated bronze framed panels and (at the corner) the bronze cladding.

WALLS 37

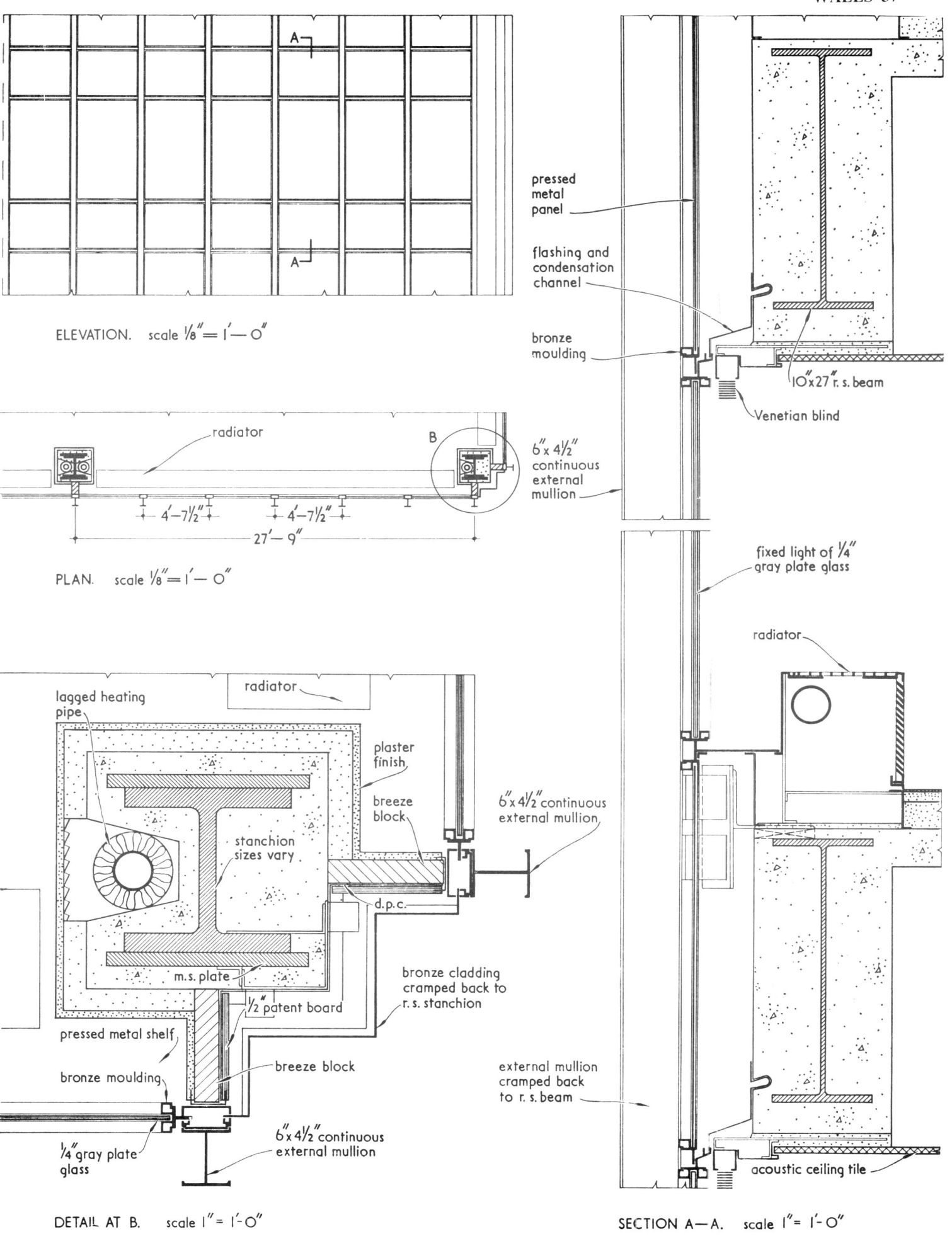

ELEVATION. scale 1/8" = 1'-0"

PLAN. scale 1/8" = 1'-0"

DETAIL AT B. scale 1" = 1'-0"

SECTION A—A. scale 1" = 1'-0"

- radiator
- 4'-7½"
- 27'-9"
- B
- 6" x 4½" continuous external mullion
- lagged heating pipe
- plaster finish
- breeze block
- stanchion sizes vary
- 6" x 4½" continuous external mullion
- d.p.c.
- m.s. plate
- ½" patent board
- pressed metal shelf
- bronze moulding
- breeze block
- bronze cladding cramped back to r.s. stanchion
- ¼" gray plate glass
- 6" x 4½" continuous external mullion
- pressed metal panel
- flashing and condensation channel
- bronze moulding
- 10" x 27" r.s. beam
- Venetian blind
- fixed light of ¼" gray plate glass
- radiator
- external mullion cramped back to r.s. beam
- acoustic ceiling tile

38 WALLS

CURTAIN WALL: DEPARTMENT STORE IN DENVER, COLORADO, U.S.A.
DESIGNED BY I. M. PEI *(Material supplied by Felix Moore)*

This 'windowless' aluminium curtain wall is built of panels 16 ft. 6 in. high by 9 ft. 0 in. wide. The panel stiffeners, of the 'bulked form' characteristic of aluminium, project on the outside of the wall, as the panels are designed to present a fairface surface internally. All visible surfaces of the aluminium, both inside and out, are gold-anodised.

WALLS 39

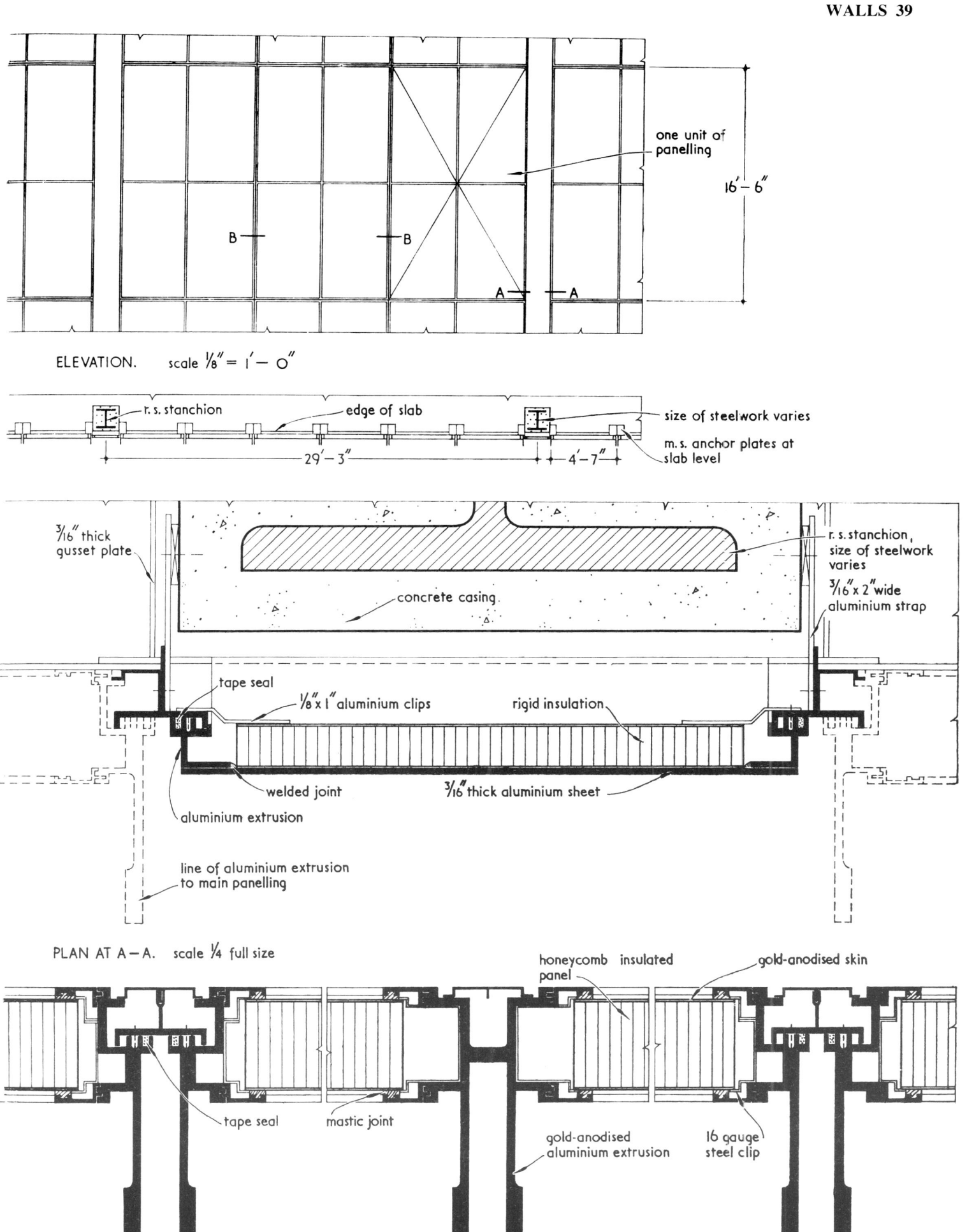

ELEVATION. scale ⅛" = 1'−0"

- one unit of panelling
- 16'−6"
- r.s. stanchion
- edge of slab
- size of steelwork varies
- m.s. anchor plates at slab level
- 29'−3"
- 4'−7"

- ³⁄₁₆" thick gusset plate
- concrete casing
- r.s. stanchion, size of steelwork varies
- ³⁄₁₆" x 2" wide aluminium strap
- tape seal
- ⅛" x 1" aluminium clips
- rigid insulation
- welded joint
- ³⁄₁₆" thick aluminium sheet
- aluminium extrusion
- line of aluminium extrusion to main panelling

PLAN AT A−A. scale ¼ full size

- honeycomb insulated panel
- gold-anodised skin
- tape seal
- mastic joint
- gold-anodised aluminium extrusion
- 16 gauge steel clip

PLAN AT B−B. scale ¼ full size

40 WALLS

CURTAIN WALL: OFFICES IN CREVE COEUR, MISSOURI, U.S.A.
DESIGNED BY VINCENT G. KLING   (*Material supplied by W. H. Roberts*)

The opaque surfaces are wholly of aluminium. The mullions of the façades visible in the photograph are made of tapering aluminium box sections bolted top and bottom to the main structure. On the façades which fall at right angles to these, the main steel stanchions project in front of the curtain and are faced with prefabricated aluminium panels with insulated backing.

WALLS 41

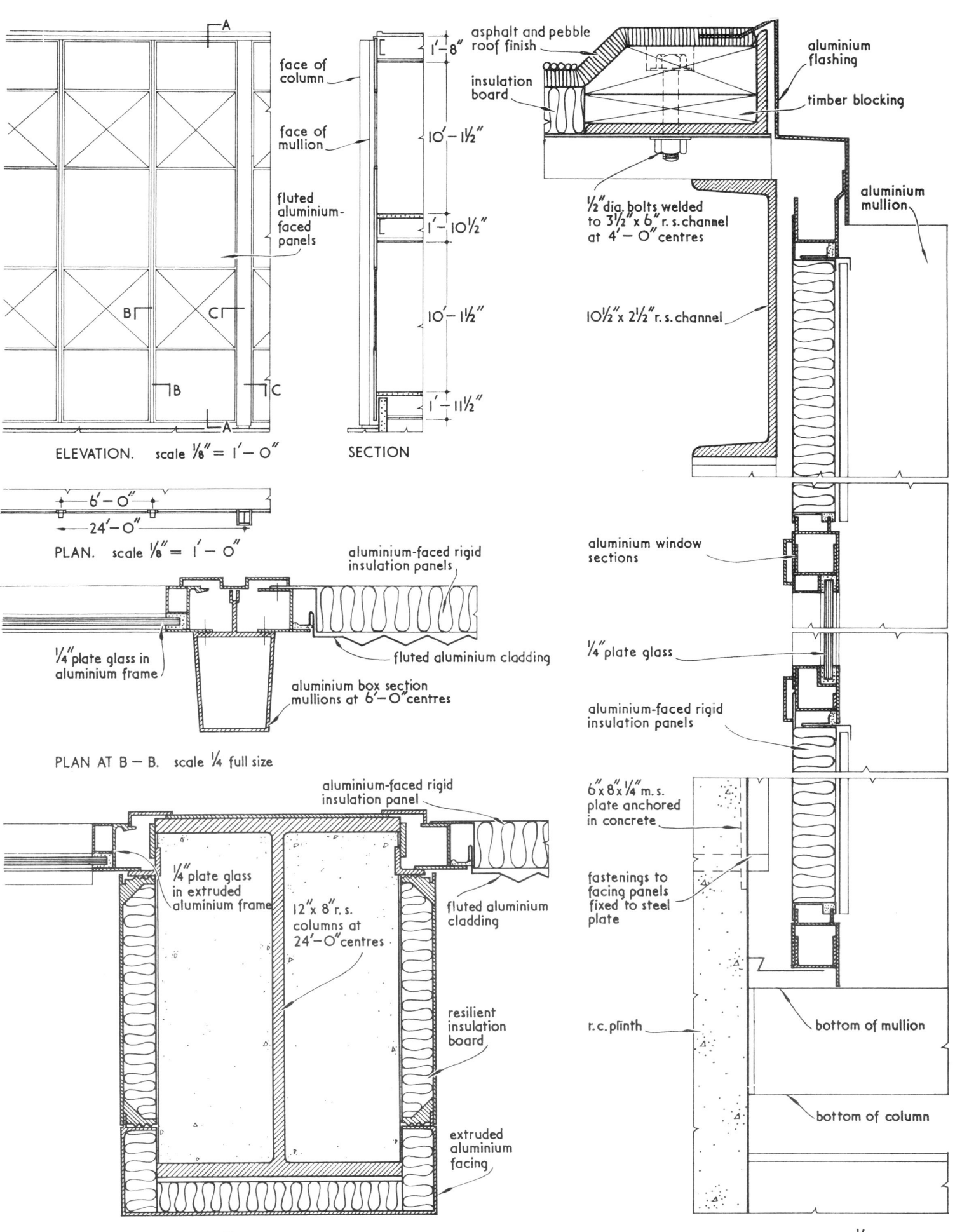

ELEVATION. scale ⅛" = 1'-0"

SECTION

- face of column
- face of mullion
- fluted aluminium-faced panels
- 1'-8"
- 10'-1½"
- 1'-10½"
- 10'-1½"
- 1'-11½"

PLAN. scale ⅛" = 1'-0"
- 6'-0"
- 24'-0"

PLAN AT B—B. scale ¼ full size
- ¼" plate glass in aluminium frame
- aluminium-faced rigid insulation panels
- fluted aluminium cladding
- aluminium box section mullions at 6'-0" centres

PLAN AT C—C. scale ¼ full size
- aluminium-faced rigid insulation panel
- ¼" plate glass in extruded aluminium frame
- 12" x 8" r.s. columns at 24'-0" centres
- fluted aluminium cladding
- resilient insulation board
- extruded aluminium facing

SECTION A—A. scale ¼ full size
- asphalt and pebble roof finish
- insulation board
- aluminium flashing
- timber blocking
- ½" dia. bolts welded to 3½" x 6" r.s. channel at 4'-0" centres
- 10½" x 2½" r.s. channel
- aluminium mullion
- aluminium window sections
- ¼" plate glass
- aluminium-faced rigid insulation panels
- 6" x 8" x ¼" m.s. plate anchored in concrete
- fastenings to facing panels fixed to steel plate
- r.c. plinth
- bottom of mullion
- bottom of column

42 WALLS

GLAZED WALL: OFFICES IN LONDON, N.W.1
DESIGNED BY GOLLINS, MELVIN, WARD AND PARTNERS

Among the points to notice about this curtain wall is the combination of aluminium sub-frame with heavy infill panels (here of marble), the continuance of the mullion upwards to provide support to the balustrade and (visible on the drawing only) the unusual detail at the roof edge.

WALLS 43

ELEVATION. scale 1/16"=1'-0"

- balcony rail
- opening lights
- marble panels
- entrance

PLAN. scale 1/16"=1'-0"

- windows
- marble panels
- 23'-4½"
- 11'-4¼"

PLAN B-B. scale 3/8 full size

- glazing nib
- marble panel
- sliding sash
- aluminium bead
- rubber seal
- aluminium mullion section

PLAN C-C. scale 3/8 full size

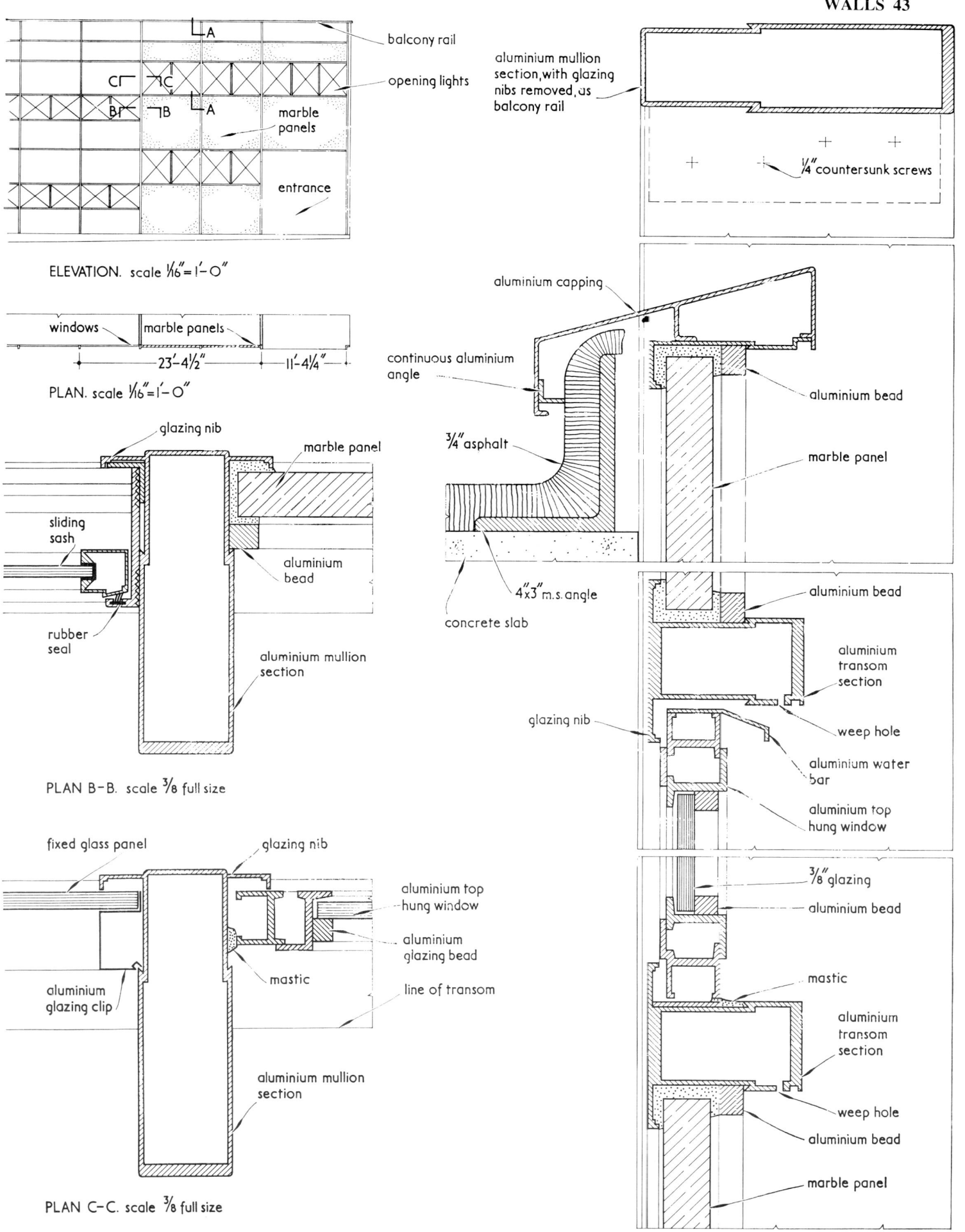

- fixed glass panel
- glazing nib
- aluminium top hung window
- aluminium glazing bead
- mastic
- line of transom
- aluminium glazing clip
- aluminium mullion section

SECTION A-A. scale 3/8 full size

- aluminium mullion section, with glazing nibs removed, as balcony rail
- ¼" countersunk screws
- aluminium capping
- continuous aluminium angle
- aluminium bead
- ¾" asphalt
- marble panel
- 4"x3" m.s. angle
- concrete slab
- aluminium bead
- aluminium transom section
- weep hole
- glazing nib
- aluminium water bar
- aluminium top hung window
- 3/8" glazing
- aluminium bead
- mastic
- aluminium transom section
- weep hole
- aluminium bead
- marble panel

44 WALLS

CURTAIN WALL: DECKEL BUILDING, PLINGANSER STREET, MUNICH, GERMANY
DESIGNED BY PROF. DR. ING. WALTER HENN *(Material supplied by Francis Duffy)*

This aluminium clad façade is the most skilfully designed that we have seen. Note the forward projection of the cladding panels to cover and conceal the external blind boxes and the method of running the aluminium mullion in a recess between panels. Presumably staining will be largely confined to the channels where it will be least visible. Also the fact that the glass-holding parts of the subframe are behind and not on the same plane as the mullion permits exceptionally thin verticals on elevation.

WALLS 45

ELEVATION scale ⅛" = 1'-0"

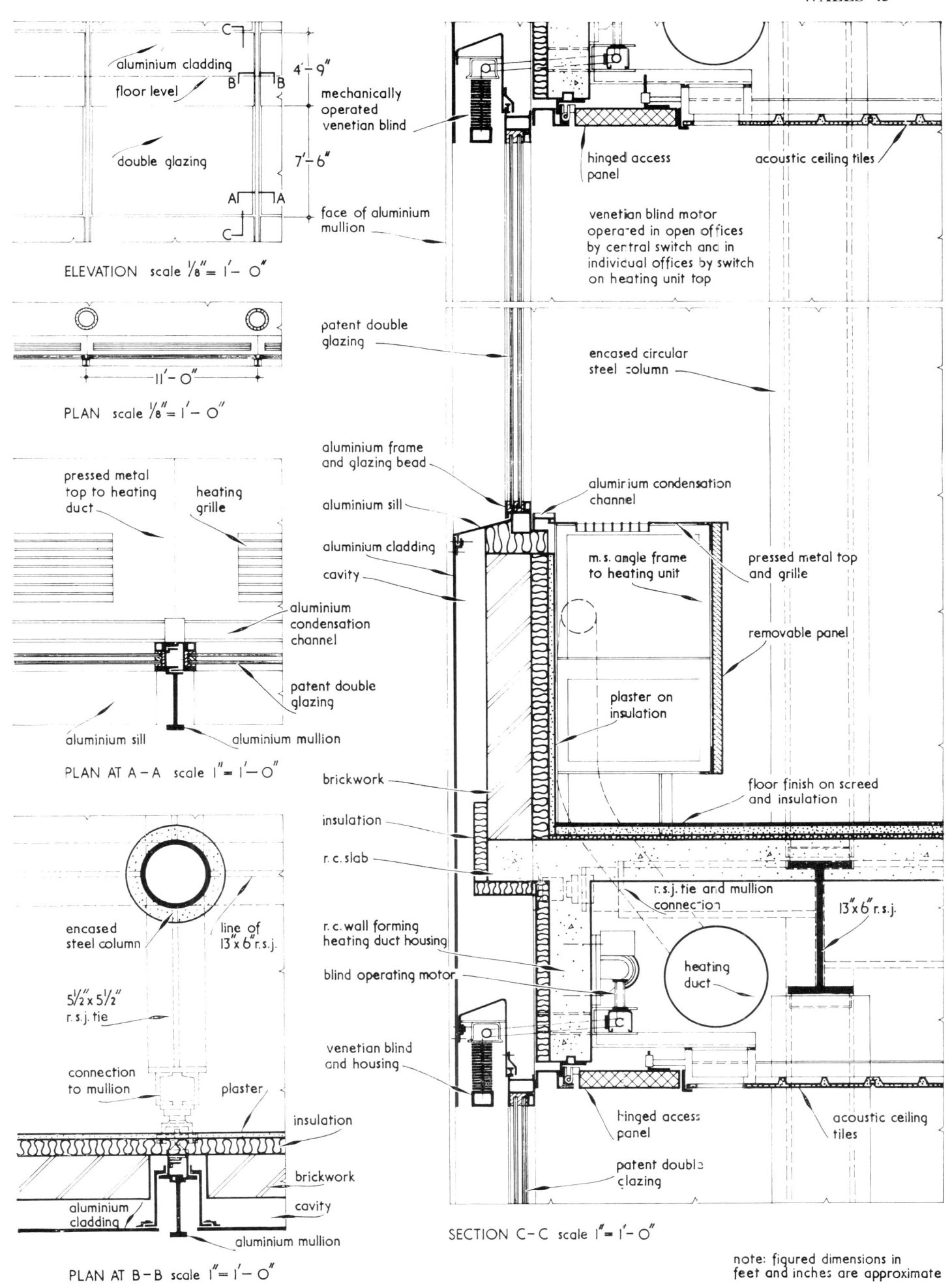

- aluminium cladding
- floor level
- 4'-9"
- mechanically operated venetian blind
- 7'-6"
- double glazing
- face of aluminium mullion

PLAN scale ⅛" = 1'-0"

- 11'-0"

PLAN AT A–A scale 1" = 1'-0"

- pressed metal top to heating duct
- heating grille
- aluminium sill
- aluminium mullion
- aluminium condensation channel
- patent double glazing

PLAN AT B–B scale 1" = 1'-0"

- encased steel column
- line of 13"x 6" r.s.j.
- 5½"x 5½" r.s.j. tie
- connection to mullion
- plaster
- insulation
- brickwork
- cavity
- aluminium cladding
- aluminium mullion

SECTION C–C scale 1" = 1'-0"

- hinged access panel
- acoustic ceiling tiles
- venetian blind motor operated in open offices by central switch and in individual offices by switch on heating unit top
- patent double glazing
- encased circular steel column
- aluminium frame and glazing bead
- aluminium sill
- aluminium condensation channel
- aluminium cladding
- cavity
- m.s. angle frame to heating unit
- pressed metal top and grille
- removable panel
- plaster on insulation
- brickwork
- insulation
- r.c. slab
- r.c. wall forming heating duct housing
- blind operating motor
- venetian blind and housing
- floor finish on screed and insulation
- r.s.j. tie and mullion connection
- 13"x 6" r.s.j.
- heating duct
- hinged access panel
- acoustic ceiling tiles
- patent double glazing

note: figured dimensions in feet and inches are approximate

46 WALLS

CURTAIN WALL: EMBASSY IN ATHENS, GREECE
DESIGNED BY WALTER GROPIUS   (*Material supplied by Garbis Urégian*)

This detail shows standard American practice regarding trim in curtain walling.

WALLS 47

ELEVATION. scale 1/16" = 1'-0"

SECTION. scale 1/16" = 1'-0"

23'-0"

PLAN AT A–A. scale 3/16 full size

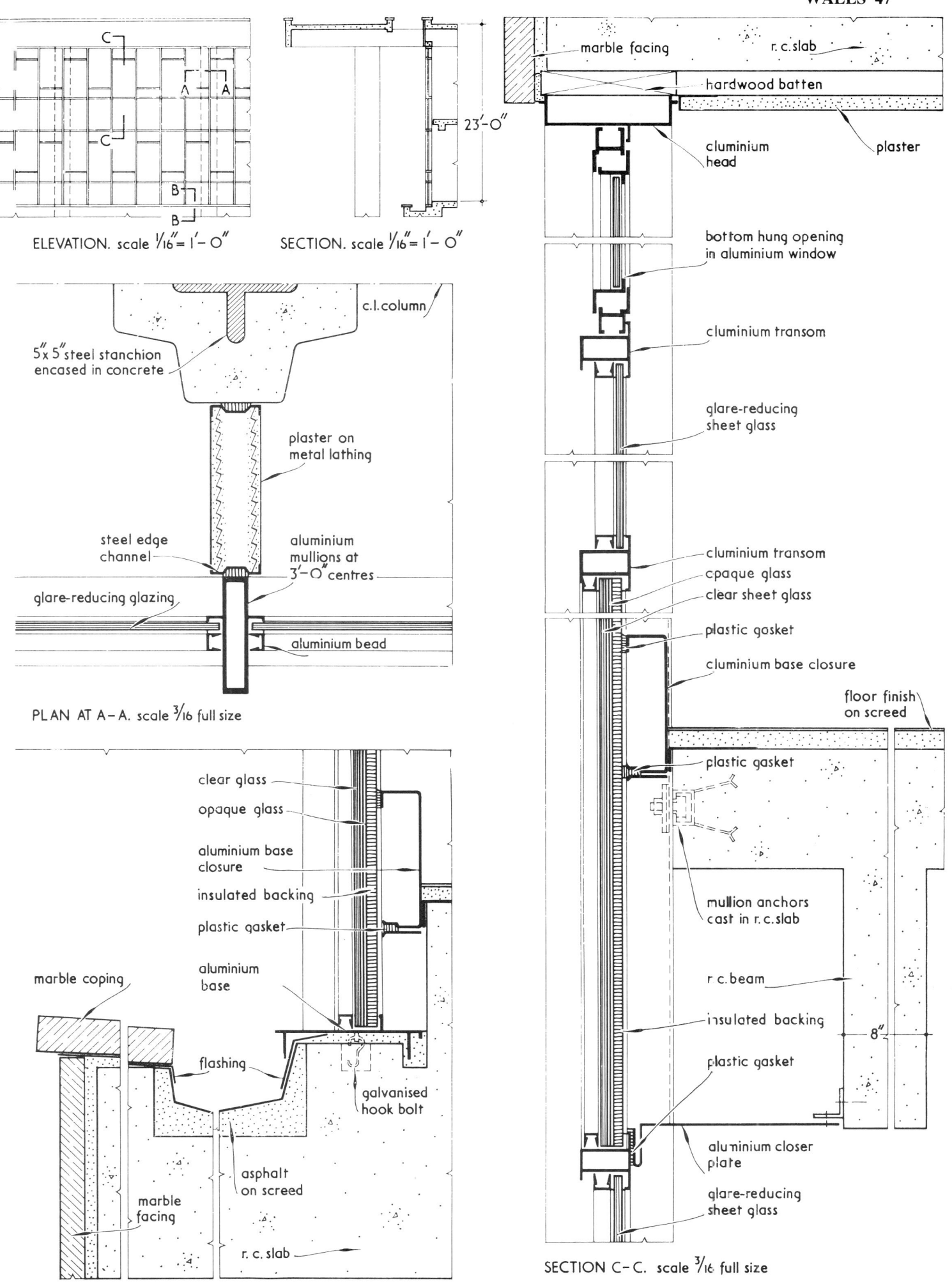

- c.i. column
- 5"x 5" steel stanchion encased in concrete
- plaster on metal lathing
- steel edge channel
- aluminium mullions at 3'-0" centres
- glare-reducing glazing
- aluminium bead

SECTION B–B. scale 3/16 full size

- clear glass
- opaque glass
- aluminium base closure
- insulated backing
- plastic gasket
- aluminium base
- marble coping
- flashing
- galvanised hook bolt
- asphalt on screed
- marble facing
- r.c. slab

SECTION C–C. scale 3/16 full size

- marble facing
- r.c. slab
- hardwood batten
- plaster
- aluminium head
- bottom hung opening in aluminium window
- aluminium transom
- glare-reducing sheet glass
- aluminium transom
- opaque glass
- clear sheet glass
- plastic gasket
- aluminium base closure
- floor finish on screed
- plastic gasket
- mullion anchors cast in r.c. slab
- r.c. beam
- insulated backing
- 8"
- plastic gasket
- aluminium closer plate
- glare-reducing sheet glass

note: figured dimensions in feet and inches are approximate

48 WALLS

GLAZED WALL: MUSEUM OF FINE ARTS, EXPO, OSAKA, JAPAN
DESIGNED BY KIYOSHI KAWASAKI   (*Material supplied by Jeremy Dodd*)

This glazed wall is composed of 12 mm toughened glass panels, each 2·7 m square. These are secured at their corners by cruciform steel clamps which in turn are bolted to the nodal points of the tubular space frame behind. The photograph is taken from the inside and the circular discs form part of the lighting fittings.

WALLS 49

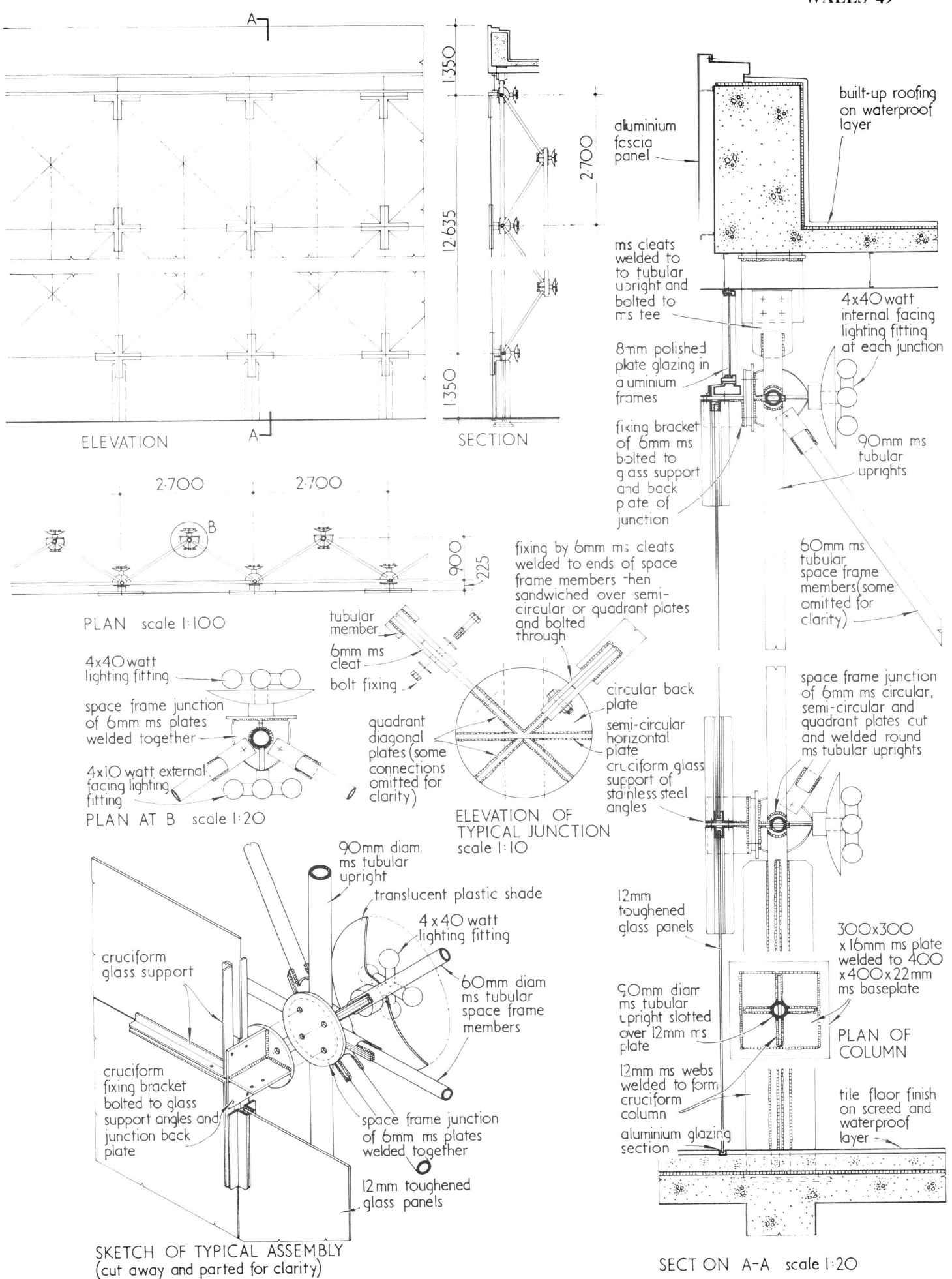

ELEVATION

SECTION

PLAN scale 1:100

PLAN AT B scale 1:20

- 4×40 watt lighting fitting
- space frame junction of 6mm ms plates welded together
- 4×10 watt external facing lighting fitting

ELEVATION OF TYPICAL JUNCTION scale 1:10

- tubular member
- 6mm ms cleat
- bolt fixing
- fixing by 6mm ms cleats welded to ends of space frame members then sandwiched over semi-circular or quadrant plates and bolted through
- quadrant diagonal plates (some connections omitted for clarity)
- circular back plate
- semi-circular horizontal plate
- cruciform glass support of stainless steel angles

SKETCH OF TYPICAL ASSEMBLY
(cut away and parted for clarity)

- 90mm diam ms tubular upright
- translucent plastic shade
- 4×40 watt lighting fitting
- 60mm diam ms tubular space frame members
- space frame junction of 6mm ms plates welded together
- 12mm toughened glass panels
- cruciform glass support
- cruciform fixing bracket bolted to glass support angles and junction back plate

SECTION A-A scale 1:20

- built-up roofing on waterproof layer
- aluminium fascia panel
- ms cleats welded to tubular upright and bolted to ms tee
- 4×40 watt internal facing lighting fitting at each junction
- 8mm polished plate glazing in aluminium frames
- fixing bracket of 6mm ms bolted to glass support and back plate of junction
- 90mm ms tubular uprights
- 60mm ms tubular space frame members (some omitted for clarity)
- space frame junction of 6mm ms circular, semi-circular and quadrant plates cut and welded round ms tubular uprights
- 12mm toughened glass panels
- 90mm diam ms tubular upright slotted over 12mm ms plate
- 12mm ms webs welded to form cruciform column
- aluminium glazing section
- 300×300×16mm ms plate welded to 400×400×22mm ms baseplate

PLAN OF COLUMN

- tile floor finish on screed and waterproof layer

50 WALLS

FAÇADE: TIME AND LIFE BUILDING, CHICAGO, USA
DESIGNED BY HARRY WEESE AND ASSOCIATES (*Material collected by Alan Mossman*)

As can be seen in the drawing, the building has a reinforced concrete structure, clad in weathering stee sheet. The design was much influenced by American office-letting conventions, according to which floor space is charged to the glass line, and by the desire to reduce to a minimum the space on plan taken up by air-conditioning ducts and services runs.

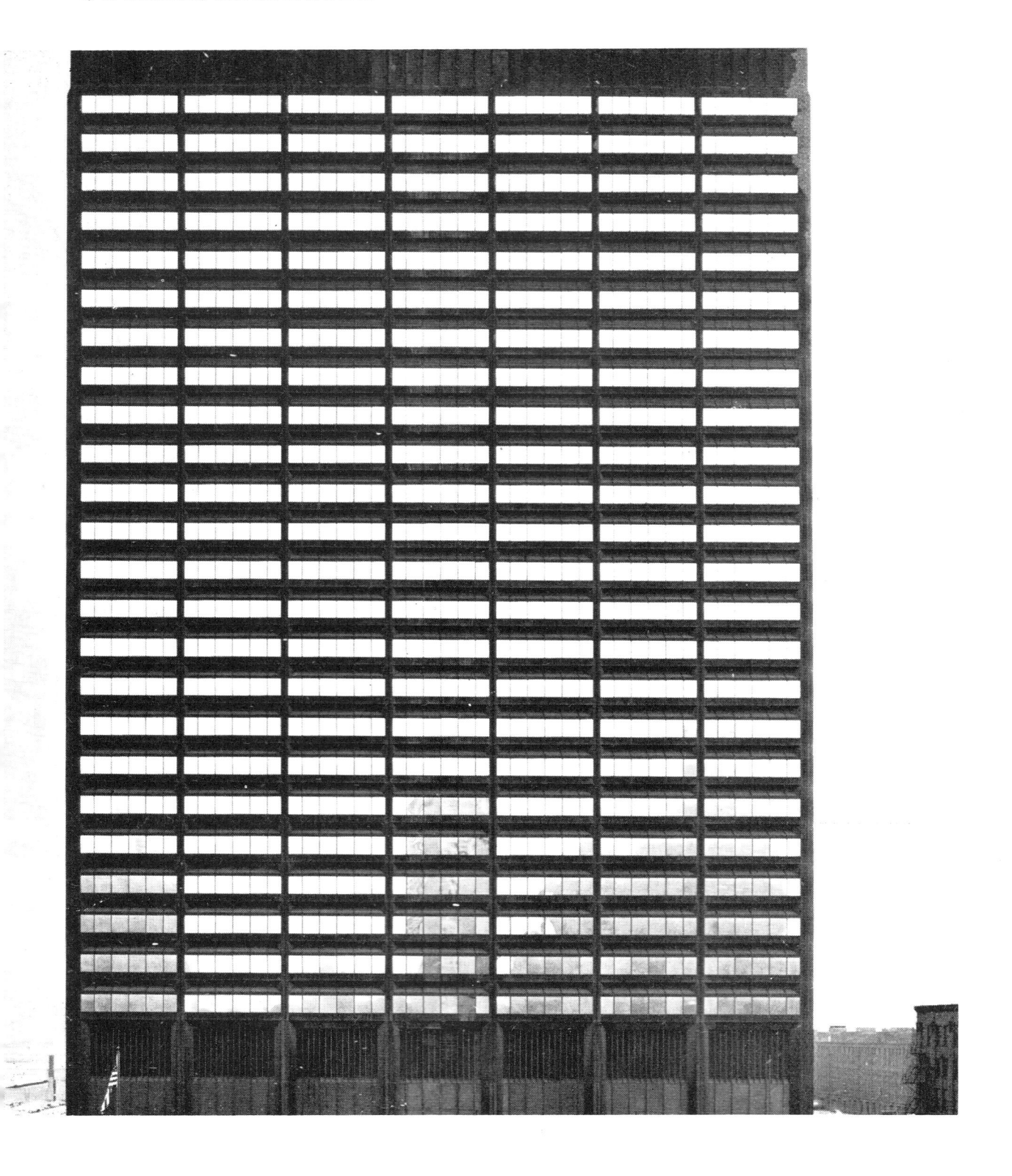

WALLS 51

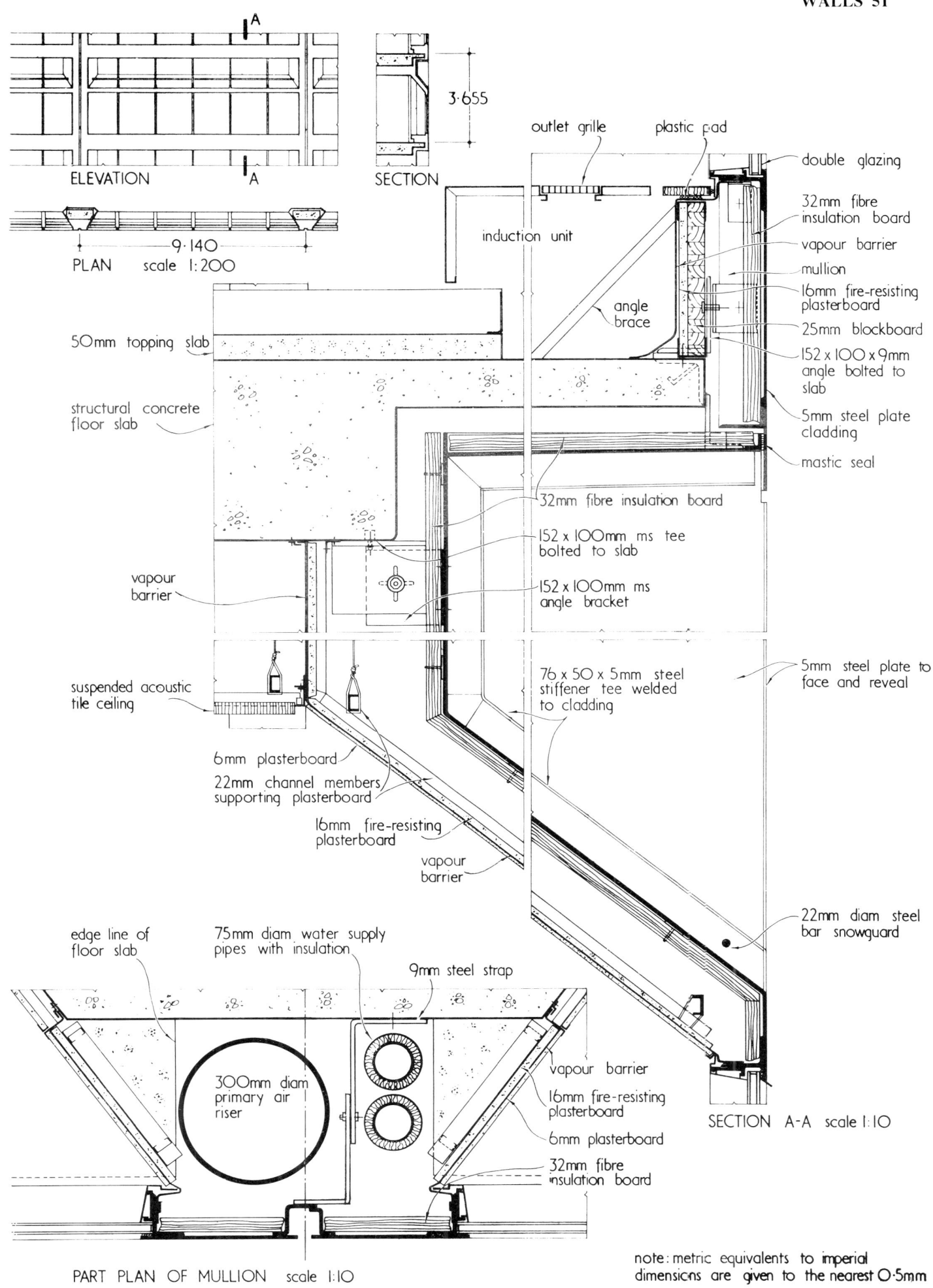

ELEVATION

PLAN scale 1:200

9.140

SECTION

3.655

- outlet grille
- plastic pad
- double glazing
- 32mm fibre insulation board
- vapour barrier
- mullion
- 16mm fire-resisting plasterboard
- 25mm blockboard
- 152 x 100 x 9mm angle bolted to slab
- 5mm steel plate cladding
- induction unit
- angle brace
- 50mm topping slab
- structural concrete floor slab
- mastic seal
- 32mm fibre insulation board
- 152 x 100mm ms tee bolted to slab
- 152 x 100mm ms angle bracket
- vapour barrier
- 76 x 50 x 5mm steel stiffener tee welded to cladding
- 5mm steel plate to face and reveal
- suspended acoustic tile ceiling
- 6mm plasterboard
- 22mm channel members supporting plasterboard
- 16mm fire-resisting plasterboard
- vapour barrier
- 22mm diam steel bar snowguard

SECTION A-A scale 1:10

- edge line of floor slab
- 75mm diam water supply pipes with insulation
- 9mm steel strap
- 300mm diam primary air riser
- vapour barrier
- 16mm fire-resisting plasterboard
- 6mm plasterboard
- 32mm fibre insulation board

PART PLAN OF MULLION scale 1:10

note: metric equivalents to imperial dimensions are given to the nearest 0·5mm

52 WALLS

WINDOW WALL: OAKLAND COLISEUM ARENA, NIMITZ FREEWAY, OAKLAND, CALIFORNIA
DESIGNED BY SKIDMORE, OWINGS AND MERRILL   (*Material supplied by Duncan Macintosh*)

The window wall is supported by vertical lattice trusses which lie behind (not *by the diagonal concrete members which support the ring beam and roof*). *The wall is built up of aluminium frame units, each 28ft × 3ft 6in (8.534m × 1.067m) and each lattice truss supports two units, one above the other. Each frame unit is attached to the supporting truss at the top and, as it is merely restrained at the bottom and at three intermediate points, it is free to expand downwards and sideways. The glass is held in synthetic rubber structural gaskets.*

WALLS 53

ELEVATION
- vertical joist
- horizontal cross bracing
- 1·524
- 17·221
- ·762
- 2·438

SECTION

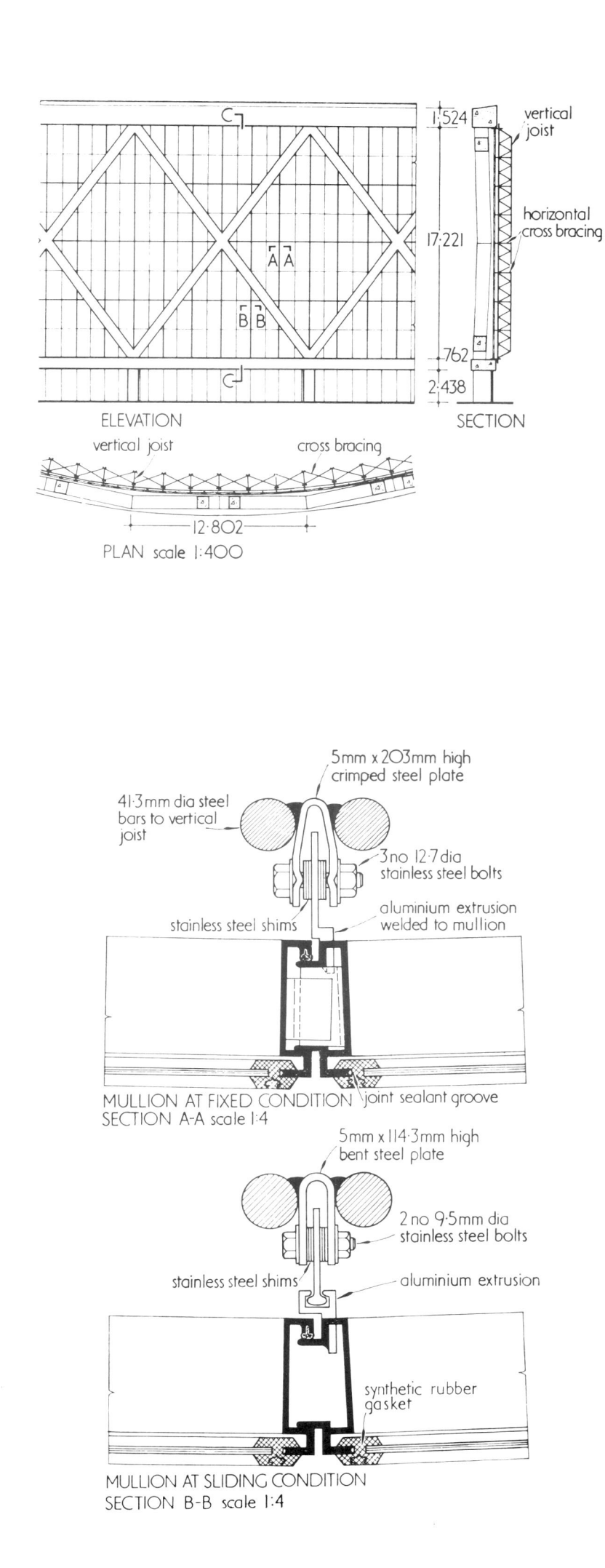

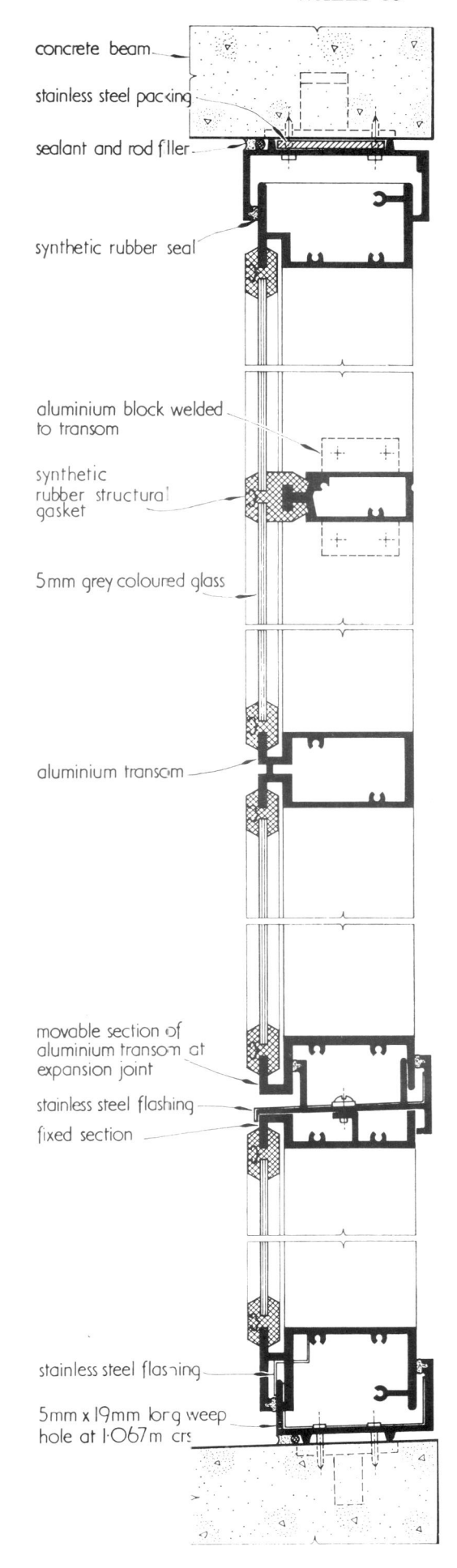

PLAN scale 1:400
- vertical joist
- cross bracing
- 12·802

MULLION AT FIXED CONDITION SECTION A-A scale 1:4
- 5mm x 203mm high crimped steel plate
- 41·3mm dia steel bars to vertical joist
- 3 no 12·7 dia stainless steel bolts
- stainless steel shims
- aluminium extrusion welded to mullion
- joint sealant groove

MULLION AT SLIDING CONDITION SECTION B-B scale 1:4
- 5mm x 114·3mm high bent steel plate
- 2 no 9·5mm dia stainless steel bolts
- stainless steel shims
- aluminium extrusion
- synthetic rubber gasket

SECTION C-C scale 1:4
- concrete beam
- stainless steel packing
- sealant and rod filler
- synthetic rubber seal
- aluminium block welded to transom
- synthetic rubber structural gasket
- 5mm grey coloured glass
- aluminium transom
- movable section of aluminium transom at expansion joint
- stainless steel flashing
- fixed section
- stainless steel flashing
- 5mm x 19mm long weep hole at 1·067m crs

54 WALLS

GLAZED WALL: EXHIBITION HALL IN ROTTERDAM, HOLLAND
DESIGNED BY J. H. VAN DEN BROEK AND J. B. BAKEMA (*Material supplied by R. Watts and R. Padovan*)

This most ingenious version of a glazed wall effects a complete visual divorce between the mullions, formed by r.s.j.s lying some 5 in. behind the glass line, and the transoms which are formed by continuous lines of 4-in. by 3-in. timber stiffened by m.s. angles. The vertical divisions between the sheets of glass are covered by the useful expedient of steel-cored lead cames.

WALLS 55

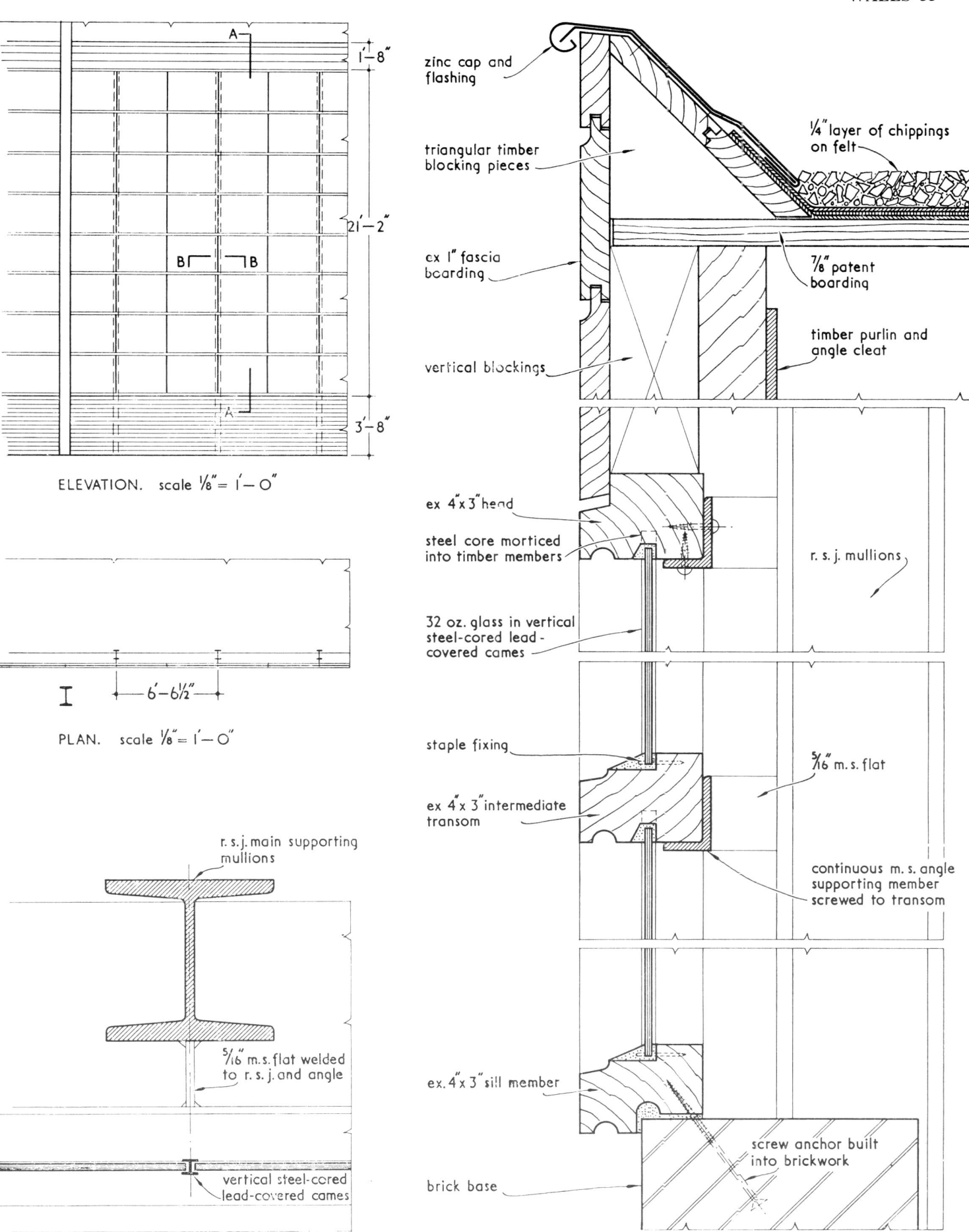

ELEVATION. scale ⅛" = 1'—0"

- 1'-8"
- 21'-2"
- 3'-8"

PLAN. scale ⅛" = 1'—0"

6'-6½"

PLAN AT B—B. scale ¼ full size

- r.s.j. main supporting mullions
- 5/16" m.s. flat welded to r.s.j. and angle
- vertical steel-cored lead-covered cames

SECTION A—A. scale ¼ full size

- zinc cap and flashing
- triangular timber blocking pieces
- ex 1" fascia boarding
- vertical blockings
- ex 4"x 3" head
- steel core morticed into timber members
- 32 oz. glass in vertical steel-cored lead-covered cames
- staple fixing
- ex 4"x 3" intermediate transom
- ex. 4"x 3" sill member
- brick base
- ¼" layer of chippings on felt
- ⅞" patent boarding
- timber purlin and angle cleat
- r.s.j. mullions
- 5/16" m.s. flat
- continuous m.s. angle supporting member screwed to transom
- screw anchor built into brickwork

note: figured dimensions in feet and inches are approximate

GLASS WALL TO BOILER HOUSE: FACTORY AT HEMEL HEMPSTEAD, HERTS
DESIGNED BY OVE ARUP AND PARTNERS; PHILIP DOWSON AND FRANCIS PYM (architects-in-charge)

The equipment—the calorifiers, the pipe runs and the oil-fired boiler itself—is sufficiently lagged to make heat loss through the glass of no account. A half-inch gap is left to right and left of each glazed wall to let air into the boiler. But, as this was found insufficient, a louvred ventilator was inserted in the boiler-house door. An incidental advantage of glazed walling in this context is that it is simple to take down a few sections when any of the larger pieces of equipment have to be renewed.

WALLS 57

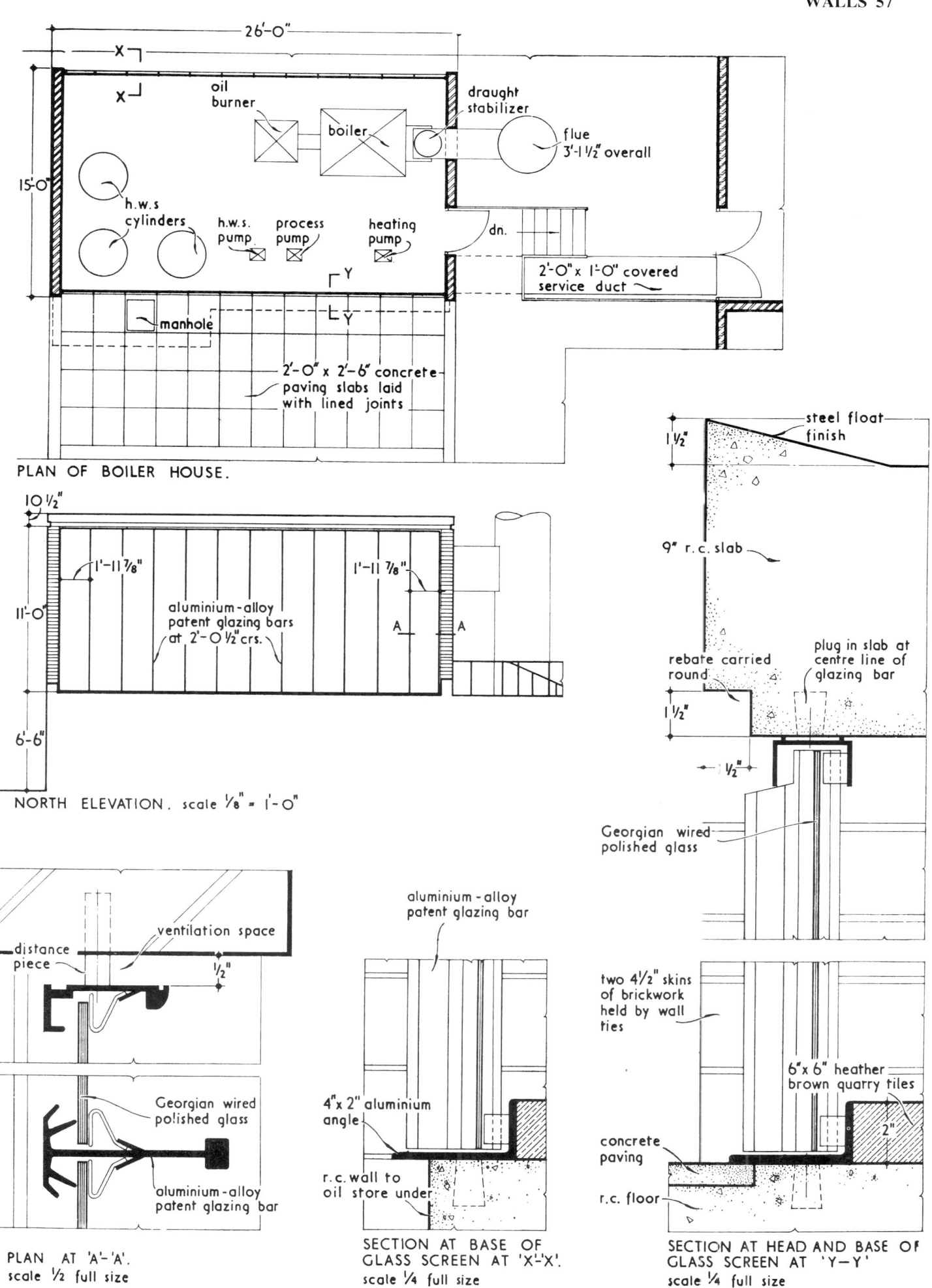

PLAN OF BOILER HOUSE.

Labels: 26'-0"; 15'-0"; oil burner; boiler; draught stabilizer; flue 3'-1½" overall; h.w.s cylinders; h.w.s pump; process pump; heating pump; dn.; 2'-0" x 1'-0" covered service duct; manhole; 2'-0" x 2'-6" concrete paving slabs laid with lined joints.

NORTH ELEVATION. scale ⅛" = 1'-0"

Labels: 10½"; 11'-0"; 6'-6"; 1'-11⅞"; aluminium-alloy patent glazing bars at 2'-0½" crs.; A—A.

PLAN AT 'A'-'A'. scale ½ full size

Labels: distance piece; ventilation space; ½"; Georgian wired polished glass; aluminium-alloy patent glazing bar.

SECTION AT BASE OF GLASS SCREEN AT 'X'-'X'. scale ¼ full size

Labels: aluminium-alloy patent glazing bar; 4" x 2" aluminium angle; r.c. wall to oil store under.

SECTION AT HEAD AND BASE OF GLASS SCREEN AT 'Y-Y' scale ¼ full size

Labels: steel float finish; 1½"; 9" r.c. slab; rebate carried round; plug in slab at centre line of glazing bar; 1½"; ½"; Georgian wired polished glass; two 4½" skins of brickwork held by wall ties; 6" x 6" heather brown quarry tiles; concrete paving; r.c. floor; 2".

58 WALLS

SCREENS: OFFICE BUILDING IN DON MILLS, ONTARIO, CANADA
DESIGNED BY JOHN B. PARKIN ASSOCIATES (*Material supplied by Felix Moore*)

This detail is an example of the accommodation of screens within a traditional concrete-cased steel structure: the screen above shelters fully-serviced office accommodation and the screen below (which is an ingenious detail in its own right shelters the parking lot.

WALLS 59

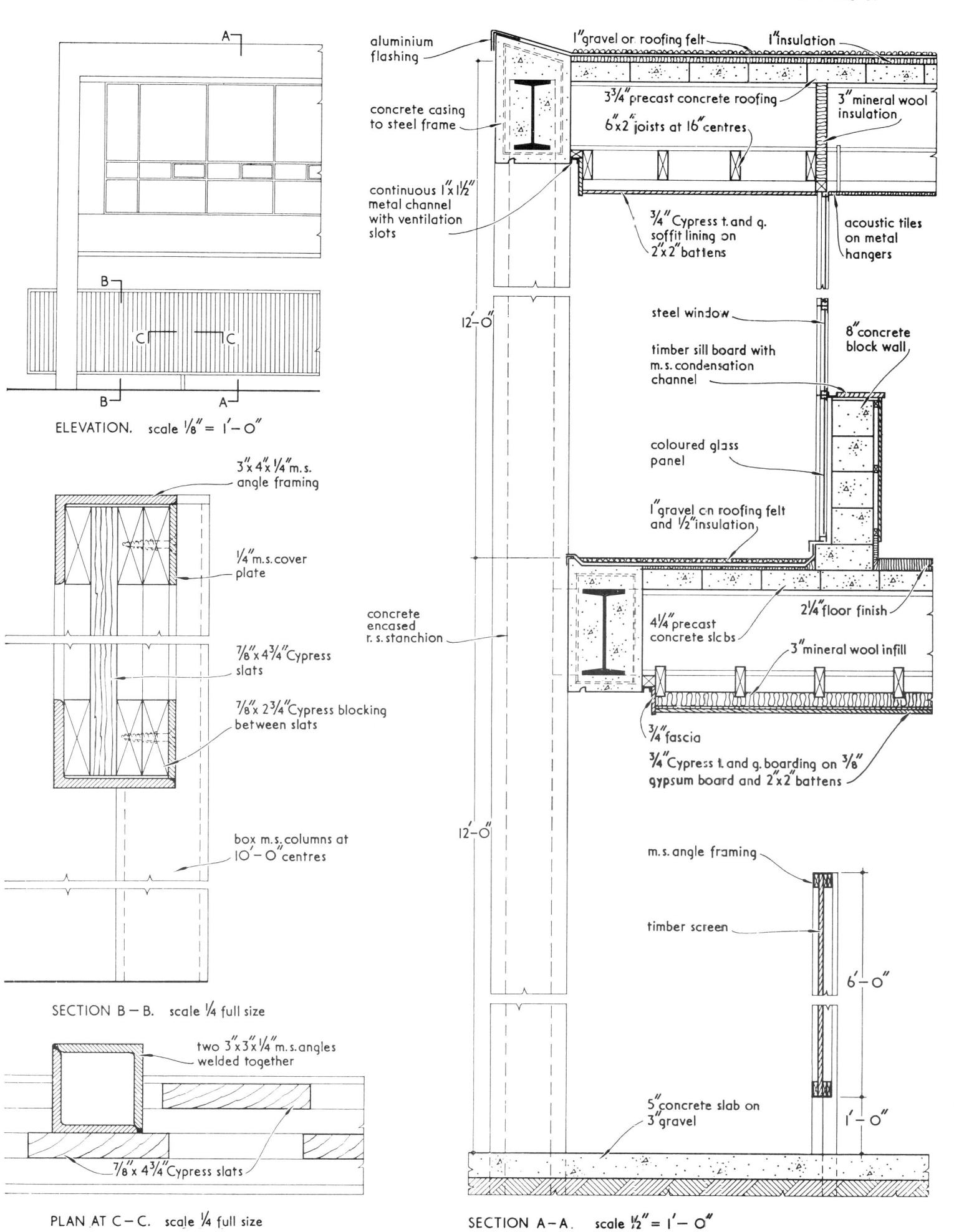

ELEVATION. scale 1/8" = 1'-0"

SECTION B—B. scale 1/4 full size

- 3"x 4"x 1/4" m.s. angle framing
- 1/4" m.s. cover plate
- 7/8" x 4 3/4" Cypress slats
- 7/8" x 2 3/4" Cypress blocking between slats
- box m.s. columns at 10'-0" centres

PLAN AT C—C. scale 1/4 full size

- two 3"x 3"x 1/4" m.s. angles welded together
- 7/8" x 4 3/4" Cypress slats

SECTION A—A. scale 1/2" = 1'-0"

- aluminium flashing
- 1" gravel or roofing felt
- 1" insulation
- concrete casing to steel frame
- 3 3/4" precast concrete roofing
- 6"x 2" joists at 16" centres
- 3" mineral wool insulation
- continuous 1"x 1 1/2" metal channel with ventilation slots
- 3/4" Cypress t. and g. soffit lining on 2"x 2" battens
- acoustic tiles on metal hangers
- steel window
- timber sill board with m.s. condensation channel
- 8" concrete block wall
- coloured glass panel
- 1" gravel on roofing felt and 1/2" insulation
- concrete encased r.s. stanchion
- 4 1/4" precast concrete slabs
- 2 1/4" floor finish
- 3" mineral wool infill
- 3/4" fascia
- 3/4" Cypress t. and g. boarding on 3/8" gypsum board and 2"x 2" battens
- m.s. angle framing
- timber screen
- 5" concrete slab on 3" gravel

12'-0"
12'-0"
6'-0"
1'-0"

60 WALLS

EXTERNAL SUN VISOR AND PLATFORM: HEAD OFFICE EXTENSION, METROPOLITAN WATER, SEWERAGE AND DRAINAGE BOARD, BATHURST STREET, SYDNEY, AUSTRALIA
DESIGNED BY McCONNEL, SMITH AND JOHNSON *(Material supplied by Marcus Mallam)*

This should be read in conjunction with the next detail on page 30. Note the fixing of visors and handrails by means of stainless steel plates attached directly to the structural steelwork but in a manner which permits movement at one end. Note also the concealment of a window cleaners' platform between the sun visor and the building face. This is perforated to permit a flow of air up the façade.

WALLS 61

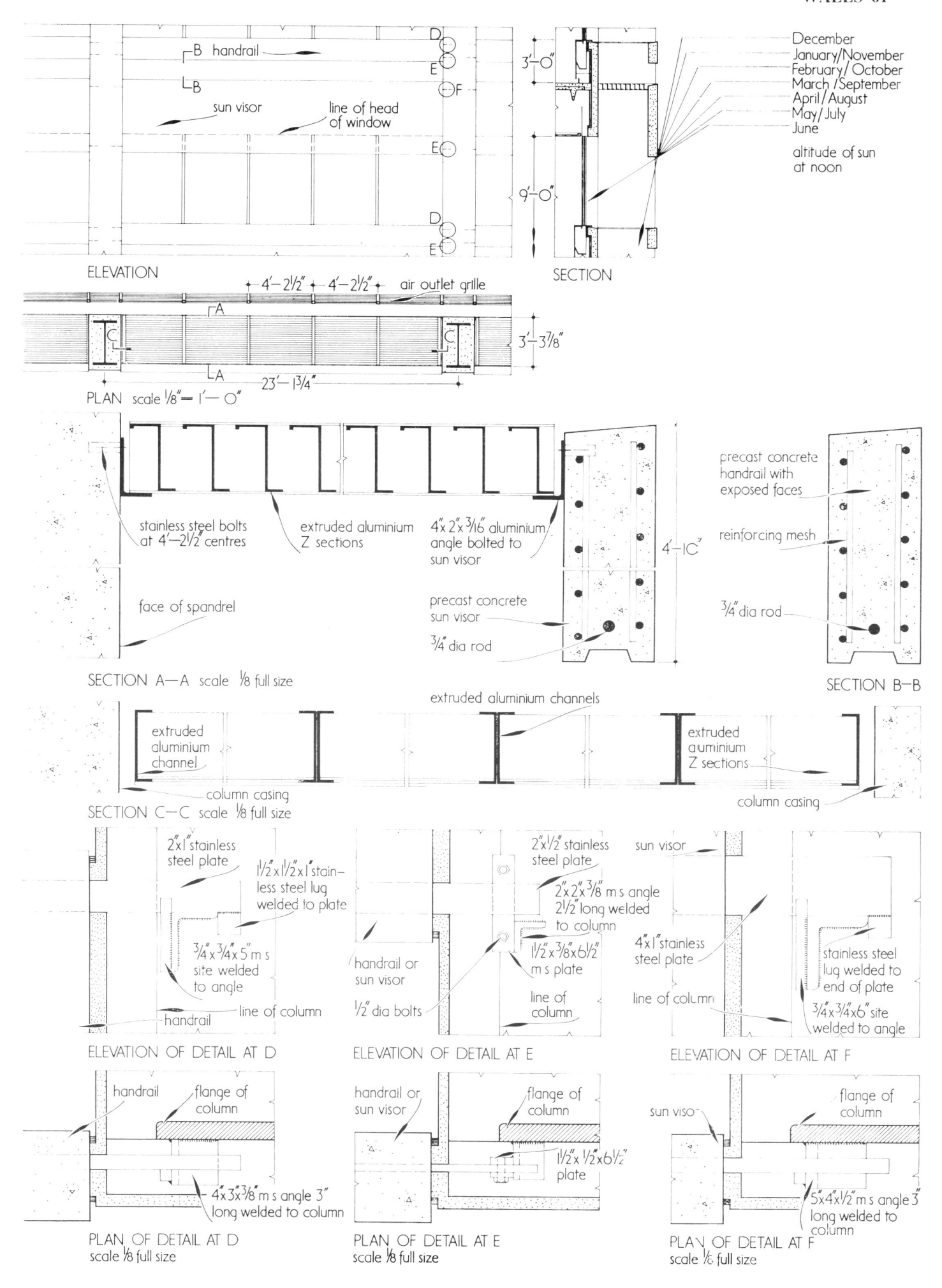

62 WALLS

EXTERNAL WALL: HEAD OFFICE EXTENSION, METROPOLITAN WATER, SEWERAGE AND DRAINAGE BOARD, BATHURST STREET, SYDNEY, AUSTRALIA
DESIGNED BY McCONNEL, SMITH AND JOHNSON. *(Material supplied by Marcus Mallam)*

This shows the inmost part of the sophisticated defence against sun penetration and glare, the external portion of which (the sun visor and platform) is illustrated on page 28. The under sill unit has a chilled water coil over which room air is drawn

WALLS 63

ELEVATION

- handrail
- sun visor
- line of head of window

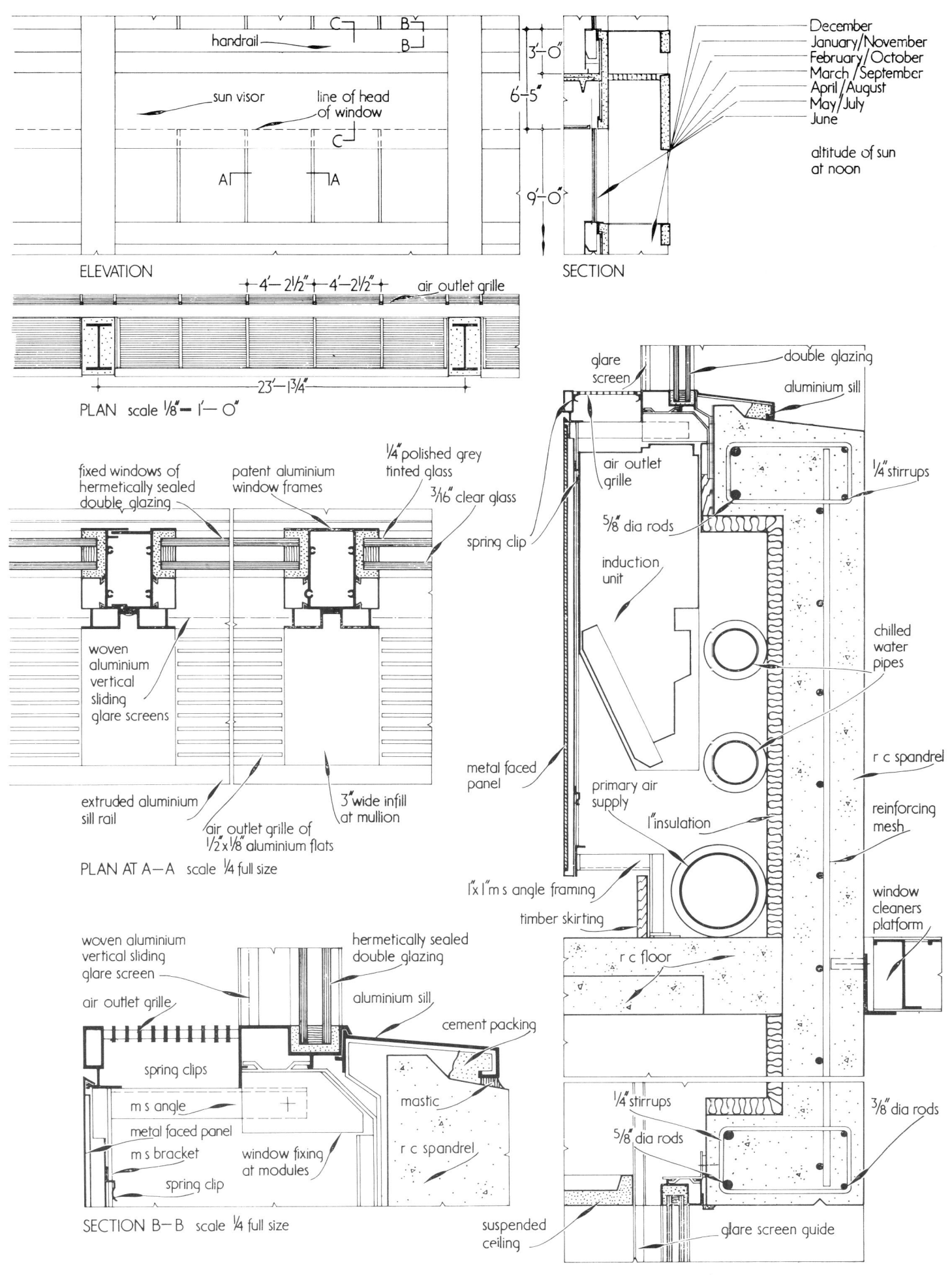

SECTION
- 3'-0"
- 6'-5"
- 9'-0"
- December
- January/November
- February/October
- March/September
- April/August
- May/July
- June

altitude of sun at noon

PLAN scale ⅛" = 1'-0"
- 4'-2½" + 4'-2½"
- 23'-1¾"
- air outlet grille

PLAN AT A—A scale ¼ full size
- fixed windows of hermetically sealed double glazing
- patent aluminium window frames
- ¼" polished grey tinted glass
- ³⁄₁₆" clear glass
- woven aluminium vertical sliding glare screens
- extruded aluminium sill rail
- 3" wide infill at mullion
- air outlet grille of ½" x ⅛" aluminium flats

SECTION B—B scale ¼ full size
- woven aluminium vertical sliding glare screen
- air outlet grille
- spring clips
- m s angle
- metal faced panel
- m s bracket
- spring clip
- hermetically sealed double glazing
- aluminium sill
- cement packing
- mastic
- r c spandrel
- window fixing at modules
- suspended ceiling

SECTION C—C scale ⅛ full size
- glare screen
- double glazing
- aluminium sill
- air outlet grille
- ¼" stirrups
- spring clip
- ⅝" dia rods
- induction unit
- chilled water pipes
- metal faced panel
- primary air supply
- 1" insulation
- r c spandrel
- reinforcing mesh
- 1" x 1" m s angle framing
- timber skirting
- window cleaners platform
- r c floor
- ¼" stirrups
- ⅝" dia rods
- ⅜" dia rods
- glare screen guide

64 BALCONIES

BALCONY AND WINDOWS: HOUSE NEAR HALLAND, SUSSEX
DESIGNED BY SERGE CHERMAYEFF

The balcony runs the length of the house, and bedrooms have access to it. It has a teak balustrade, and a slat deck, removable in sections, laid on bituminous felt roofing. The slat deck allows rainwater to run away immediately. The louvre ventilators over doors and windows are baffled in the wall thickness against direct draught and whistle

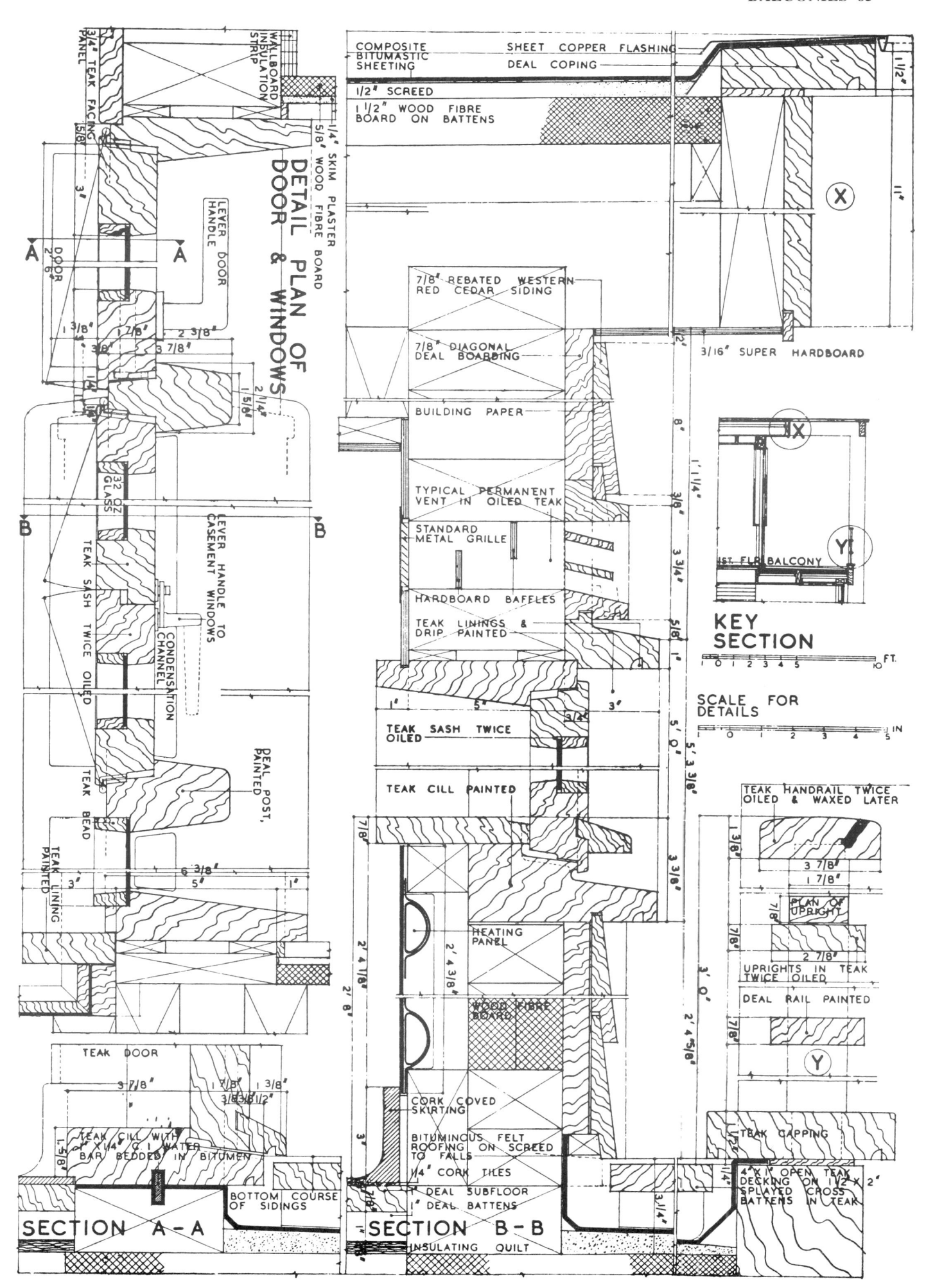

BALCONIES

66 BALCONIES

WALL AND BALCONIES: MAISONETTES IN LONDON, S.W.1
DESIGNED BY POWELL AND MOYA

Reinforced concrete slabs, connected by columns, form the top and bottom of the balconies, the latter being a continuation of the floor which divides the upper maisonettes from the lower ones

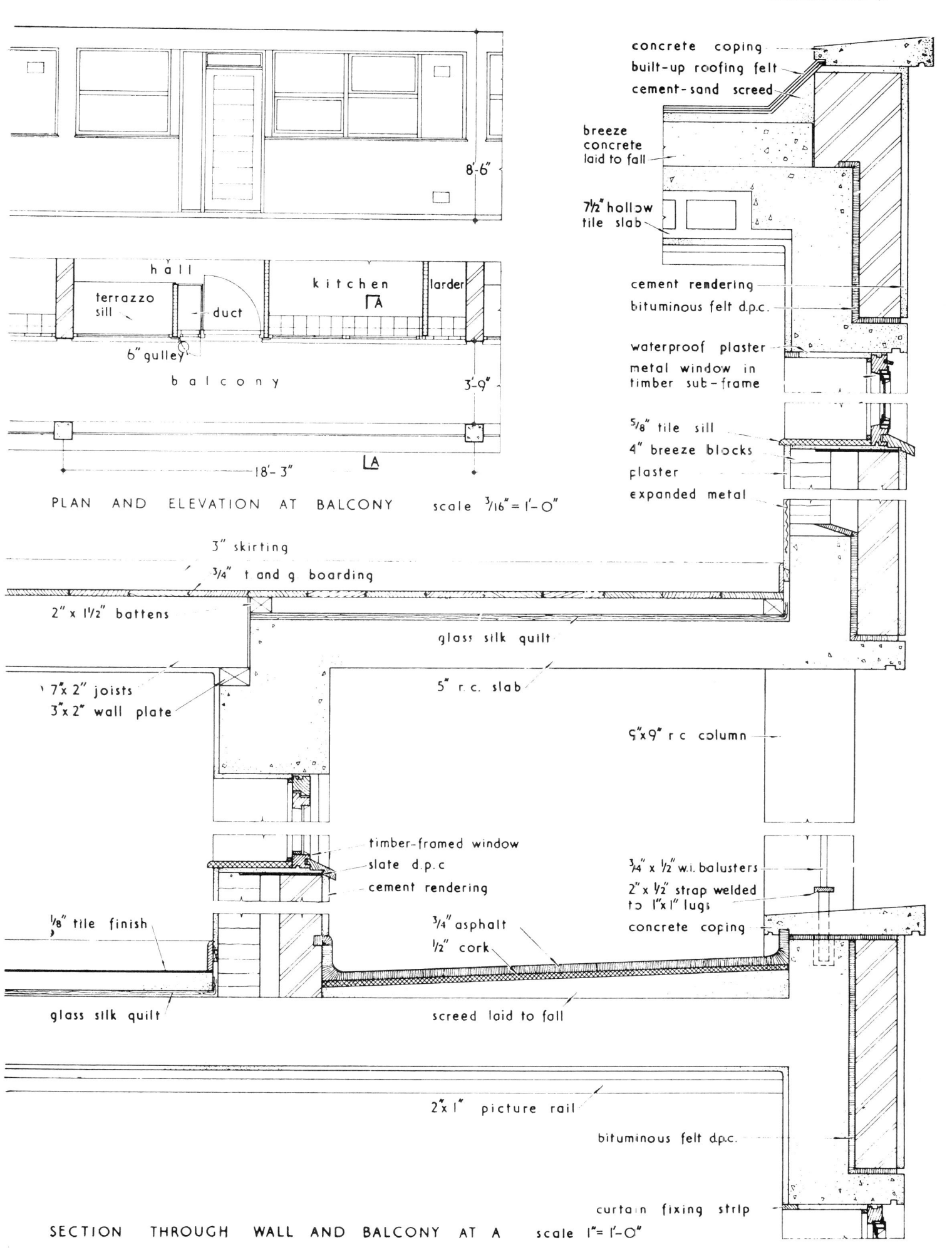

BALCONIES

PLAN AND ELEVATION AT BALCONY scale 3/16"= 1'-0"

- terrazzo sill
- hall
- duct
- 6" gulley
- kitchen
- larder
- balcony
- 8'-6"
- 3'-9"
- 18'-3"

SECTION THROUGH WALL AND BALCONY AT A scale 1"= 1'-0"

- concrete coping
- built-up roofing felt
- cement-sand screed
- breeze concrete laid to fall
- 7½" hollow tile slab
- cement rendering
- bituminous felt d.p.c.
- waterproof plaster
- metal window in timber sub-frame
- ⅝" tile sill
- 4" breeze blocks
- plaster
- expanded metal
- 3" skirting
- ¾" t and g boarding
- 2" x 1½" battens
- glass silk quilt
- 7" x 2" joists
- 3" x 2" wall plate
- 5" r.c. slab
- 9" x 9" r.c. column
- timber-framed window
- slate d.p.c
- cement rendering
- ¾" x ½" w.i. balusters
- 2" x ½" strap welded to 1" x 1" lugs
- concrete coping
- ⅛" tile finish
- ¾" asphalt
- ½" cork
- glass silk quilt
- screed laid to fall
- 2" x 1" picture rail
- bituminous felt d.p.c.
- curtain fixing strip

68 BALCONIES

BALCONIES : FLATS IN LONDON, S.W.1
DESIGNED BY POWELL AND MOYA

The Georgian-wired glass panels forming the front and sides of each balcony are held in small channels bolted through the flanges of the tee uprights, the nuts being previously welded to the insides of the channel sections.

BALCONIES 69

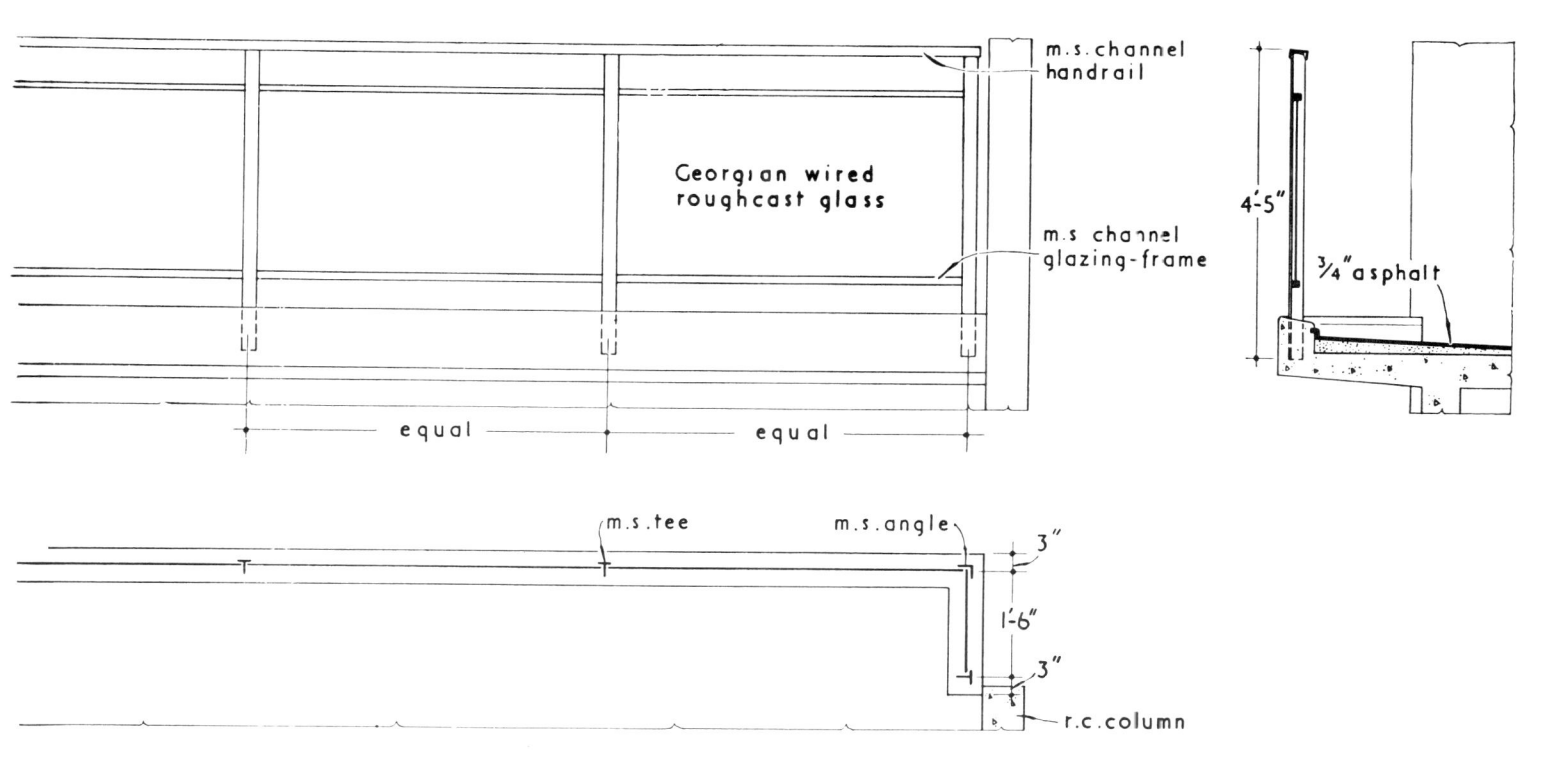

KEY ELEVATION, SECTION AND PLAN. scale 3/8" = 1'-0"

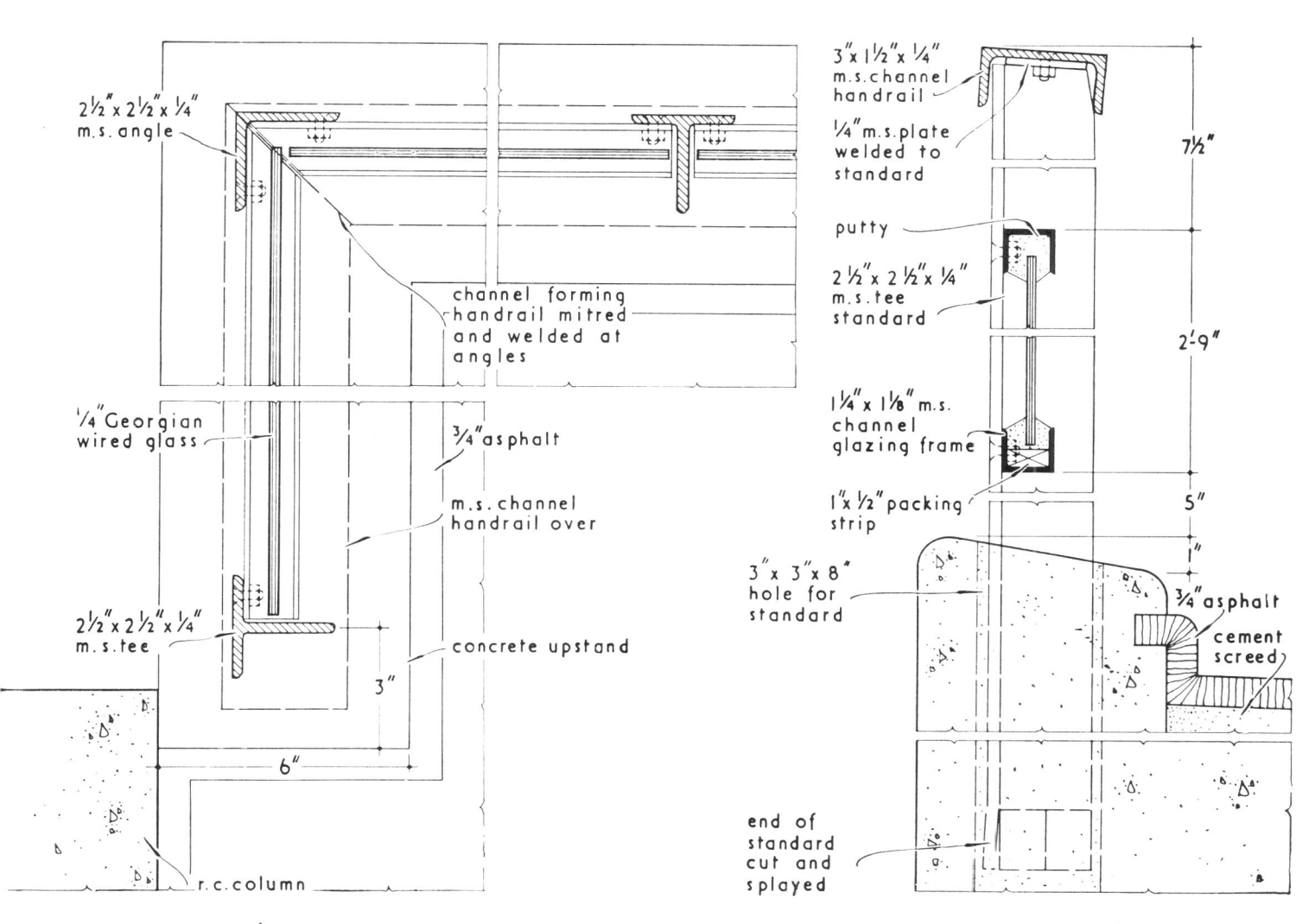

PLAN THRO' BALUSTRADE. scale 1/4 full size

TYPICAL SECTION. scale 1/4 full size

BALCONY: CRICKET PAVILION AT EAST MOLESEY, SURREY
DESIGNED BY PROFESSOR BASIL WARD (of Ramsey, Murray, White and Ward); G. P. BUZUK (site architect)

The balcony of the cricket pavilion is not cantilevered from the walls but is hung from the roof truss. Window frames are of mahogany, the capping of the balustrades of oak, the floor of the balcony of gurjun, the weatherboarding of painted softwood. Windows facing the pitch are of Georgian wired glass to guard against cricket balls. There are no opening lights on this side, cross ventilation being ensured by 1 in. diameter air holes at 6 in. centres in the hardboard lining beneath the upper windows, and by a corresponding slit in the weatherboarding.

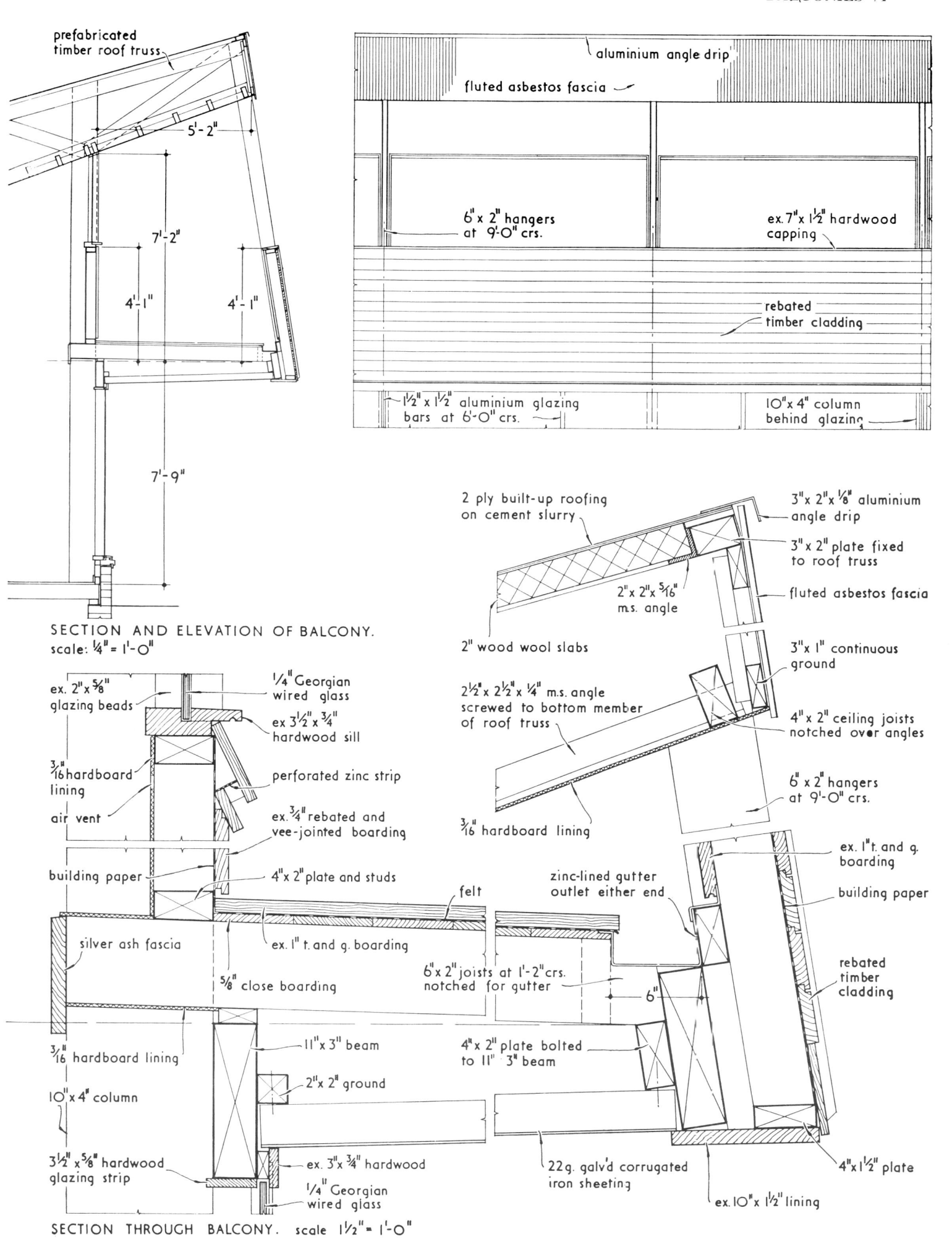

BALCONIES 71

SECTION AND ELEVATION OF BALCONY. scale: ¼" = 1'-0"

- prefabricated timber roof truss
- 5'-2"
- 7'-2"
- 4'-1"
- 4'-1"
- 7'-9"

- aluminium angle drip
- fluted asbestos fascia
- 6" x 2" hangers at 9'-0" crs.
- ex. 7" x 1½" hardwood capping
- rebated timber cladding
- 1½" x 1½" aluminium glazing bars at 6'-0" crs.
- 10" x 4" column behind glazing

SECTION THROUGH BALCONY. scale 1½" = 1'-0"

- ex. 2" x ⅝" glazing beads
- ¼" Georgian wired glass
- ex 3½" x ¾" hardwood sill
- ³⁄₁₆" hardboard lining
- perforated zinc strip
- air vent
- ex. ¾" rebated and vee-jointed boarding
- building paper
- 4" x 2" plate and studs
- silver ash fascia
- ex. 1" t. and g. boarding
- ⅝" close boarding
- ³⁄₁₆" hardboard lining
- 11" x 3" beam
- 2" x 2" ground
- 10" x 4" column
- 3½" x ⅝" hardwood glazing strip
- ex. 3" x ¾" hardwood
- ¼" Georgian wired glass

- 2 ply built-up roofing on cement slurry
- 2" x 2" x ⁵⁄₁₆" m.s. angle
- 2" wood wool slabs
- 2½" x 2½" x ¼" m.s. angle screwed to bottom member of roof truss
- ³⁄₁₆" hardboard lining
- felt
- zinc-lined gutter outlet either end
- 6" x 2" joists at 1'-2" crs. notched for gutter
- 4" x 2" plate bolted to 11" x 3" beam
- 6"
- 22 g. galv'd corrugated iron sheeting

- 3" x 2" x ⅛" aluminium angle drip
- 3" x 2" plate fixed to roof truss
- fluted asbestos fascia
- 3" x 1" continuous ground
- 4" x 2" ceiling joists notched over angles
- 6" x 2" hangers at 9'-0" crs.
- ex. 1" t. and g. boarding
- building paper
- rebated timber cladding
- 4" x 1½" plate
- ex. 10" x 1½" lining

72 BALCONIES

BALCONY BALUSTRADE: SCHOOL IN LONDON, E.5
DESIGNED BY J. M. AUSTIN-SMITH AND PARTNERS

Detailed points to notice about this balustrade are the cranking of the supports to give an external face flush with the brickwork, the use of welding to give neat junctions to the mild steel members, and the grouting of the uprights into tubes cast in the structural floor. The fascia and balcony edge are painted.

BALCONIES 73

ELEVATION.

9'-0"
6"
9'-0"

PLAN. scale 1/8" = 1'-0"

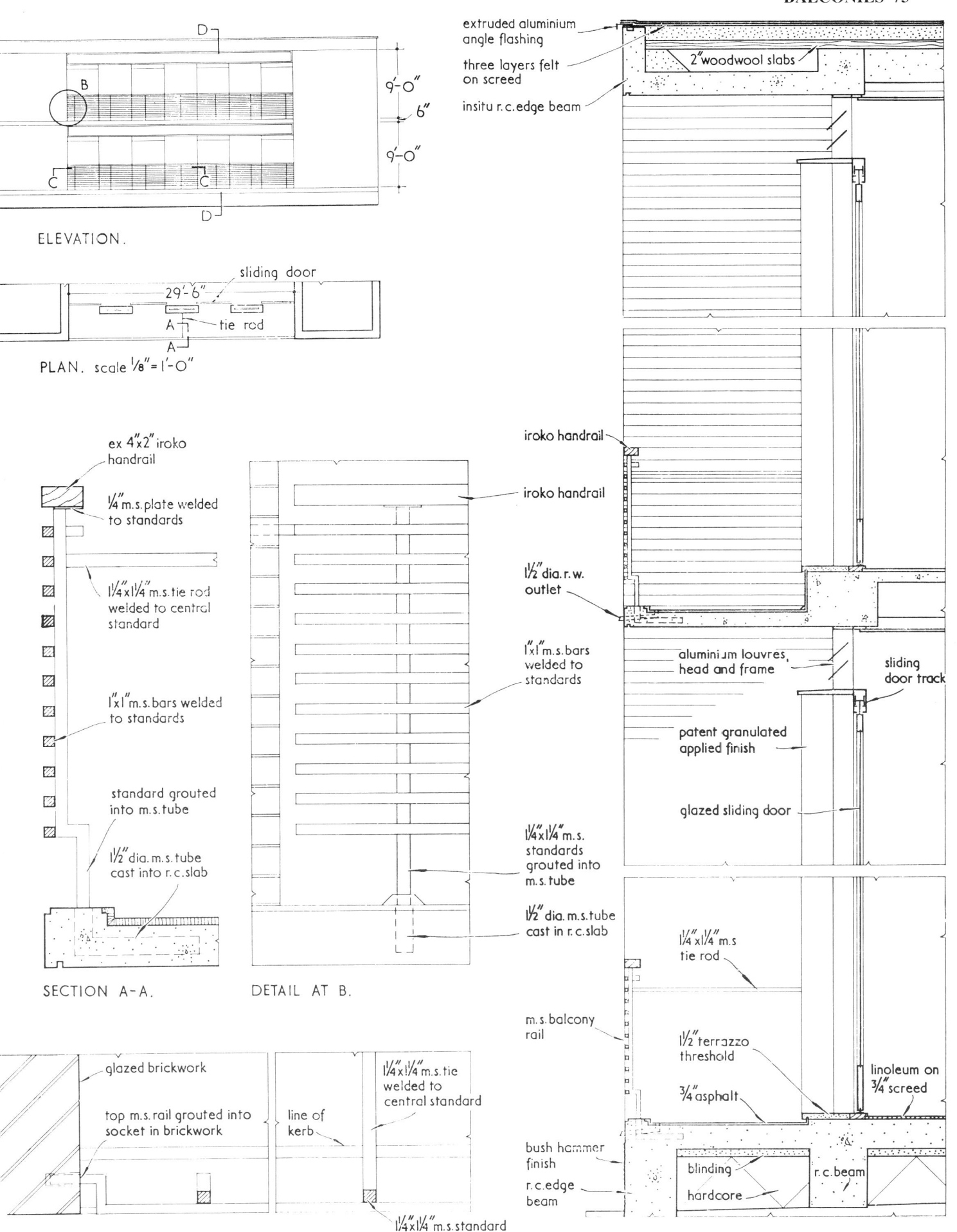

sliding door
29'-6"
tie rod

SECTION A-A.

ex 4"x2" iroko handrail
1/4" m.s. plate welded to standards
1/4"x1/4" m.s. tie rod welded to central standard
1"x1" m.s. bars welded to standards
standard grouted into m.s. tube
1½" dia. m.s. tube cast into r.c. slab

DETAIL AT B.

1"x1" m.s. bars welded to standards
1/4"x1/4" m.s. standards grouted into m.s. tube
1½" dia. m.s. tube cast in r.c. slab

PLAN C-C. scale 1" = 1'-0"

glazed brickwork
top m.s. rail grouted into socket in brickwork
line of kerb
1/4"x1/4" m.s. tie welded to central standard
1/4"x1/4" m.s. standard

SECTION D-D. scale 3/8" = 1'-0"

extruded aluminium angle flashing
three layers felt on screed
2" woodwool slabs
insitu r.c. edge beam
iroko handrail
iroko handrail
1½" dia. r.w. outlet
aluminium louvres, head and frame
sliding door track
patent granulated applied finish
glazed sliding door
1/4"x1/4" m.s. tie rod
m.s. balcony rail
1½" terrazzo threshold
3/4" asphalt
linoleum on 3/4" screed
bush hammer finish
r.c. edge beam
blinding
hardcore
r.c. beam

74 BALCONIES

BALCONIES: FLATS IN HELSINKI, FINLAND
DESIGNED BY VILJO REVELL

(*Material supplied by H. S. Sami*)

Each precast concrete balcony is formed as a tray and is supported at each end on cross walls. Note the projection of a highly-insulated larder into the balcony space.

BALCONIES

ELEVATION. scale 1/8" = 1'-0"

- louvres
- 7'-11"
- 1'-4"
- louvres and balustrade omitted
- larder
- 2" r.c. step

PLAN. scale 1/8" = 1'-0"

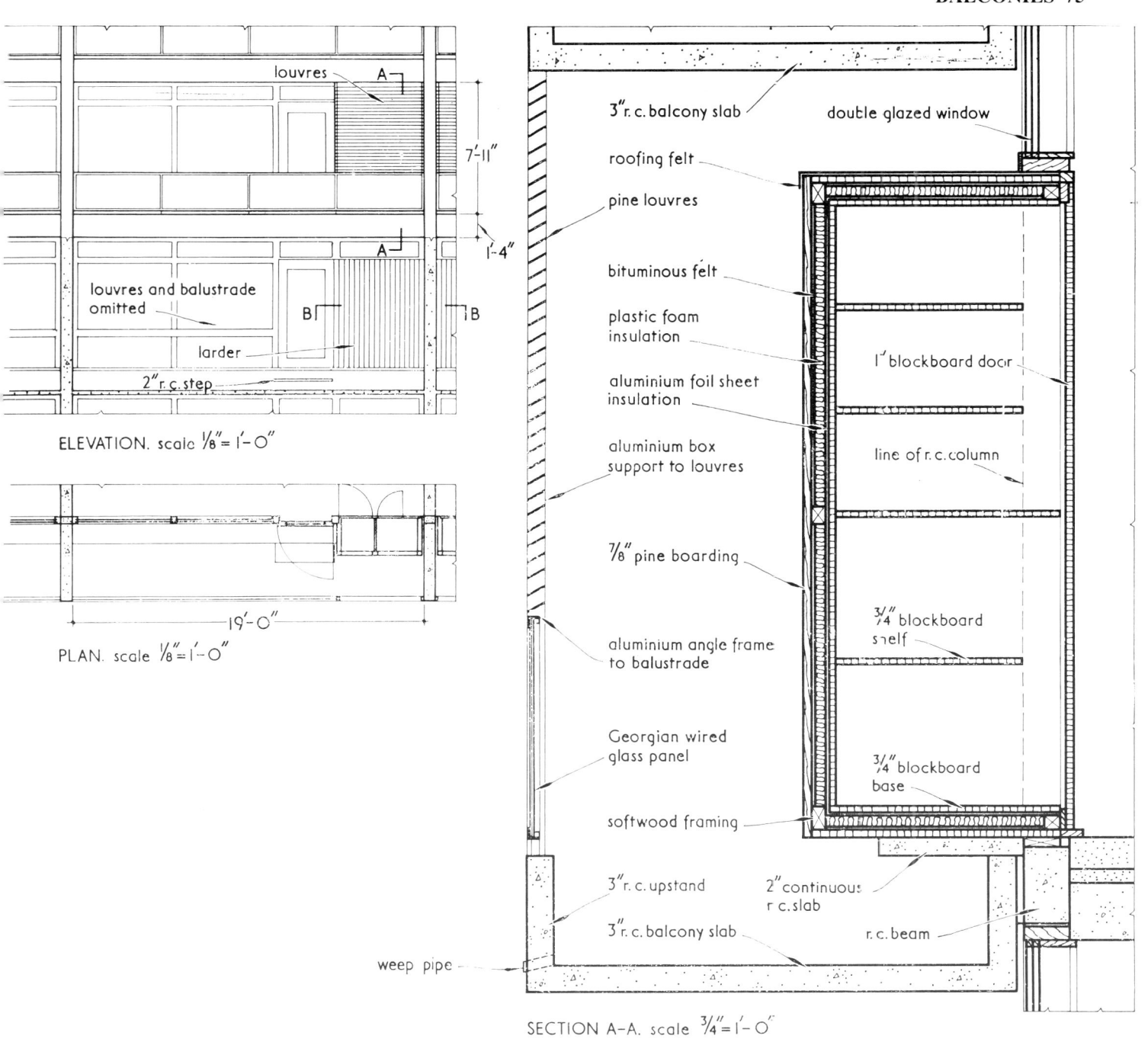

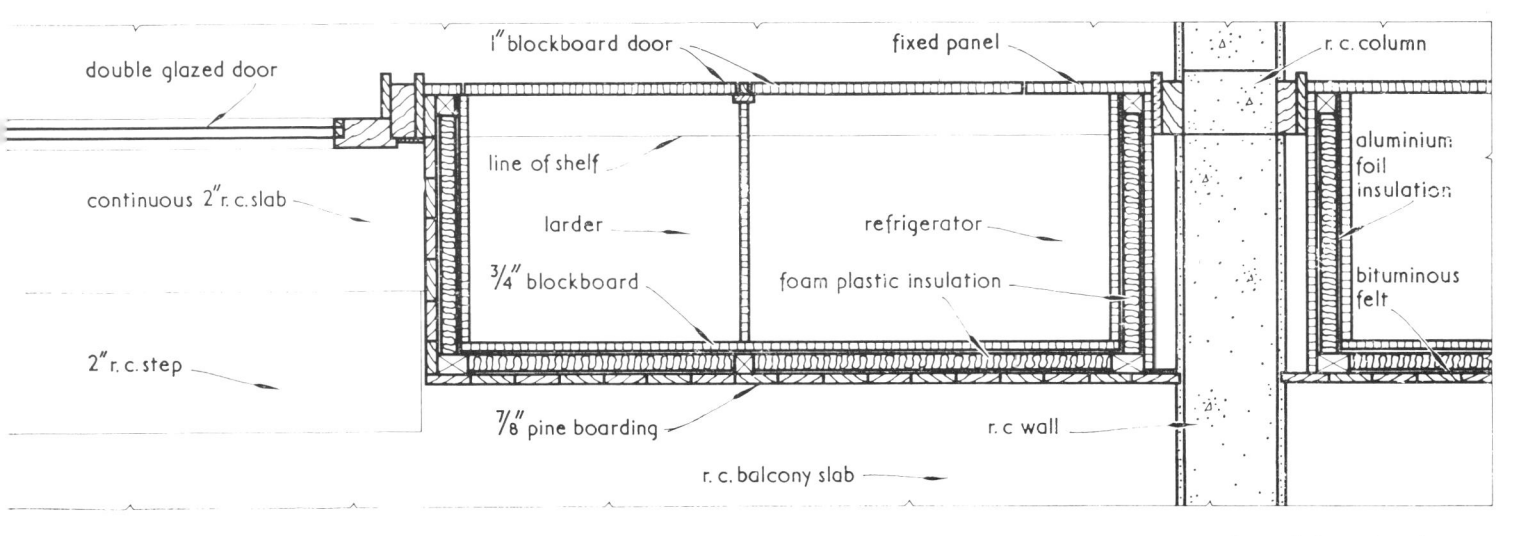

- 19'-0"

SECTION A-A. scale 3/4" = 1'-0"

- 3" r.c. balcony slab
- double glazed window
- roofing felt
- pine louvres
- bituminous felt
- plastic foam insulation
- 1" blockboard door
- aluminium foil sheet insulation
- aluminium box support to louvres
- line of r.c. column
- 7/8" pine boarding
- 3/4" blockboard shelf
- aluminium angle frame to balustrade
- Georgian wired glass panel
- 3/4" blockboard base
- softwood framing
- 3" r.c. upstand
- 2" continuous r.c. slab
- 3" r.c. balcony slab
- r.c. beam
- weep pipe

PLAN AT B-B. scale 3/4" = 1'-0"

- double glazed door
- 1" blockboard door
- fixed panel
- r.c. column
- continuous 2" r.c. slab
- line of shelf
- larder
- refrigerator
- aluminium foil insulation
- 3/4" blockboard
- foam plastic insulation
- bituminous felt
- 2" r.c. step
- 7/8" pine boarding
- r.c. wall
- r.c. balcony slab

note: figured dimensions in feet and inches are approximate

76 BALCONIES

BALCONY FAÇADE: TOWN HALL, ASKER, NR OSLO, NORWAY
DESIGNED BY NILS SLAATTO AND KJELL LUND (*Material supplied by J. B. Patterson*)

The shallow balconies on this building serve as escape routes in case of fire. Note the downstand balcony front to limit sun penetration and (on the detail photograph) a discreet and successful use of the traditional device of a recessed moulding at the top and bottom edges of the balcony front.

BALCONIES 77

ELEVATION

SECTION

PLAN scale 1:200

PLAN AT B-B scale 1:5

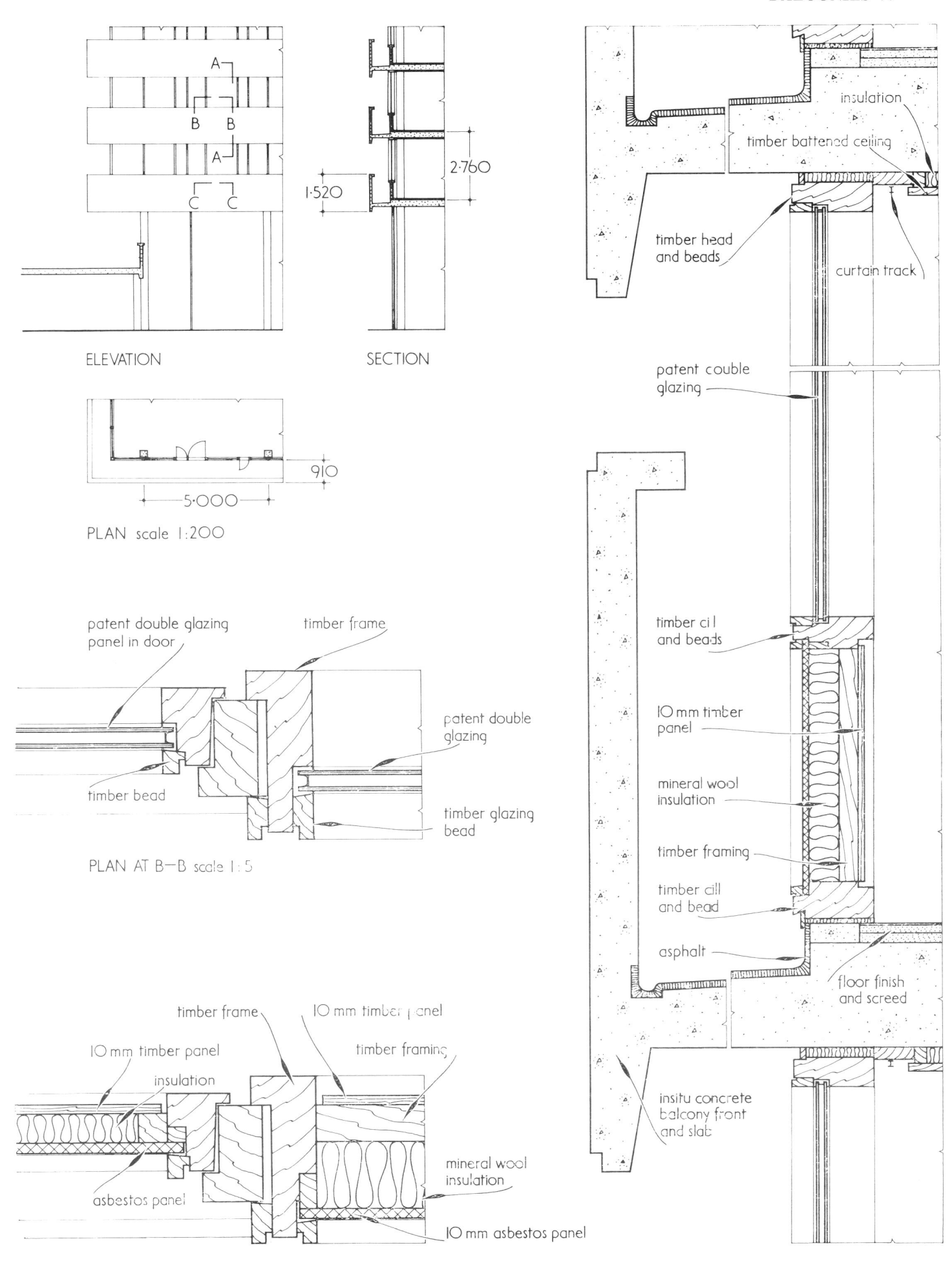

PLAN AT C-C scale 1:5

SECTION A-A scale 1:10

78 STAIRCASES

SPIRAL STAIRCASE: OFFICES IN COPENHAGEN, DENMARK
DESIGNED BY ESKE KRISTENSEN AND E. BARFOED   (*Material supplied by Michael Sadler*)

An interesting variation of the precast concrete newel stair incorporaitng a riser and a slight thickening at the string to receive the balusters. It is a tribute to the fine quality of the precast concrete work that the incorporation of a wrought timber canopy does not look out of place. A detail of subsidiary interest (which can be appreciated from the drawing only) is the tanking for the adjoining flower bed.

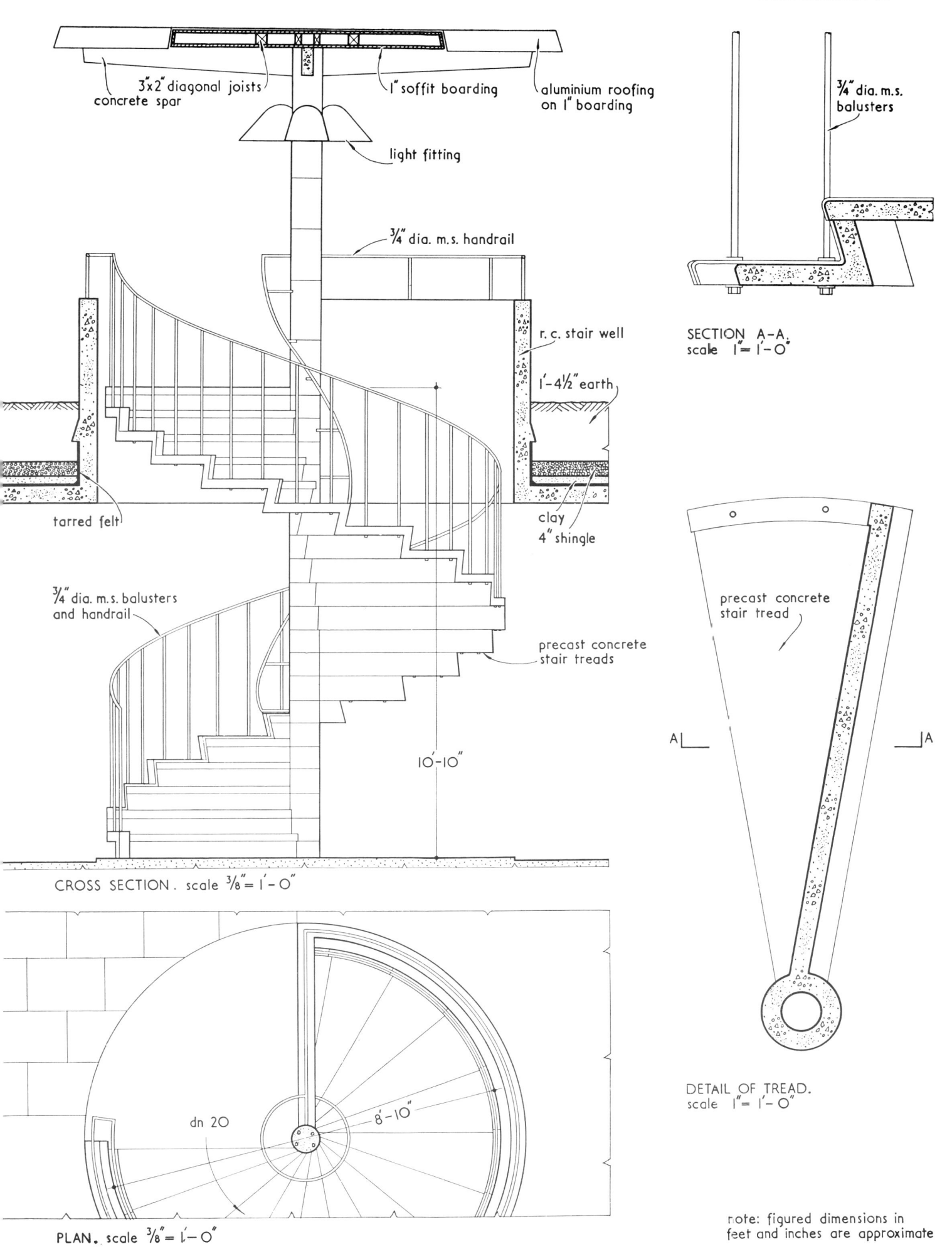

STAIRCASES 79

3"x2" diagonal joists
concrete spar
1" soffit boarding
aluminium roofing on 1" boarding
light fitting
¾" dia. m.s. handrail
r.c. stair well
1'-4½" earth
tarred felt
clay
4" shingle
¾" dia. m.s. balusters and handrail
precast concrete stair treads
10'-10"

CROSS SECTION. scale ⅜"= 1'-0"

dn 20
8'-10"

PLAN. scale ⅜"= 1'-0"

¾" dia. m.s. balusters

SECTION A-A.
scale 1"= 1'-0"

precast concrete stair tread

A| |A

DETAIL OF TREAD.
scale 1"= 1'-0"

note: figured dimensions in feet and inches are approximate

80 STAIRCASES

FIRE ESCAPE STAIRCASE: TOWER IN GENEVA, SWITZERLAND
**DESIGNED BY A. BORDIGONI, J. GROS, A. DE SAUSSURE
AND R. FLEURY**

(*Material supplied by Dariush Borbor*)

The erection sequence was, first, to fix the precast spiral treads; second, to weld the steel uprights to steel angles cast into the treads taking one rise at a time; third, to lower each curved precast baluster slab on to steel angles welded to the flanges of the uprights and grout in. A further length of steel upright was then bolted on and the cycle repeated. English readers will envy the quality and precision of the curved panels.

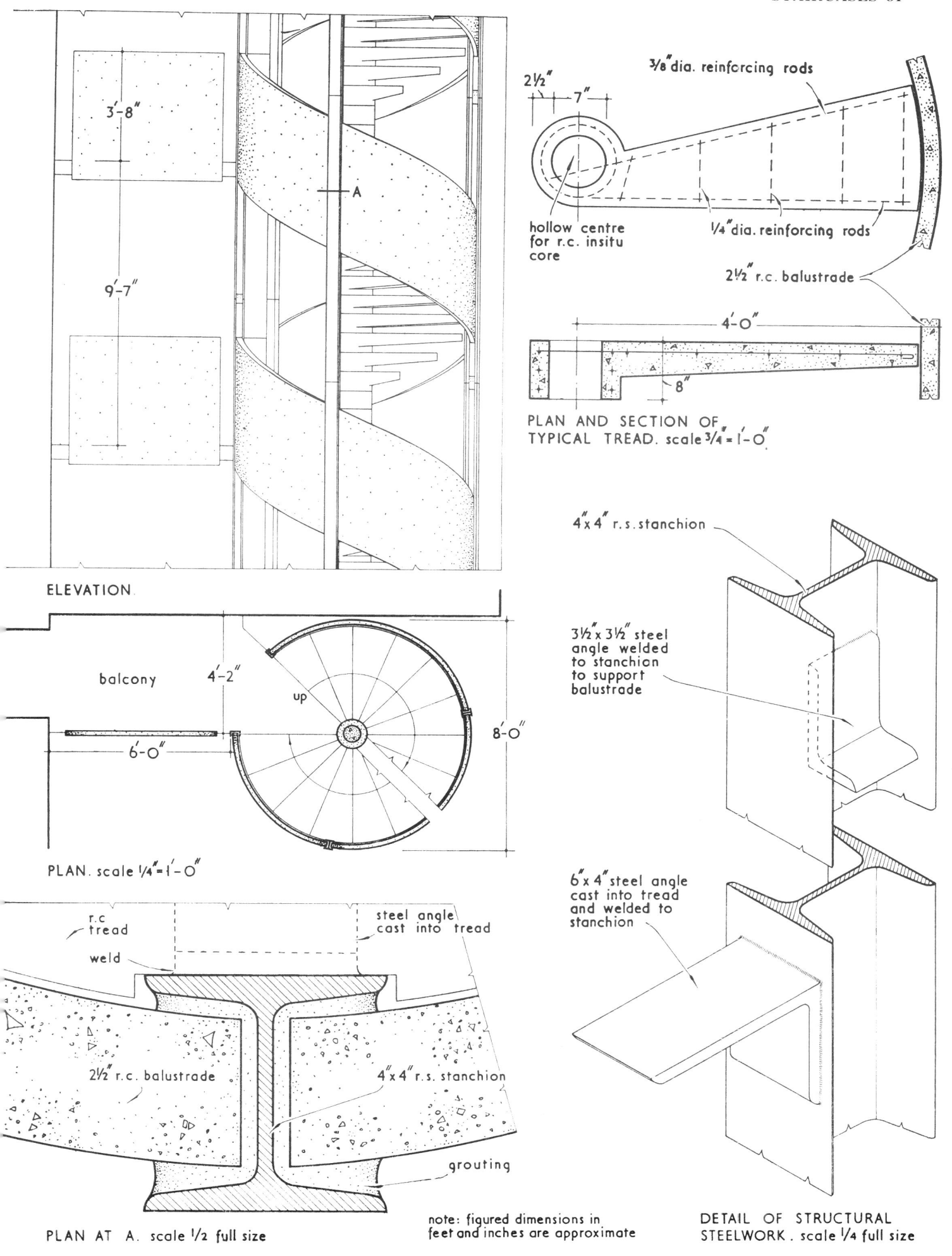

STAIRCASES 81

ELEVATION

balcony — 4'-2" — up — 8'-0"
— 6'-0" —

PLAN. scale 1/4" = 1'-0"

r.c tread — steel angle cast into tread
weld
2½" r.c. balustrade
4"×4" r.s. stanchion
grouting

PLAN AT A. scale 1/2 full size

2½" — 7"
3/8" dia. reinforcing rods
hollow centre for r.c. insitu core
¼" dia. reinforcing rods
2½" r.c. balustrade
— 4'-0" —
8"

PLAN AND SECTION OF TYPICAL TREAD. scale 3/4" = 1'-0"

4"×4" r.s. stanchion

3½"×3½" steel angle welded to stanchion to support balustrade

6"×4" steel angle cast into tread and welded to stanchion

note: figured dimensions in feet and inches are approximate

DETAIL OF STRUCTURAL STEELWORK. scale 1/4 full size

82 ROOFS

ROOF: FACTORY AT HEMEL HEMPSTEAD, HERTS
DESIGNED BY OVE ARUP AND PARTNERS; PHILIP DOWSON AND FRANCIS PYM (architects-in-charge)

This Detail shows one method of freeing the wide span industrial roof from the display of 'knitting' (i.e., the multiplicity of small scale engineering parts) which is all too common. The ceiling of ⅜-in. asbestos board conceals a system of composite stressed skin timber and steel triangular space frames. Steel is used for the top and bottom booms to take the main bending stresses of tension and compression. These booms are joined by timber triangulated struts glued and screwed to the steel. The ⅜-in. ply decking, on which the roofing felt is supported, being glued to the timber struts, acts as a flange for the junctions and a web for the two canted sides of the space frame.

ROOFS 83

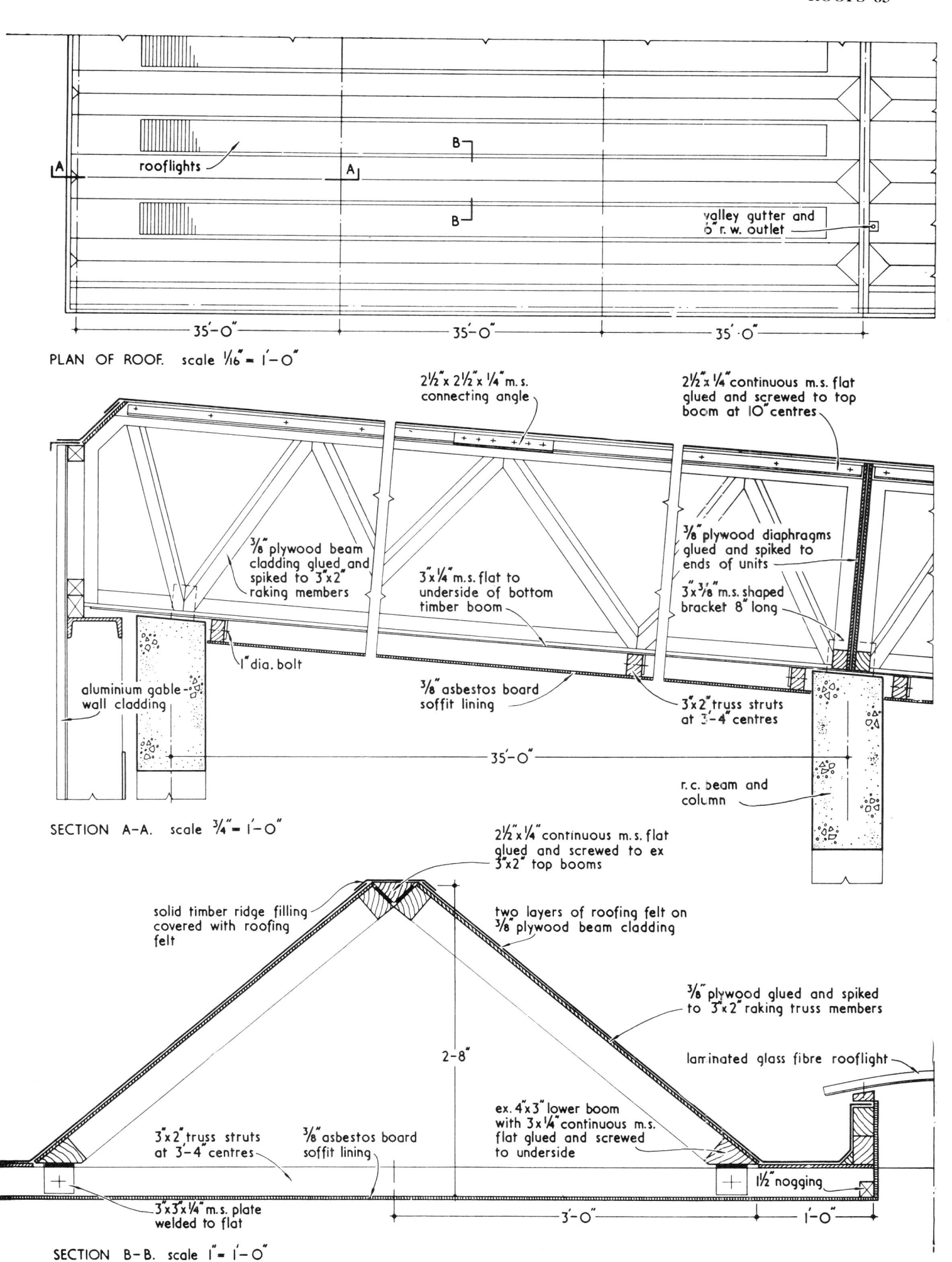

PLAN OF ROOF. scale 1/16" = 1'-0"

- rooflights
- valley gutter and 6" r.w. outlet
- 35'-0" / 35'-0" / 35'-0"

SECTION A-A. scale 3/4" = 1'-0"

- 2½" x 2½" x ¼" m.s. connecting angle
- 2½" x ¼" continuous m.s. flat glued and screwed to top boom at 10" centres
- 3/8" plywood beam cladding glued and spiked to 3"x 2" raking members
- 3" x ¼" m.s. flat to underside of bottom timber boom
- 3/8" plywood diaphragms glued and spiked to ends of units
- 3" x 3/8" m.s. shaped bracket 8" long
- 1" dia. bolt
- aluminium gable wall cladding
- 3/8" asbestos board soffit lining
- 3"x 2" truss struts at 3'-4" centres
- 35'-0"
- r.c. beam and column

SECTION B-B. scale 1" = 1'-0"

- 2½" x ¼" continuous m.s. flat glued and screwed to ex 3"x 2" top booms
- solid timber ridge filling covered with roofing felt
- two layers of roofing felt on 3/8" plywood beam cladding
- 3/8" plywood glued and spiked to 3"x 2" raking truss members
- laminated glass fibre rooflight
- 3"x 2" truss struts at 3'-4" centres
- 3/8" asbestos board soffit lining
- ex. 4"x 3" lower boom with 3"x ¼" continuous m.s. flat glued and screwed to underside
- 1½" nogging
- 3"x 3"x ¼" m.s. plate welded to flat
- 2'-8"
- 3'-0" / 1'-0"

84 ROOFS

ROOF TRUSS: CHAPEL AT OTANIEMI, FINLAND
DESIGNED BY HEIKKI SIREN *(Material supplied by Imre Weores)*

This celebrated roof truss is a good example of the expression proper to timber. Technical interest lies in the liberal use of mild steel tie and fishplates to reduce the size of the timber sections. Note the unobtrusive fixing of the lights at the foot of each post.

ROOFS 85

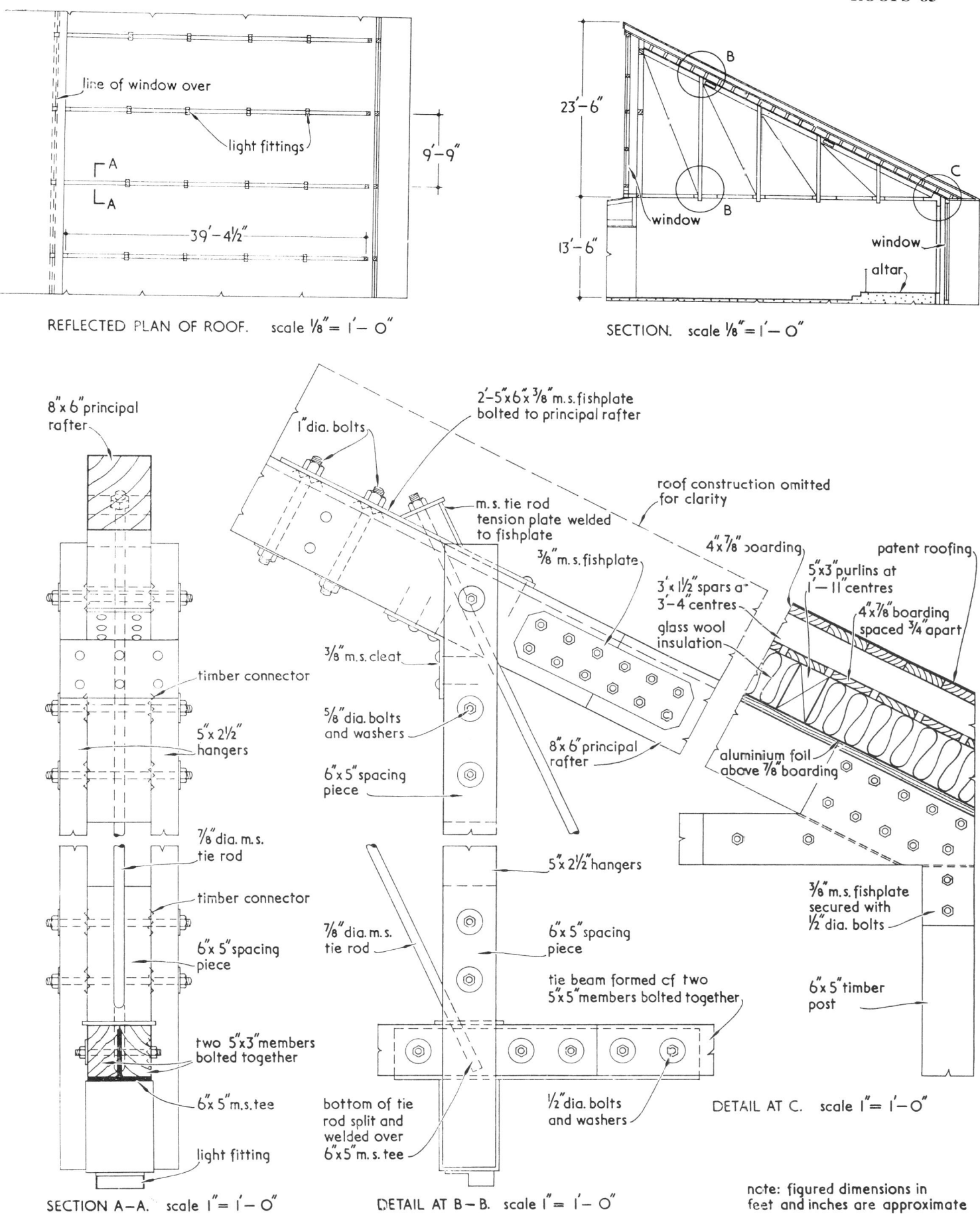

86 ROOFS

ROOF: FACTORY IN DUBLIN
DESIGNED BY OVE ARUP AND PARTNERS

The form of this roof was determined in the first instance by the decision to economise on walling by having a low eaves line, while still giving sufficient height for the overhead gantries; and in the second instance by the desire for a structure which would be strong enough to take the loads required by the gantries and would give support at sufficiently close centres for the roof purlins, while still giving an effect of lightness. This second aim was achieved by combining two systems of trussing into one: heavy trusses (both transverse and lateral) to take the gantry loads, and lighter trusses to take the purlins. The former are painted black and the latter white to clarify the structural pattern.

ROOFS 87

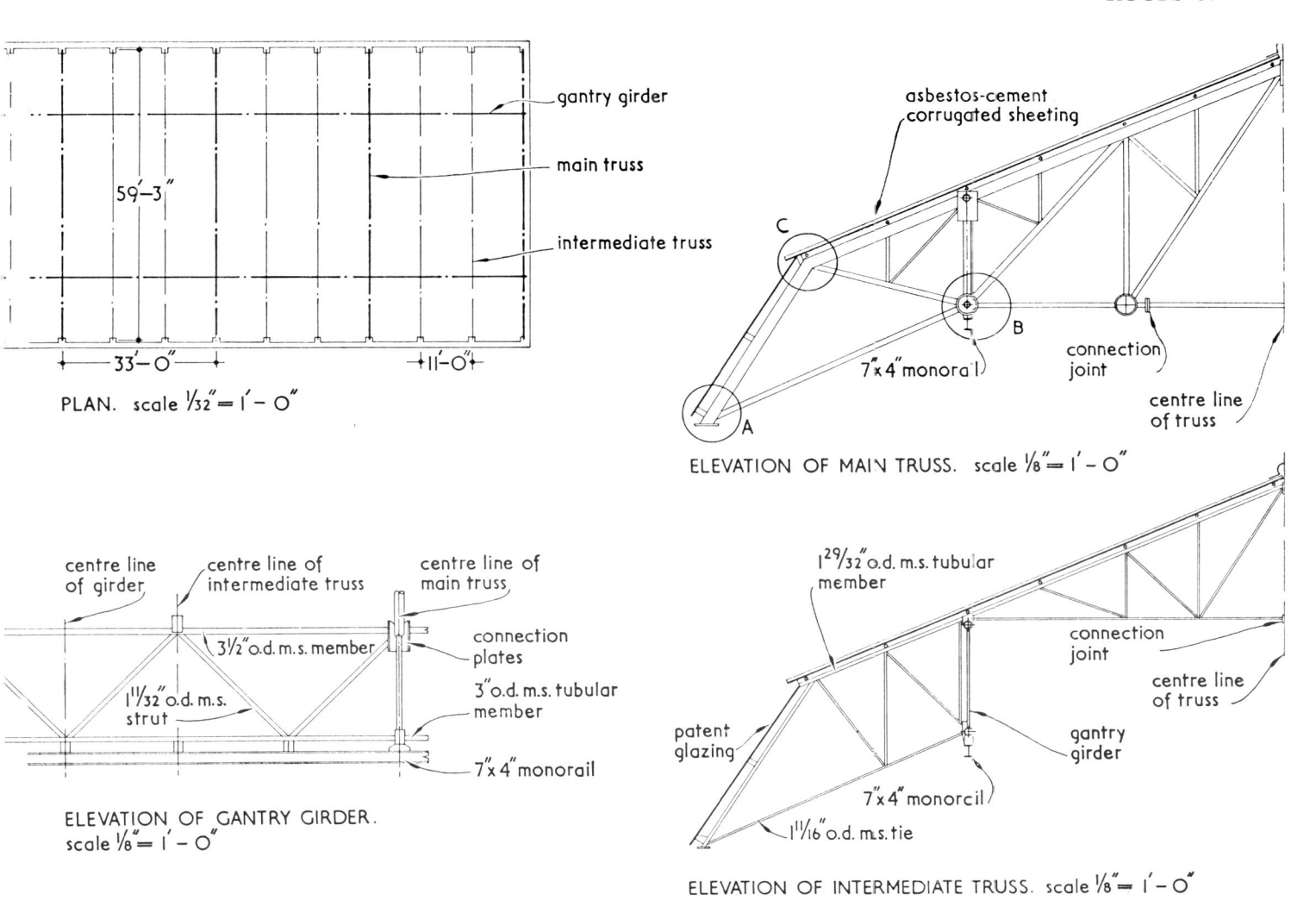

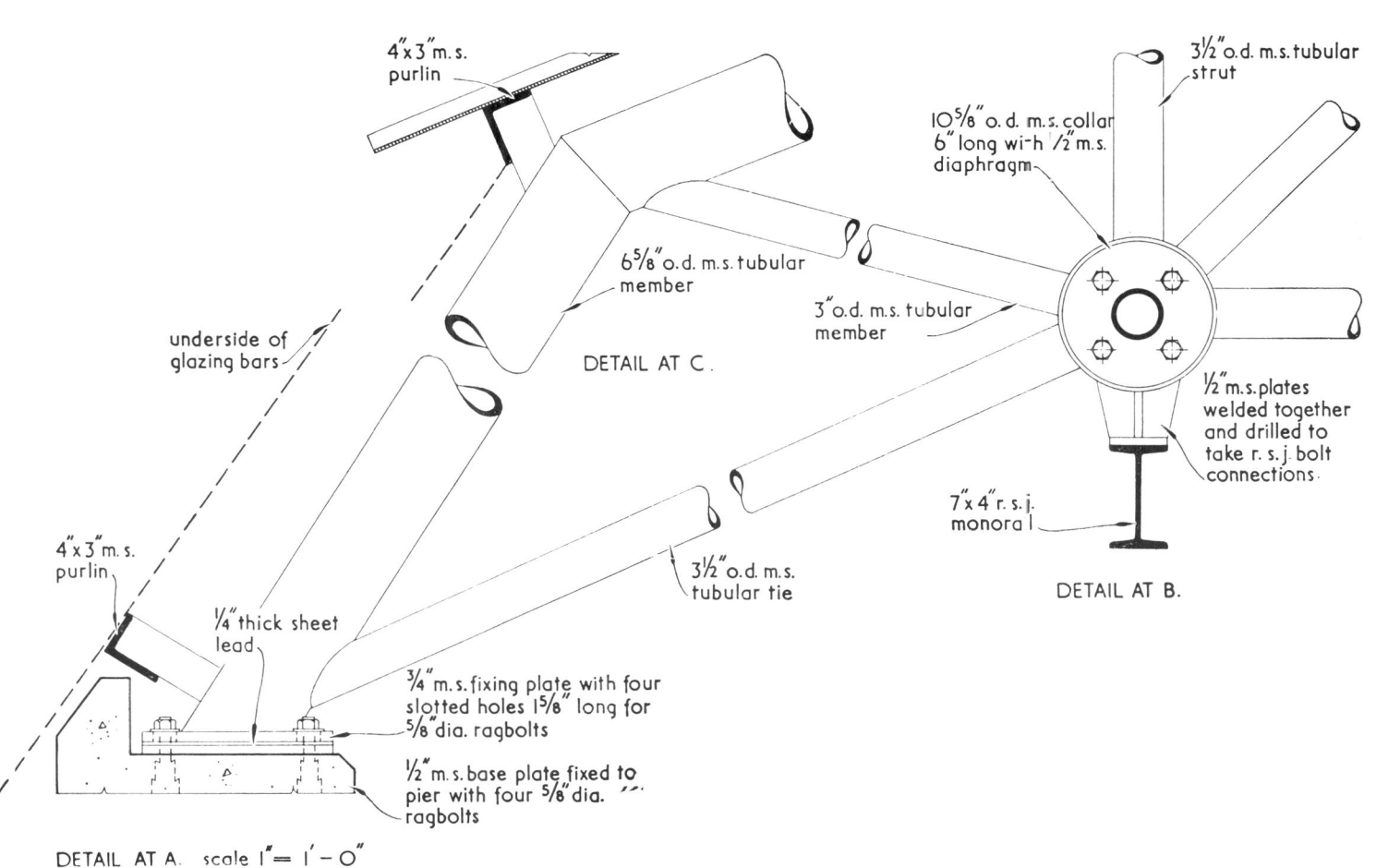

ROOF: FACTORY AT POOLE, DORSET
DESIGNED BY FARMER AND DARK

The space frames for the roof glazing consist of tubular members welded to 6-in. by 3-in. angles at the base, and at the apex to a box section of 5-in. by 2½-in. channels. The remainder of the roof is of channel-reinforced wood-wool slabs, screeded and finished with roofing felt.

ROOFS 89

SECTION A—A. scale ¼"= 1'— 0"

SECTION

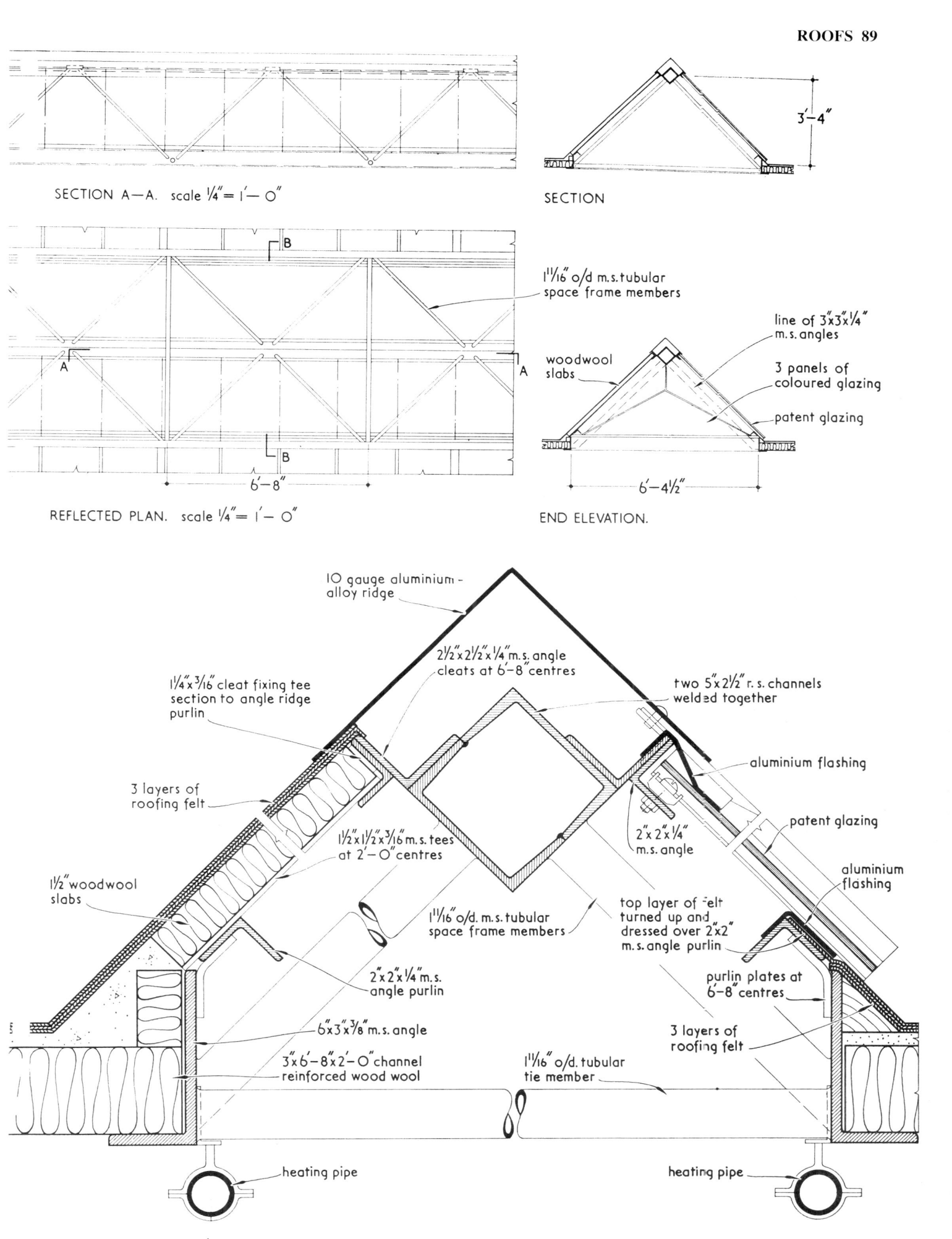

REFLECTED PLAN. scale ¼"= 1'— 0"

- 1¹¹⁄₁₆" o/d m.s. tubular space frame members
- line of 3"x3"x¼" m.s. angles
- 3 panels of coloured glazing
- patent glazing
- woodwool slabs

3'-4"

6'-4½"

END ELEVATION.

6'-8"

SECTION B—B. scale ¼ full size

- 10 gauge aluminium-alloy ridge
- 2½"x2½"x¼" m.s. angle cleats at 6'-8" centres
- 1¼"x³⁄₁₆" cleat fixing tee section to angle ridge purlin
- two 5"x2½" r.s. channels welded together
- 3 layers of roofing felt
- aluminium flashing
- 1½"x1½"x³⁄₁₆" m.s. tees at 2'-0" centres
- 2"x2"x¼" m.s. angle
- patent glazing
- 1½" woodwool slabs
- 1¹¹⁄₁₆" o/d m.s. tubular space frame members
- aluminium flashing
- top layer of felt turned up and dressed over 2"x2" m.s. angle purlin
- 2"x2"x¼" m.s. angle purlin
- purlin plates at 6'-8" centres
- 6"x3"x⅜" m.s. angle
- 3"x6'-8"x2'-0" channel reinforced wood wool
- 3 layers of roofing felt
- 1¹¹⁄₁₆" o/d. tubular tie member
- heating pipe
- heating pipe

MONITOR ROOF: FACTORY IN LONDON, E.8
DESIGNED BY WALTER SEGAL

This monitor truss is an excellent example of how, by using common unspecialized components intelligently, a result can be produced which is neater and cheaper than using more elaborate products which the industry offers for this purpose. The 38-ft. span trusses which form the sides of these monitors are made from 3 in. by 3 in. by ¼ in. angles, 1½ in. by 1½ in. by ¼ in. tees, and steel rods (which vary in diameter between ½ in. and ¾ in. according to their position). Note the welding of an additional strip of angle to the bottom boom to support the wood-wool slabs.

ROOFS 91

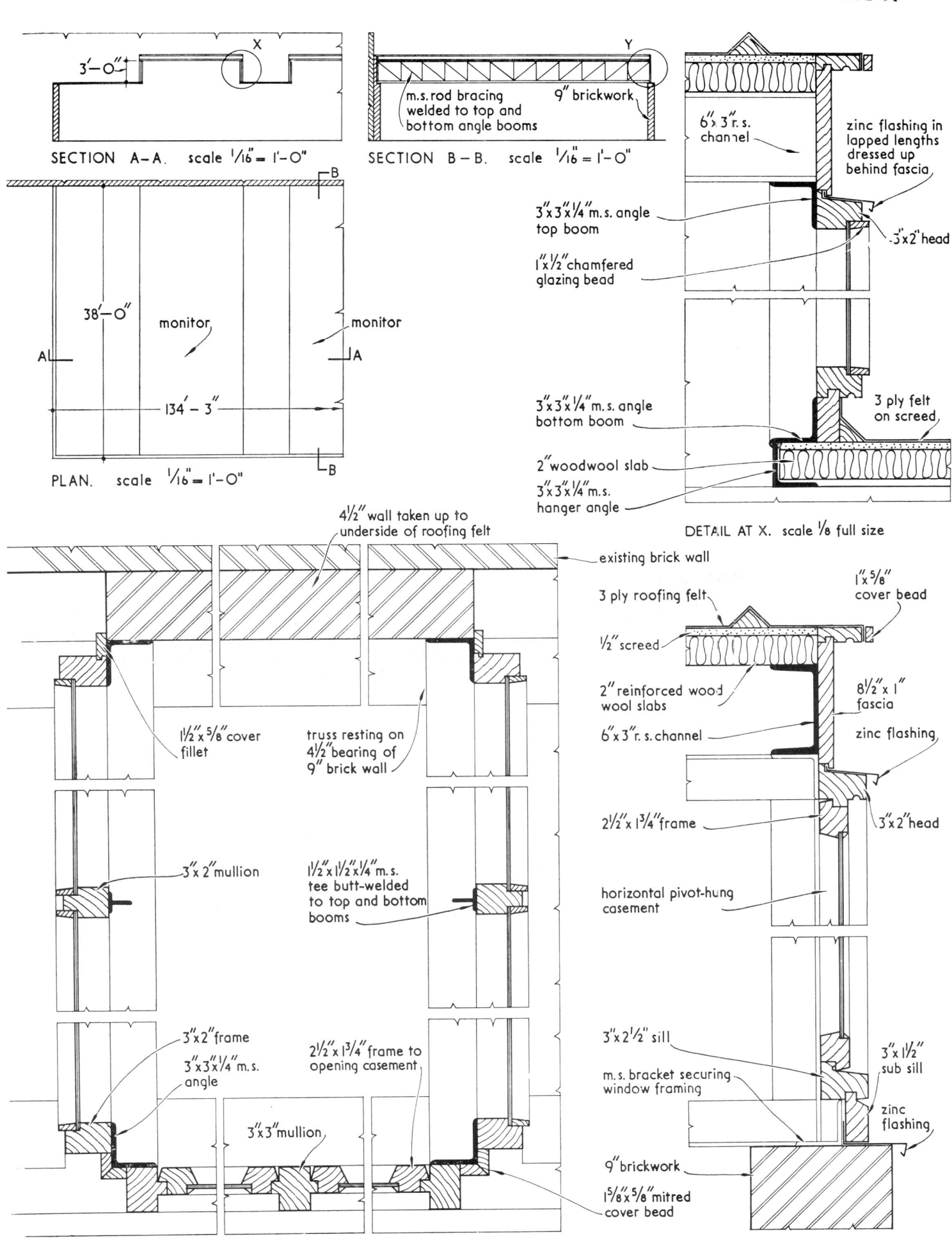

92 ROOFS

MONITOR ROOF: FACTORY AT GOTHAM, NOTTS
DESIGNED BY BARTLETT AND GRAY

The basis of the construction in this detail is a lattice girder spanning the width of the building and supporting the cranked r.s.j. framing to the monitor roofs. One end of the r.s.j. bears on the top flange of the lattice girder and the opposite end, for the next bay, bears on the bottom flange.

ROOFS 93

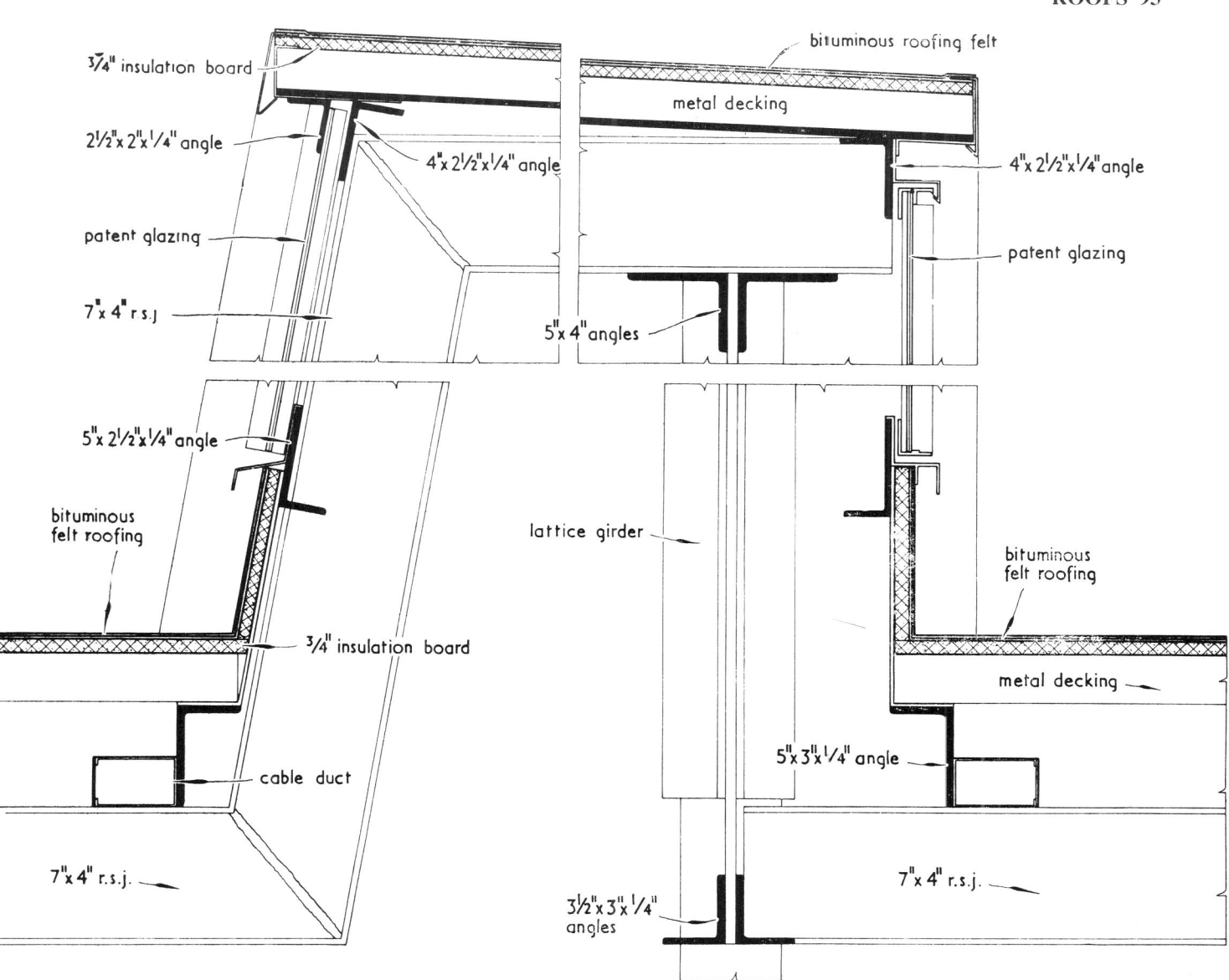

VERTICAL SECTION THRO' MONITOR. scale: 1½"= 1'-0"

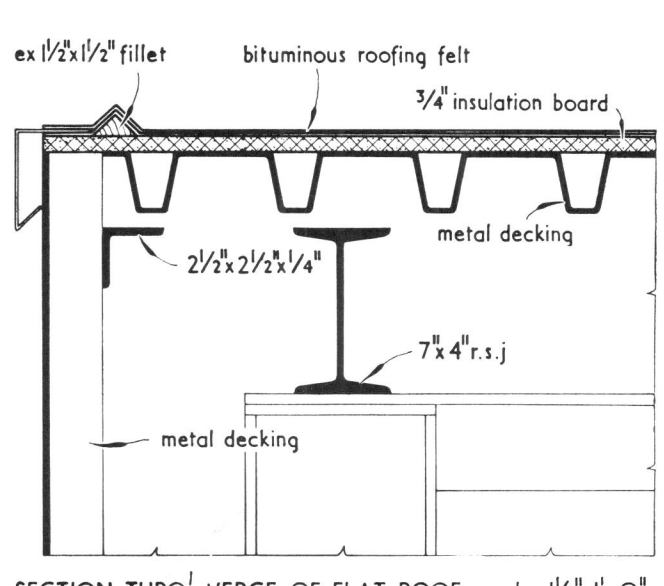

SECTION THRO' VERGE OF FLAT ROOF. scale: 1½"=1'-0"

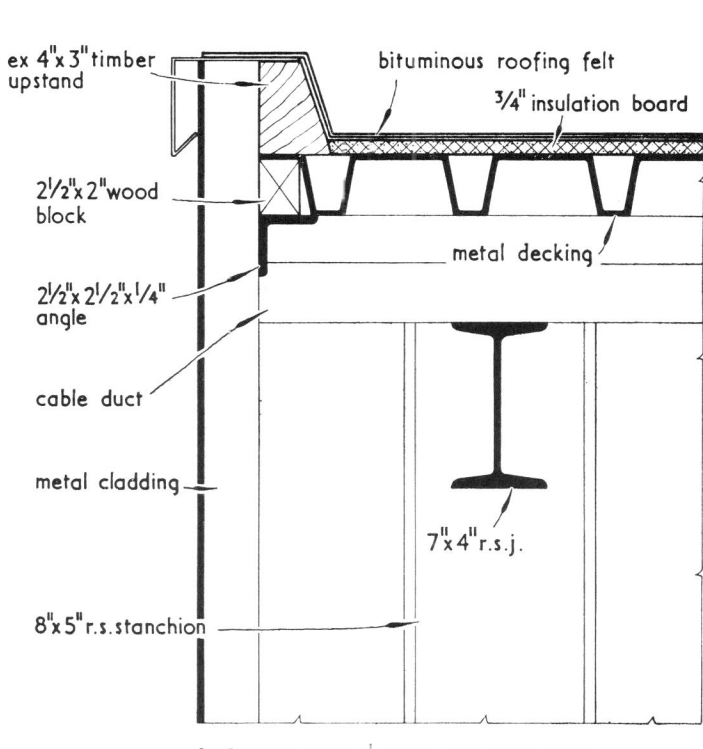

SECTION THRO' END OF MONITOR.

94 ROOFS

TIMBER ROOF: FARM NEAR STUTTON, SUFFOLK
DESIGNED BY C. H. SMITH AND PARTNER

This roof over a cattleyard covers an area 60 ft. by 40 ft. and is supported on two pairs of posts and four single posts, of which only two are in the yard itself. The posts are transmission poles set 4 ft. in the ground: edge beams are in Douglas fir. The roof itself comprises two layers of 5 in. by 1 in. tongued and grooved European redwood boarding. The bottom layer is parallel with the tie rods, the top layer at right angles to it and between the two is a thin aluminium membrane. All timber was pressure-creosoted before delivery to the site and all bolts, nails, coach screws and other fastenings are galvanized. The whole structure is designed and built to withstand exposure.

ROOFS 95

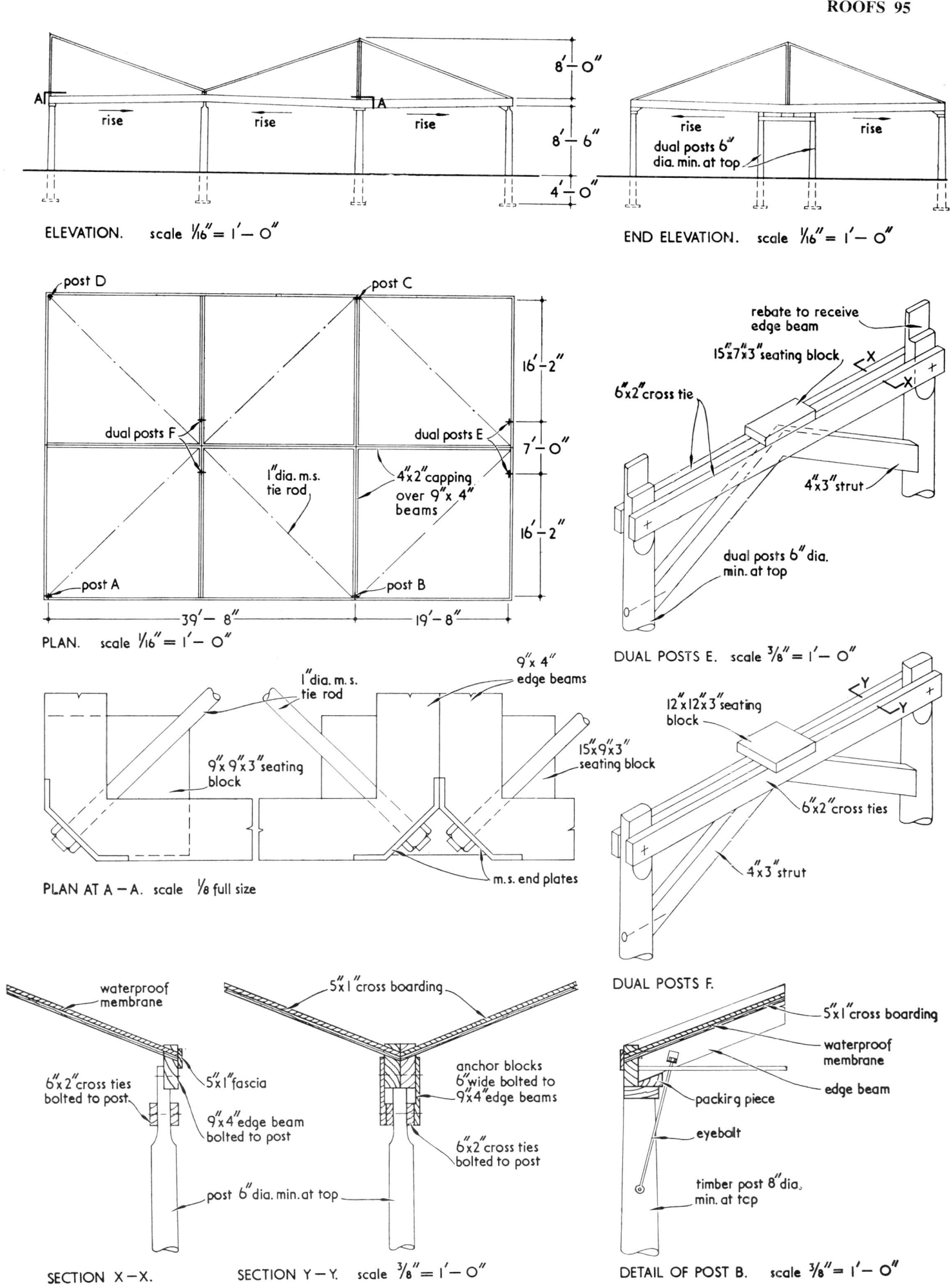

ELEVATION. scale 1/16" = 1' - 0"

END ELEVATION. scale 1/16" = 1' - 0"

PLAN. scale 1/16" = 1' - 0"

PLAN AT A – A. scale 1/8 full size

DUAL POSTS E. scale 3/8" = 1' - 0"

DUAL POSTS F.

SECTION X – X.

SECTION Y – Y. scale 3/8" = 1' - 0"

DETAIL OF POST B. scale 3/8" = 1' - 0"

96 ROOFS

ROOF: MUSIC BOWL IN MELBOURNE, AUSTRALIA
DESIGNED BY YUNCKEN, FREEMAN BROTHERS, GRIFFITHS AND SIMPSON

The form of roof was chosen not to provide shelter but to deflect the sound of traffic. The two masts are of steel cased in glass fibre and have ball-and-socket joints at the foot to permit movement. The main cable supporting the roof is 568 ft. long and weighs 40 tons. The roof covering is of ½-in. plywood in 25-ft. by 7-ft. sheets, faced with satin aluminium. These are bolted to the secondary, transverse cables, polythene and nylon washers being used in the joints to damp sound caused by movement of the structure. The building was relatively cheap: the total cost being about £A200,000 (i.e. £160,000).

ROOFS 97

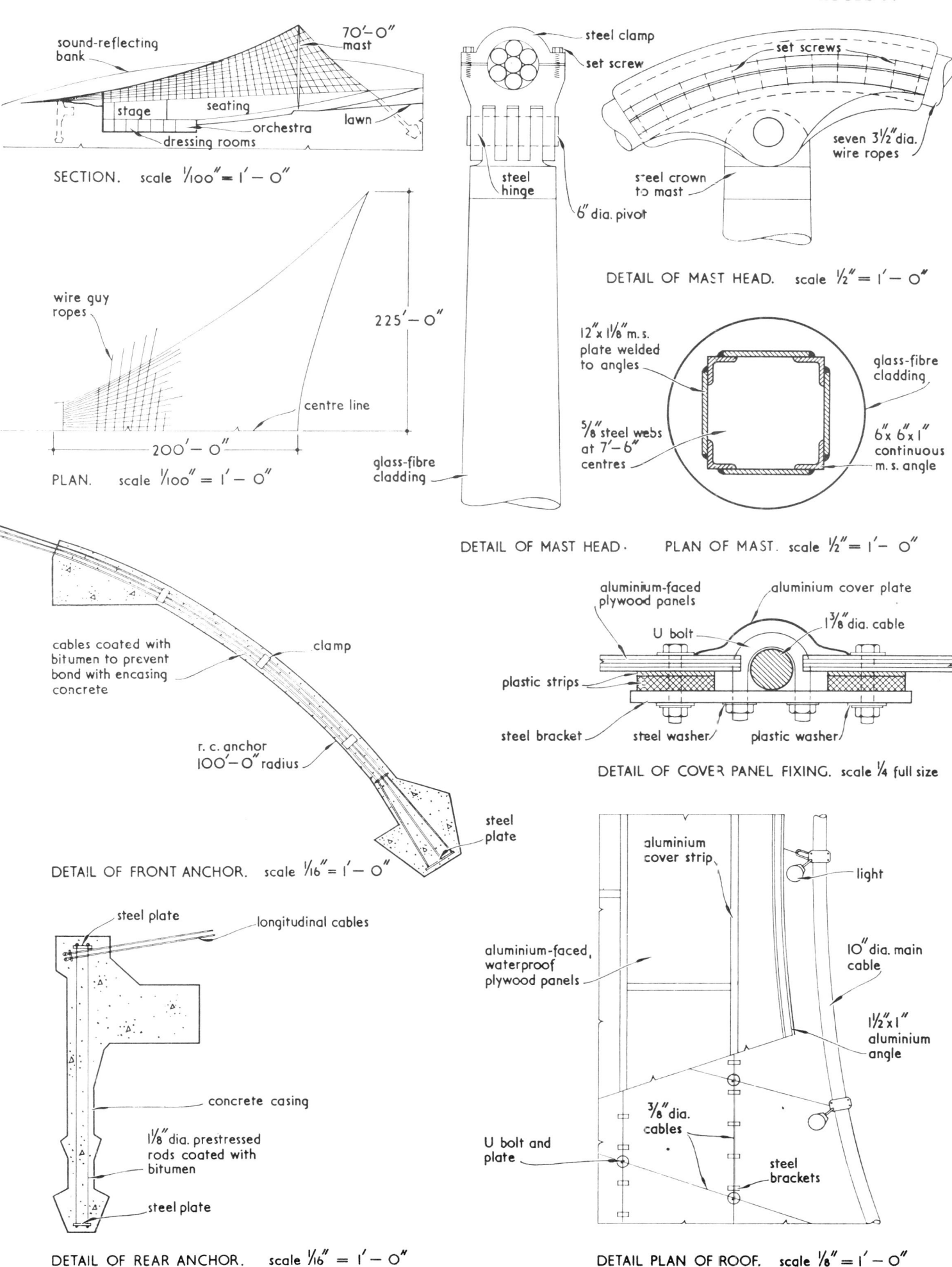

SECTION. scale 1/100" = 1'-0"

Labels: sound-reflecting bank; 70'-0" mast; stage; seating; orchestra; lawn; dressing rooms

PLAN. scale 1/100" = 1'-0"

Labels: wire guy ropes; 225'-0"; centre line; 200'-0"

DETAIL OF MAST HEAD. scale 1/2" = 1'-0"

Labels: steel clamp; set screws; set screw; seven 3½" dia. wire ropes; steel crown to mast; steel hinge; 6" dia. pivot; glass-fibre cladding

DETAIL OF MAST HEAD. PLAN OF MAST. scale 1/2" = 1'-0"

Labels: 12" x 1⅛" m.s. plate welded to angles; glass-fibre cladding; ⅝" steel webs at 7'-6" centres; 6" x 6" x 1" continuous m.s. angle

DETAIL OF FRONT ANCHOR. scale 1/16" = 1'-0"

Labels: cables coated with bitumen to prevent bond with encasing concrete; clamp; r.c. anchor 100'-0" radius; steel plate

DETAIL OF COVER PANEL FIXING. scale ¼ full size

Labels: aluminium-faced plywood panels; aluminium cover plate; U bolt; 1⅜" dia. cable; plastic strips; steel bracket; steel washer; plastic washer

DETAIL OF REAR ANCHOR. scale 1/16" = 1'-0"

Labels: steel plate; longitudinal cables; concrete casing; 1⅛" dia. prestressed rods coated with bitumen; steel plate

DETAIL PLAN OF ROOF. scale 1/8" = 1'-0"

Labels: aluminium cover strip; light; aluminium-faced, waterproof plywood panels; 10" dia. main cable; 1½" x 1" aluminium angle; ⅜" dia. cables; U bolt and plate; steel brackets

NORTHLIGHT ROOF: FACTORY IN GOSSAU, SWITZERLAND
DESIGNED BY DANZEISEN AND VOSER

(Material supplied by Dariush Borbor)

The arrangement of natural lighting and drainage on a factory roof, formed of a series of tilted semi-circular shells, is shown here. Following the usual Continental practice, the concrete shells are heavily insulated and the insulation is protected by corrugated asbestos-cement sheeting.

ROOFS 99

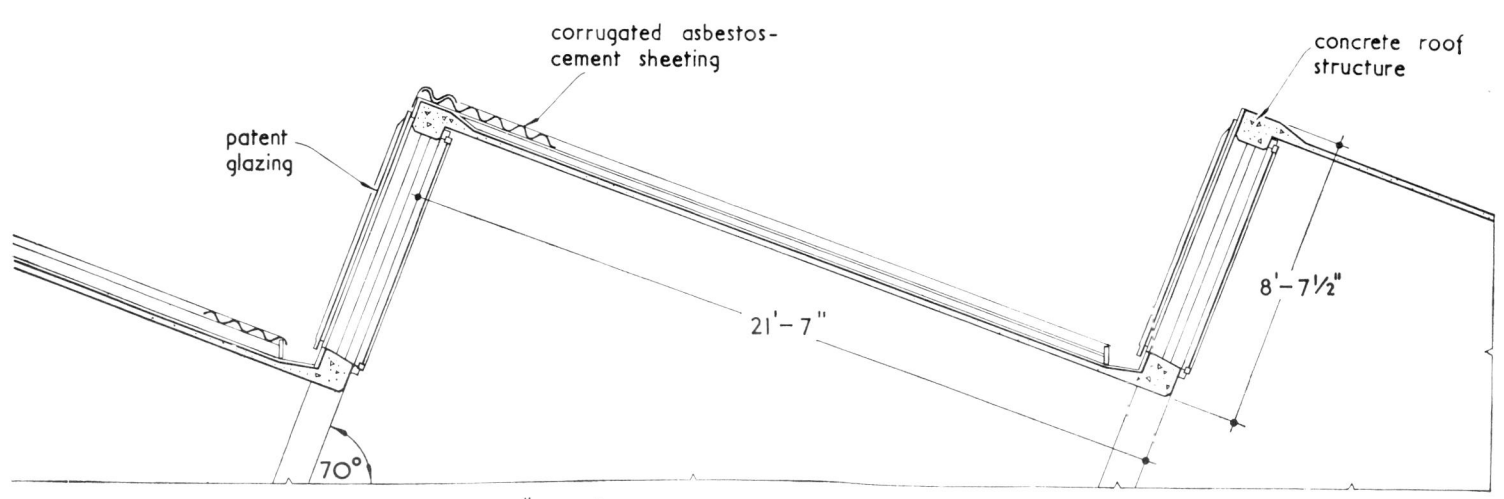

LONGITUDINAL SECTION. scale 3/16" = 1'-0"

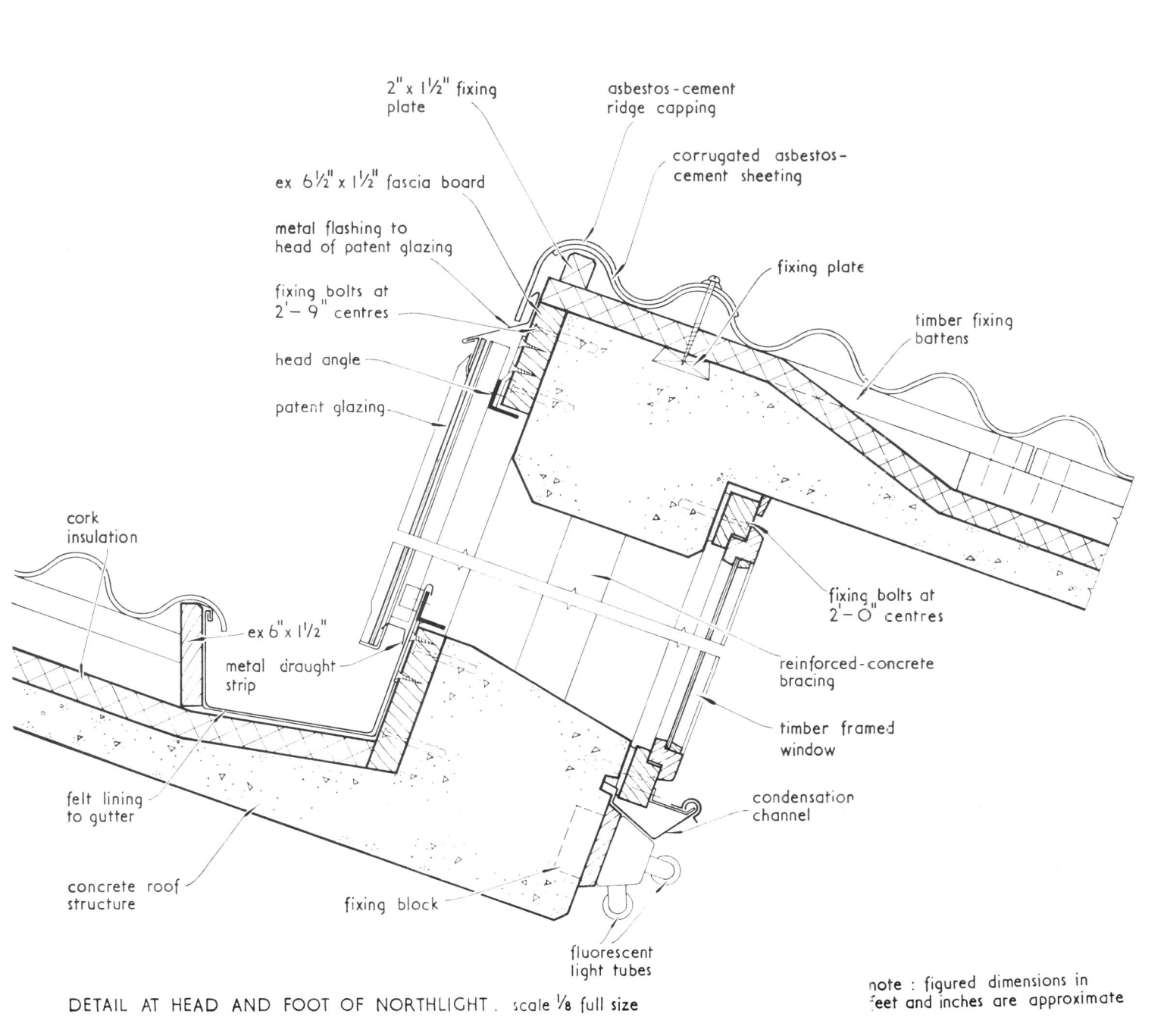

- patent glazing
- corrugated asbestos-cement sheeting
- concrete roof structure
- 21'-7"
- 8'-7½"
- 70°

DETAIL AT HEAD AND FOOT OF NORTHLIGHT. scale ⅛ full size

- 2" x 1½" fixing plate
- asbestos-cement ridge capping
- ex 6½" x 1½" fascia board
- corrugated asbestos-cement sheeting
- metal flashing to head of patent glazing
- fixing plate
- fixing bolts at 2'-9" centres
- timber fixing battens
- head angle
- patent glazing
- cork insulation
- ex 6" x 1½"
- metal draught strip
- fixing bolts at 2'-0" centres
- reinforced-concrete bracing
- timber framed window
- felt lining to gutter
- condensation channel
- concrete roof structure
- fixing block
- fluorescent light tubes

note: figured dimensions in feet and inches are approximate

100 ROOFS

TIMBER ROOF: SNACK BAR NEAR ATHENS, GREECE
DESIGNED BY P. A. SAKELLARIOS, E. VOUREKAS AND P. VASILIADES (*Material supplied by G. Urégian*)

The wide spans of this version of the butterfly roof are made possible by the systematic use of mild steel plates. These are normally concealed from view, but, when visible, are countersunk into the joist thickness. Note the use of brackets at the foot of all posts to ensure that the timber does not come into contact with the ground at any point.

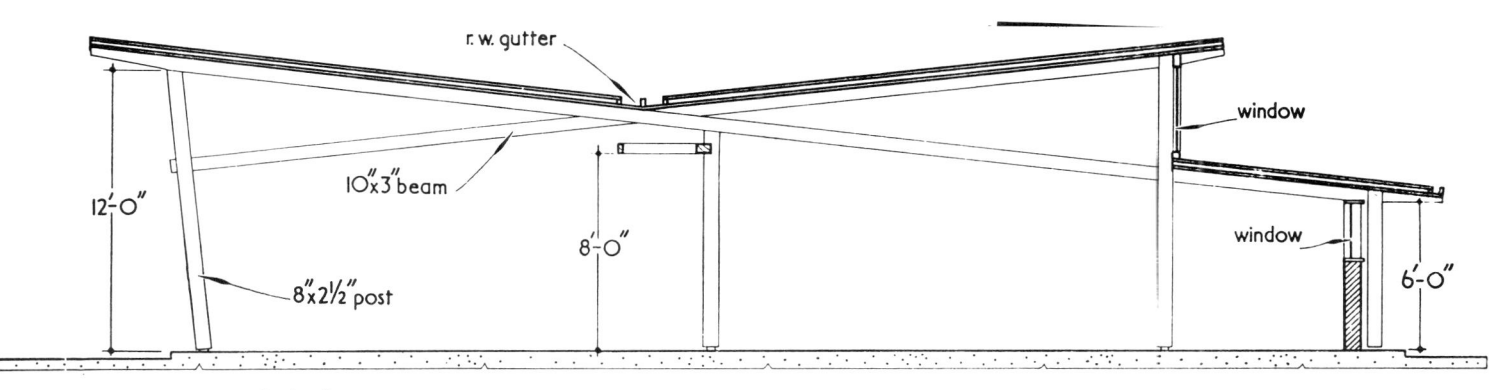

ROOFS 101

SECTION. scale 1/8"=1'-0"

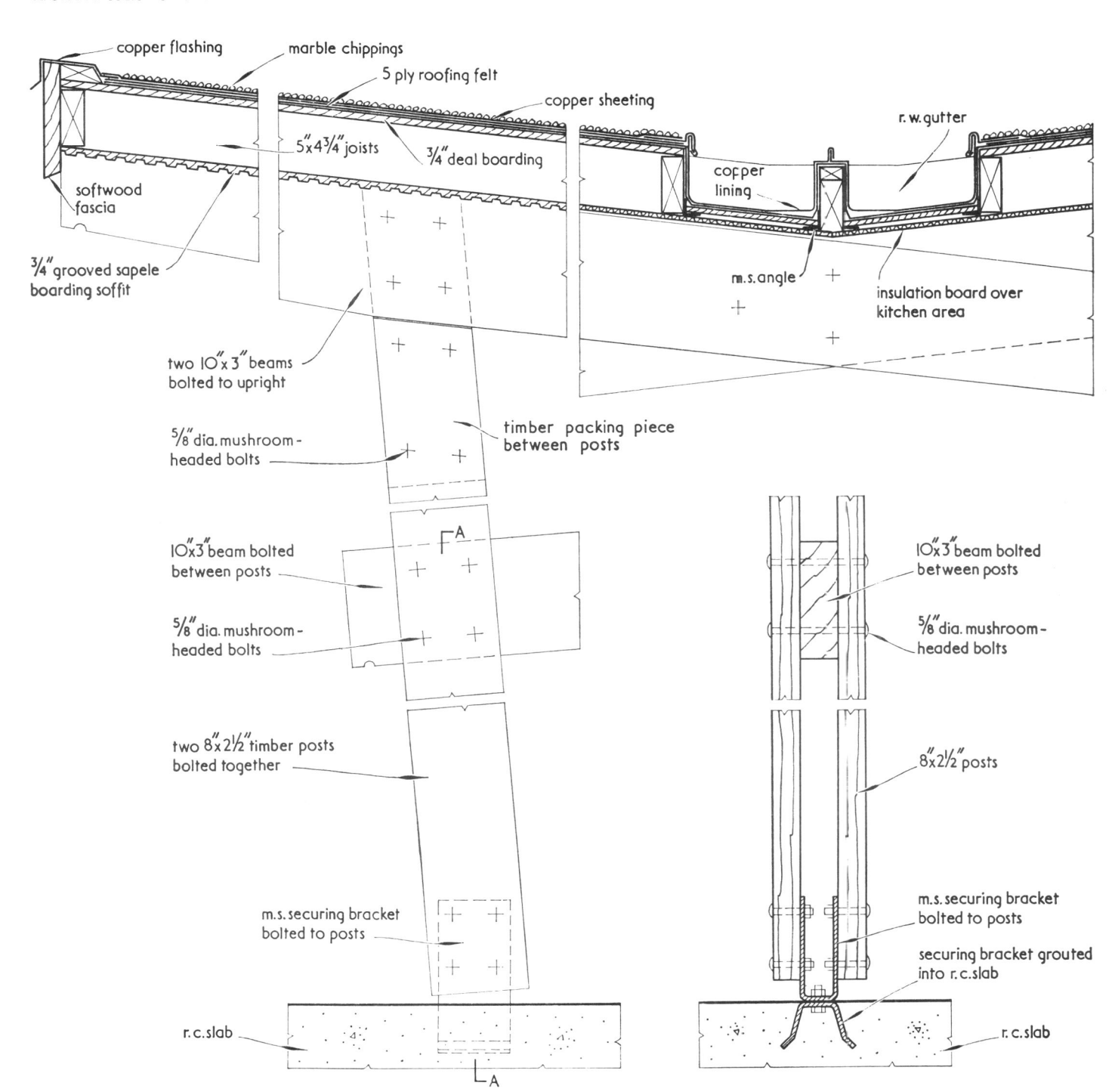

- r.w. gutter
- 10"x3" beam
- 8"x2½" post
- 12'-0"
- 8'-0"
- 6'-0"
- window

DETAIL SECTION. scale 1"=1'-0"

- copper flashing
- marble chippings
- 5 ply roofing felt
- copper sheeting
- 5"x4¾" joists
- ¾" deal boarding
- softwood fascia
- ¾" grooved sapele boarding soffit
- r.w. gutter
- copper lining
- m.s. angle
- insulation board over kitchen area
- two 10"x3" beams bolted to upright
- ⅝" dia. mushroom-headed bolts
- timber packing piece between posts
- 10"x3" beam bolted between posts
- ⅝" dia. mushroom-headed bolts
- two 8"x2½" timber posts bolted together
- m.s. securing bracket bolted to posts
- r.c. slab

SECTION A-A.

- 10"x3" beam bolted between posts
- ⅝" dia. mushroom-headed bolts
- 8"x2½" posts
- m.s. securing bracket bolted to posts
- securing bracket grouted into r.c. slab
- r.c. slab

note: figured dimensions in feet and inches are approximate

102 ROOFS

MONITOR ROOF: LIBRARY AT ST. AUSTELL, CORNWALL
DESIGNED BY F. KENNETH HICKLIN (architect to the Cornwall County Council)

A competent solution is provided, by this example, to the problem of detailing the junctions between a number of different materials. In this case patent glazing, felt roofing and weatherboards are used.

ROOFS 103

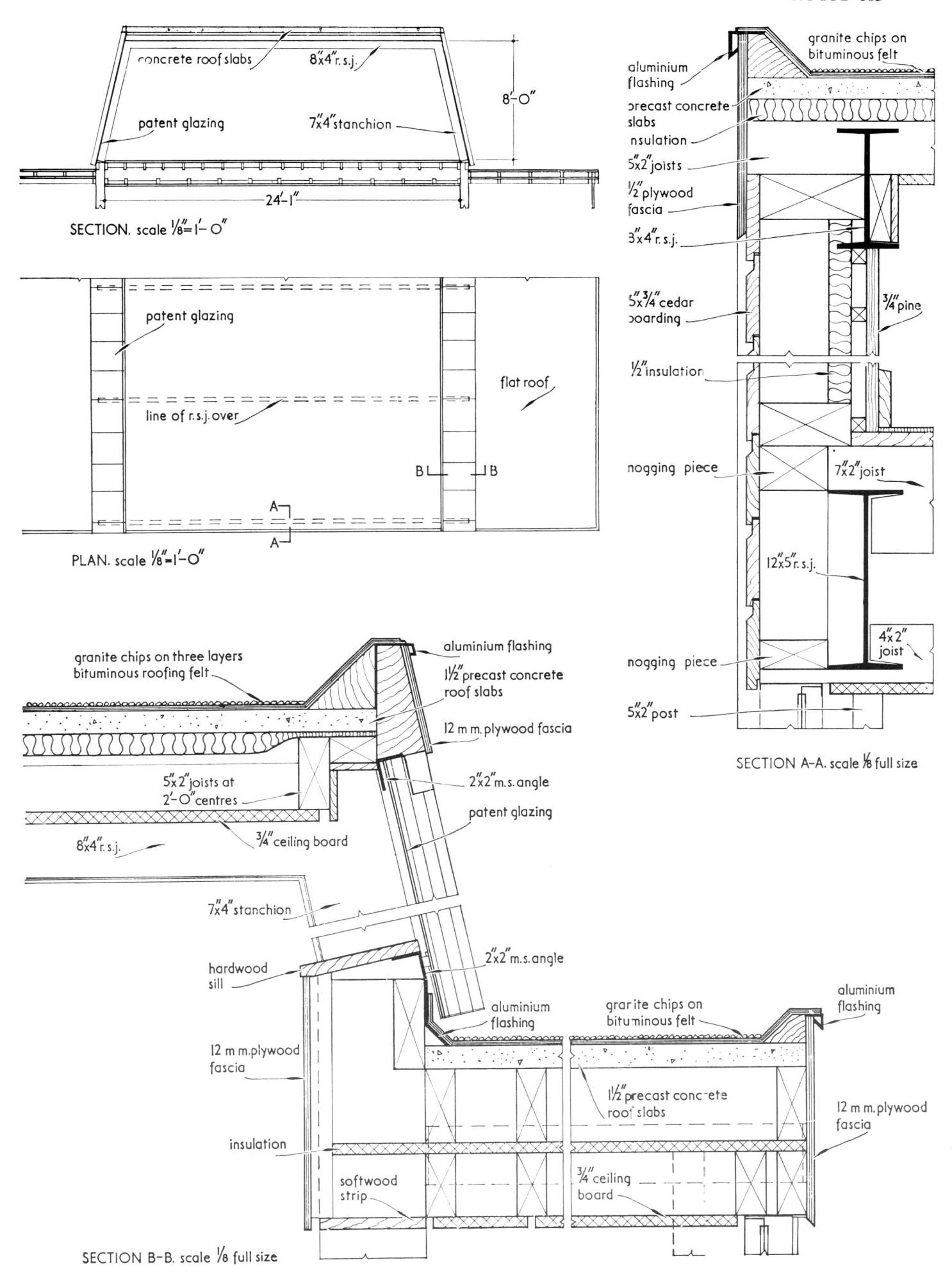

104 ROOFS

ROOF: KINDERGARTEN AT ST IVES, SYDNEY, AUSTRALIA
DESIGNED BY CALLARD, CLARKE AND JACKSON

This low pitched deeply overhanging roof produces an overshadowing that is welcome in the intense sunlight of Australia. It will be noticed that the roof covering is relatively heavy: a necessary precaution for so flat a pitch.

ROOFS 105

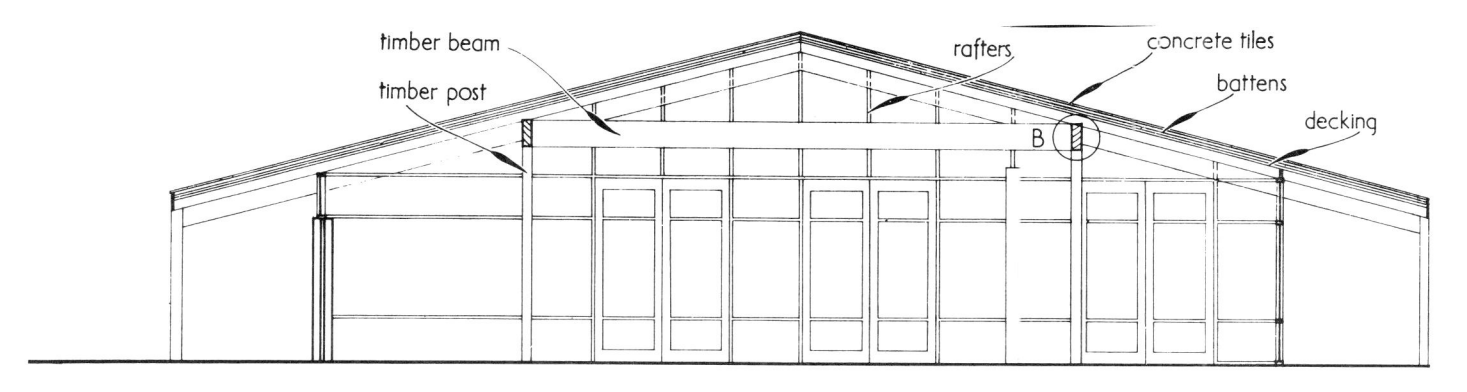

SECTION

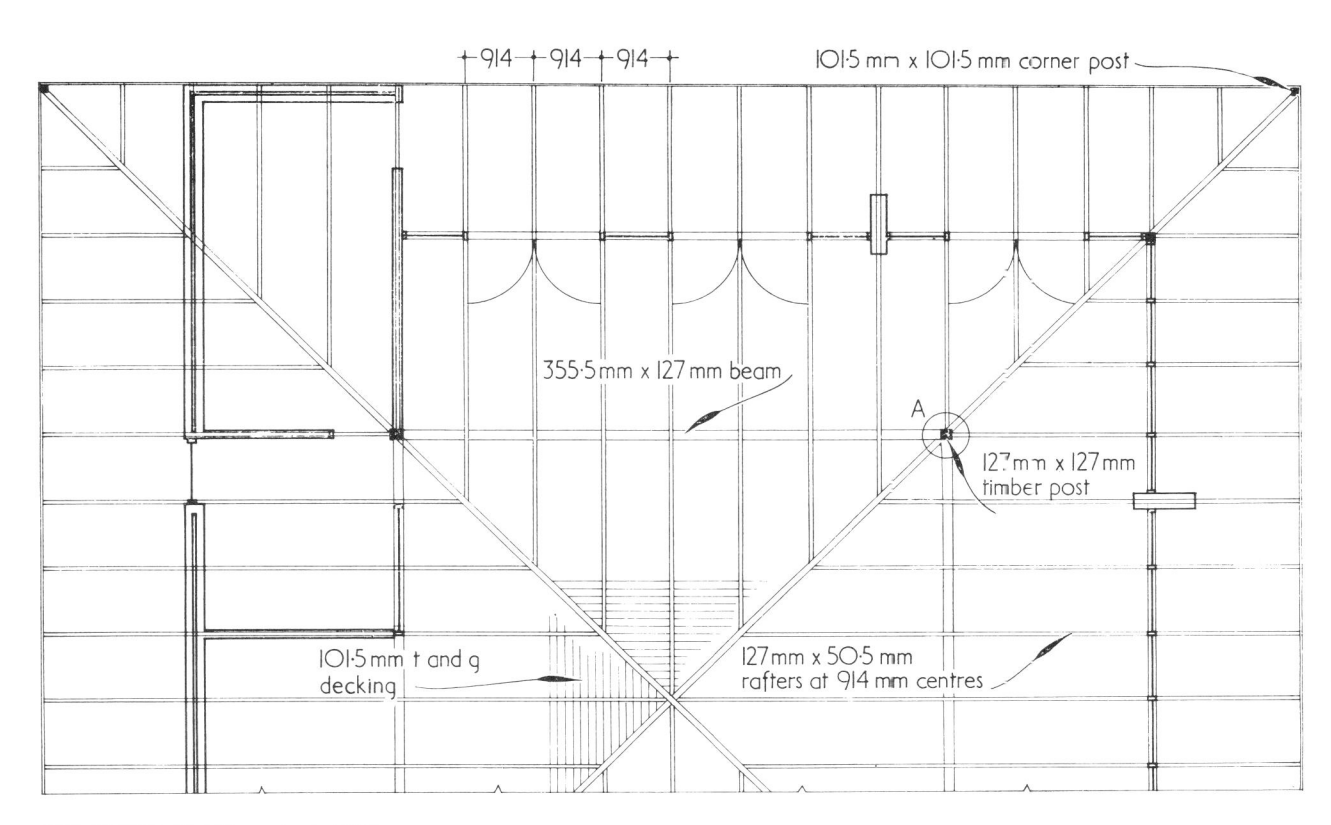

REFLECTED PLAN scale 1:100

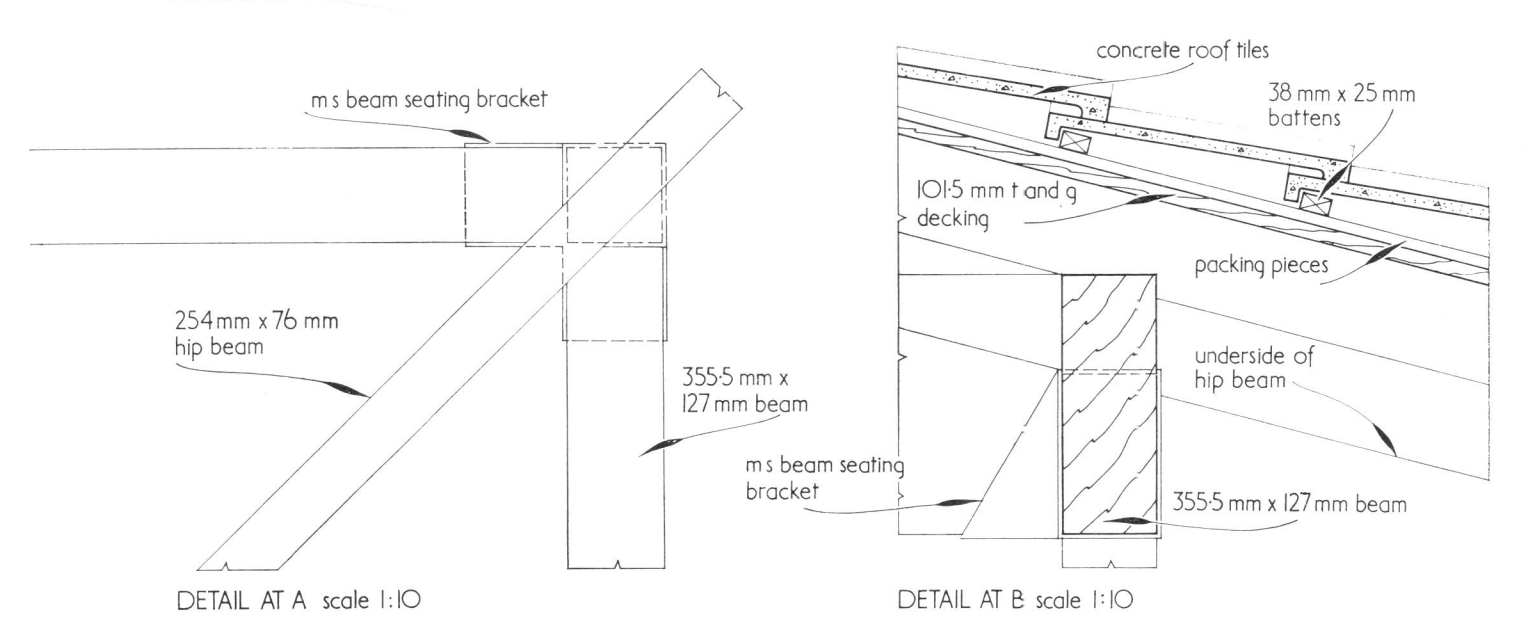

DETAIL AT A scale 1:10

DETAIL AT B scale 1:10

note: metric equivalents of imperial dimensions are given to the nearest 0·5 mm

106 ROOFS

ROOF: FACTORY BUILDING AT VICH, BARCELONA, SPAIN
DESIGNED BY MIGUEL FISAC (*Material supplied by Gil del Palacio*)

An example of skill and finesse in handling precast, post-tensioned concrete units. The projecting fin keeps out direct sunlight and the curved lip serves as a gutter. The beams are secured against lateral movement at the abutments.

ROOFS 107

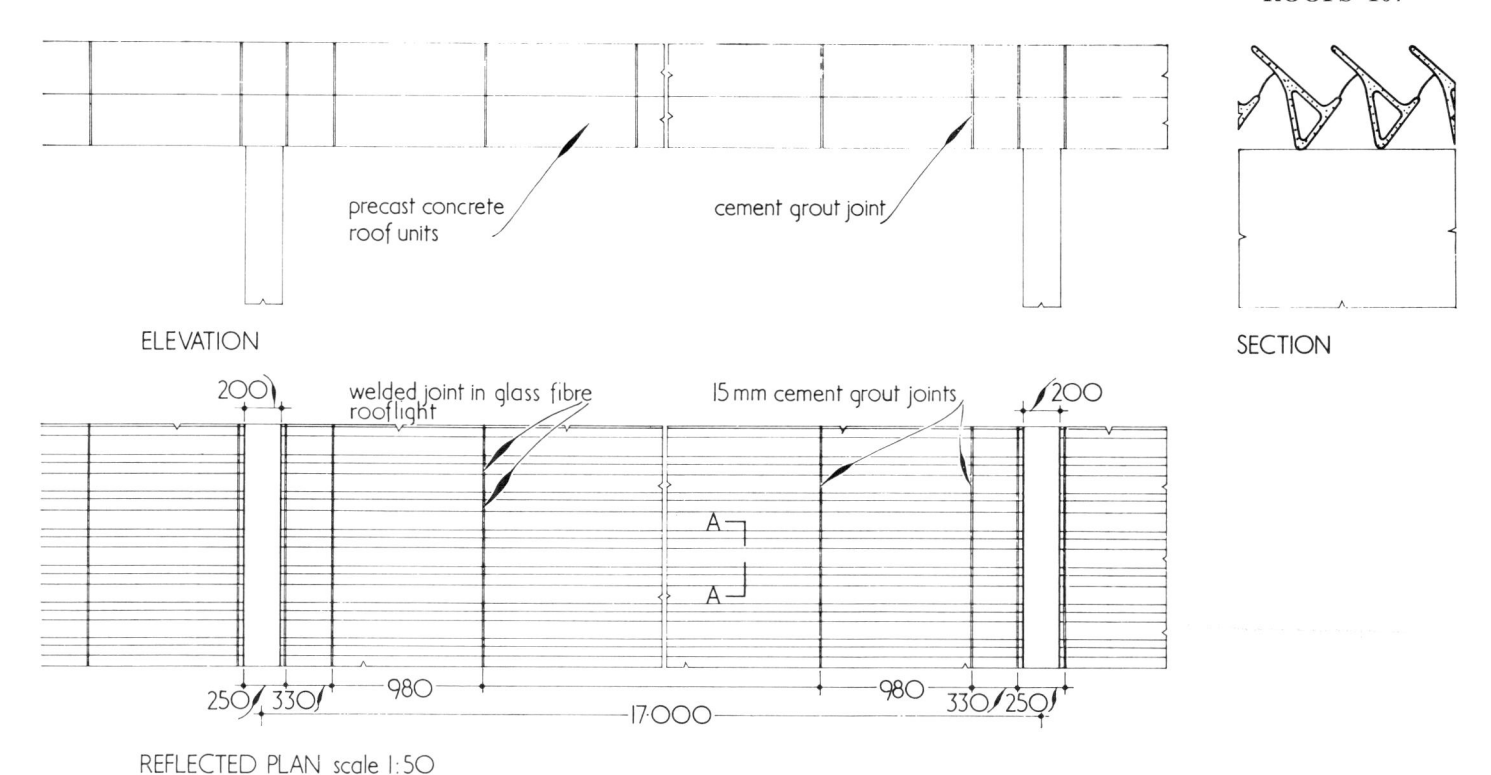

ELEVATION

- precast concrete roof units
- cement grout joint

SECTION

REFLECTED PLAN scale 1:50

- 200
- welded joint in glass fibre rooflight
- 15 mm cement grout joints
- 200
- 250 / 330
- 980
- 17·000
- 980
- 330 / 250

SECTION A–A scale 1:5

- 5 mm diam rod
- glass fibre rooflight bedded in mastic
- precast concrete roof unit
- horizontal joints in rooflights welded
- 6 mm diam rod
- 9 mm diam post-tensioned cable

108 ROOFS

ROOFLIGHT: COMMUNITY HALL AT HATFIELD
DESIGNED BY LIONEL BRETT AND KENNETH BOYD

A lantern light with glazing at 45° has been contrived over the ridge of a 22½° pitched roof. The ridge board of the roof penetrates the framing of the lantern and is visible from below. The lantern is sheathed in super-purity aluminium to match the patented " clip-on " type aluminium covering used on the main roof. The object was to obtain a structure which, while giving a large glass area, would be light in weight but very strong.

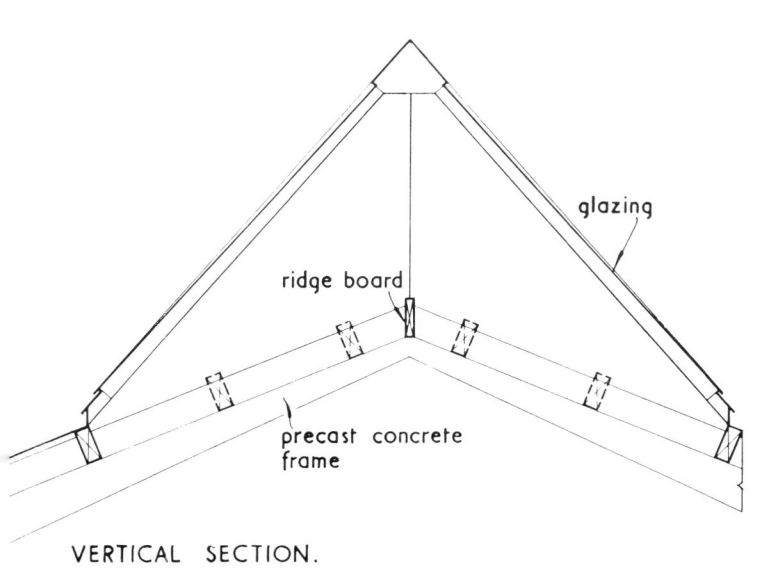

ROOFS 109

VERTICAL SECTION.
- ridge board
- glazing
- precast concrete frame

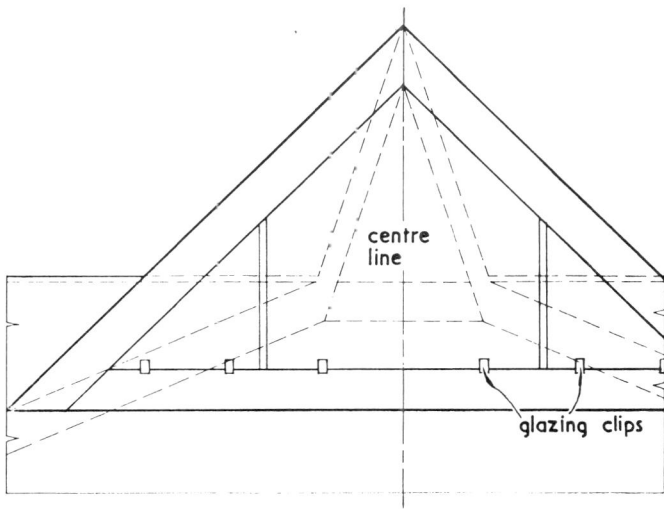

PART ELEVATION OF LANTERN LIGHT. scale 3/8" = 1'-0"
- centre line
- glazing clips

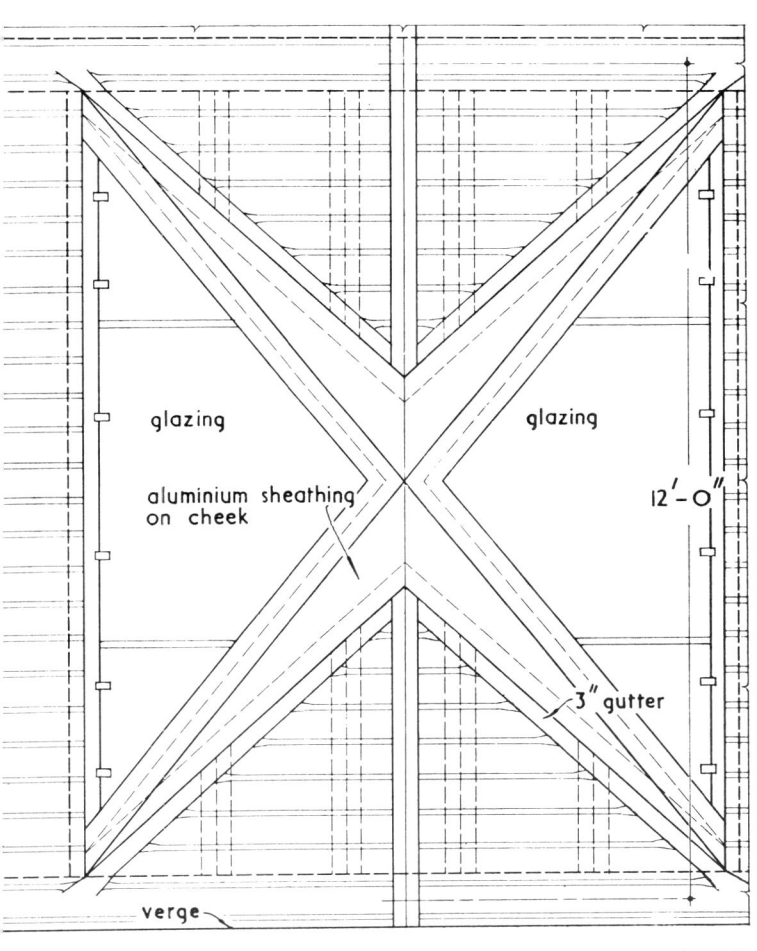

PLAN OF ROOF LANTERN LIGHT. scale 3/8" = 1'-0"
- glazing
- aluminium sheathing on cheek
- 12'-0"
- 3" gutter
- verge

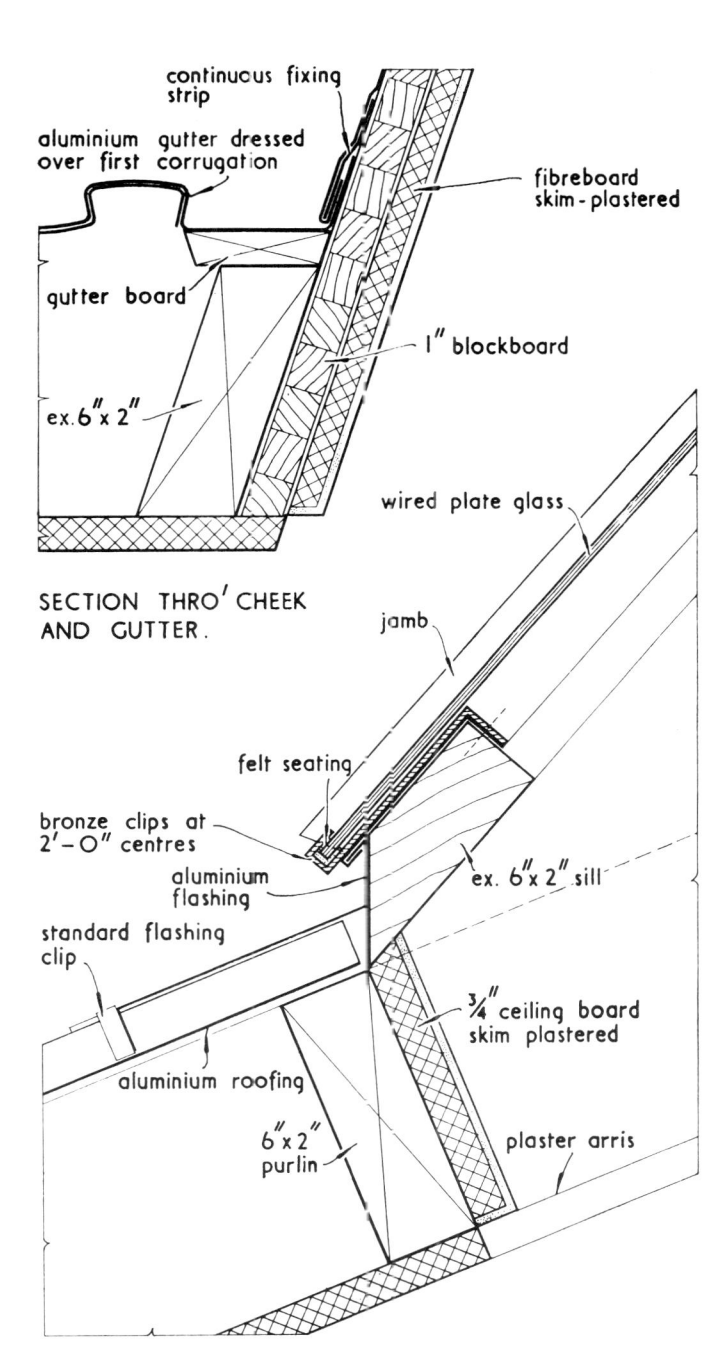

SECTION THRO' CHEEK AND GUTTER.
- continuous fixing strip
- aluminium gutter dressed over first corrugation
- fibreboard skim-plastered
- gutter board
- 1" blockboard
- ex. 6" x 2"

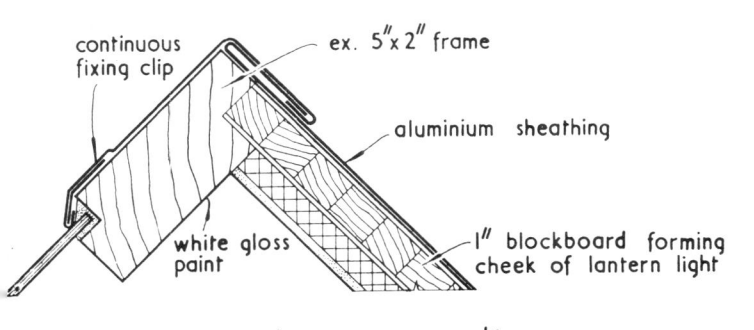

SECTION THRO' JAMB. scale 1/4 full size
- continuous fixing clip
- ex. 5" x 2" frame
- aluminium sheathing
- white gloss paint
- 1" blockboard forming cheek of lantern light

VERTICAL SECTION THRO' SILL OF LANTERN LIGHT.
- wired plate glass
- jamb
- felt seating
- bronze clips at 2'-0" centres
- aluminium flashing
- ex. 6" x 2" sill
- standard flashing clip
- 3/4" ceiling board skim plastered
- aluminium roofing
- 6" x 2" purlin
- plaster arris

110 ROOFS

MONITOR ROOFLIGHT: ART GALLERY IN COPENHAGEN, DENMARK
DESIGNED BY JØRGEN BO AND VILHELM WOHLERT   *(Material supplied by George Kew)*

A splendid example of careful timber detailing. Note such refinements as the coincidence of joints in the boarding with the centre lines of mullions, the avoidance of visible glazing beads, recessed cover joints at corner (on the drawing) and the Continental preference for building up of mullions and window frames from a number of small sections.

ROOFS 111

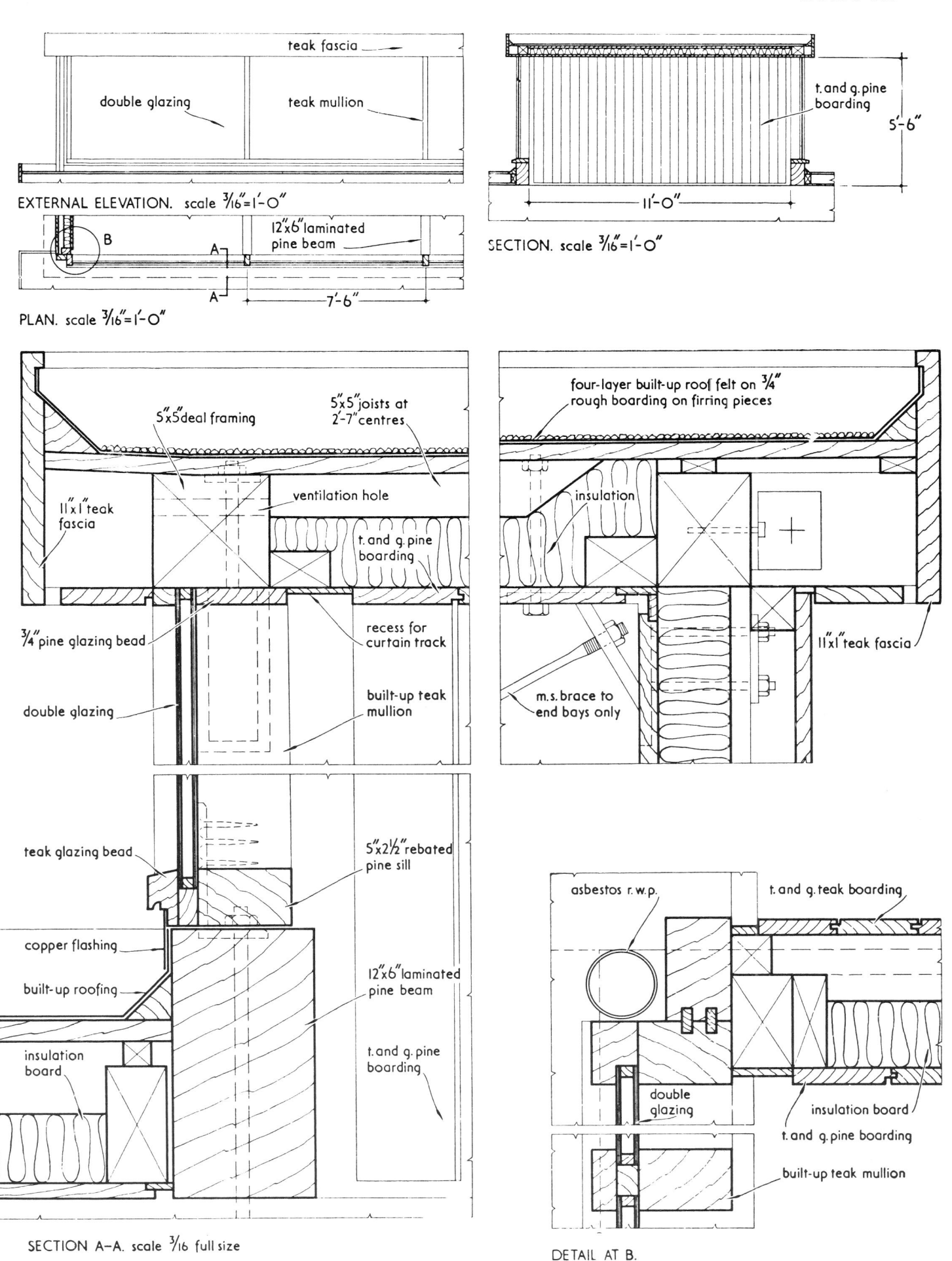

EXTERNAL ELEVATION. scale 3/16"=1'-0"
- teak fascia
- double glazing
- teak mullion

PLAN. scale 3/16"=1'-0"
- 12"x6" laminated pine beam
- 7'-6"

SECTION. scale 3/16"=1'-0"
- t. and g. pine boarding
- 5'-6"
- 11'-0"

SECTION A–A. scale 3/16 full size
- 5"x5" deal framing
- 5"x5" joists at 2'-7" centres
- 11"x1" teak fascia
- ventilation hole
- t. and g. pine boarding
- 3/4" pine glazing bead
- recess for curtain track
- double glazing
- built-up teak mullion
- teak glazing bead
- 5"x2½" rebated pine sill
- copper flashing
- built-up roofing
- 12"x6" laminated pine beam
- insulation board
- t. and g. pine boarding

- four-layer built-up roof felt on 3/4" rough boarding on firring pieces
- insulation
- m.s. brace to end bays only
- 11"x1" teak fascia

DETAIL AT B.
- asbestos r.w.p.
- t. and g. teak boarding
- double glazing
- insulation board
- t. and g. pine boarding
- built-up teak mullion

note: figured dimensions in feet and inches are approximate

LAYLIGHT: MONASTIC CHURCH AT SAUNEN, OBWALDEN, SWITZERLAND
DESIGNED BY NAEF, STUDER AND STUDER
in association with G. ZIMMERMAN

(*Material supplied by John Eger*)

This peripheral laylight is designed to throw light on the walls of the church but to be out of line of sight of most of the congregation. Though heavily insulated, the roof structure is very light. Note the heating pipes within to prevent down-draught and heating cables outside to keep the internal gutter free of ice.

ROOFS 113

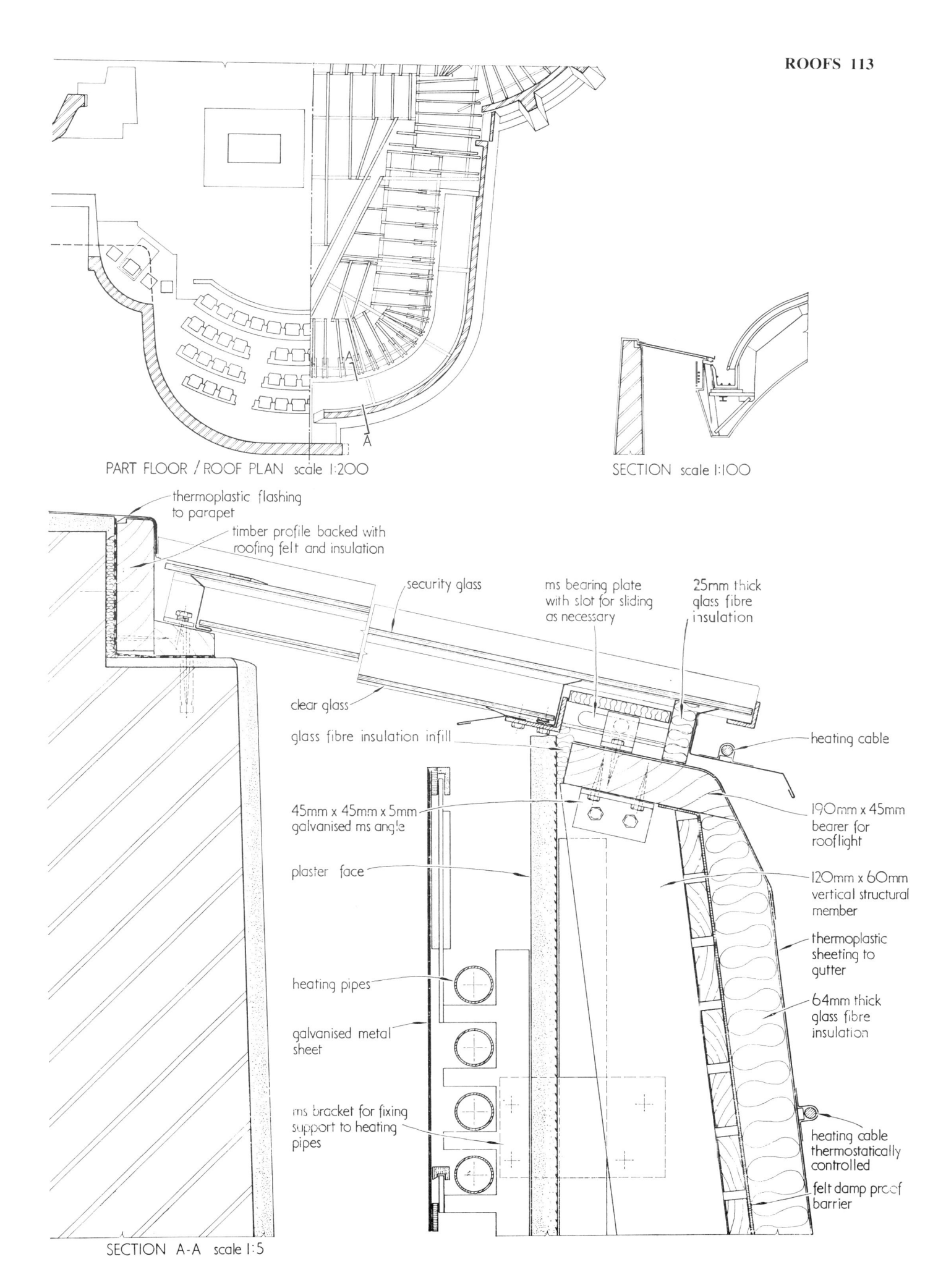

PART FLOOR / ROOF PLAN scale 1:200

SECTION scale 1:100

SECTION A-A scale 1:5

- thermoplastic flashing to parapet
- timber profile backed with roofing felt and insulation
- security glass
- ms bearing plate with slot for sliding as necessary
- 25mm thick glass fibre insulation
- clear glass
- glass fibre insulation infill
- heating cable
- 45mm x 45mm x 5mm galvanised ms angle
- plaster face
- 190mm x 45mm bearer for rooflight
- 120mm x 60mm vertical structural member
- thermoplastic sheeting to gutter
- heating pipes
- galvanised metal sheet
- 64mm thick glass fibre insulation
- ms bracket for fixing support to heating pipes
- heating cable thermostatically controlled
- felt damp proof barrier

114 WINDOWS

WINDOW WALL IN CAFETERIA: LABORATORY BUILDING IN ILLINOIS
DESIGNED BY HOLABIRD AND ROOT AND BURGEE AND ASSOCIATES

The wall of this cafeteria consists of ¼ in. plate glass panels 13 ft. 7 in. in height supported by steel mullions at 10 ft. centres

WINDOWS 115

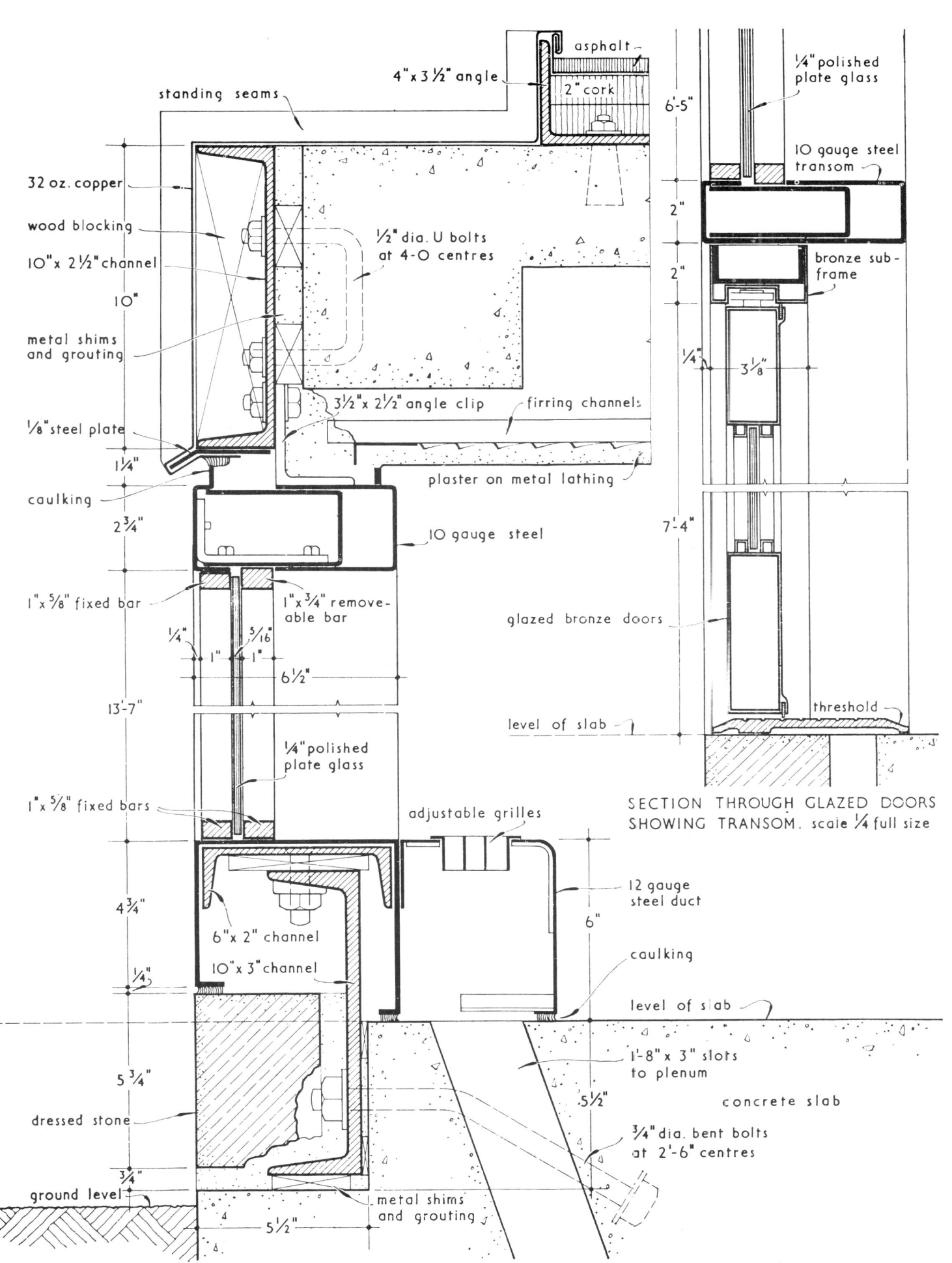

SECTION THROUGH EXTERNAL WALL SHOWING HEAD AND SILL OF WINDOW. scale ¼ full size

SECTION THROUGH GLAZED DOORS SHOWING TRANSOM. scale ¼ full size

116 WINDOWS

SLIDING WINDOWS: HOUSE AT KINGSTON, SURREY
DESIGNED BY E. MAXWELL FRY

Externally a sunblind runs the whole length of the living room windows, and there is a flower box in reinforced concrete. The illustration below shows the interior of the living room. Concealed below the window level there are specially designed electric convection heaters

WINDOWS 117

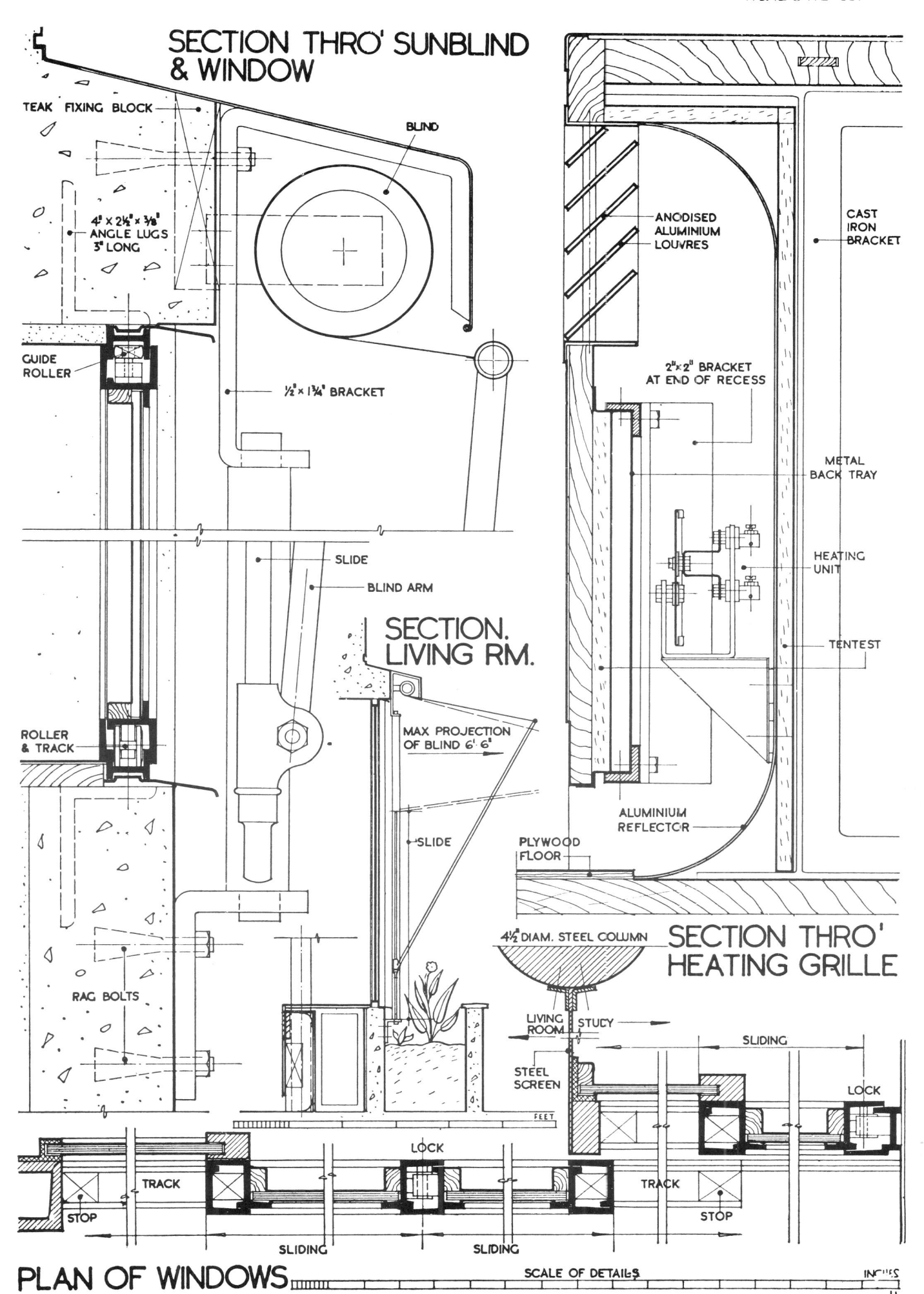

SECTION THRO' SUNBLIND & WINDOW

- TEAK FIXING BLOCK
- BLIND
- 4" × 2½" × ⅜" ANGLE LUGS 3" LONG
- GUIDE ROLLER
- ½" × 1¾" BRACKET
- SLIDE
- BLIND ARM
- ROLLER & TRACK
- RAG BOLTS

SECTION. LIVING RM.

- MAX PROJECTION OF BLIND 6'-6"
- SLIDE

SECTION THRO' HEATING GRILLE

- ANODISED ALUMINIUM LOUVRES
- CAST IRON BRACKET
- 2" × 2" BRACKET AT END OF RECESS
- METAL BACK TRAY
- HEATING UNIT
- TENTEST
- ALUMINIUM REFLECTOR
- PLYWOOD FLOOR
- 4½" DIAM. STEEL COLUMN
- LIVING ROOM / STUDY
- STEEL SCREEN
- SLIDING
- LOCK

PLAN OF WINDOWS

- STOP
- TRACK
- LOCK
- SLIDING
- SLIDING
- TRACK
- STOP

SCALE OF DETAILS — INCHES

J.L.

118 WINDOWS

WINDOWS: FLATS IN LONDON, S.W.1
DESIGNED BY POWELL AND MOYA

These glazed panels are from the front façade of the same building illustrated on page 104. It will be noticed that there is no mullion; the two main opening lights in each unit close one against the other. The opaque panels beneath the windows are glazed on the outside and closed with plywood on the inside. The outside face of this plywood is painted cypress green (5·0 G 2/2) on all panels with rubber-based paint. The brick and concrete surfaces surrounding the panel are painted one coat of bituminous paint to a depth of 1 ft. from the outside face of the building. A seat-cum-shelf of West African mahogany is fixed behind the window, with a radiator beneath. Permanent ventilation is provided over the head of the panel frame which is separated from the structure by blocking pieces with gaps between.

WINDOWS 119

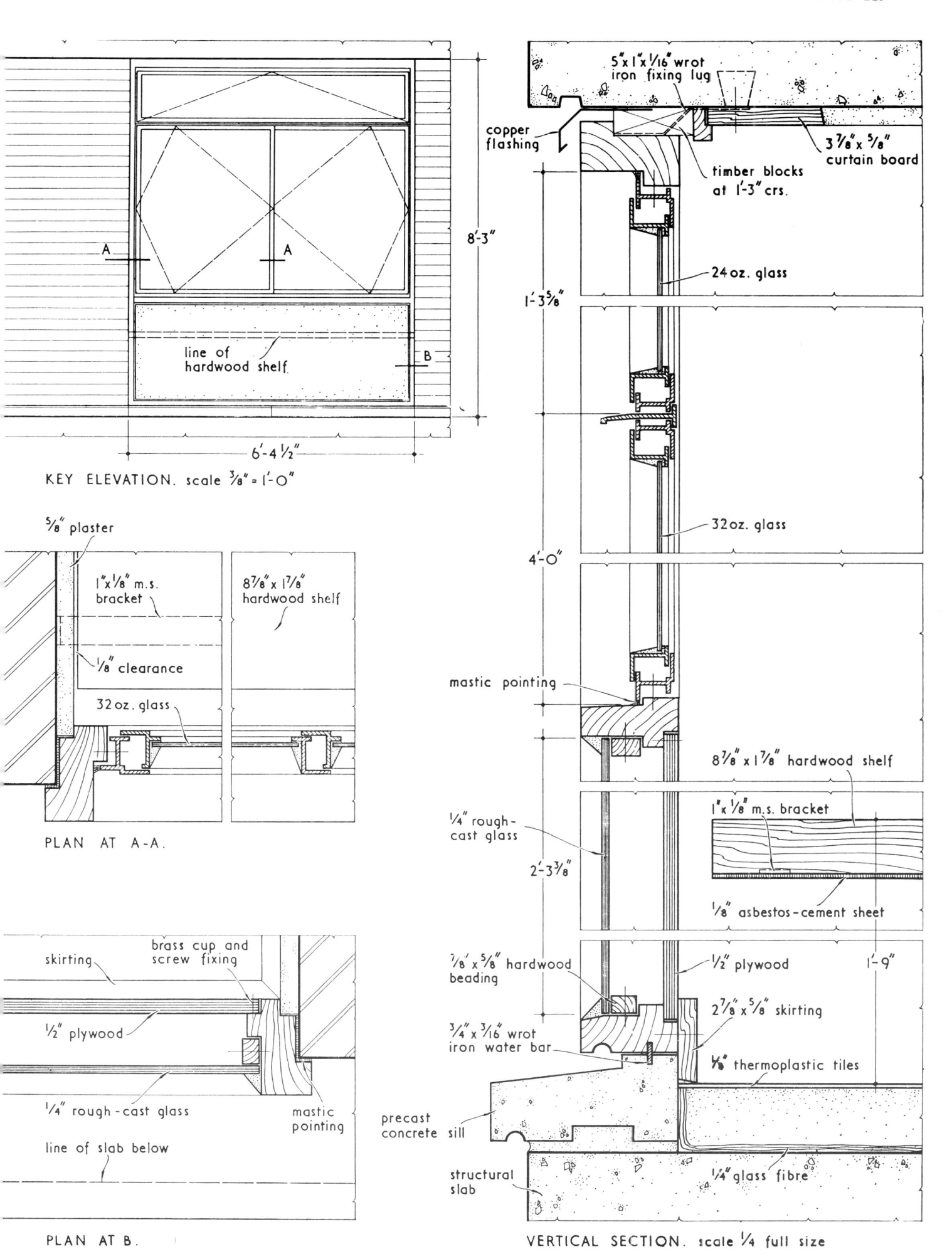

KEY ELEVATION. scale 3/8" = 1'-0"

PLAN AT A-A.

PLAN AT B.

VERTICAL SECTION. scale 1/4 full size

GLAZED WALL: SURGERY, DOCTOR'S HOUSE AT DETROIT, MICHIGAN, U.S.A.
DESIGNED BY LEINWEBER, YAMASAKI AND HELLMUTH (*Material supplied by Tim Sturgis*)

The welded steel frame, which includes an 8 in. × 4 in. angle to serve as eaves beam and fascia, is bolted to the concrete foundation. The line of holes under the eaves beam gives ventilation to the roof and is covered by screen rings to prevent the entry of insects.

WINDOWS 121

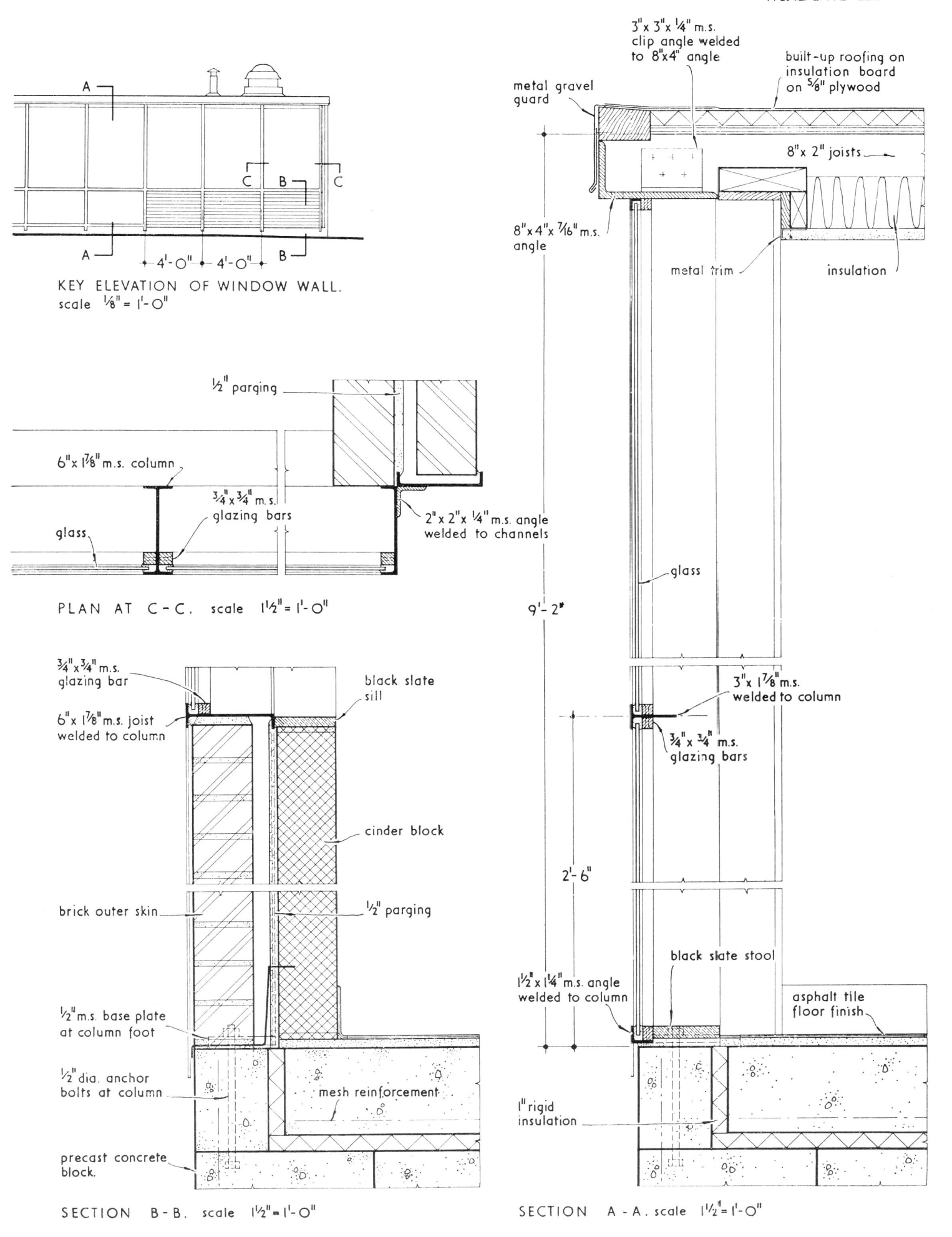

KEY ELEVATION OF WINDOW WALL.
scale 1/8" = 1'-0"

- A
- C B C
- 4'-0" 4'-0"

PLAN AT C-C. scale 1 1/2" = 1'-0"

- 1/2" parging
- 6" x 1 7/8" m.s. column
- 3/4" x 3/4" m.s. glazing bars
- 2" x 2" x 1/4" m.s. angle welded to channels
- glass

SECTION B-B. scale 1 1/2" = 1'-0"

- 3/4" x 3/4" m.s. glazing bar
- 6" x 1 7/8" m.s. joist welded to column
- black slate sill
- cinder block
- brick outer skin
- 1/2" parging
- 1/2" m.s. base plate at column foot
- 1/2" dia. anchor bolts at column
- mesh reinforcement
- precast concrete block.

SECTION A-A. scale 1 1/2" = 1'-0"

- 3" x 3" x 1/4" m.s. clip angle welded to 8" x 4" angle
- metal gravel guard
- built-up roofing on insulation board on 5/8" plywood
- 8" x 2" joists
- 8" x 4" x 7/16" m.s. angle
- metal trim
- insulation
- glass
- 9'-2"
- 3" x 1 7/8" m.s. welded to column
- 3/4" x 3/4" m.s. glazing bars
- 2'-6"
- black slate stool
- 1 1/2" x 1 1/4" m.s. angle welded to column
- asphalt tile floor finish
- 1" rigid insulation

122 WINDOWS

WINDOWS: SCHOOL IN LONDON, W.C.1
DESIGNED BY HUBERT BENNETT (architect to the London County Council)

The fenestration on this building shows the triumphant technical realisation of one of the earliest ideas of the modern movement. Note the bedding of the glass in aluminium cames and in a timber frame flush with the concrete.

WINDOWS 123

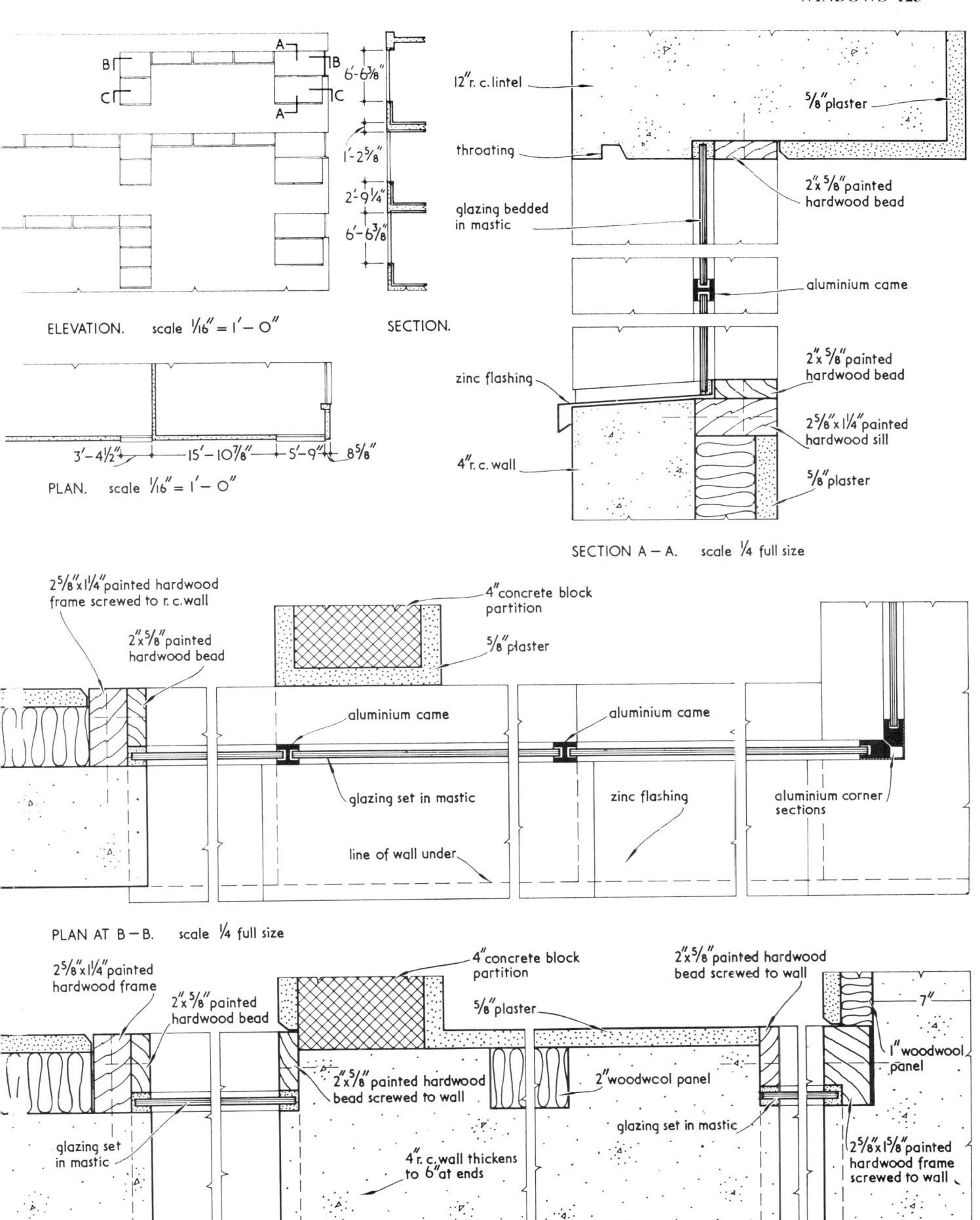

124 WINDOWS

DISPLAY WINDOW: SWEDEN HOUSE, STOCKHOLM, SWEDEN
DESIGNED BY PROFESSOR SVEN MARKELIUS

The originality of these double glazed oriels lies in the sloping glazed head and foot. These allow light to strike in and give views out, both at unaccustomed angles. Oriels are heated by warm air entering at the base and by radiators contained within the splayed upstands at the sides.

WINDOWS 125

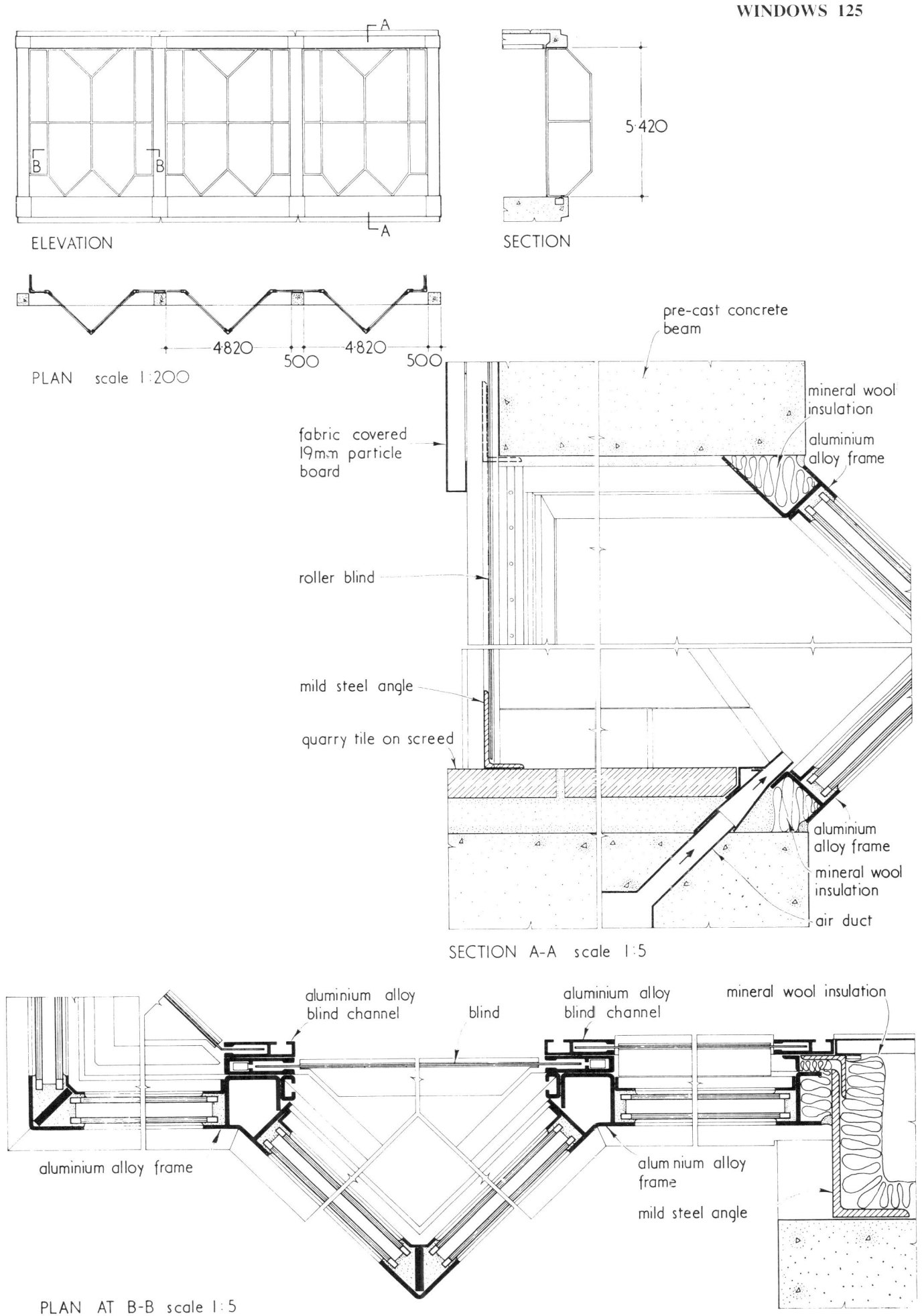

ELEVATION

SECTION

5.420

PLAN scale 1:200

4.820 500 4.820 500

pre-cast concrete beam

mineral wool insulation

aluminium alloy frame

fabric covered 19mm particle board

roller blind

mild steel angle

quarry tile on screed

aluminium alloy frame

mineral wool insulation

air duct

SECTION A-A scale 1:5

aluminium alloy blind channel

blind

aluminium alloy blind channel

mineral wool insulation

aluminium alloy frame

aluminium alloy frame

mild steel angle

PLAN AT B-B scale 1:5

126 WINDOWS

GLAZED WALL: HOUSE AT DUSSELDORF, GERMANY
DESIGNED BY B. M. PFAU (*Material supplied by Barrie Sheldon*)

An unusual example of the use of steel in domestic detailing to produce an effect of extreme lightness and simplicity. Though it is barely visible in the photograph, a glazed canopy extends outwards from the horizontal member at first floor height. Within a depth of about 8 inches are accommodated the gutter for this canopy, the overhead gear for the sliding doors and the furled venetian blinds.

WINDOWS 127

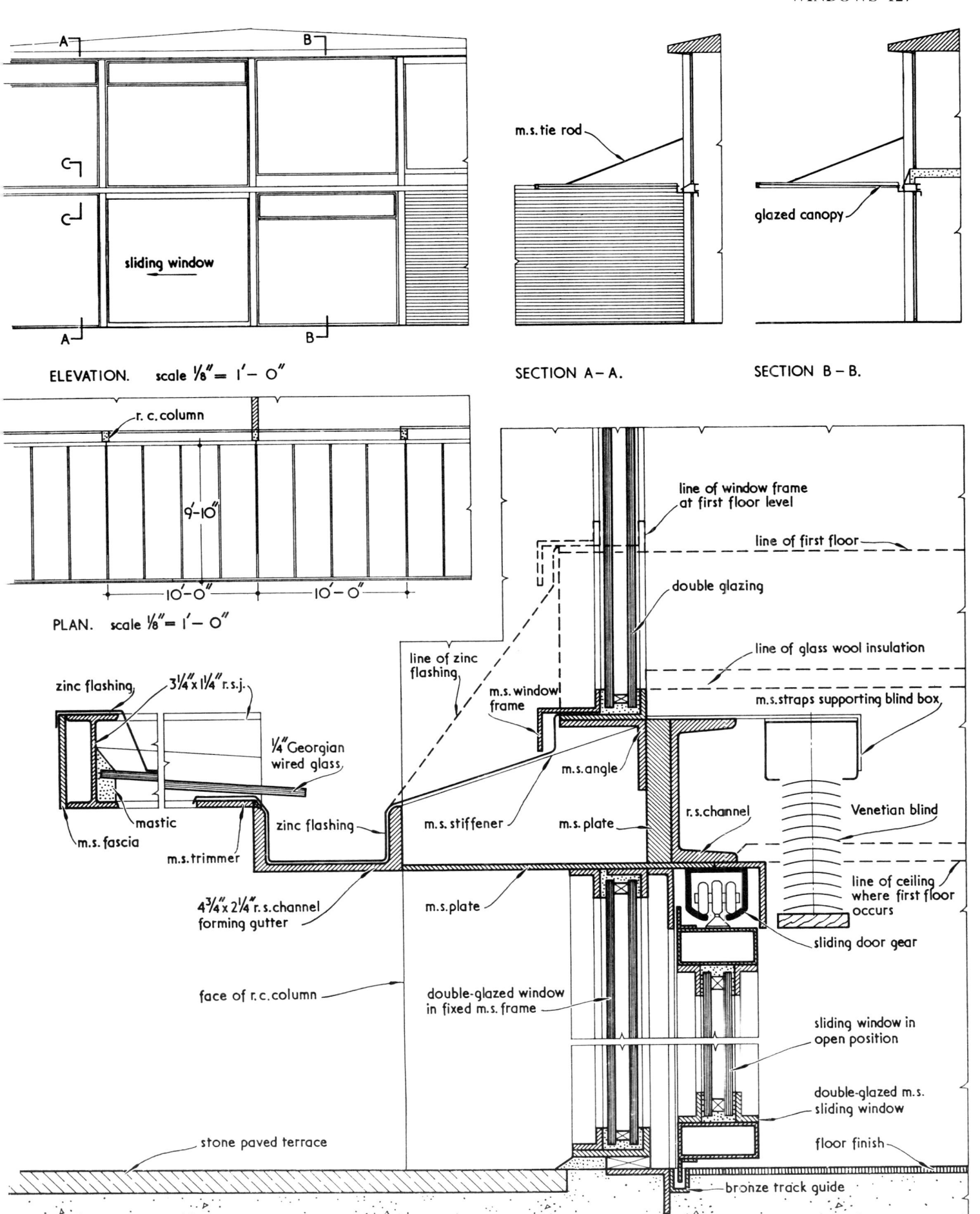

ELEVATION. scale ⅛" = 1'-0"

SECTION A-A.

SECTION B-B.

- m.s. tie rod
- glazed canopy

PLAN. scale ⅛" = 1'-0"
- r.c. column
- 9'-10"
- 10'-0"
- 10'-0"

SECTION C-C. scale ¼ full size

- zinc flashing
- 3¼" x 1¼" r.s.j.
- ¼" Georgian wired glass
- mastic
- m.s. fascia
- m.s. trimmer
- zinc flashing
- 4¾" x 2¼" r.s. channel forming gutter
- line of zinc flashing
- m.s. window frame
- m.s. stiffener
- m.s. angle
- m.s. plate
- face of r.c. column
- m.s. plate
- double-glazed window in fixed m.s. frame
- stone paved terrace
- line of window frame at first floor level
- line of first floor
- double glazing
- line of glass wool insulation
- m.s. straps supporting blind box
- Venetian blind
- r.s. channel
- line of ceiling where first floor occurs
- sliding door gear
- sliding window in open position
- double-glazed m.s. sliding window
- floor finish
- bronze track guide

note: figured dimensions in feet and inches are approximate

WINDOW WALL : SCHOOL AT OLDBURY, WORCESTER
DESIGNED BY F. R. S. YORKE, E. ROSENBERG AND C. S. MARDALL IN ASSOCIATION WITH F. W. B. YORKE AND H. M. BARKER

The chief interest in this detail centres around the hardwood sun-baffle and in the flashing which was required at the point of junction of its supporting bracket with the stanchion. The precast concrete slabs which comprise the cladding are attached direct to the stanchions at points which do not appear on the drawings.

WINDOWS 129

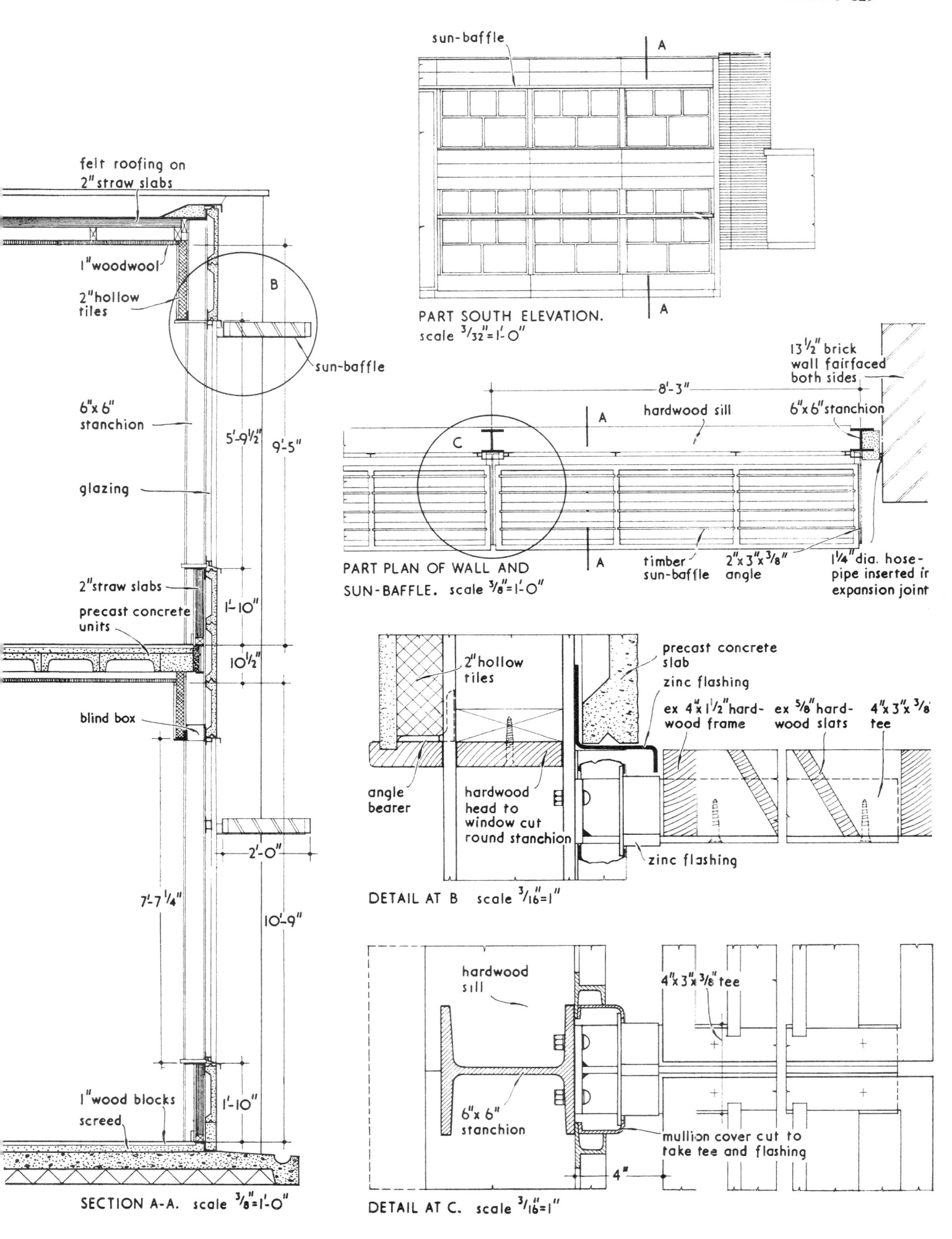

Labels on Section A-A (left diagram):
- felt roofing on 2" straw slabs
- 1" woodwool
- 2" hollow tiles
- sun-baffle
- 6"x 6" stanchion
- glazing
- 2" straw slabs
- precast concrete units
- blind box
- 1" wood blocks screed

Dimensions: 5'-9½", 9'-5", 1'-10", 10½", 2'-0", 7'-7¼", 10'-9", 1'-10"

SECTION A-A. scale ⅜"=1'-0"

PART SOUTH ELEVATION. scale 3/32"=1'-0"
- sun-baffle

PART PLAN OF WALL AND SUN-BAFFLE. scale ⅜"=1'-0"
- 13½" brick wall fairfaced both sides
- hardwood sill
- 6"x 6" stanchion
- timber sun-baffle
- 2"x 3"x ⅜" angle
- 1¼" dia. hose-pipe inserted in expansion joint
- 8'-3"

DETAIL AT B scale 3/16"=1"
- 2" hollow tiles
- precast concrete slab
- zinc flashing
- ex 4"x 1½" hardwood frame
- ex ⅝" hardwood slats
- 4"x 3"x ⅜" tee
- angle bearer
- hardwood head to window cut round stanchion
- zinc flashing

DETAIL AT C. scale 3/16"=1"
- hardwood sill
- 4"x 3"x ⅜" tee
- 6"x 6" stanchion
- mullion cover cut to take tee and flashing
- 4"

WINDOW: HOSPITAL AT SWINDON
DESIGNED BY POWELL AND MOYA

The original purpose of the fin-like mullions of this window was to direct the gaze of those inside towards the magnificent distant view. This purpose has not been perfectly fulfilled, but the window remains an interesting example of detailing in steel. The steel members are sufficiently slight to give the open-air sense which comes from structure-to-structure glazing, yet they are sufficiently frequent and substantial to make an architectural plane and not merely a void.

WINDOWS 131

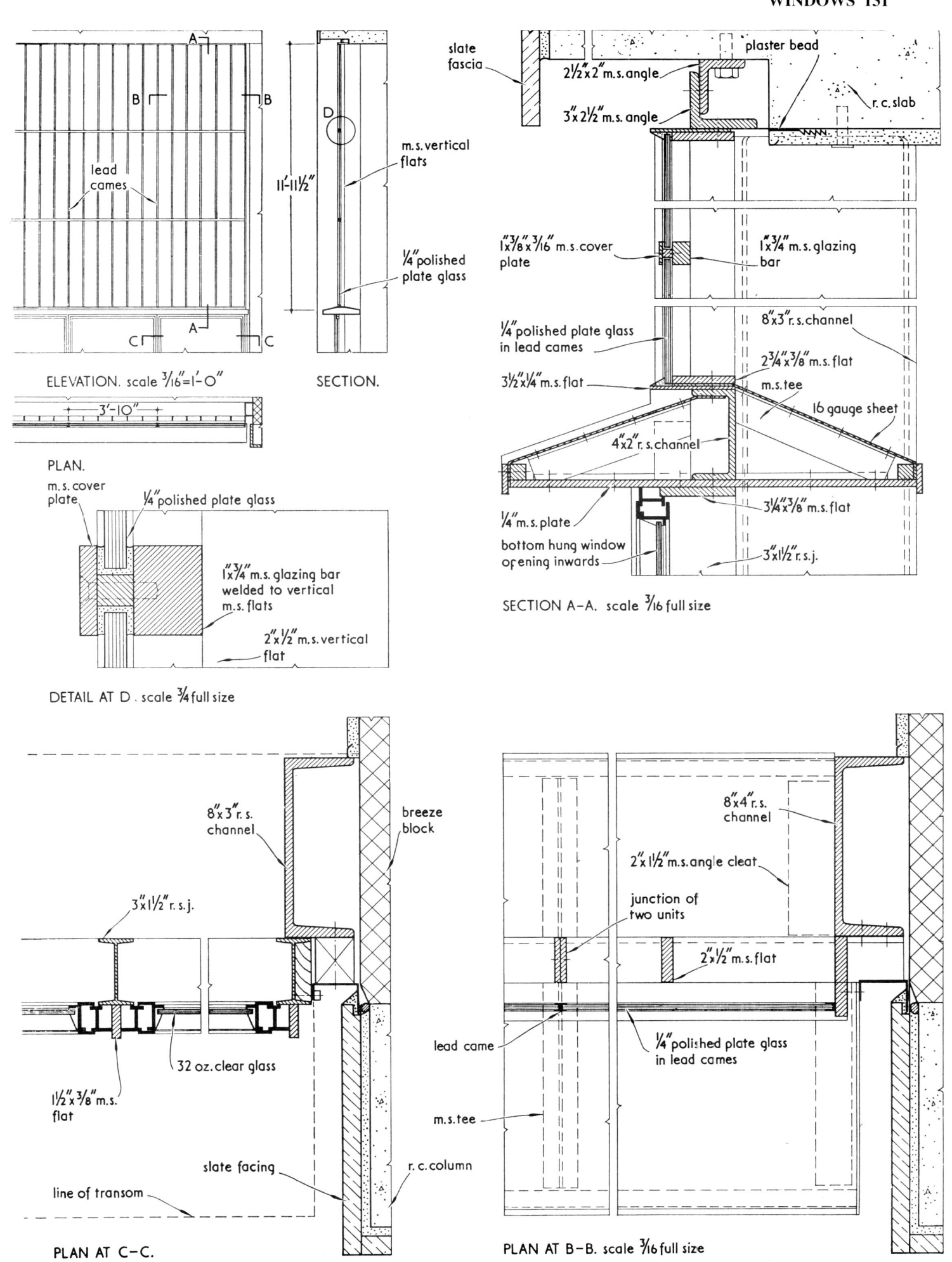

SLIDING WINDOWS: HOUSE NEAR HALLAND, SUSSEX
DESIGNED BY SERGE CHERMAYEFF

The garden front is divided by the timber framework into six bays, five with sliding windows and one with a fixed window section. The teak window frames enable the sections to be fined down to almost steel-frame dimensions. There are heating panels under the artificial stone extension of the terrace paving, and in the ceiling above

WINDOWS

WALLBOARD CEILING — **FACE PLATE OF HEATING PANEL**
CURTAIN RAIL FINISHED MATT NICKEL

1ST FLOOR BALCONY
GROUND FLOOR — TERRACE

KEY SECTION

0 1 2 3 4 5 · 10 · 15 FT.

STUDY | LIVING ROOM | DINING ROOM
SLIDING | FIXED | SLIDING | SLIDING | SLIDING | SLIDING

KEY PLAN

10 5 0 10 20 30 40 50 FT.

DETAIL SECTION X-X THRO' SLIDING WINDOWS

RECESSED BRASS CHANNEL GUIDES: ROLLERS REMOVED FROM END OF SLIDING SASH BY DOVETAIL PLATE FIXING

SPRING STRIP DRAUGHT EXCLUDER

1/4" POLISHED PLATE GLAZING BEDDED IN RED LEAD AND GOLDSIZE

1" TEAK SASHBAR

CENTRE HUNG VENT ON FRICTION PIVOTS: BRONZE FRAME WITH 1/4" POLISHED PLATE GLAZING

BOW HANDLE ON BACKPLATE FINISHED MATT NICKEL

12" x 5" JARRAH COLUMN

BALL BEARING RUNNERS

BRONZE THREE WAY TRACK: RUNNERS IN BRONZE WITH SMALL WEEP HOLES AT INTERVALS

DETAIL SECTION THRO' FIXED WINDOW

1/2" TUBES AS WEEPS THROUGH BRONZE CHANNEL

2" STONE PAVING

ARTIFICIAL STONE FLOORING
HEATING PANEL
ASBESTOS
SCREED

BLACK RUBBER BUFFER — SLIDING DOOR
STUDY | LIVING ROOM
DEAL LINING, PAINTED
DEAL BLOCKING PIECE, PAINTED
1/4" POLISHED PLATE GLAZING BEDDED IN RED LEAD & GOLDSIZE
BOW HANDLE ON BACKPLATE FINISHED MATT NICKEL

BRONZE CILL PLATE WITH 1" RAISED STRIPS

BRONZE CENTRE HUNG VENT ON FRICTION PIVOTS. 4" GRIP HANDLES FIXED 4" FROM PIVOT C/C

BLACK RUBBER BUFFER

SLIDING & FIXED SASHES IN TEAK, TWICE OILED

TRACK FOR SLIDING WINDOW

1/2" DEAL LINING, PAINTED

DETAIL PLAN OF WINDOWS

0 1 2 3 4 5 6 7 8 9 10 INS.

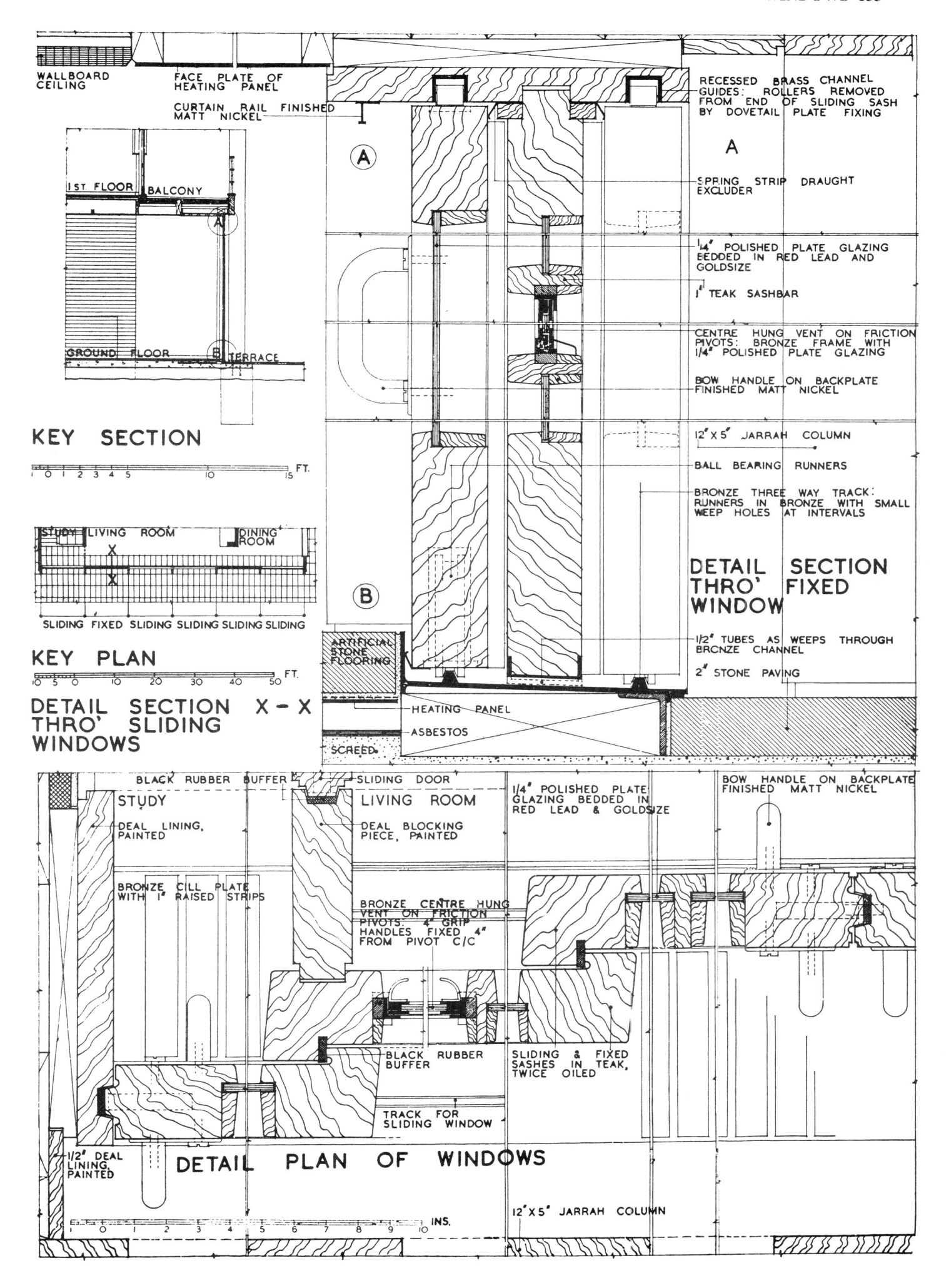

12" x 5" JARRAH COLUMN

BAY WINDOW: STUDIO IN BRISTOL
DESIGNED BY R. TOWNING HILL AND PARTNERS

The bay window has been built into an existing brick-faced stone wall and is supported on a framework composed of three lengths of 4-in. by 2-in. m.s. channel. This framework, which is mitred and welded at the joints, is bolted down to a concrete sub-floor inside the building and, outside, provides the forward edge to the bay. The glazing in the bay front is in the form of a fixed light in ¼-in. polished plate glass to give the maximum unobstructed view from the room behind.

WINDOWS 135

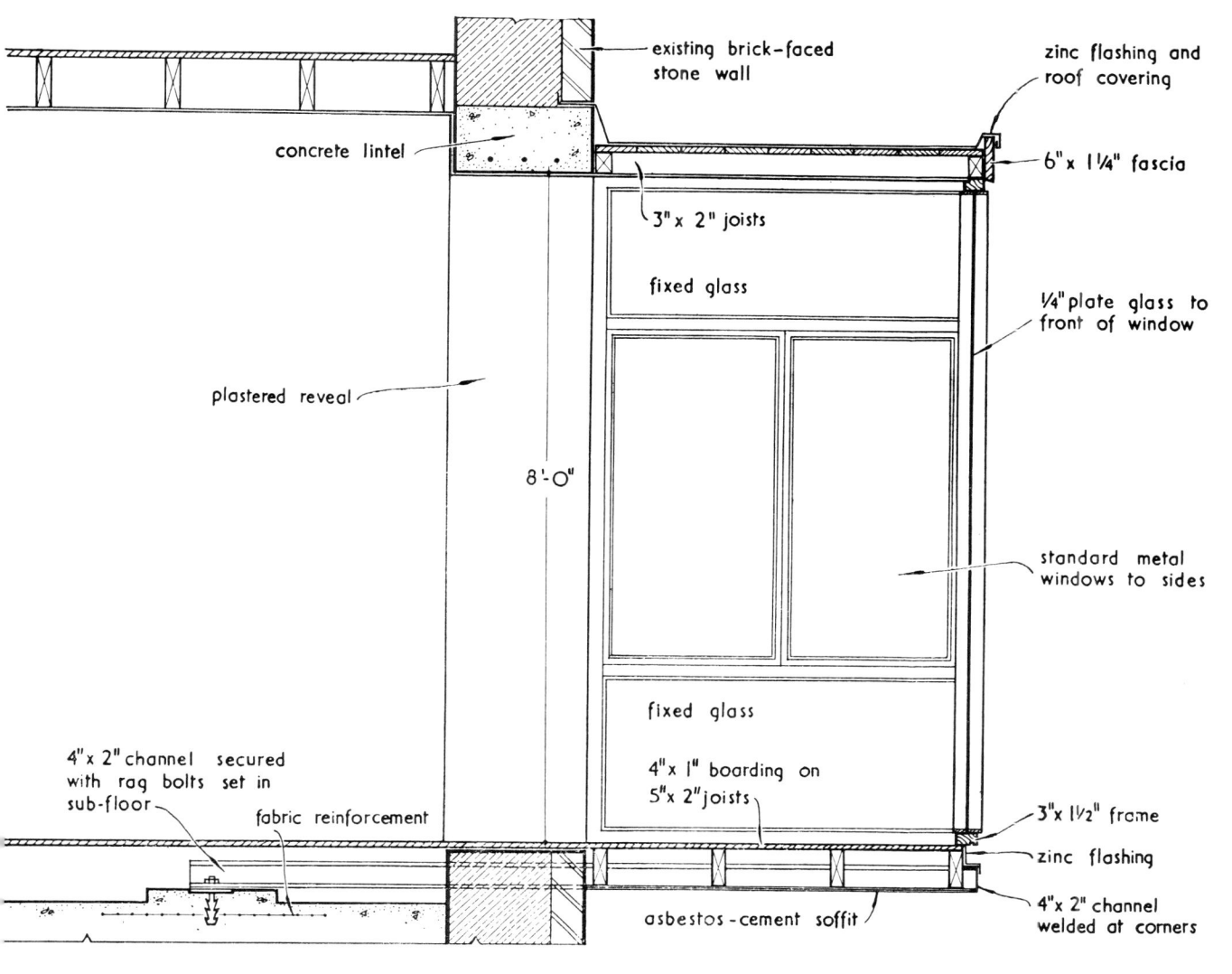

SECTION THROUGH CANTILEVERED WINDOW. scale ½" = 1'-0"

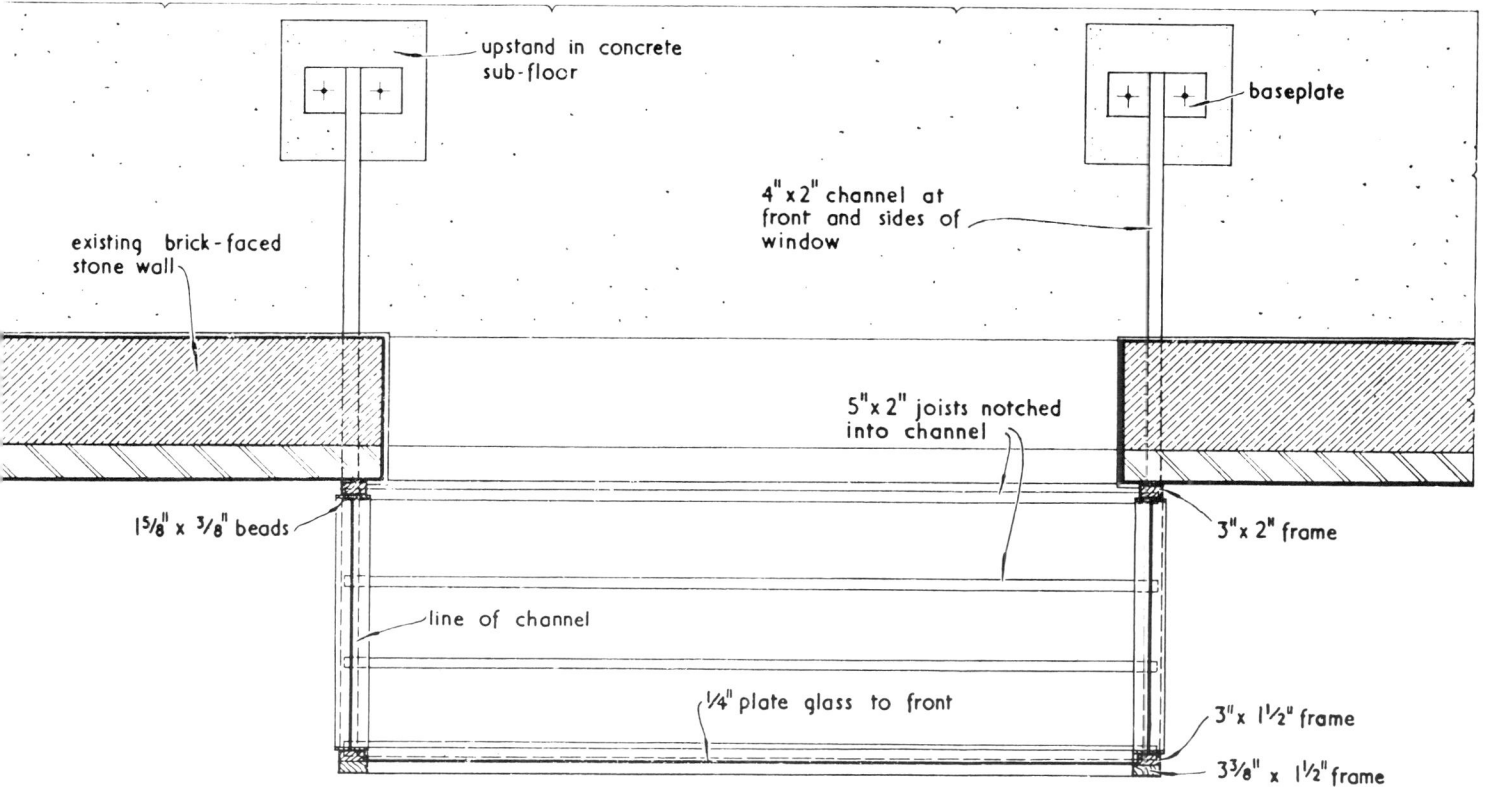

PLAN OF CANTILEVERED WINDOW. scale ½" = 1'-0"

COMMITTEE ROOM WINDOW: OFFICES IN LONDON, W.C.1
DESIGNED BY DAVID DU R. ABERDEEN AND PARTNERS

The smaller lights are straight on plan but the large lights and sill are curved (radius: 97 ft. 9 in.). The gear is of interest: the large lights swing on friction pivots but are locked by rotating bars in the mullions. When swung inwards for cleaning, they are held by a bronze dog-leash hook in the head which clips over an eye on the bottom transom. Top and bottom lights are held open by a pair of secret folding-arm stays and secured when closed by a budget lock.

WINDOWS 137

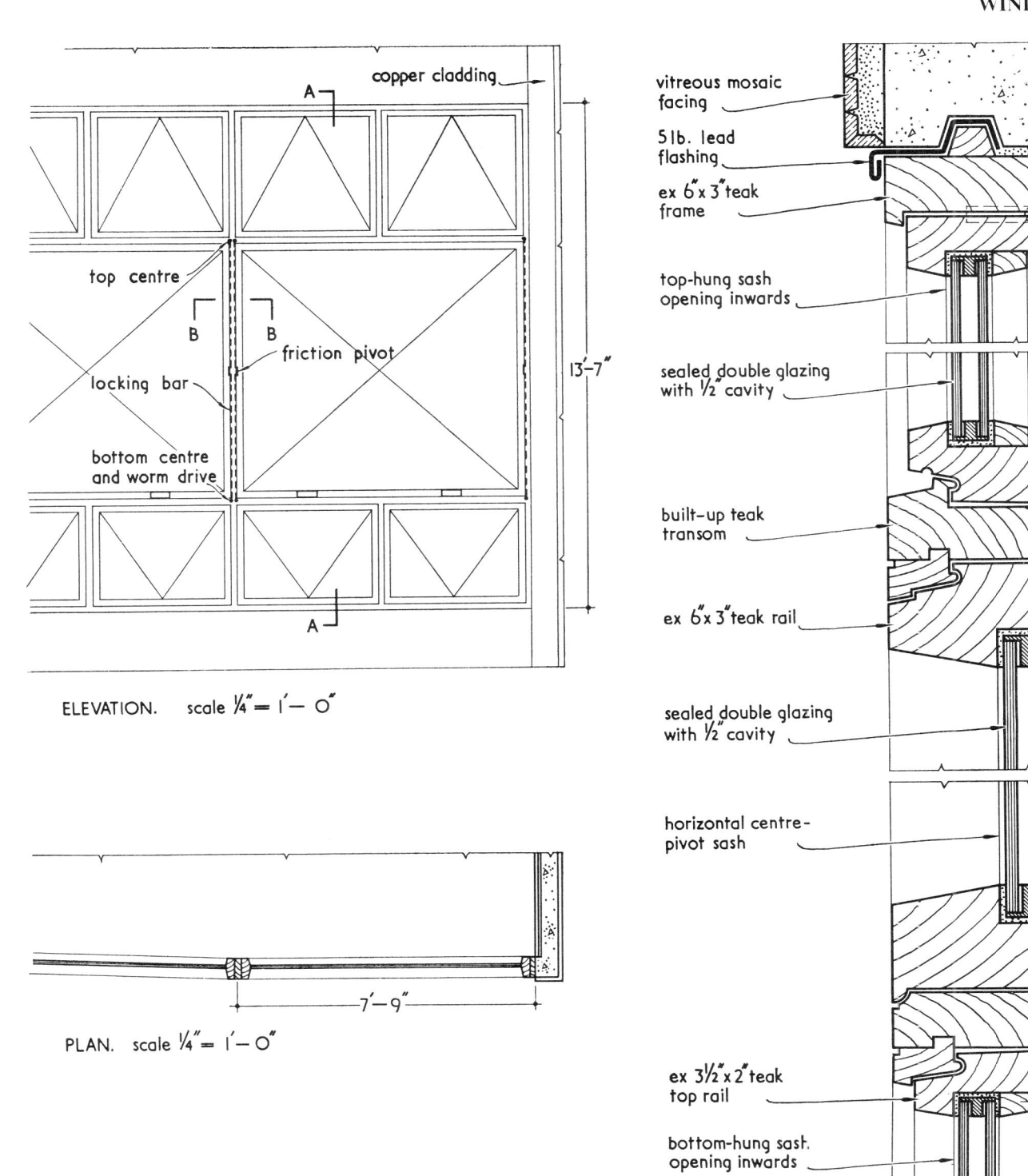

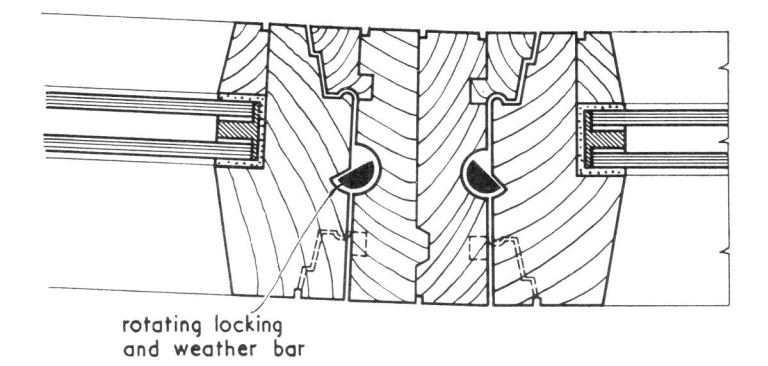

ELEVATION. scale ¼" = 1'—0"

- copper cladding
- A
- top centre
- friction pivot
- locking bar
- bottom centre and worm drive
- 13'—7"

PLAN. scale ¼" = 1'—0"

- 7'—9"

PLAN AT B—B. scale ¼ full size

- rotating locking and weather bar

SECTION A—A. scale ¼ full size

- vitreous mosaic facing
- 5 lb. lead flashing
- ex 6" x 3" teak frame
- top-hung sash opening inwards
- sealed double glazing with ½" cavity
- built-up teak transom
- ex 6" x 3" teak rail
- sealed double glazing with ½" cavity
- horizontal centre-pivot sash
- ex 3½" x 2" teak top rail
- bottom-hung sash opening inwards
- ⅝" x ⅜" bronze protection bars
- ex 3½" x 2½" bottom rail
- ex 7" x 2" teak sill
- bronze flashing
- blocking

138 WINDOWS

WINDOW IN FLAT: COLLEGE AT OXFORD
DESIGNED BY ARCHITECTS' CO-PARTNERSHIP

This window in the caretaker's flat has Georgian wired glass in the fixed lower light and the panel above the opening is one slab of slate grooved for decorative effect.

WINDOWS 139

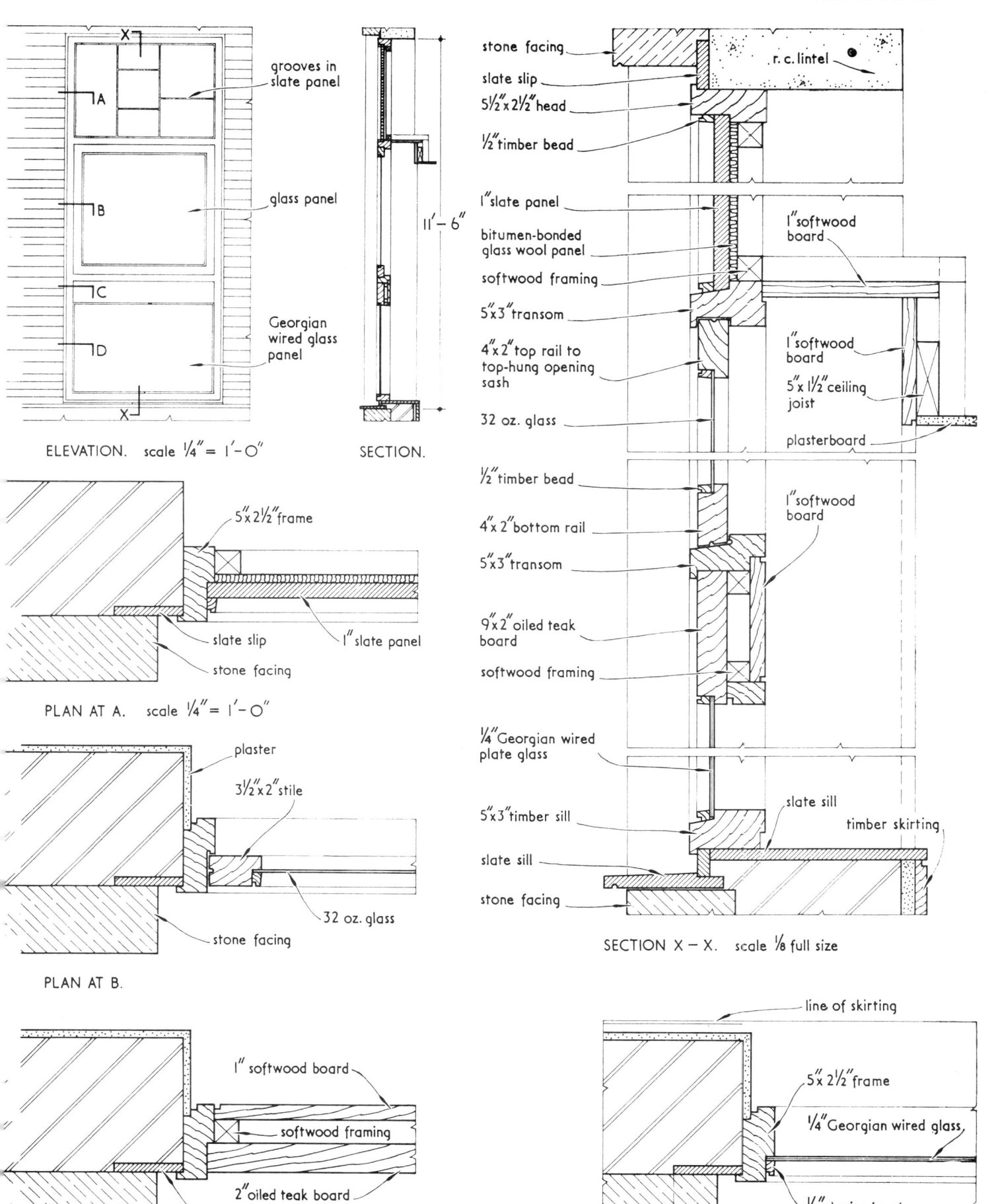

ELEVATION. scale ¼" = 1'-0"

- grooves in slate panel
- glass panel
- Georgian wired glass panel

SECTION. 11'-6"

PLAN AT A. scale ¼" = 1'-0"
- 5" x 2½" frame
- slate slip
- 1" slate panel
- stone facing

PLAN AT B.
- plaster
- 3½" x 2" stile
- 32 oz. glass
- stone facing

PLAN AT C. 5'-0"
- 1" softwood board
- softwood framing
- 2" oiled teak board
- slate slip

SECTION X – X. scale ⅛ full size
- stone facing
- slate slip
- 5½" x 2½" head
- ½" timber bead
- 1" slate panel
- bitumen-bonded glass wool panel
- softwood framing
- 5" x 3" transom
- 4" x 2" top rail to top-hung opening sash
- 32 oz. glass
- ½" timber bead
- 4" x 2" bottom rail
- 5" x 3" transom
- 9" x 2" oiled teak board
- softwood framing
- ¼" Georgian wired plate glass
- 5" x 3" timber sill
- slate sill
- stone facing
- r.c. lintel
- 1" softwood board
- 1" softwood board
- 5" x 1½" ceiling joist
- plasterboard
- 1" softwood board
- slate sill
- timber skirting

PLAN AT D.
- line of skirting
- 5" x 2½" frame
- ¼" Georgian wired glass
- ½" glazing bead
- line of sill

140 WINDOWS

WINDOW: COLLEGE AT OXFORD
DESIGNED BY ARCHITECTS' CO-PARTNERSHIP

This version of the traditional sash has two fixed lights, one top and one bottom, and a vertical sliding sash between. Note the simplification of detail at the sill and the use of a bead to form an outside flange for the sliding sash.

WINDOWS 141

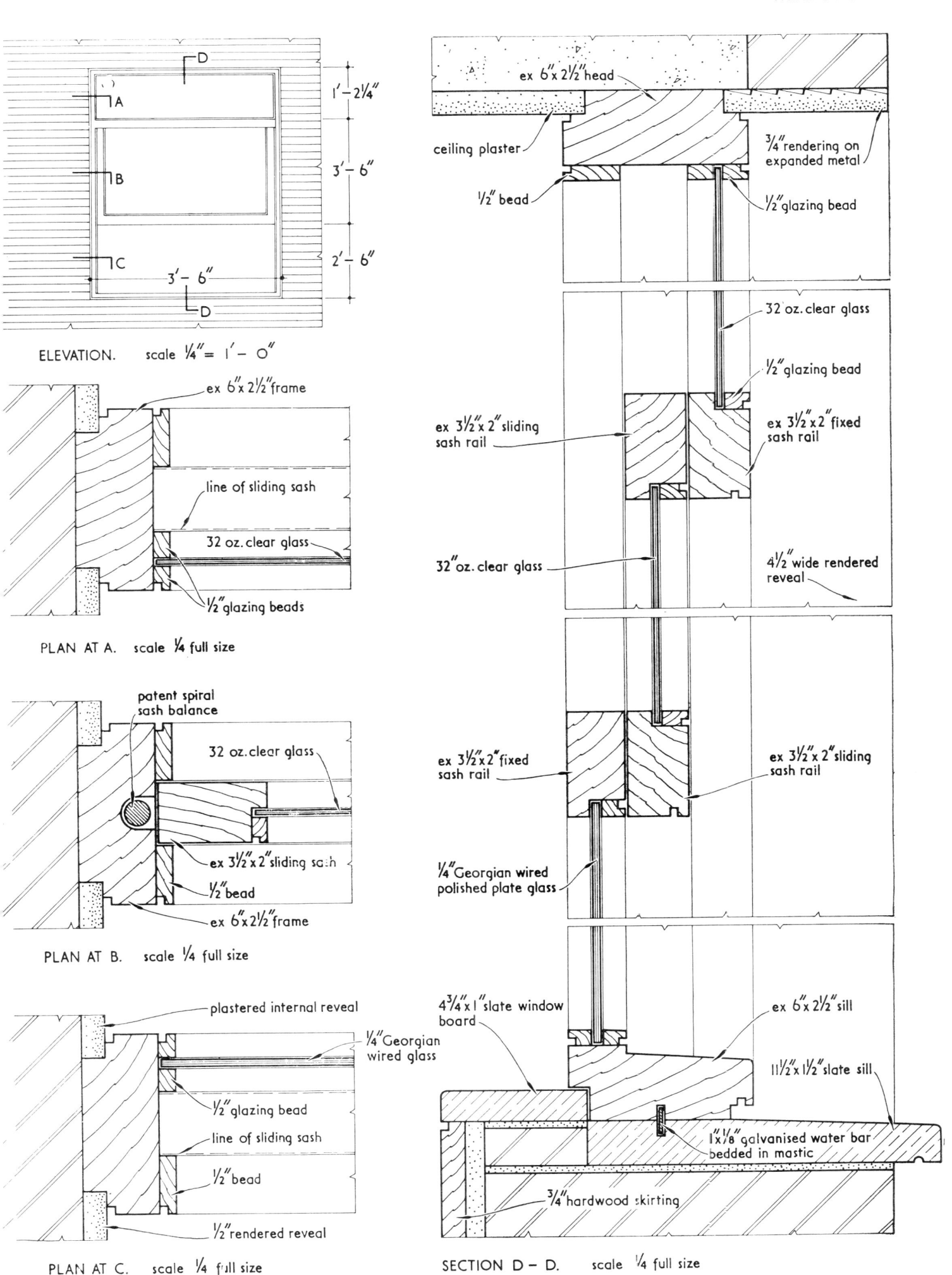

142 WINDOWS

GLAZED WALL: HOSPITAL AT SWINDON
DESIGNED BY POWELL AND MOYA

This is an ingenious example of how to give a fully-glazed storey-wall a strong horizontal emphasis. This is achieved by recessing the mullions behind the glass face, by holding the glass at head, sill and transom and by effecting the vertical joint between panes with lead cames.

WINDOWS 143

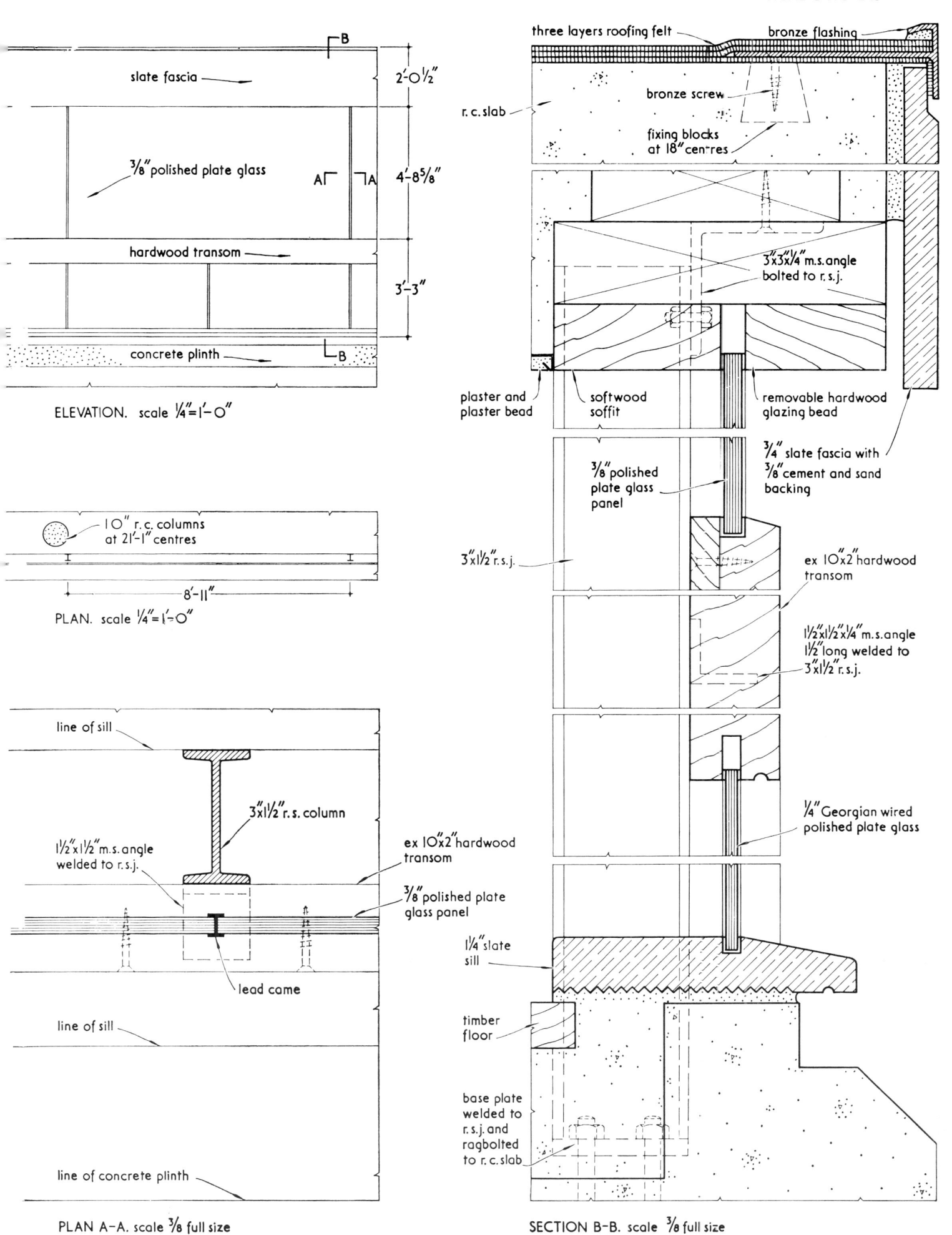

ELEVATION. scale ¼"=1'–0"

- slate fascia
- ⅜" polished plate glass
- hardwood transom
- concrete plinth
- 2'–0½"
- 4'–8⅝"
- 3'–3"

PLAN. scale ¼"=1'–0"

- 10" r.c. columns at 21'–1" centres
- 8'–11"

PLAN A–A. scale ⅜ full size

- line of sill
- 3"x1½" r.s. column
- 1½"x1½" m.s. angle welded to r.s.j.
- ex 10"x2" hardwood transom
- ⅜" polished plate glass panel
- lead came
- line of sill
- line of concrete plinth

SECTION B–B. scale ⅜ full size

- three layers roofing felt
- bronze flashing
- r.c. slab
- bronze screw
- fixing blocks at 18" centres
- 3"x3"x¼" m.s. angle bolted to r.s.j.
- plaster and plaster bead
- softwood soffit
- removable hardwood glazing bead
- ⅜" polished plate glass panel
- ¾" slate fascia with ⅜" cement and sand backing
- 3"x1½" r.s.j.
- ex 10"x2" hardwood transom
- 1½"x1½"x¼" m.s. angle 1½" long welded to 3"x1½" r.s.j.
- ¼" Georgian wired polished plate glass
- 1¼" slate sill
- timber floor
- base plate welded to r.s.j. and ragbolted to r.c. slab

WINDOW: COLLEGE IN LONDON, S.W.7
DESIGNED BY RICHARD SHEPPARD, ROBSON AND PARTNERS

Constructed throughout in teak, these windows are the full width of the room with a maximum opening area of half this width by a height of 5 ft.

WINDOWS 145

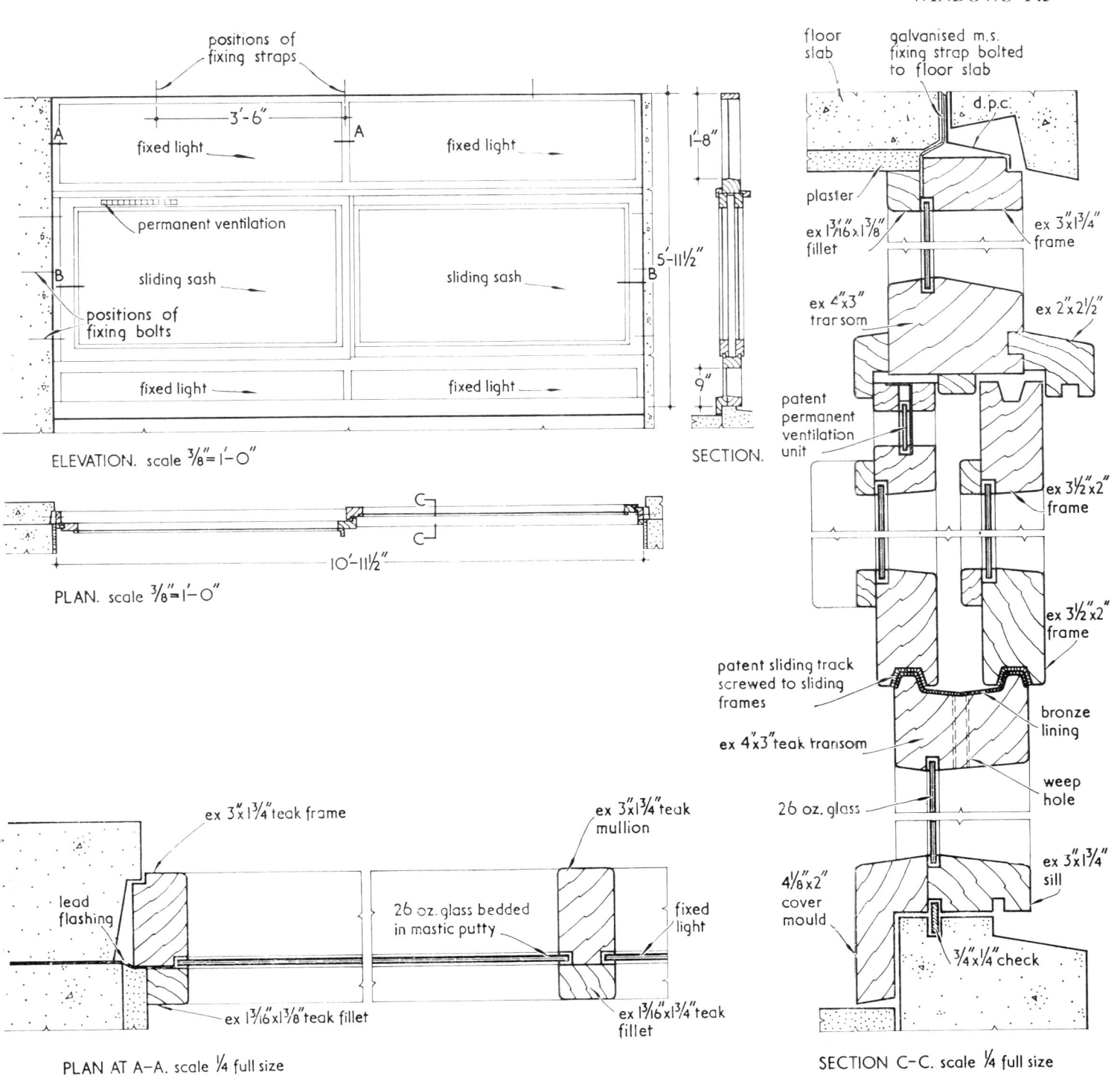

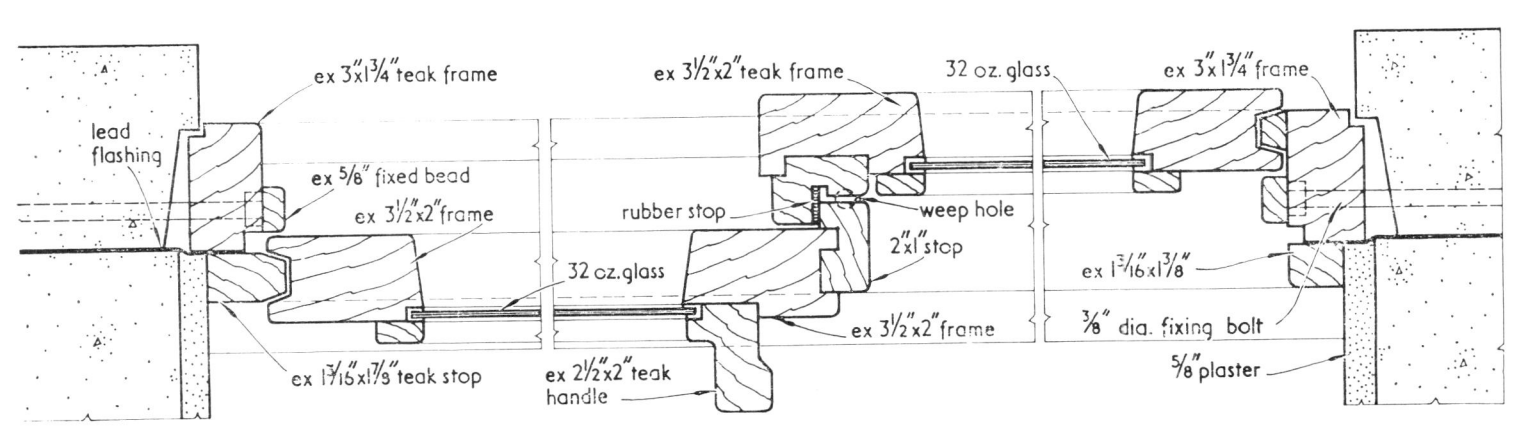

146 WINDOWS

GLAZED WALL: HOUSE AT UPPSALA, SWEDEN
DESIGNED BY HANS MATELL, VIKING GÖRANSSON,
CARL-ERIC NOHLDÉN, ULLA HANSEN-CAMPBELL

(*Material supplied by C. B. Wilcher*)

A noteworthy attempt is here made, in the context of domestic architecture, to reconcile a high standard of insulation with large areas of glazing. Note (on the drawing) the holes in the transoms to ventilate the outer air space in the triple glazing, the warm air duct behind the skirting to eliminate down-draught and the plastic moisture barriers in the mullions.

WINDOWS 147

KEY ELEVATION. scale $1/8" = 1'-0"$

- triple glazing
- $10'-4\frac{1}{2}"$
- $6'-9"$
- $3'-3"$ (×4)

SECTION A-A scale $1" = 1'-0"$

- aluminium sheet roofing
- $2" \times 2"$ framing
- rafter
- aluminium guttering in aluminium bracket
- $3" \times 1"$ Norwegian spruce boarding
- $3'-3\frac{1}{2}"$

SECTION B-B. scale ½ full size

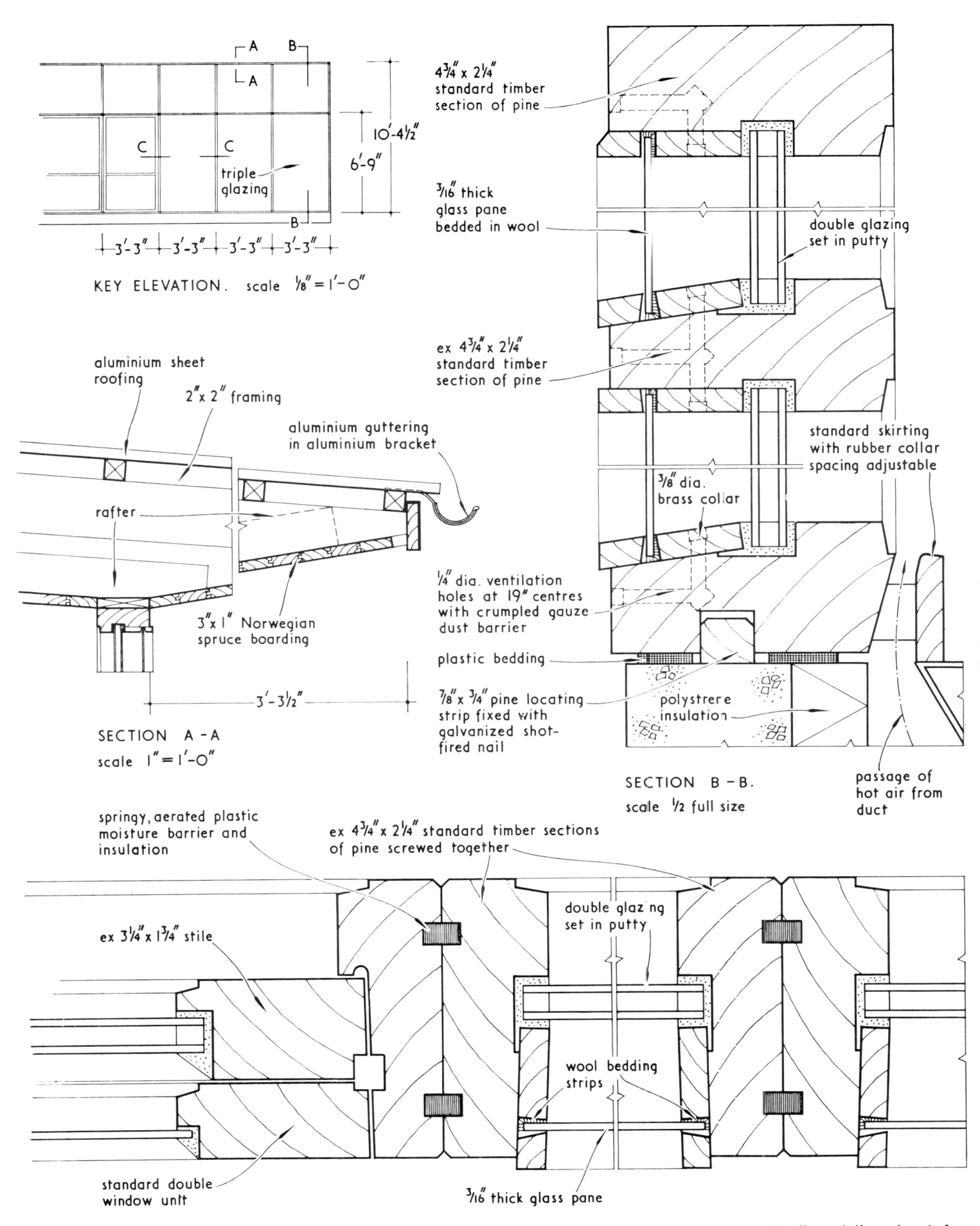

- $4\frac{3}{4}" \times 2\frac{1}{4}"$ standard timber section of pine
- $3/16"$ thick glass pane bedded in wool
- double glazing set in putty
- ex $4\frac{3}{4}" \times 2\frac{1}{4}"$ standard timber section of pine
- standard skirting with rubber collar spacing adjustable
- $3/8"$ dia. brass collar
- $1/4"$ dia. ventilation holes at 19" centres with crumpled gauze dust barrier
- plastic bedding
- $7/8" \times 3/4"$ pine locating strip fixed with galvanized shot-fired nail
- polystrere insulation
- passage of hot air from duct

PLAN C-C. scale ½ full size

- springy, aerated plastic moisture barrier and insulation
- ex $4\frac{3}{4}" \times 2\frac{1}{4}"$ standard timber sections of pine screwed together
- ex $3\frac{1}{4}" \times 1\frac{3}{4}"$ stile
- double glazing set in putty
- wool bedding strips
- standard double window unit
- $3/16"$ thick glass pane

note: figured dimensions in feet and inches are approximate

148 WINDOWS

BAY WINDOWS : HOUSE IN LONDON, N.W. 3
DESIGNED BY ARCHITECTS' CO-PARTNERSHIP

New windows have been fitted in two floors of a three-storey Victorian bay. R.c. in-situ beams, cranked to the shape of the bay, have been inserted at first and second floor levels, and are supported at the outside angles of the bay by 3-in. diameter mild steel tubes. The sash windows are hung in spring balances.

WINDOWS 149

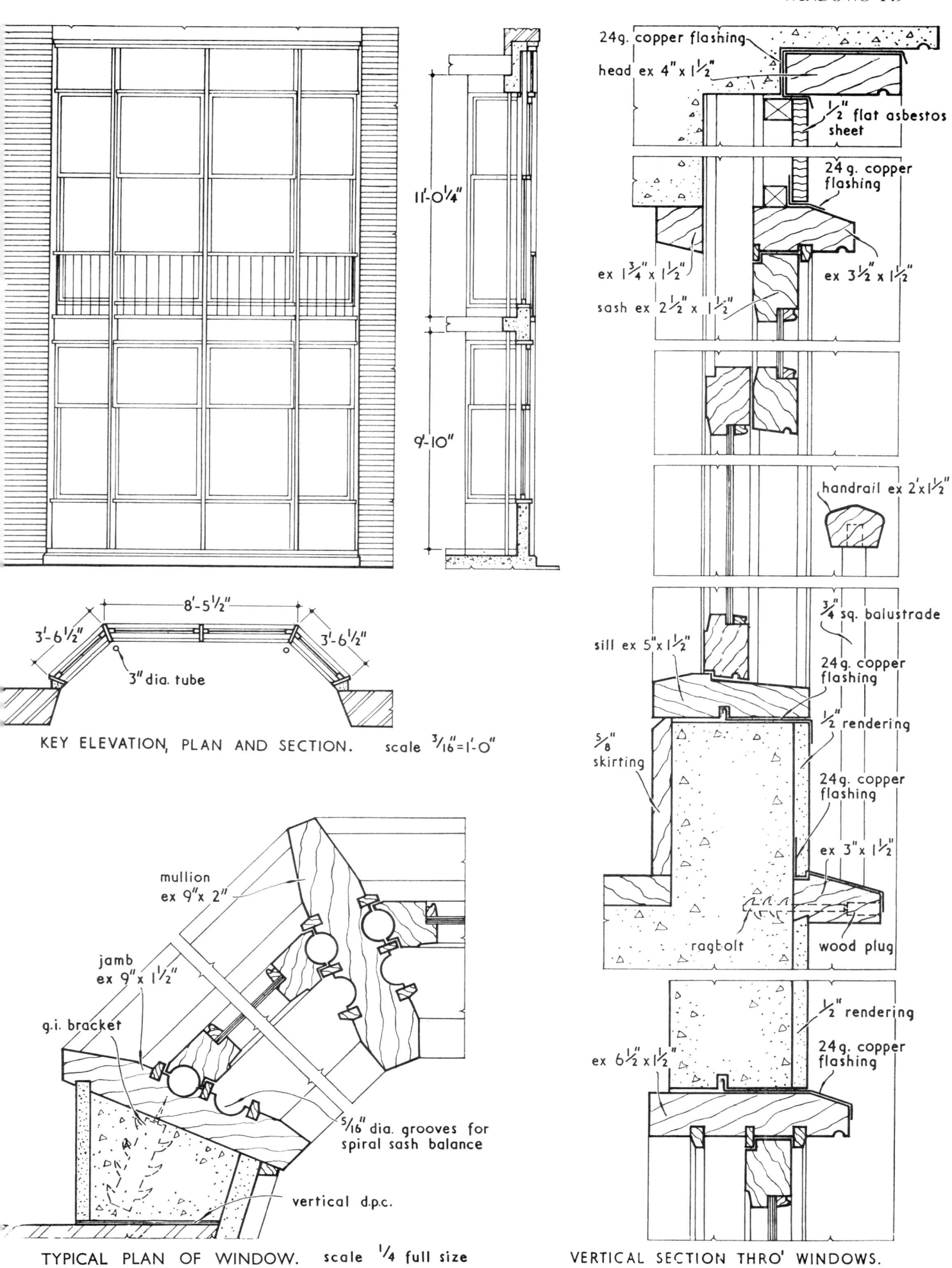

KEY ELEVATION, PLAN AND SECTION. scale ³⁄₁₆"=1'-0"

TYPICAL PLAN OF WINDOW. scale ¼ full size

- mullion ex 9" x 2"
- jamb ex 9" x 1½"
- g.i. bracket
- ⁵⁄₁₆" dia. grooves for spiral sash balance
- vertical d.p.c.
- 3" dia. tube
- 8'-5½"
- 3'-6½"
- 3'-6½"
- 11'-0¼"
- 9'-10"

VERTICAL SECTION THRO' WINDOWS.

- 24g. copper flashing
- head ex 4" x 1½"
- ½" flat asbestos sheet
- 24 g. copper flashing
- ex 1¾" x 1½"
- ex 3½" x 1½"
- sash ex 2½" x 1½"
- handrail ex 2" x 1½"
- ¾" sq. balustrade
- sill ex 5" x 1½"
- 24g. copper flashing
- ½" rendering
- ⅝" skirting
- 24g. copper flashing
- ex 3" x 1½"
- ragbolt
- wood plug
- ½" rendering
- 24g. copper flashing
- ex 6½" x 1½"

150 WINDOWS

RANGE OF WINDOWS: OFFICES IN LONDON, N.W.9
DESIGNED BY WALTER SEGAL

The use of 9-in. brick piers and the consequent impossibility of getting a true face on both reveals led the architect to lay the back of the gurjun frame flush with the face of the brickwork. Gurjun gives a minimum of movement when used externally. The fixed frames, built up in horizontal units of two windows each, are secured to the brickwork by 8-in. by 2½-in. by ⅛-in. cramps, two on either side of each window. The vertical strips connecting the two ranges of window are morticed top and bottom into the adjoining frames.

WINDOWS 151

PLAN AND ELEVATION OF WINDOW. scale ¼" = 1'0"

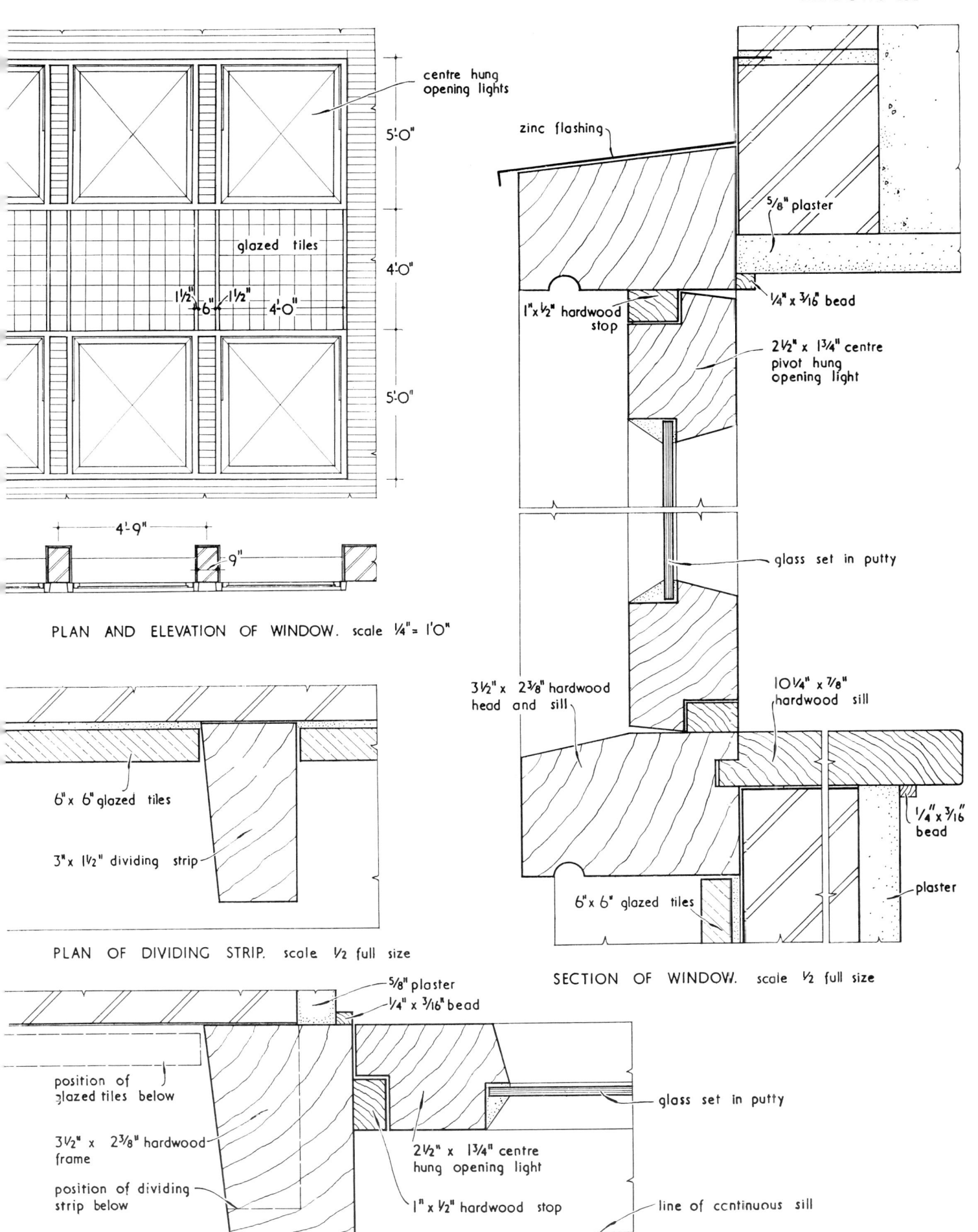

- centre hung opening lights
- glazed tiles

PLAN OF DIVIDING STRIP. scale ½ full size

- 6" x 6" glazed tiles
- 3" x 1½" dividing strip

PLAN OF WINDOW. scale ½ full size

- position of glazed tiles below
- 3½" x 2⅜" hardwood frame
- position of dividing strip below
- ⅝" plaster
- ¼" x 3/16" bead
- 2½" x 1¾" centre hung opening light
- 1" x ½" hardwood stop
- glass set in putty
- line of continuous sill

SECTION OF WINDOW. scale ½ full size

- zinc flashing
- ⅝" plaster
- 1" x ½" hardwood stop
- ¼" x 3/16" bead
- 2½" x 1¾" centre pivot hung opening light
- glass set in putty
- 3½" x 2⅜" hardwood head and sill
- 10¼" x ⅞" hardwood sill
- 6" x 6" glazed tiles
- ¼" x 3/16" bead
- plaster

152 WINDOWS

WINDOWS: HOSPITAL IN LONDON, S.E.1
DESIGNED BY W. G. HOLFORD AND L. G. CREED

A factor determining the fenestration of this very skilful façade was the need to screen the bench tops, which lie directly behind the windows, from draughts from the opening lights. Therefore the opening lights were stopped about a foot above bench level and a strip of fixed lights inserted. Because this type of double window is so effective in stopping draughts when shut, a line of ventilation slots was inserted above the head. Woodwork is teak, varnished inside, oiled outside; strings are Westmorland slate, and the panels beneath the windows are oyster grey vitreous mosaic. The ground floor arcades form part of the existing building.

WINDOWS 153

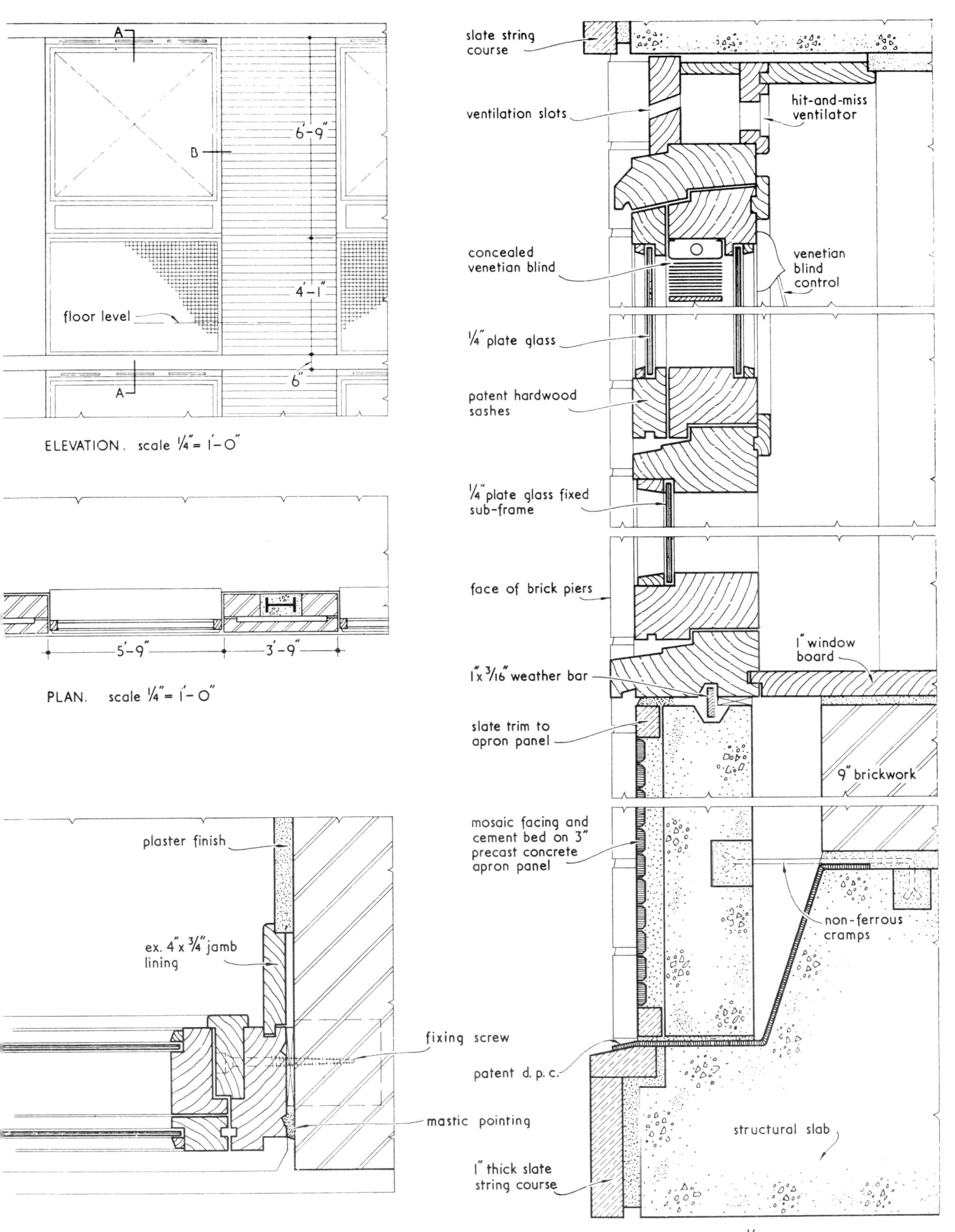

ELEVATION. scale ¼" = 1'-0"

- 6'-9"
- 4'-1"
- 6"
- floor level
- A
- B

PLAN. scale ¼" = 1'-0"

- 5'-9"
- 3'-9"

PLAN AT B. scale ¼ full size

- plaster finish
- ex. 4" x ¾" jamb lining
- fixing screw
- mastic pointing

SECTION A–A. scale ¼ full size

- slate string course
- ventilation slots
- hit-and-miss ventilator
- concealed venetian blind
- venetian blind control
- ¼" plate glass
- patent hardwood sashes
- ¼" plate glass fixed sub-frame
- face of brick piers
- 1" window board
- 1" x 3/16" weather bar
- slate trim to apron panel
- 9" brickwork
- mosaic facing and cement bed on 3" precast concrete apron panel
- non-ferrous cramps
- patent d.p.c.
- structural slab
- 1" thick slate string course

154 WINDOWS

WINDOWS: FLATS IN LONDON, S.W.1
DESIGNED BY WALTER SEGAL

This very individual window treatment uses a pre-fabricated framing (gurjun) of a type recalling the subframe of a curtain wall. This is applied to the brick face and secured by ties. It will be noticed the brick panels are of two colours—which again brings out the analogy with the glass curtain and gives an effect of lightness unusual in a brick-faced building. This arrangement of the window framing is economical, and gives an extra wide sill and uninterrupted reveals.

WINDOWS

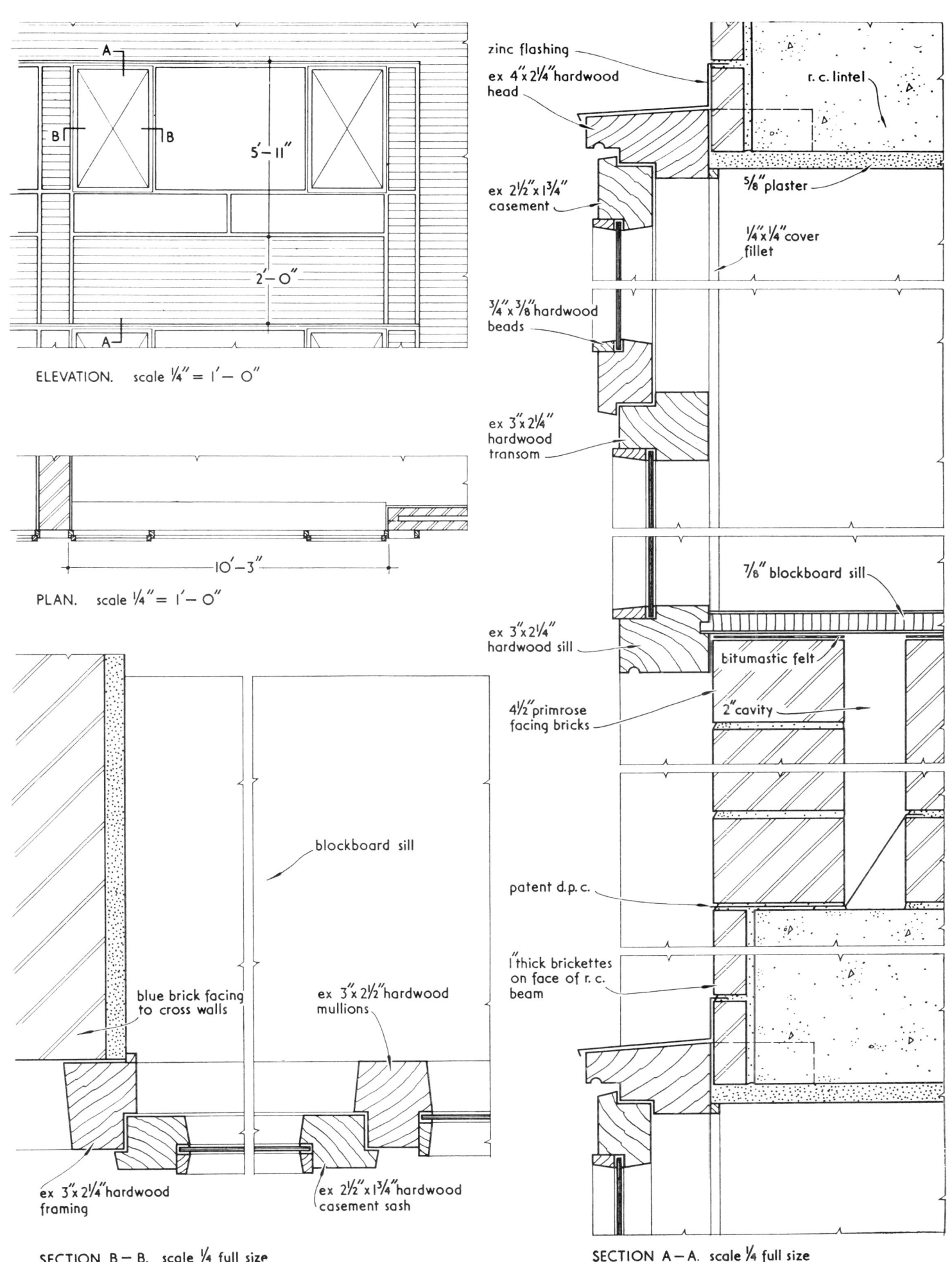

ELEVATION. scale ¼" = 1'−0"

PLAN. scale ¼" = 1'−0"

SECTION B−B. scale ¼ full size

- ex 3"×2¼" hardwood framing
- blue brick facing to cross walls
- blockboard sill
- ex 3"×2½" hardwood mullions
- ex 2½"×1¾" hardwood casement sash

SECTION A−A. scale ¼ full size

- zinc flashing
- ex 4"×2¼" hardwood head
- r. c. lintel
- ex 2½"×1¾" casement
- ⅝" plaster
- ¼"×¼" cover fillet
- ¾"×⅜" hardwood beads
- ex 3"×2¼" hardwood transom
- ⅞" blockboard sill
- ex 3"×2¼" hardwood sill
- bitumastic felt
- 4½" primrose facing bricks
- 2" cavity
- patent d.p.c.
- 1" thick brickettes on face of r. c. beam

156 WINDOWS

WINDOWS: FLATS IN LONDON, S.W.3
DESIGNED BY WALTER SEGAL

Points to notice about this façade are the reduction of the sill to a visual minimum by the use of a coved quarry tile and the insertion of permanent ventilation above the window head. The front façade of this building is illustrated on the preceding two pages.

WINDOWS 157

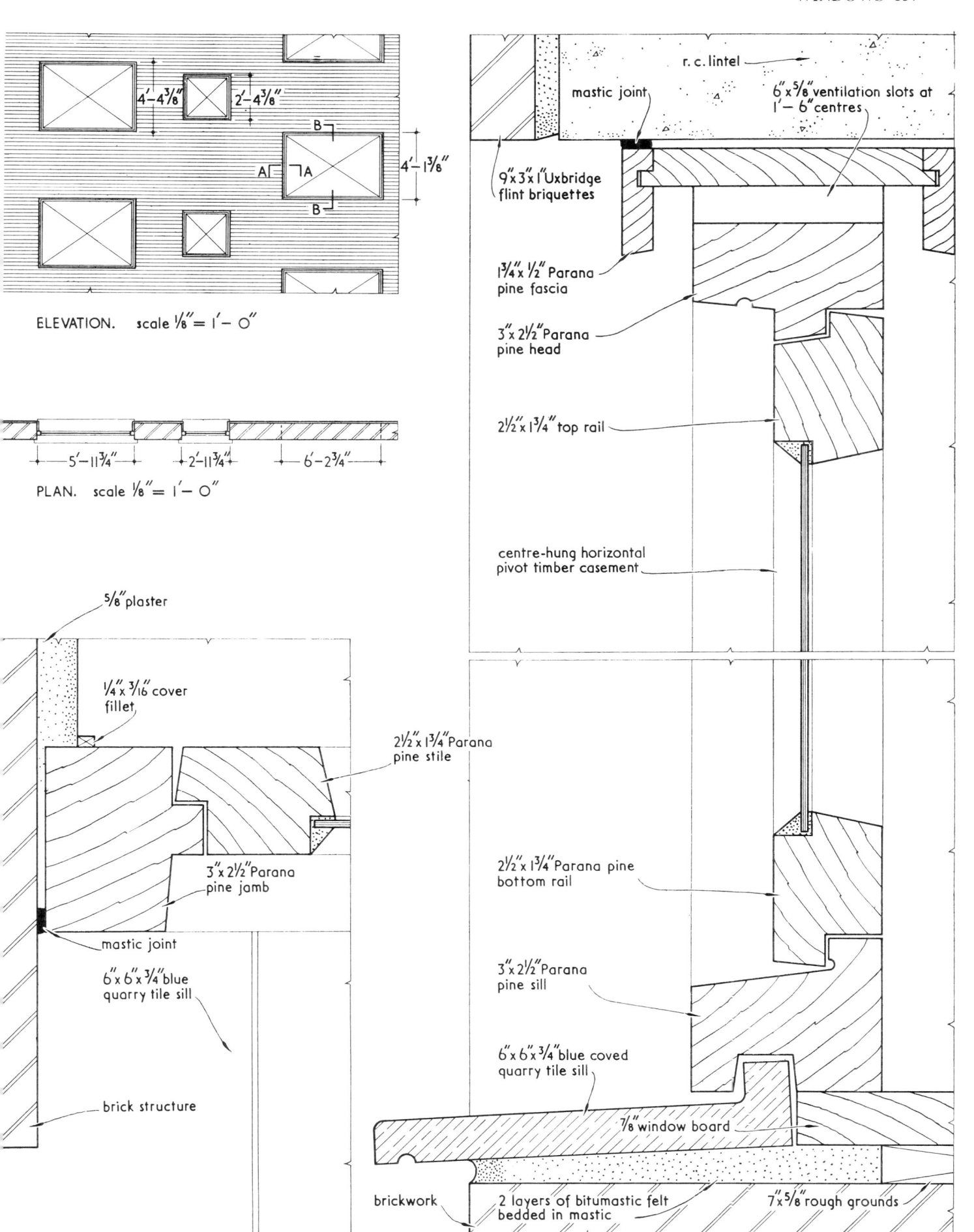

ELEVATION. scale ⅛"= 1'- 0"

4'-4⅜"   2'-4⅜"   4'-1⅜"

PLAN. scale ⅛"= 1'- 0"

5'-11¾"   2'-11¾"   6'-2¾"

PLAN AT A—A. scale ½ full size

- ⅝" plaster
- ¼"x³⁄₁₆" cover fillet
- 2½"x 1¾" Parana pine stile
- 3"x 2½" Parana pine jamb
- mastic joint
- 6"x 6"x ¾" blue quarry tile sill
- brick structure

SECTION B—B. scale ½ full size

- r.c. lintel
- mastic joint
- 6"x ⅝" ventilation slots at 1'-6" centres
- 9"x 3"x 1" Uxbridge flint briquettes
- 1¾"x ½" Parana pine fascia
- 3"x 2½" Parana pine head
- 2½"x 1¾" top rail
- centre-hung horizontal pivot timber casement
- 2½"x 1¾" Parana pine bottom rail
- 3"x 2½" Parana pine sill
- 6"x 6"x ¾" blue coved quarry tile sill
- ⅞" window board
- brickwork
- 2 layers of bitumastic felt bedded in mastic
- 7"x ⅝" rough grounds

WINDOW: SCHOOL AT AMERSHAM, BUCKS
DESIGNED BY THE CHIEF ARCHITECT'S DEPARTMENT, M.O.E.,
in collaboration with THE COUNTY ARCHITECT, Buckinghamshire County Council
J. S. B. COATMAN, MARY B. CROWLEY, DAVID L. MEDD and C. E. D. WOOSTER (architects-in-charge)

This timber detailing has been designed to make easy junctions with traditional loadbearing structure. Note the use of glass louvres to give maximum ventilation areas, while avoiding the obstruction of wood frames, and the splayed reveal to catch the light and provide a gradation of light between the sky and interior surfaces.

WINDOWS 159

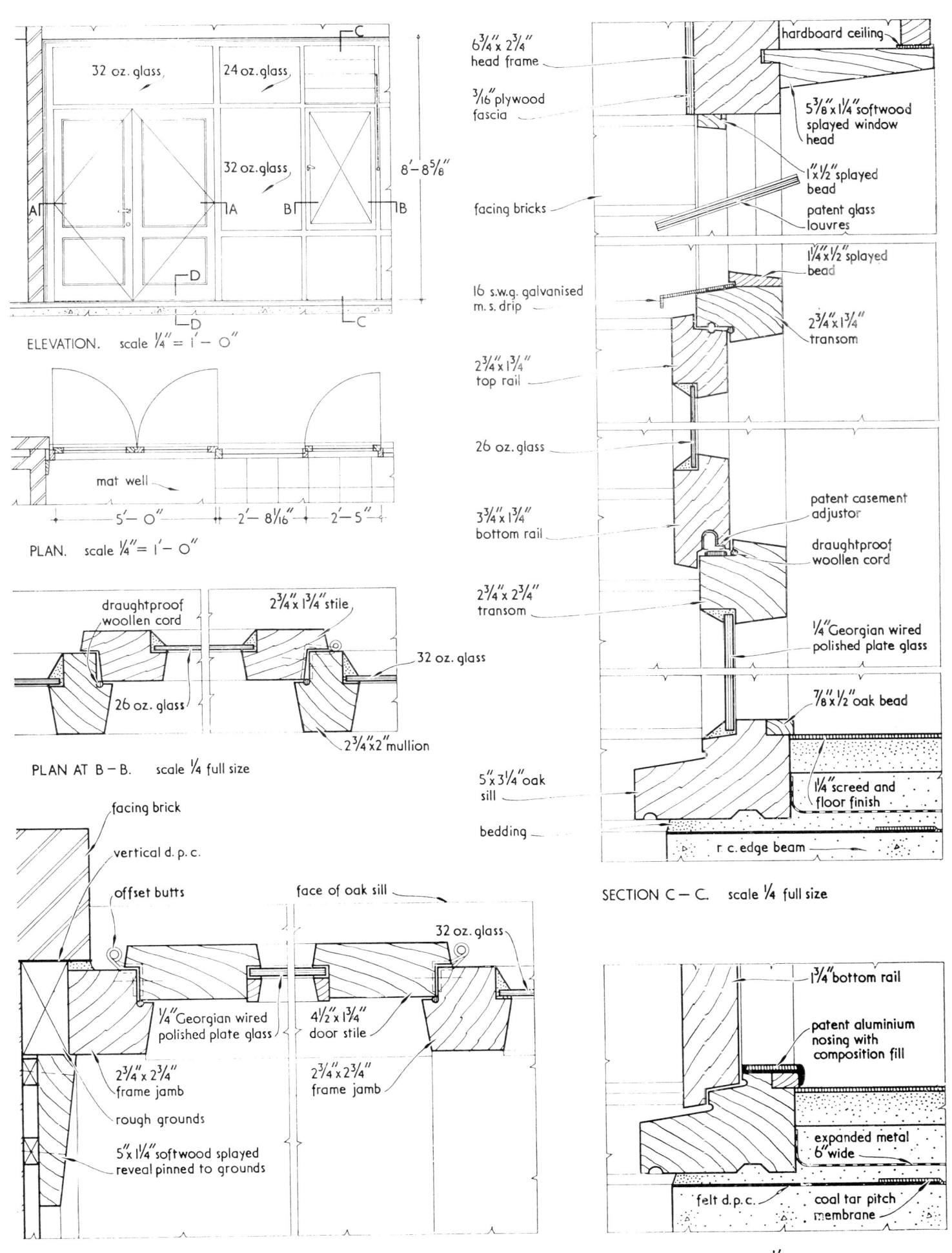

WINDOWS: OFFICES IN HELSINKI, FINLAND
DESIGNED BY ALVAR AALTO

(*Material supplied by Jan Thompson*)

This must show one of the most sophisticated uses of the horizontal brick under-sill panel. Note how the proportion of window height to wall height has been altered by cranking the floor slab upwards. This permits light to fall into the room at a more favourable angle and gives the windows a better proportion, without altering either the height of the sill relative to the floor or the height of the ceiling. Since the height of the windows and copper flashings is greater than the height of the brickwork, the design evades the 'streaky bacon' effect which occurs when the heights are nearly equal. (See English blocks of flats, circa 1930–35.)

WINDOWS 161

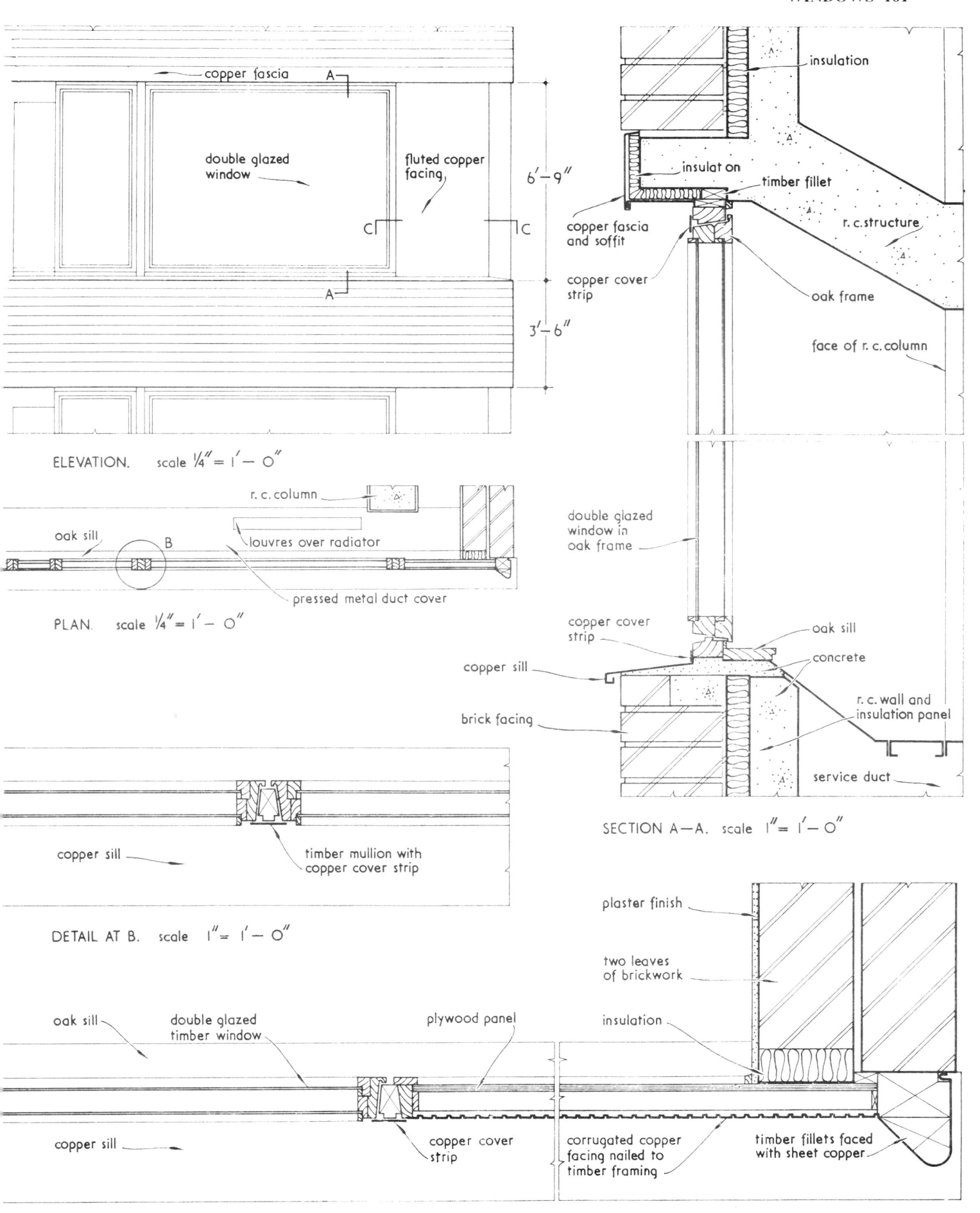

ELEVATION. scale ¼" = 1' − 0"

- copper fascia
- double glazed window
- fluted copper facing
- 6' − 9"
- 3' − 6"

PLAN. scale ¼" = 1' − 0"

- oak sill
- r.c. column
- louvres over radiator
- pressed metal duct cover

DETAIL AT B. scale 1" = 1' − 0"

- copper sill
- timber mullion with copper cover strip

PLAN AT C—C. scale 1" = 1' − 0"

- oak sill
- double glazed timber window
- plywood panel
- copper sill
- copper cover strip
- corrugated copper facing nailed to timber framing
- plaster finish
- two leaves of brickwork
- insulation
- timber fillets faced with sheet copper

SECTION A—A. scale 1" = 1' − 0"

- insulation
- insulation
- timber fillet
- copper fascia and soffit
- r.c. structure
- copper cover strip
- oak frame
- face of r.c. column
- double glazed window in oak frame
- copper cover strip
- oak sill
- copper sill
- concrete
- brick facing
- r.c. wall and insulation panel
- service duct

note: figured dimensions in feet and inches are approximate

162 WINDOWS

EXTERNAL WALL: OFFICES IN HELSINKI, FINLAND
DESIGNED BY ALVAR AALTO (*Material supplied by David I. C. Lea*)

An added neatness comes from using copper trim at sill and head, and the method of providing edge insulation while still supporting the brick panels on projecting nibs is of interest. The window in the drawing is a fixed one; but it can be dismantled for cleaning and, afterwards, it can be reassembled on the ground with its frame, and lifted again into position. Ventilation is obtained by opening the lower portion of the side-hung copper-clad panel (see section D-D); the top portion does not open.

WINDOWS 163

ELEVATION. scale ⅜"=1'-0"

SECTION.

SECTION AT A. scale ¼ full size
- oak bead
- pine head with oak facing
- all oak members of frame are made up from two sections

PLAN AT B-B. scale ¼ full size
- copper strip
- copper glazing bead
- pressed copper sheet

SECTION AT C. scale ¼ full size
- pine frame
- oak sill
- woodwool insulation

- cork insulation
- sheet copper facing
- sheet copper soffit
- copper strip
- pressed copper sheet
- softwood boarding
- 1¾" woodwool

- softwood packing
- brass screw
- softwood framing
- softwood boarding
- pine framing

- copper strip
- sheet copper sill

SECTION D-D. scale ¼ full size

note: figured dimensions in feet and inches are approximate

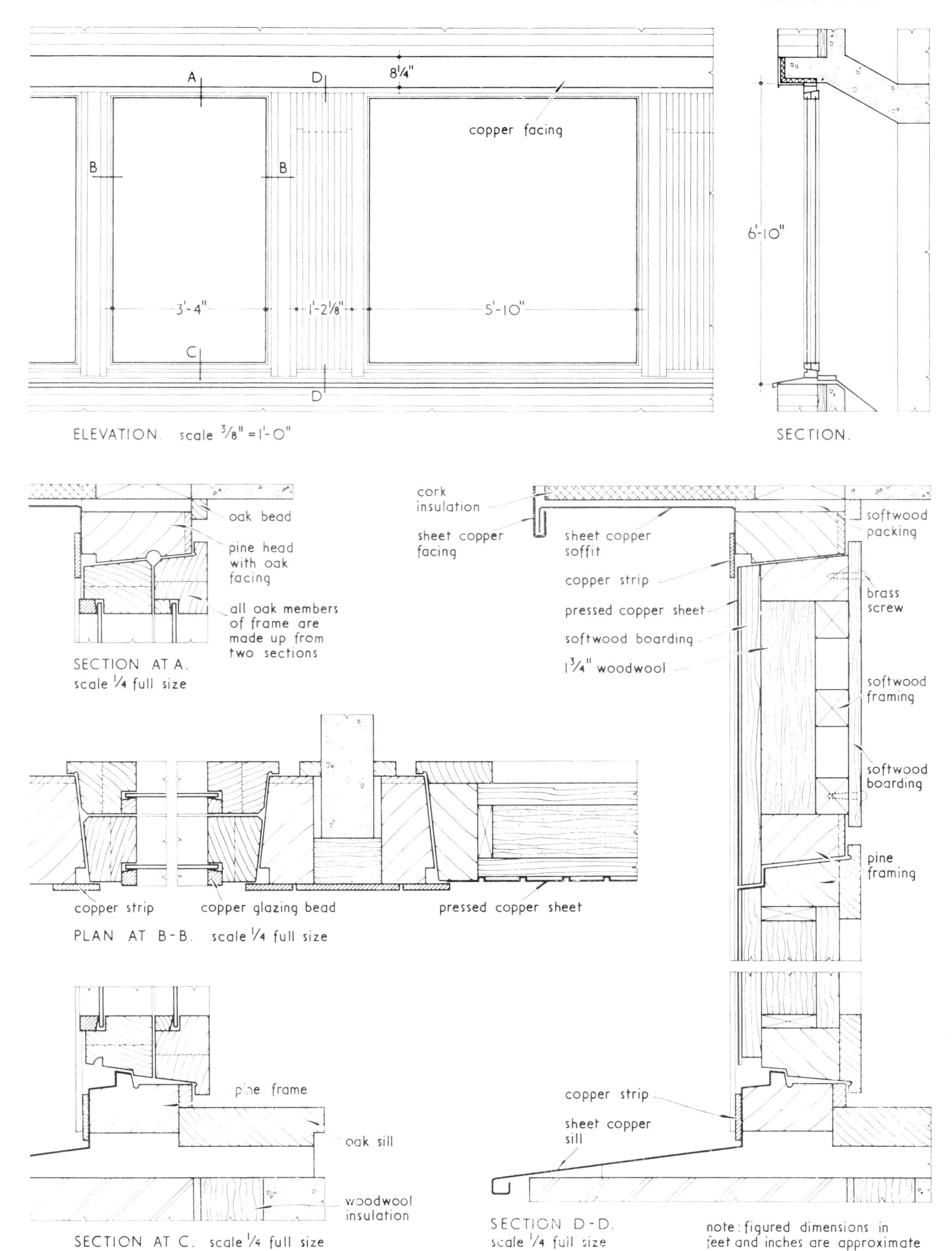

164 WINDOWS

GLAZED WALL: OFFICES IN ATHENS, GREECE
DESIGNED BY DOXIADES ASSOCIATES   *(Material supplied by Garbis Urégian)*

The need for speedy erection coupled with economy has produced a neat, simple solution free of all unnecessary embellishment. Particularly noticeable is the clean, functional simplicity of the timber sections.

WINDOWS 165

ELEVATION. scale ¼"= 1'-0"

PLAN. scale ⅛"= 1'-0"

PLAN AT A-A. scale ⅛ full size

- position of blind
- line of preformed aluminium sill
- line of concrete sill

PLAN AT B-B. scale ⅛ full size

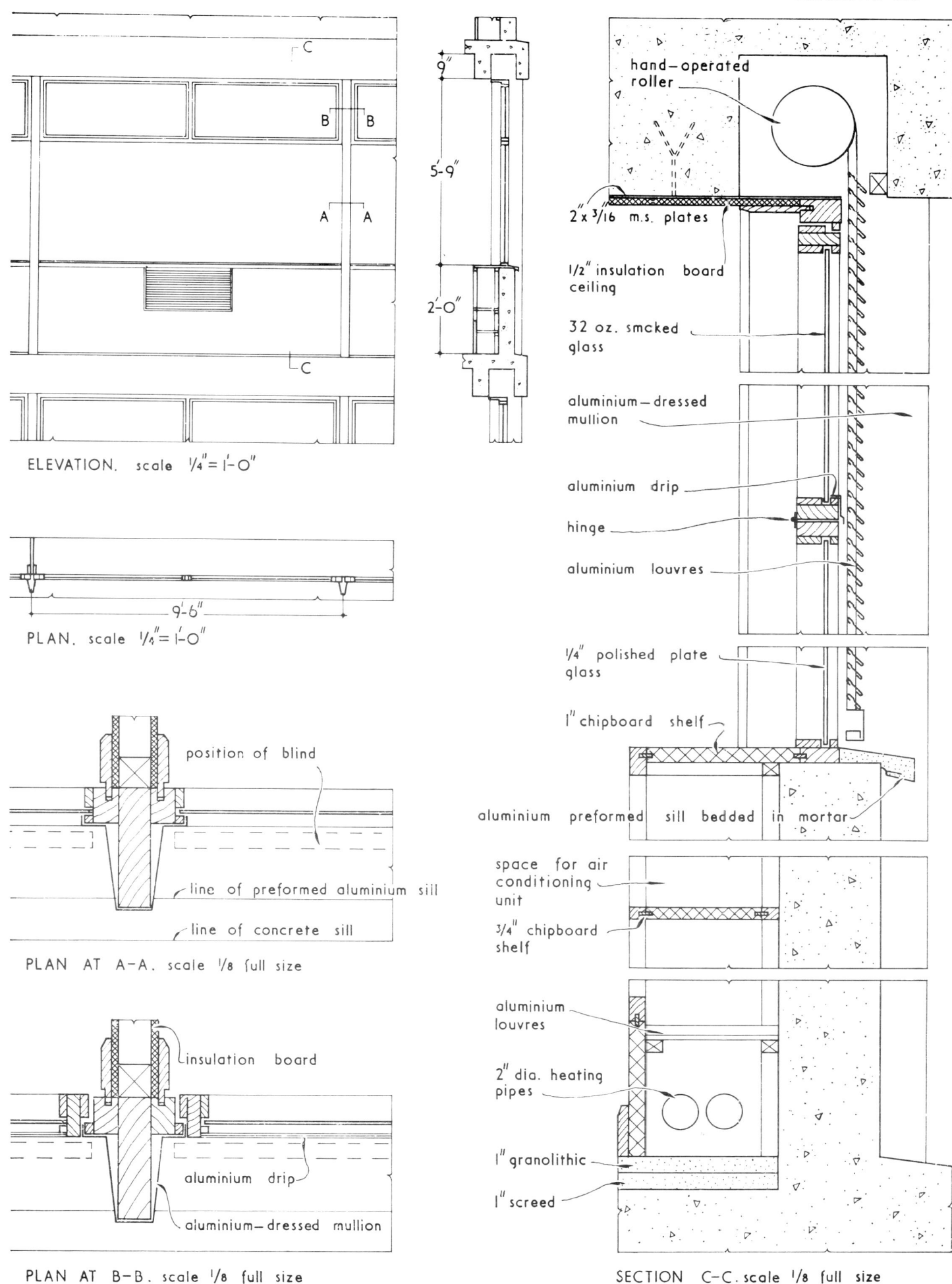

- insulation board
- aluminium drip
- aluminium-dressed mullion

SECTION C-C. scale ⅛ full size
note: figured dimensions in feet and inches are approximate

- hand-operated roller
- 2" x 3/16 m.s. plates
- ½" insulation board ceiling
- 32 oz. smoked glass
- aluminium-dressed mullion
- aluminium drip
- hinge
- aluminium louvres
- ¼" polished plate glass
- 1" chipboard shelf
- aluminium preformed sill bedded in mortar
- space for air conditioning unit
- ¾" chipboard shelf
- aluminium louvres
- 2" dia. heating pipes
- 1" granolithic
- 1" screed

WINDOW AND DOOR, AUDIOMETRY ROOM : HOSPITAL IN LONDON, W.C.1
DESIGNED BY EASTON AND ROBERTSON

The window and door to the audiometry room are both of double construction. Each door panel consists of two skins of acoustic board with slag wool between, veneered on the outer side of the door with teak.

WINDOWS 167

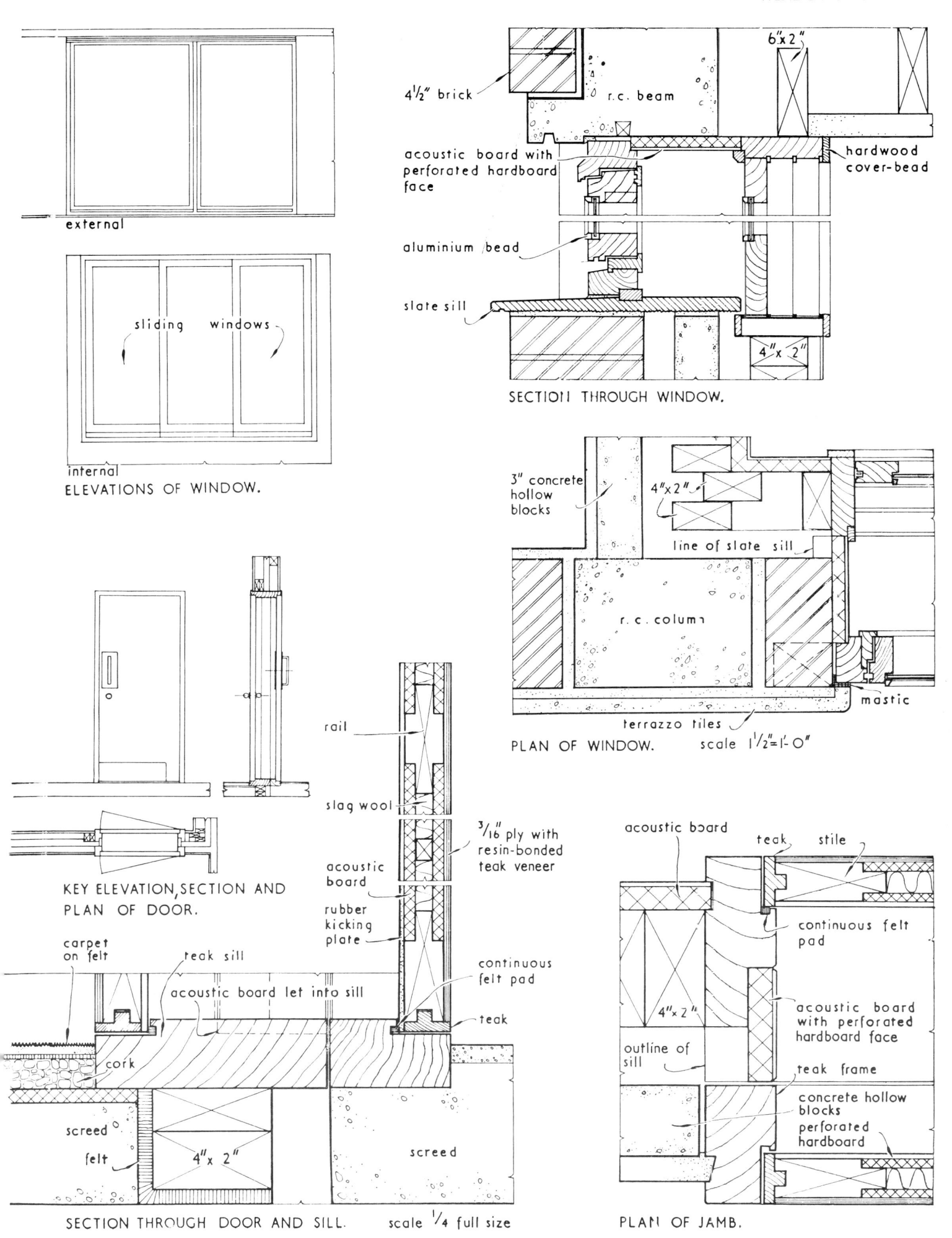

ELEVATIONS OF WINDOW.
- external
- internal / sliding windows

SECTION THROUGH WINDOW.
- 4½" brick
- r.c. beam
- 6" x 2"
- acoustic board with perforated hardboard face
- hardwood cover-bead
- aluminium bead
- slate sill
- 4" x 2"

PLAN OF WINDOW. scale 1½" = 1'-0"
- 3" concrete hollow blocks
- 4" x 2"
- line of slate sill
- r.c. column
- mastic
- terrazzo tiles

KEY ELEVATION, SECTION AND PLAN OF DOOR.

SECTION THROUGH DOOR AND SILL. scale ¼ full size
- rail
- slag wool
- 3/16" ply with resin-bonded teak veneer
- acoustic board
- rubber kicking plate
- continuous felt pad
- teak
- carpet on felt
- teak sill
- acoustic board let into sill
- cork
- screed
- felt
- 4" x 2"
- screed

PLAN OF JAMB.
- acoustic board
- teak
- stile
- continuous felt pad
- 4" x 2"
- outline of sill
- acoustic board with perforated hardboard face
- teak frame
- concrete hollow blocks
- perforated hardboard

168 WINDOWS

ACOUSTIC WINDOW: CONCERT HALL IN COPENHAGEN, DENMARK
DESIGNED BY FRITS SCHLEGEL AND HANS HANSEN *(Material supplied by D. J. Leadbetter)*

As inferred from the pin-tables outside, this window had to be well sound-proofed. This was done by double-glazing the outside window and by providing sound-absorbent surfaces between the outer and inner window frames. Every other internal light is openable for access to curtains and for cleaning.

WINDOWS 169

ELEVATION. scale 3/8" = 1'-0"

PLAN. scale 3/8" = 1'-0"

- continuous head veneered with lemonwood
- recess for curtain rail
- ex. 2"x2" lemonwood sashes
- 3/8" polished plate glass in p.v.c. strip
- double glazing
- 6'-10"
- 6 3/4"
- acoustic board in perforated metal cladding
- m.s. angle frame
- 1/4" lino. finish
- floor line

SECTION A A. scale 1/4 full size

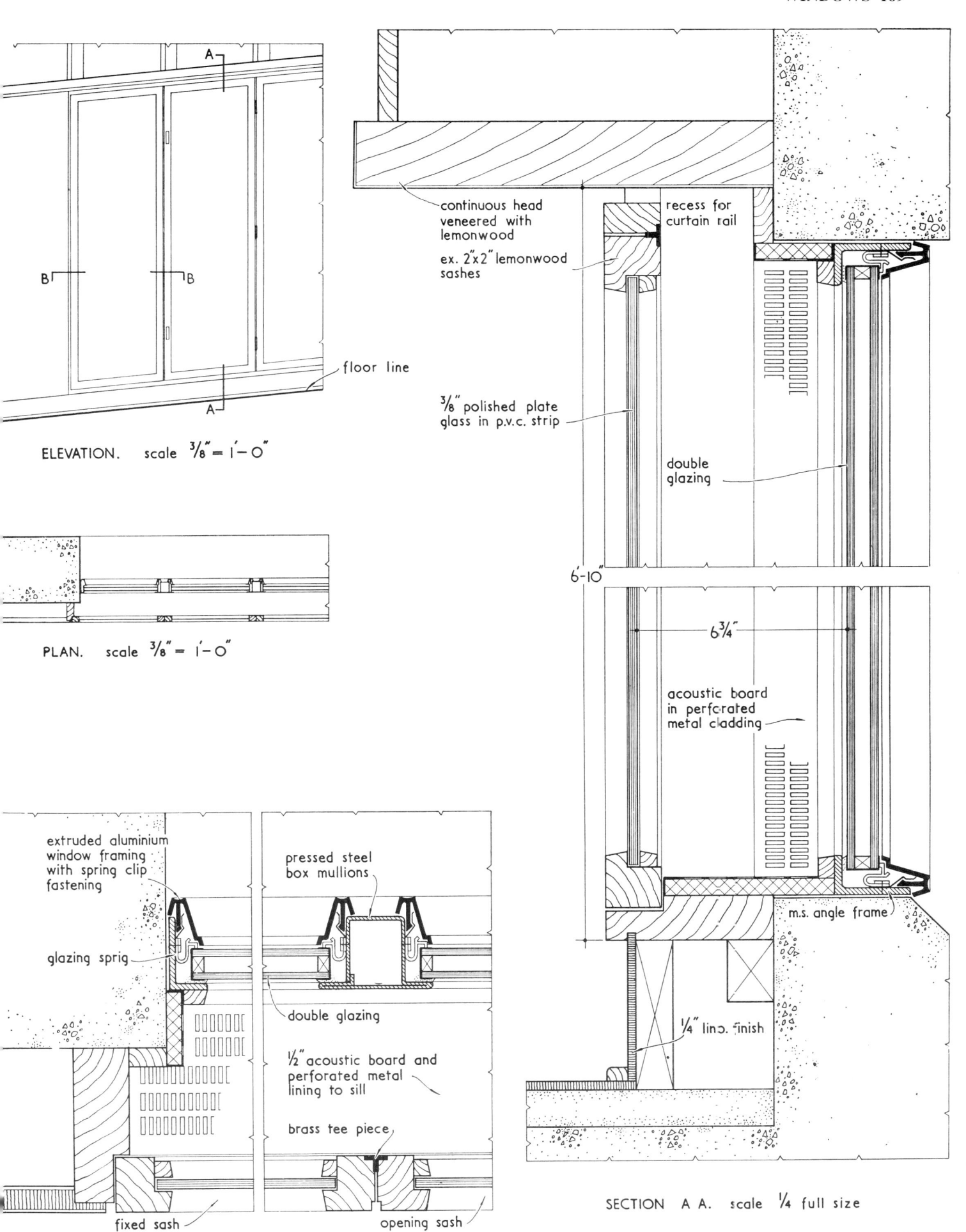

PLAN AT B-B. scale 1/4 full size

- extruded aluminium window framing with spring clip fastening
- pressed steel box mullions
- glazing sprig
- double glazing
- 1/2" acoustic board and perforated metal lining to sill
- brass tee piece
- fixed sash
- opening sash

note: figured dimensions in feet and inches are approximate

170 DOORS

GLAZED ENTRANCE DOORS AND SCREEN: SOCIETY HEADQUARTERS, LONDON, N.W.1
DESIGNED BY JOHN AND ELIZABETH EASTWICK-FIELD IN COLLABORATION WITH HUGH PITE

The entrance doors are framed in bronze and the screen is painted steel, with all glazing beads in hardwood.

DOORS 171

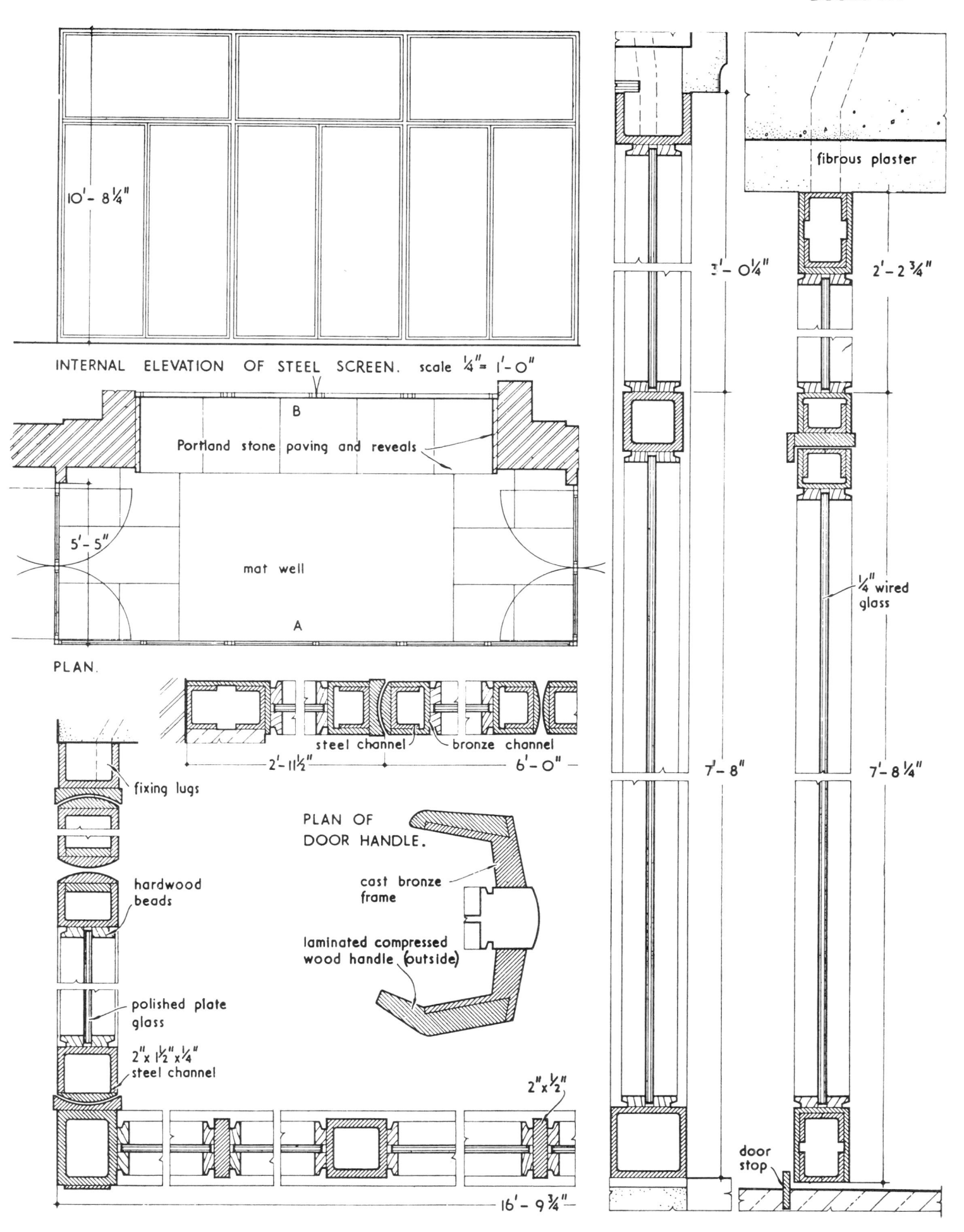

ENTRANCE DOORS: OFFICES AT BRISTOL
DESIGNED BY LEONARD MANASSEH AND PARTNERS

The framing (standard metal, painted black) and the pivots holding each door-head are screwed to blocking pieces which are scribed into and screwed to a 7 in. by 3½ in. m.s. channel of the main structure. The angle trim on the jambs are of satin-finish aluminium; the top and bottom plates of the door are satin chrome on brass. The fixing of the steel name plates required special drillings in the glass.

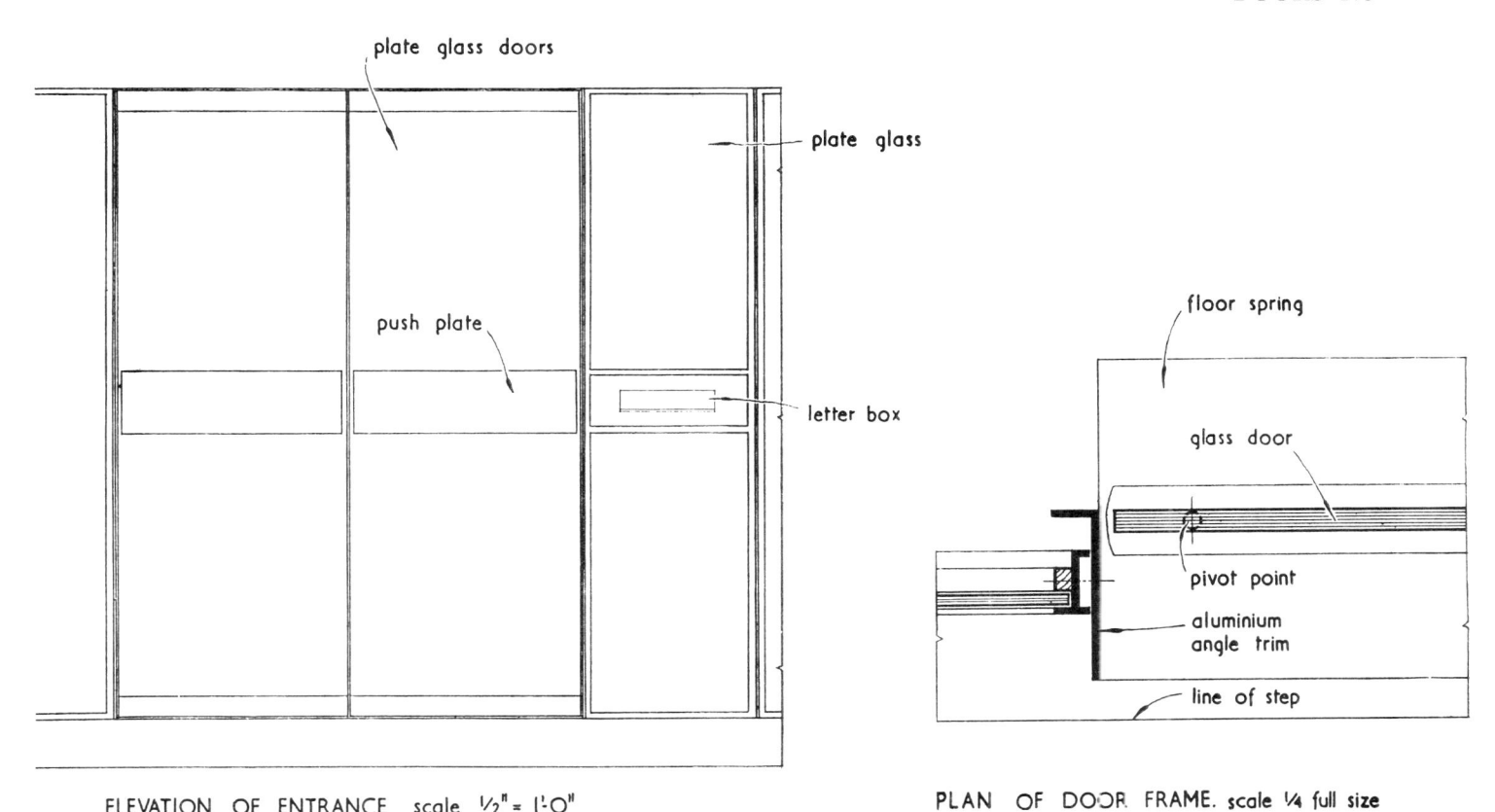

DOORS 173

ELEVATION OF ENTRANCE scale ½" = 1'-0"

- plate glass doors
- push plate
- plate glass
- letter box

PLAN OF DOOR FRAME. scale ¼ full size

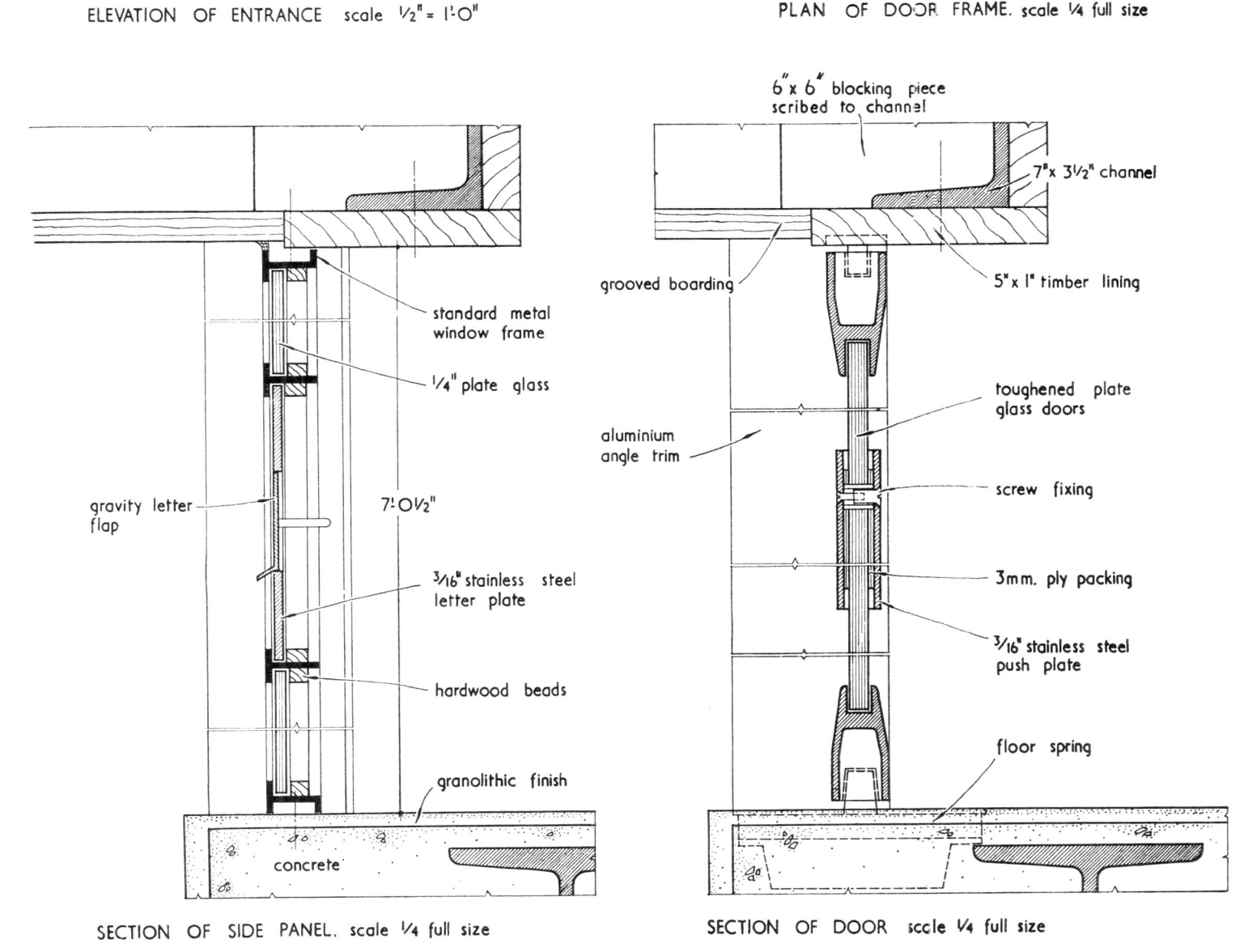

- floor spring
- glass door
- pivot point
- aluminium angle trim
- line of step

SECTION OF SIDE PANEL. scale ¼ full size

- standard metal window frame
- ¼" plate glass
- gravity letter flap
- 7'-0½"
- 3/16" stainless steel letter plate
- hardwood beads
- granolithic finish
- concrete

SECTION OF DOOR scale ¼ full size

- 6" x 6" blocking piece scribed to channel
- 7" x 3½" channel
- grooved boarding
- 5" x 1" timber lining
- aluminium angle trim
- toughened plate glass doors
- screw fixing
- 3mm. ply packing
- 3/16" stainless steel push plate
- floor spring

174 DOORS

ENTRANCE DOOR: HOSPITAL IN LONDON N.W.3
DESIGNED BY JOHN LACEY

This external door is fixed in an existing door opening. The name-plate is stove-enamelled mild steel. The cipher in the fanlight is etched on ¼-in. plate glass.

DOORS 175

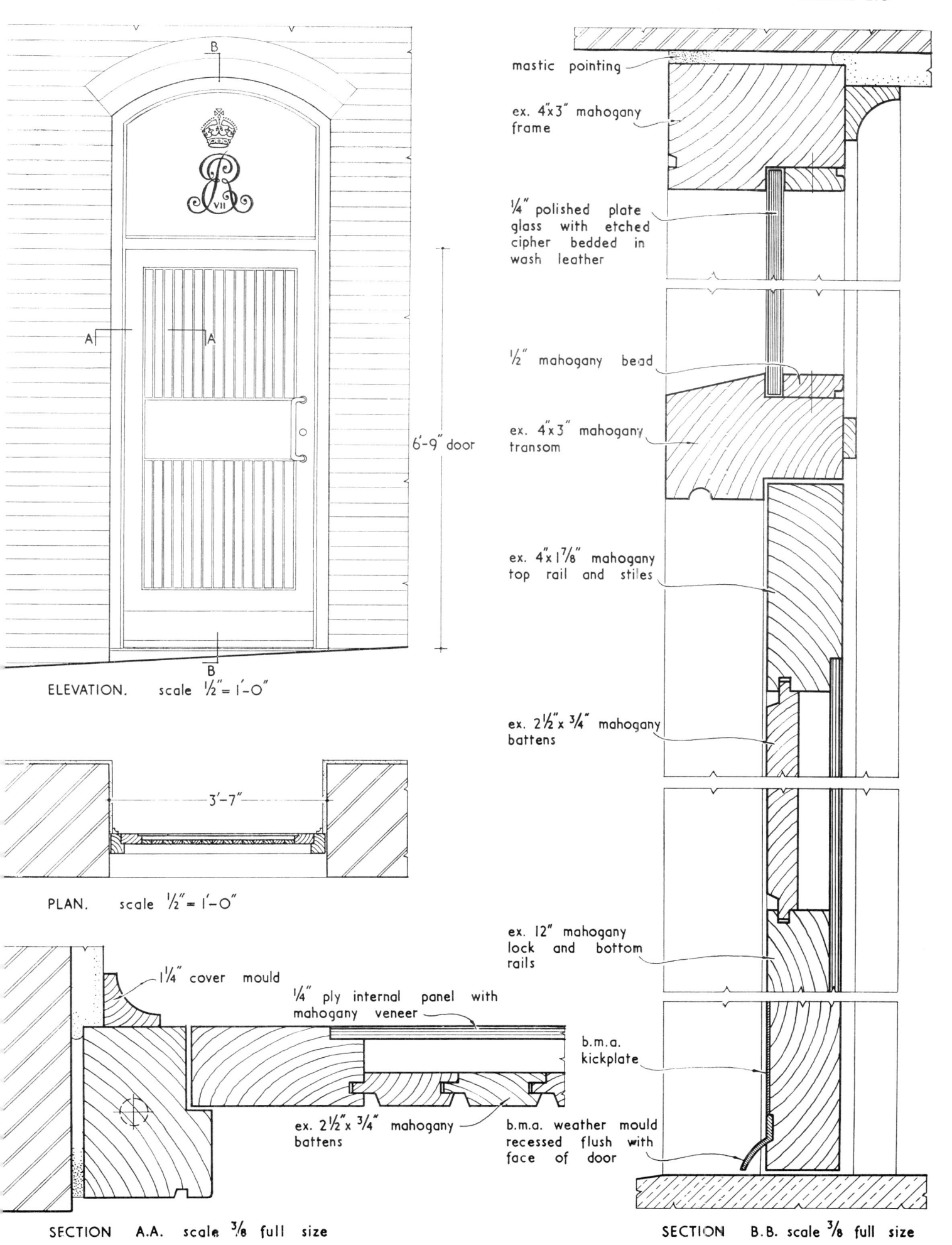

ELEVATION. scale ½" = 1'-0"

PLAN. scale ½" = 1'-0"

SECTION A.A. scale ⅜ full size

- 1¼" cover mould
- ¼" ply internal panel with mahogany veneer
- ex. 2½" x ¾" mahogany battens

6'-9" door

3'-7"

SECTION B.B. scale ⅜ full size

- mastic pointing
- ex. 4" x 3" mahogany frame
- ¼" polished plate glass with etched cipher bedded in wash leather
- ½" mahogany bead
- ex. 4" x 3" mahogany transom
- ex. 4" x 1⅞" mahogany top rail and stiles
- ex. 2½" x ¾" mahogany battens
- ex. 12" mahogany lock and bottom rails
- b.m.a. kickplate
- b.m.a. weather mould recessed flush with face of door

MAGISTRATES' ENTRANCE DOOR: MAGISTRATES' COURT AT SLOUGH, BUCKS
DESIGNED BY F. B. POOLEY (architect to the Buckinghamshire County Council)

An 'informal' door designed to read as a single unit with an adjacent solid panel. This has been realized by the use of teak slats. These have been fixed flush with the outside face and the side stiles have been rebated to simulate slats. To reinforce the effect of the pattern the rebates between slats have been stained matt black.

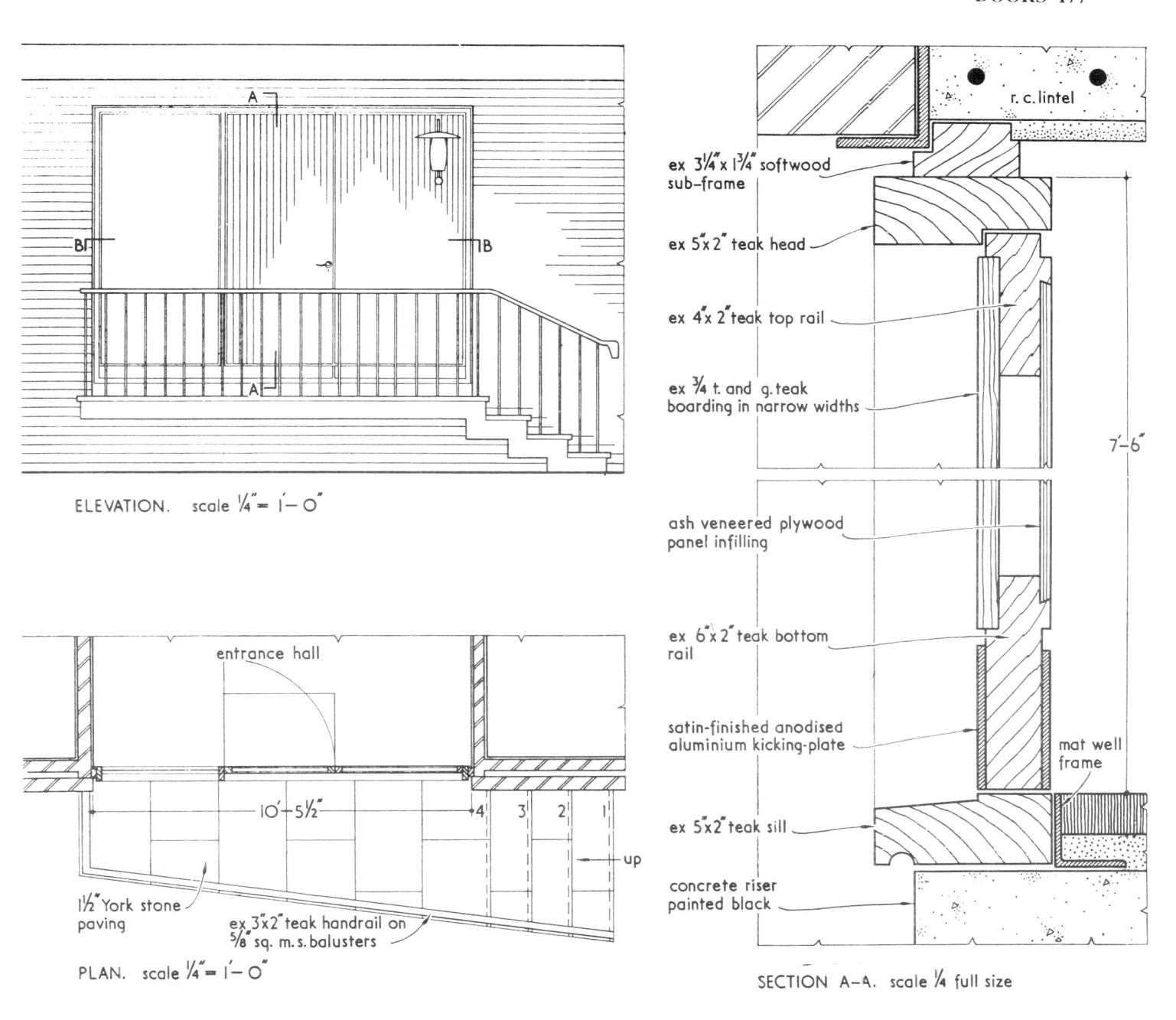

DOORS 177

ELEVATION. scale ¼" = 1'-0"

1½" York stone paving

entrance hall

10'-5½"

ex 3"x 2" teak handrail on ⅝" sq. m.s. balusters

PLAN. scale ¼" = 1'-0"

r.c. lintel

ex 3¼"x 1¾" softwood sub-frame

ex 5"x 2" teak head

ex 4"x 2" teak top rail

ex ¾" t. and g. teak boarding in narrow widths

ash veneered plywood panel infilling

ex 6"x 2" teak bottom rail

satin-finished anodised aluminium kicking-plate

ex 5"x 2" teak sill

mat well frame

concrete riser painted black

7'-6"

SECTION A–A. scale ¼ full size

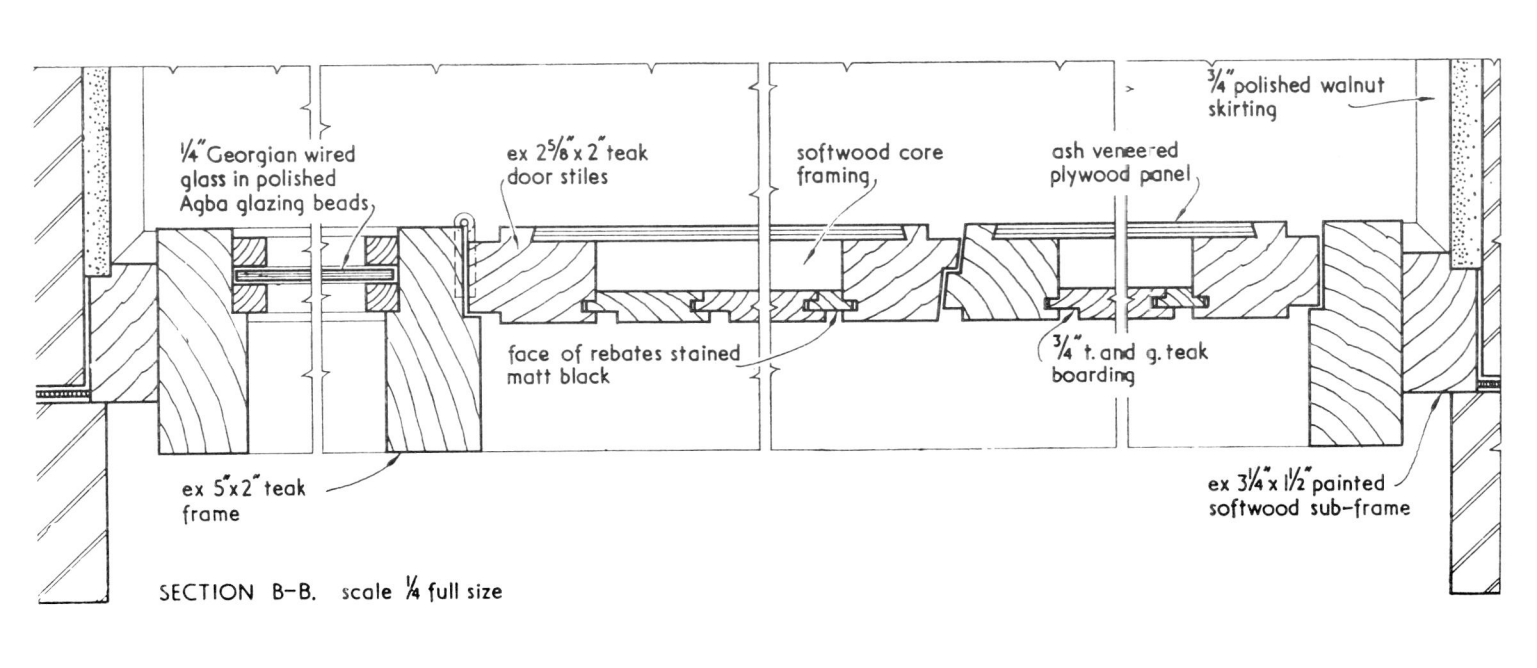

¼" Georgian wired glass in polished Agba glazing beads

ex 2⅝"x 2" teak door stiles

softwood core framing

ash veneered plywood panel

¾" polished walnut skirting

ex 5"x 2" teak frame

face of rebates stained matt black

¾" t. and g. teak boarding

ex 3¼"x 1½" painted softwood sub-frame

SECTION B–B. scale ¼ full size

178 DOORS

WROUGHT IRON GATE: COLLEGE AT OXFORD
DESIGNED BY ARCHITECTS' CO-PARTNERSHIP

This adaptation of traditional wrought ironwork has a number of points of detail which deserve study. Note the 'journal' hanging used in conjunction with a self-closing socket at the base; the avoidance of visible fixing to the brass plate; and, of course, the careful alignment of nameplate, middle rail and striking plate.

DOORS 179

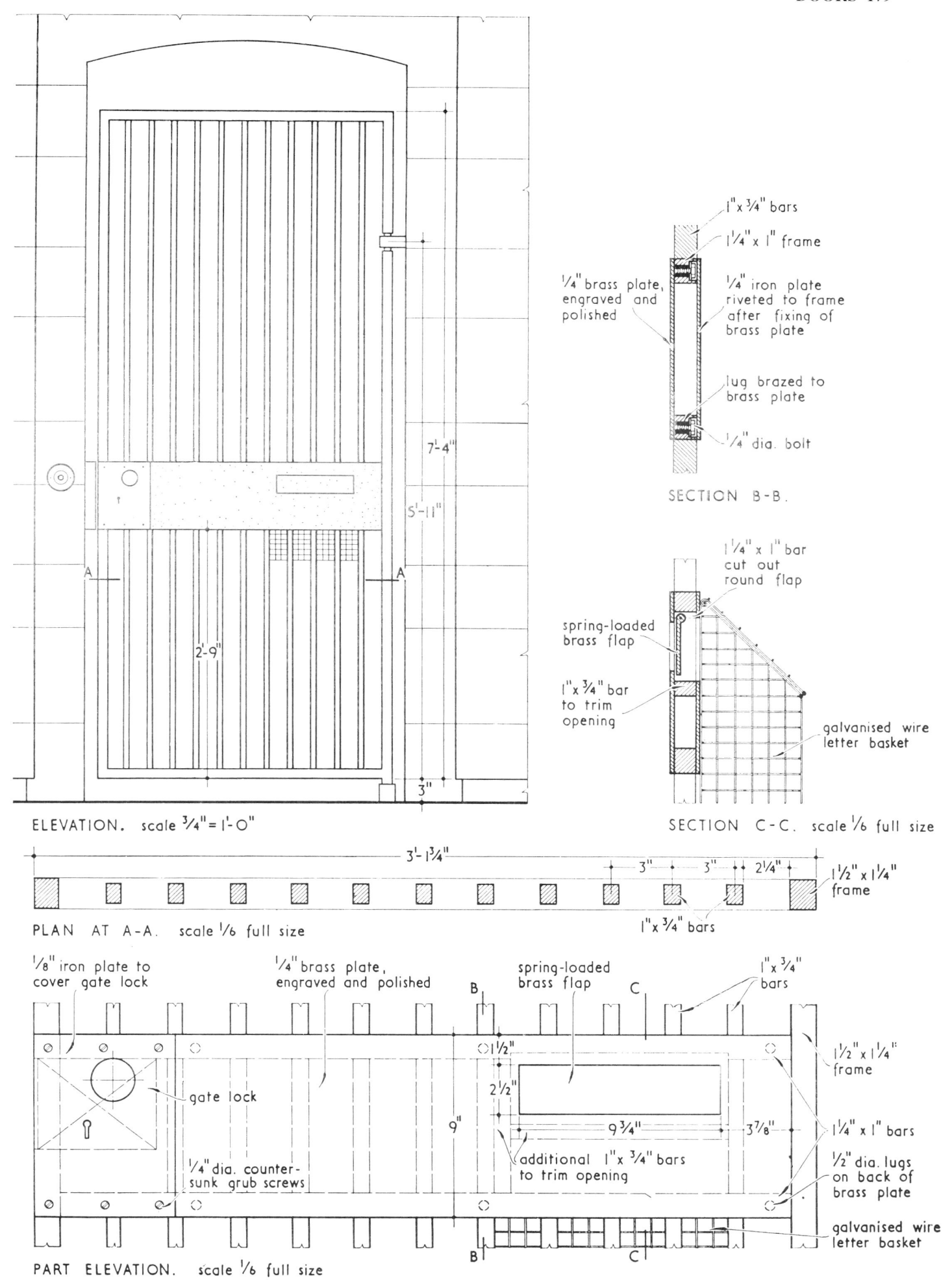

ENTRANCE DOOR TO FLAT: COLLEGE AT OXFORD
DESIGNED BY ARCHITECTS' CO-PARTNERSHIP

The problem of accommodating the dustbin has been neatly solved in this caretaker's flat. A small compartment inside the door is ventilated by a louvred panel, backed with a perforated zinc screen to exclude insects.

DOORS 181

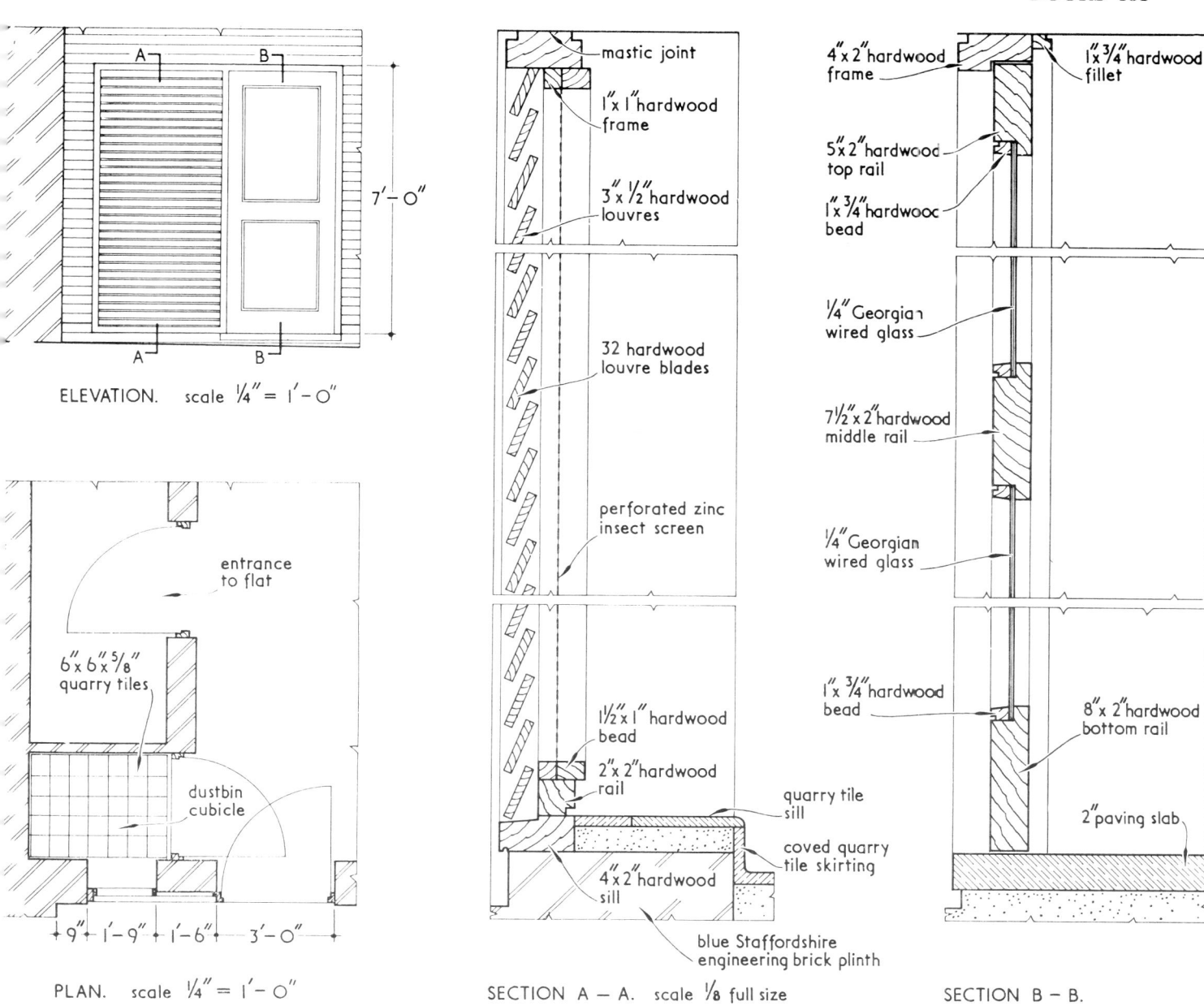

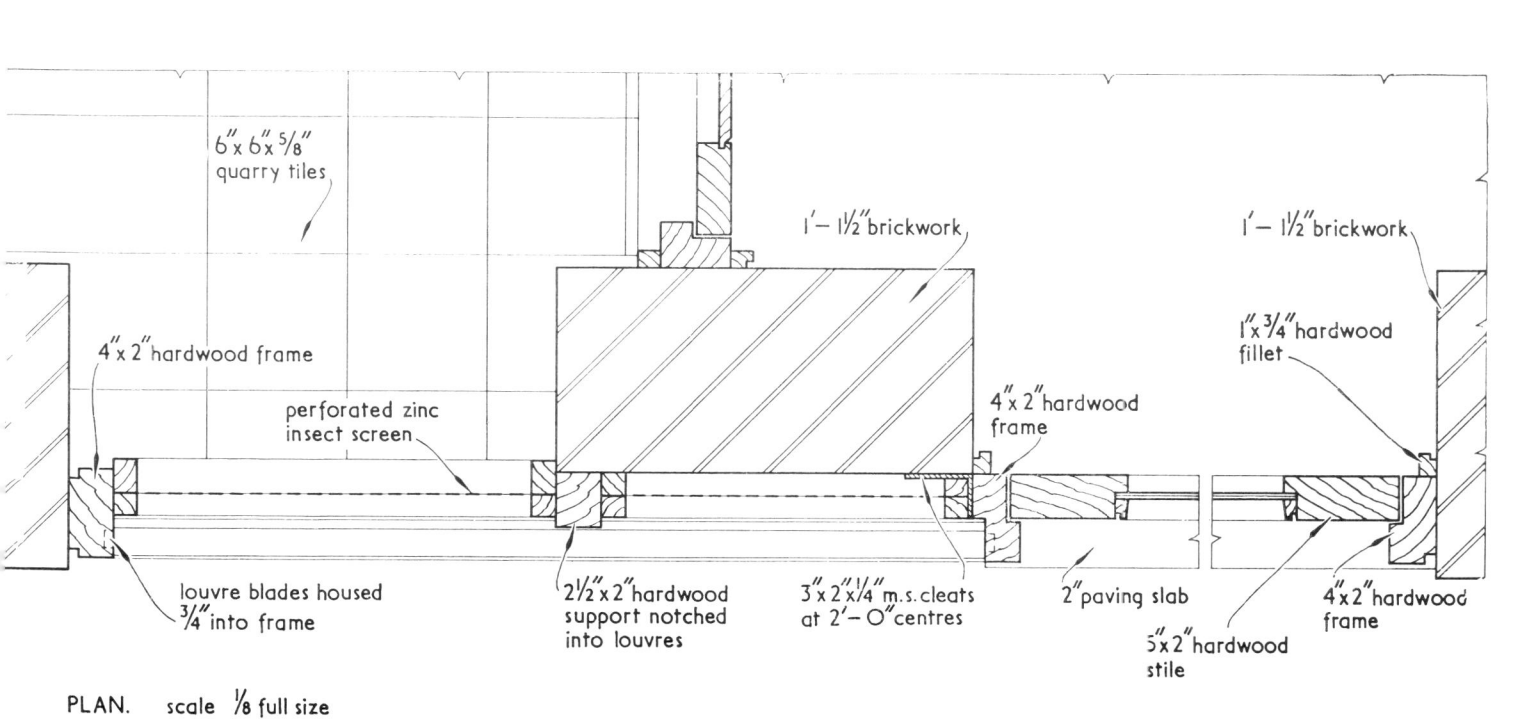

182 DOORS

DOOR AND SCREEN: COLLEGE AT OXFORD
DESIGNED BY ARCHITECTS' CO-PARTNERSHIP

A utilitarian detail, but thought out with great care. Note the construction of the concealed lintel, the aligning of the slats on the door with those above and the use of a short length of m.s. tube at the foot of the door jamb.

DOORS 183

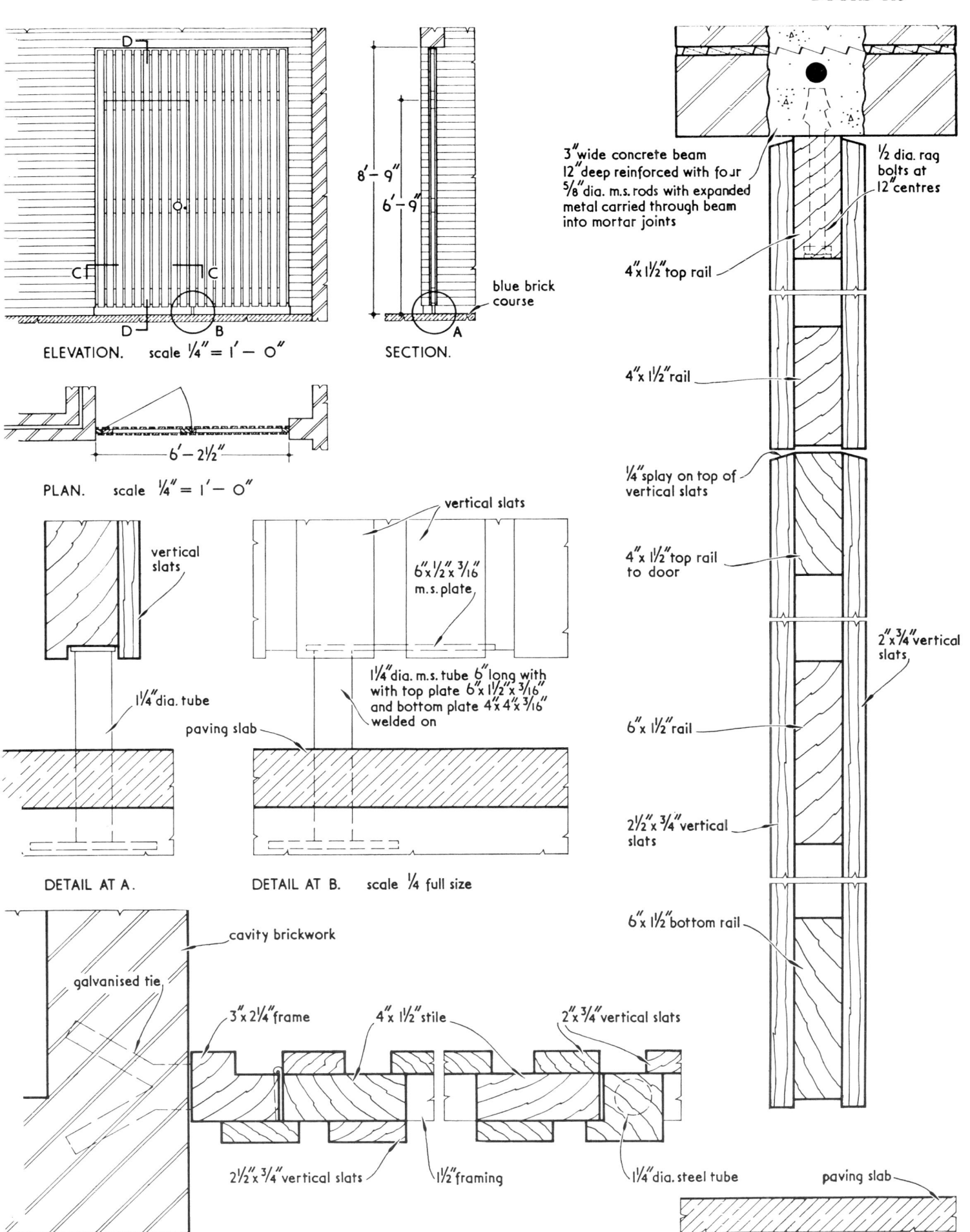

ELEVATION. scale ¼" = 1' – 0"

SECTION.

8' – 9"
6' – 9"

blue brick course

PLAN. scale ¼" = 1' – 0"

6' – 2½"

DETAIL AT A.

vertical slats

1¼" dia. tube

DETAIL AT B. scale ¼ full size

vertical slats

6" × ½" × 3/16" m.s. plate

1¼" dia. m.s. tube 6" long with top plate 6" × 1½" × 3/16" and bottom plate 4" × 4" × 3/16" welded on

paving slab

PLAN AT C – C. scale ¼ full size

cavity brickwork
galvanised tie
3" × 2¼" frame
4" × 1½" stile
2" × ¾" vertical slats
2½" × ¾" vertical slats
1½" framing
1¼" dia. steel tube

SECTION D – D. scale ¼ full size

3" wide concrete beam 12" deep reinforced with four 5/8" dia. m.s. rods with expanded metal carried through beam into mortar joints

½" dia. rag bolts at 12" centres

4" × 1½" top rail

4" × 1½" rail

¼" splay on top of vertical slats

4" × 1½" top rail to door

2" × ¾" vertical slats

6" × 1½" rail

2½" × ¾" vertical slats

6" × 1½" bottom rail

paving slab

184 DOORS

MAIN ENTRANCE DOORS: LAW COURTS, KING SAUL BOULEVARD, TEL-AVIV, ISRAEL
DESIGNED BY RECHTER AND ZARCHI *(Material supplied by Stephen Emanuel)*

These doors are a notable example of the reversal of values in entrance areas: the doors themselves appearing heavy and (when shut) impenetrable, though the screen wall in which they are set is transparent.

DOORS 185

ELEVATION

SECTION

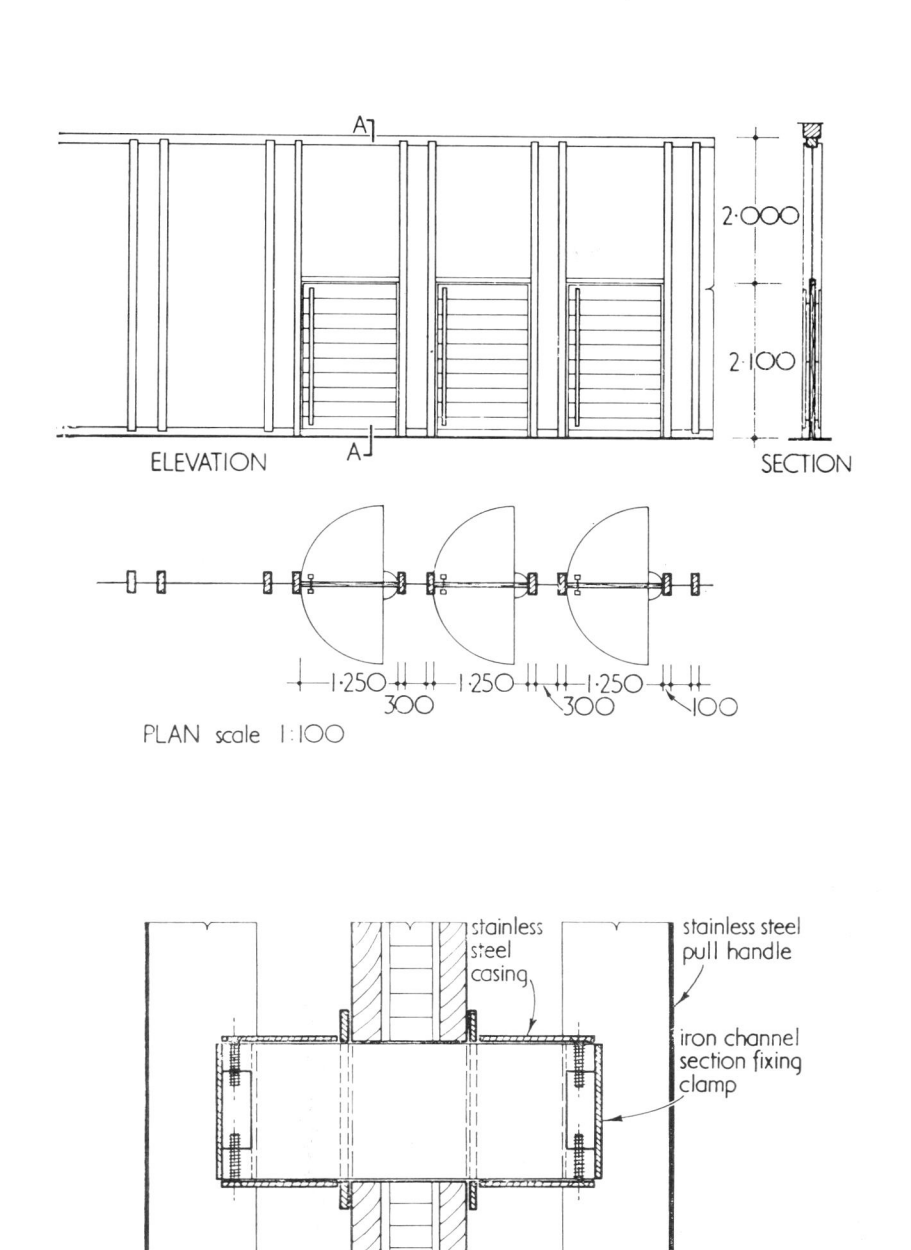

PLAN scale 1:100

1·250 300 1·250 300 1·250 100

2·000
2·100

SECTION B-B scale 1:4

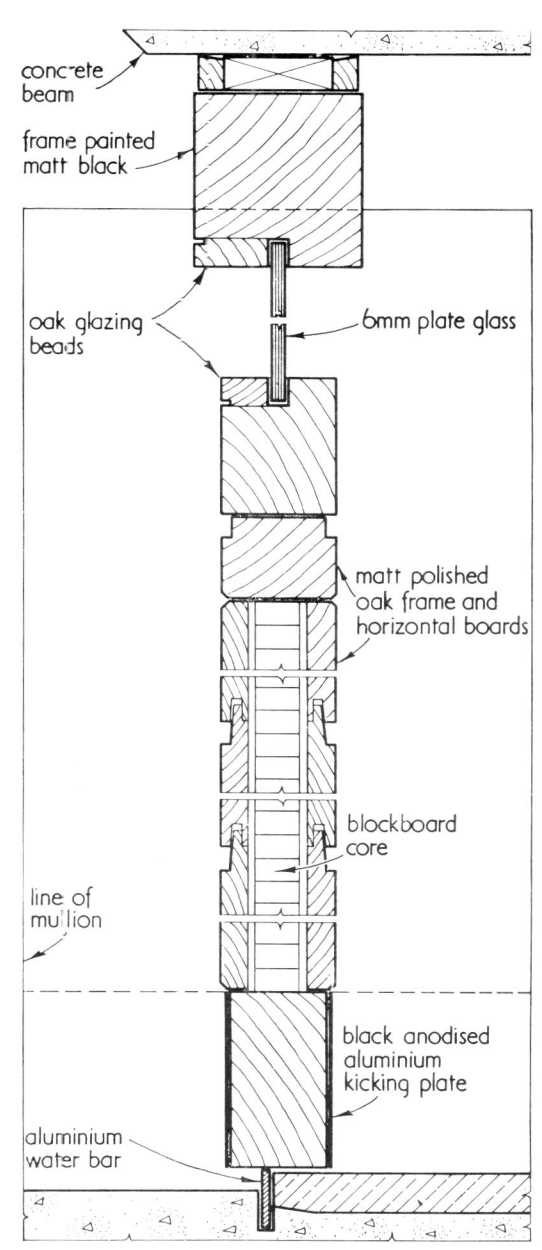

- stainless steel casing
- stainless steel pull handle
- iron channel section fixing clamp

SECTION A-A scale 1:4

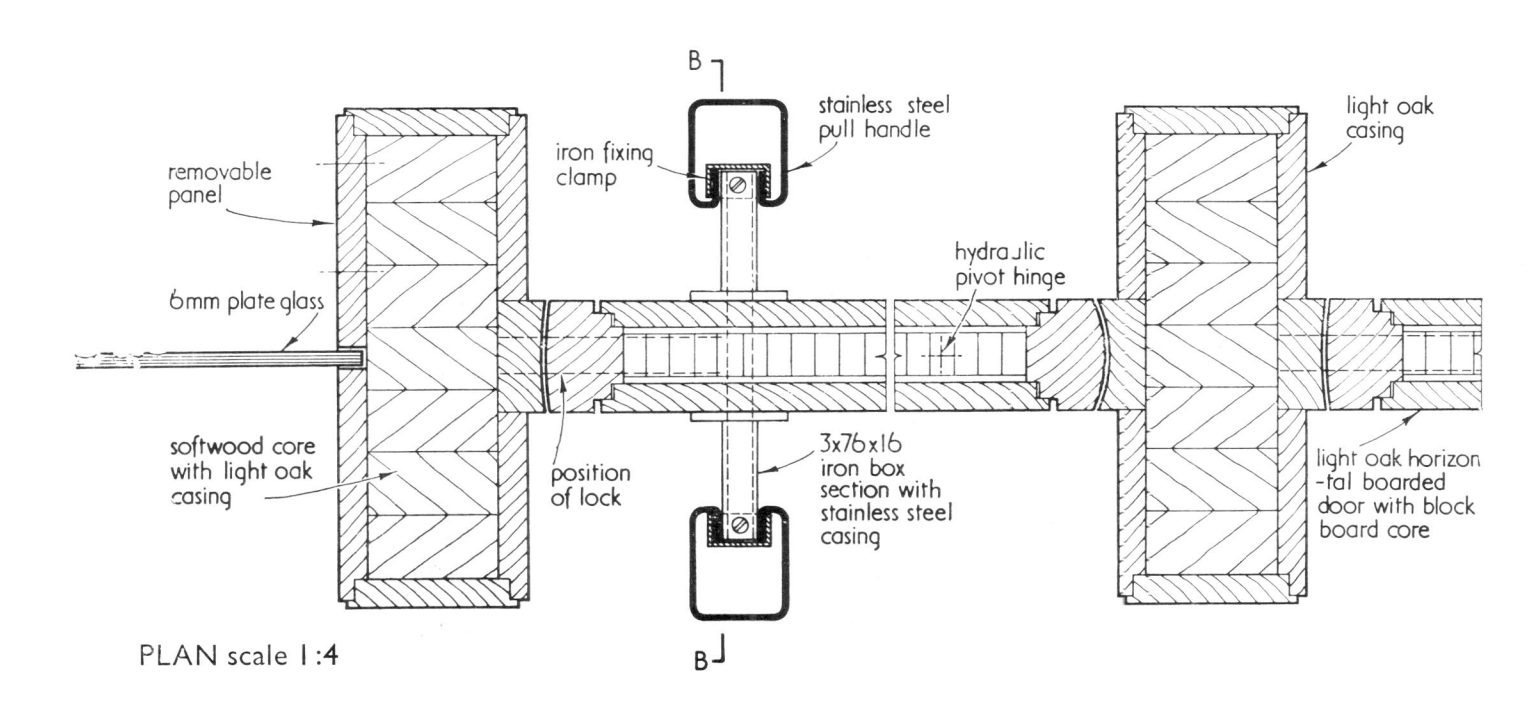

- concrete beam
- frame painted matt black
- oak glazing beads
- 6mm plate glass
- matt polished oak frame and horizontal boards
- line of mullion
- blockboard core
- black anodised aluminium kicking plate
- aluminium water bar

PLAN scale 1:4

- removable panel
- 6mm plate glass
- softwood core with light oak casing
- position of lock
- iron fixing clamp
- stainless steel pull handle
- 3×76×16 iron box section with stainless steel casing
- hydraulic pivot hinge
- light oak casing
- light oak horizontal boarded door with block board core

186 DOORS

EXTERNAL DOORS: SCHOOL AT HYVINKÄÄ, FINLAND
DESIGNED BY MARJO AND KEIJO PETAJA   *(Material supplied by David I. C. Lea)*

This pair of doors, of which the narrower leaf is required to be opened only occasionally, is a robust example of detailing: the teak boarding and the copper kicking plate are face-screwed to the framing.

DOORS 187

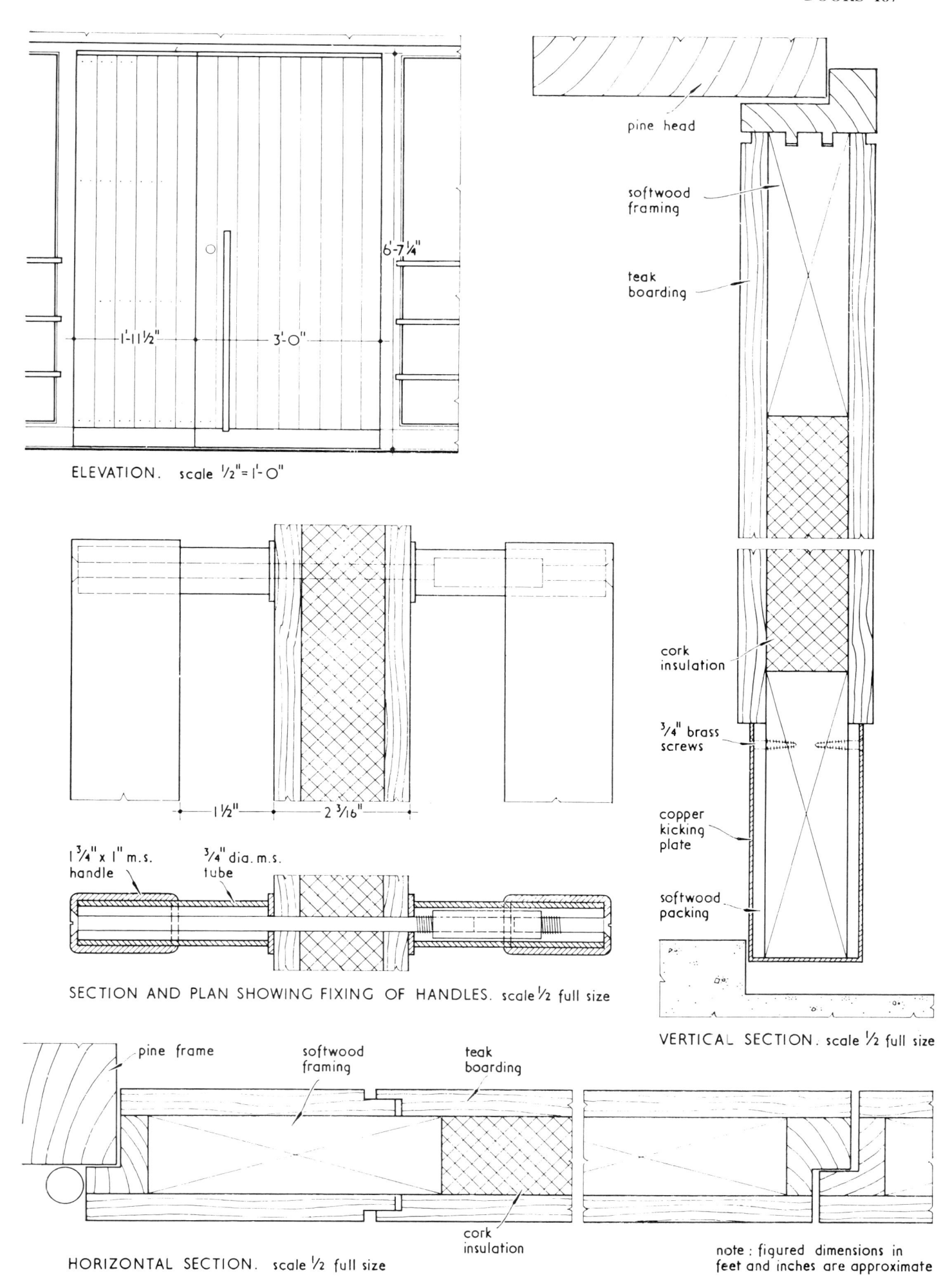

ELEVATION. scale ½"=1'-0"

1'-11½" 3'-0" 6'-7¼"

SECTION AND PLAN SHOWING FIXING OF HANDLES. scale ½ full size

1½" 2 3/16"

1¾" x 1" m.s. handle
¾" dia. m.s. tube

HORIZONTAL SECTION. scale ½ full size

pine frame
softwood framing
teak boarding
cork insulation

VERTICAL SECTION. scale ½ full size

pine head
softwood framing
teak boarding
cork insulation
¾" brass screws
copper kicking plate
softwood packing

note: figured dimensions in feet and inches are approximate

188 DOORS

SECURITY DOORS: SUMMER HOUSE AT TISVILDE, DENMARK
DESIGNED BY VILHELM WOHLERT   (*Material supplied by Keith Mallory*)

When the summer house is in use the top hung security doors are fixed by bolts to the projecting rail. In this position the white painted inside surface of these and of the side hung doors give the effect of a deep reveal.

DOORS

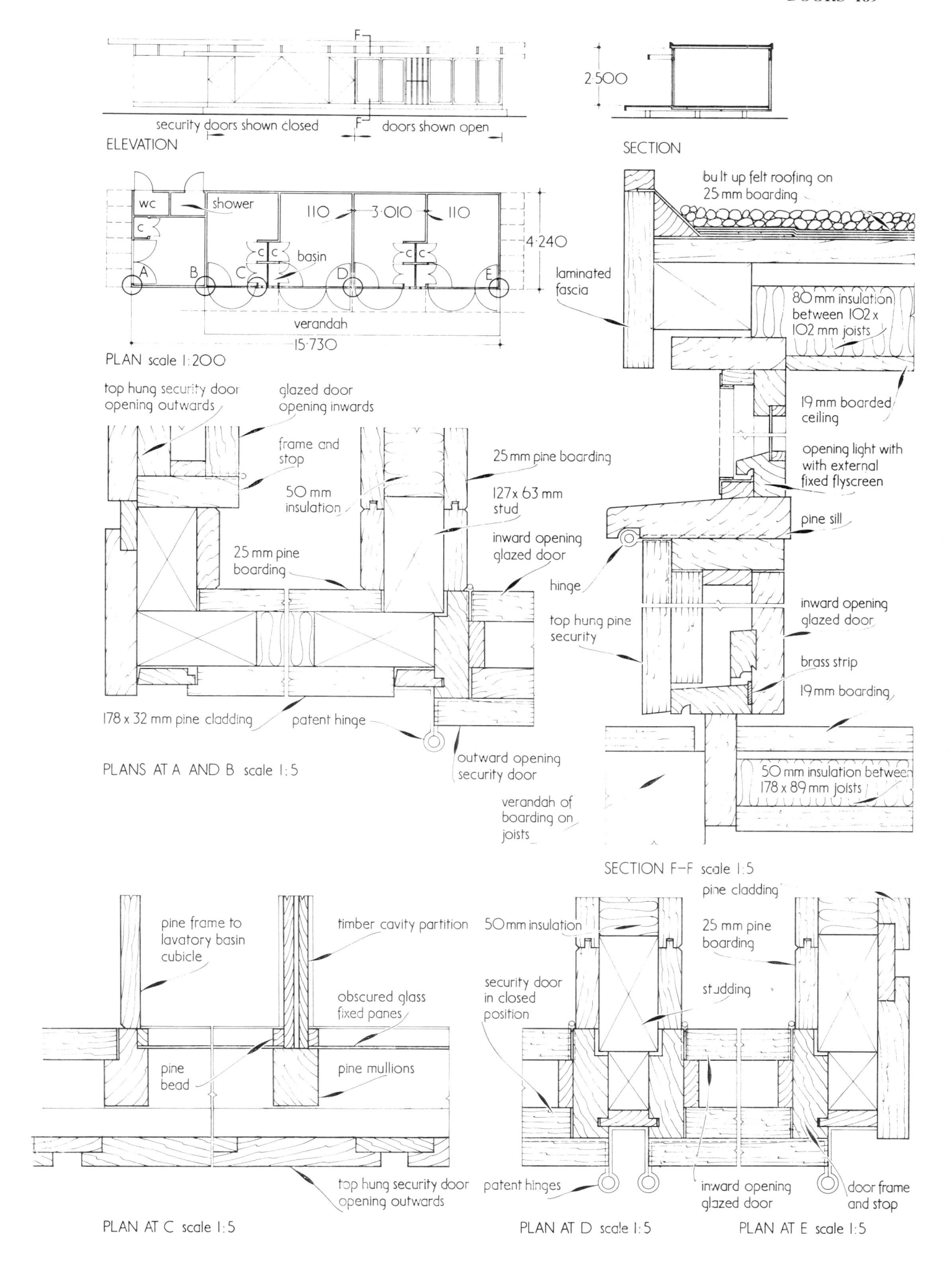

ELEVATION
- security doors shown closed
- doors shown open

SECTION — 2.500

PLAN scale 1:200
- wc
- shower
- c
- 110
- 3.010
- 110
- basin
- c c
- c c
- A, B, C, D, E
- verandah
- 15.730
- 4.240

PLANS AT A AND B scale 1:5
- top hung security door opening outwards
- glazed door opening inwards
- frame and stop
- 50 mm insulation
- 25 mm pine boarding
- 127 × 63 mm stud
- inward opening glazed door
- hinge
- top hung pine security
- 25 mm pine boarding
- 178 × 32 mm pine cladding
- patent hinge
- outward opening security door
- verandah of boarding on joists

SECTION F–F scale 1:5
- built up felt roofing on 25 mm boarding
- laminated fascia
- 80 mm insulation between 102 × 102 mm joists
- 19 mm boarded ceiling
- opening light with external fixed flyscreen
- pine sill
- inward opening glazed door
- brass strip
- 19 mm boarding
- 50 mm insulation between 178 × 89 mm joists

PLAN AT C scale 1:5
- pine frame to lavatory basin cubicle
- timber cavity partition
- obscured glass fixed panes
- pine bead
- pine mullions
- top hung security door opening outwards

PLAN AT D scale 1:5
- 50 mm insulation
- security door in closed position
- patent hinges
- inward opening glazed door

PLAN AT E scale 1:5
- pine cladding
- 25 mm pine boarding
- studding
- door frame and stop

190 DOORS

REVOLVING DOOR: GREEN CENTRE FOR EARTH SCIENCES, MASSACHUSETTS INSTITUTE OF TECHNOLOGY, CAMBRIDGE, MASS., USA
DESIGNED BY I. M. PEI AND PARTNERS   *(Material supplied by Alan Mossman)*

This revolving door and its lobby were added to an existing building to cut out the draughts coming from a windy covered way. The shaping of the sheet steel enclosure to give deep jambs on the outside makes the wind lobby compare in bulk with the surrounding structure.

DOORS 191

ELEVATION

SECTION

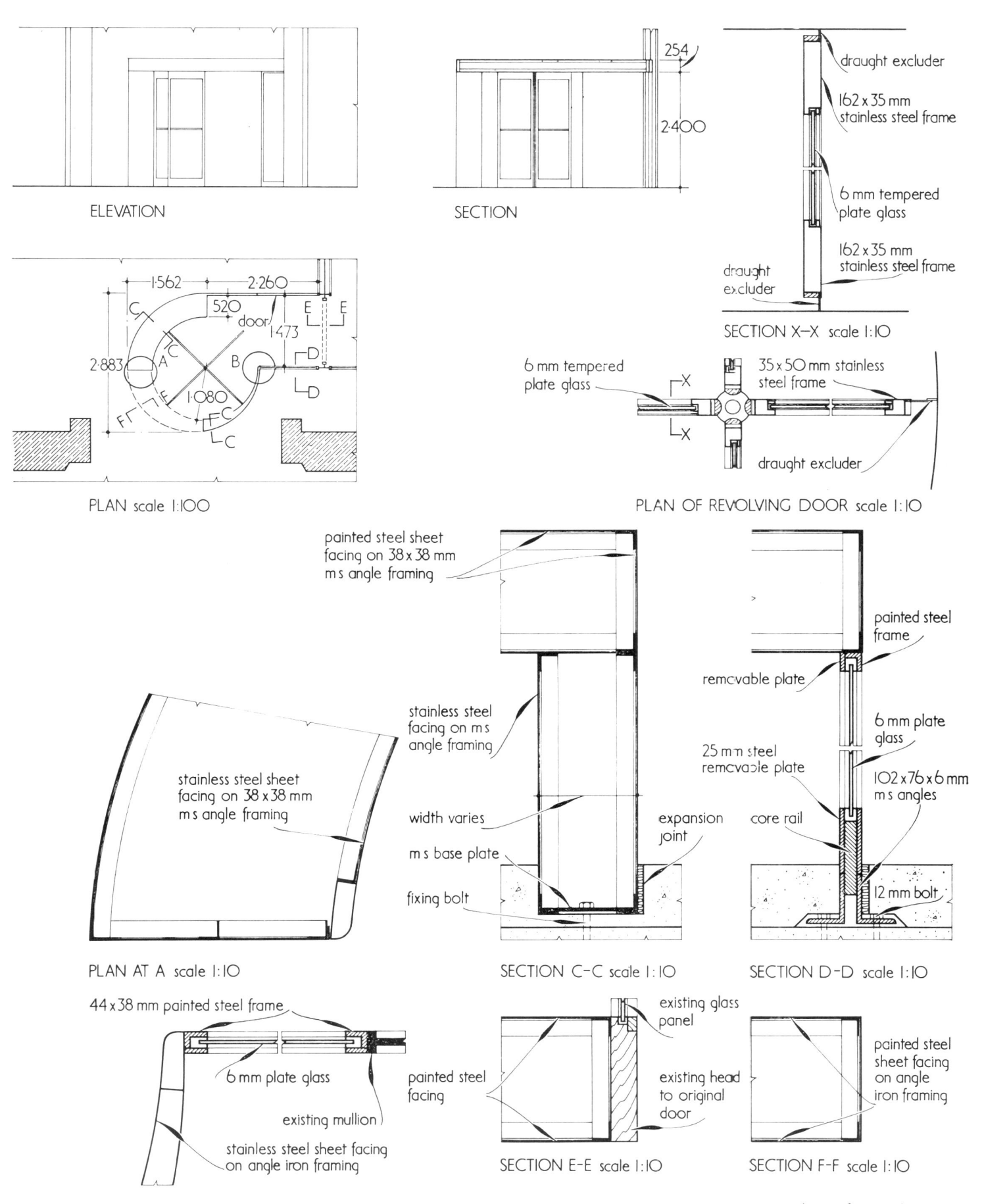

SECTION X–X scale 1:10
- draught excluder
- 162 x 35 mm stainless steel frame
- 6 mm tempered plate glass
- 162 x 35 mm stainless steel frame
- draught excluder

PLAN scale 1:100

PLAN OF REVOLVING DOOR scale 1:10
- 6 mm tempered plate glass
- 35 x 50 mm stainless steel frame
- draught excluder

PLAN AT A scale 1:10
- stainless steel sheet facing on 38 x 38 mm m s angle framing

SECTION C-C scale 1:10
- painted steel sheet facing on 38 x 38 mm m s angle framing
- stainless steel facing on m s angle framing
- width varies
- m s base plate
- fixing bolt
- expansion joint

SECTION D-D scale 1:10
- painted steel frame
- removable plate
- 6 mm plate glass
- 25 mm steel removable plate
- 102 x 76 x 6 mm m s angles
- core rail
- 12 mm bolt

PLAN AT B scale 1:10
- 44 x 38 mm painted steel frame
- 6 mm plate glass
- existing mullion
- stainless steel sheet facing on angle iron framing

SECTION E-E scale 1:10
- painted steel facing
- existing glass panel
- existing head to original door

SECTION F-F scale 1:10
- painted steel sheet facing on angle iron framing

note: metric equivalents of imperial dimensions are given to the nearest 0·5 mm

192 DOORS

GLAZED SLIDING DOORS TO SUNROOM: HOUSE IN FLORIDA
DESIGNED BY RALPH S. TWITCHELL AND PAUL RUDOLPH

The sunroom measures approximately 41 ft. by 16 ft. and the glazed sliding doors are in each of the long sides covering openings of 20 ft.

DOORS 193

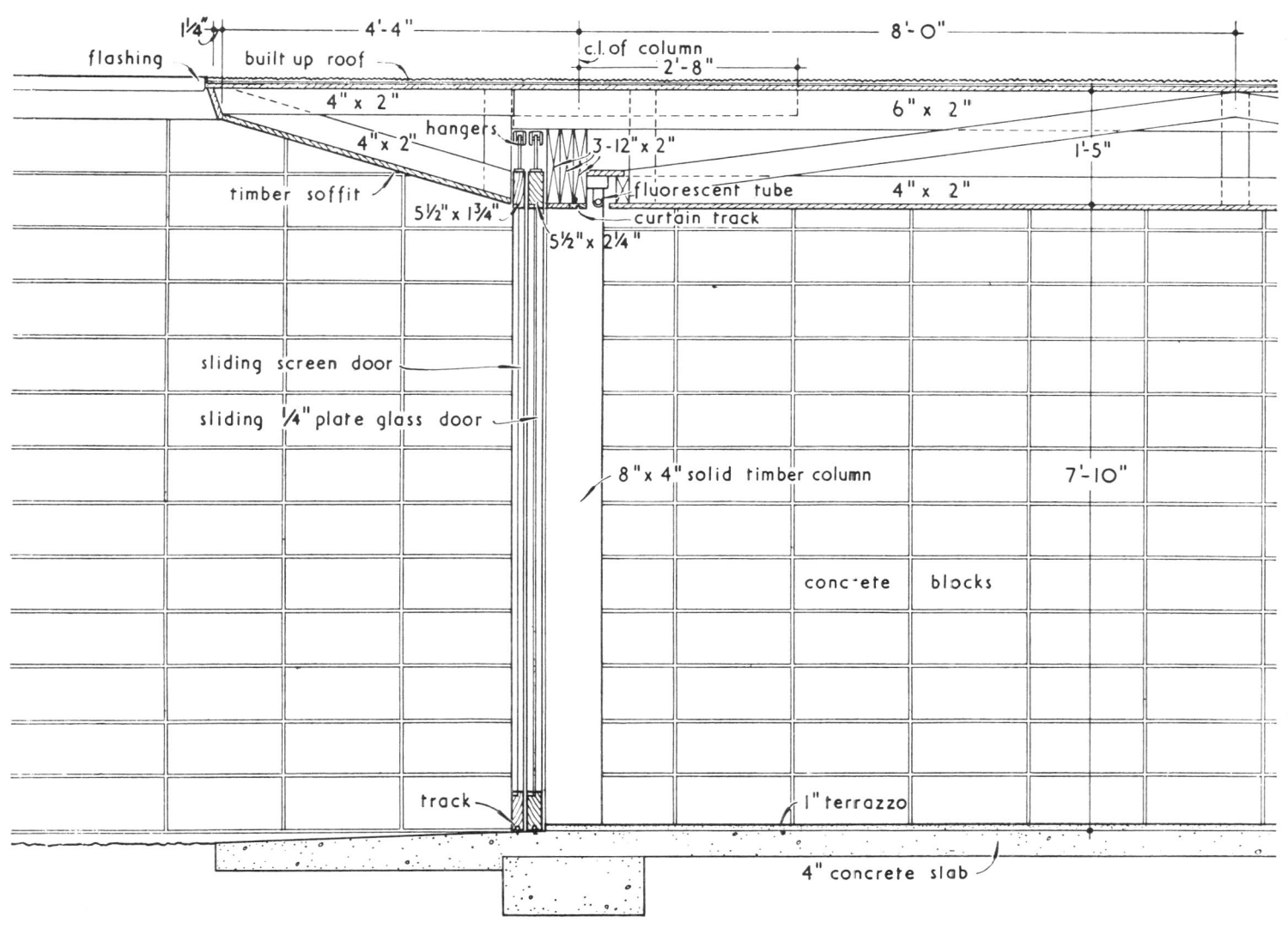

SECTION THROUGH SUNROOM LOOKING SOUTH. scale ½"= 1'-0"

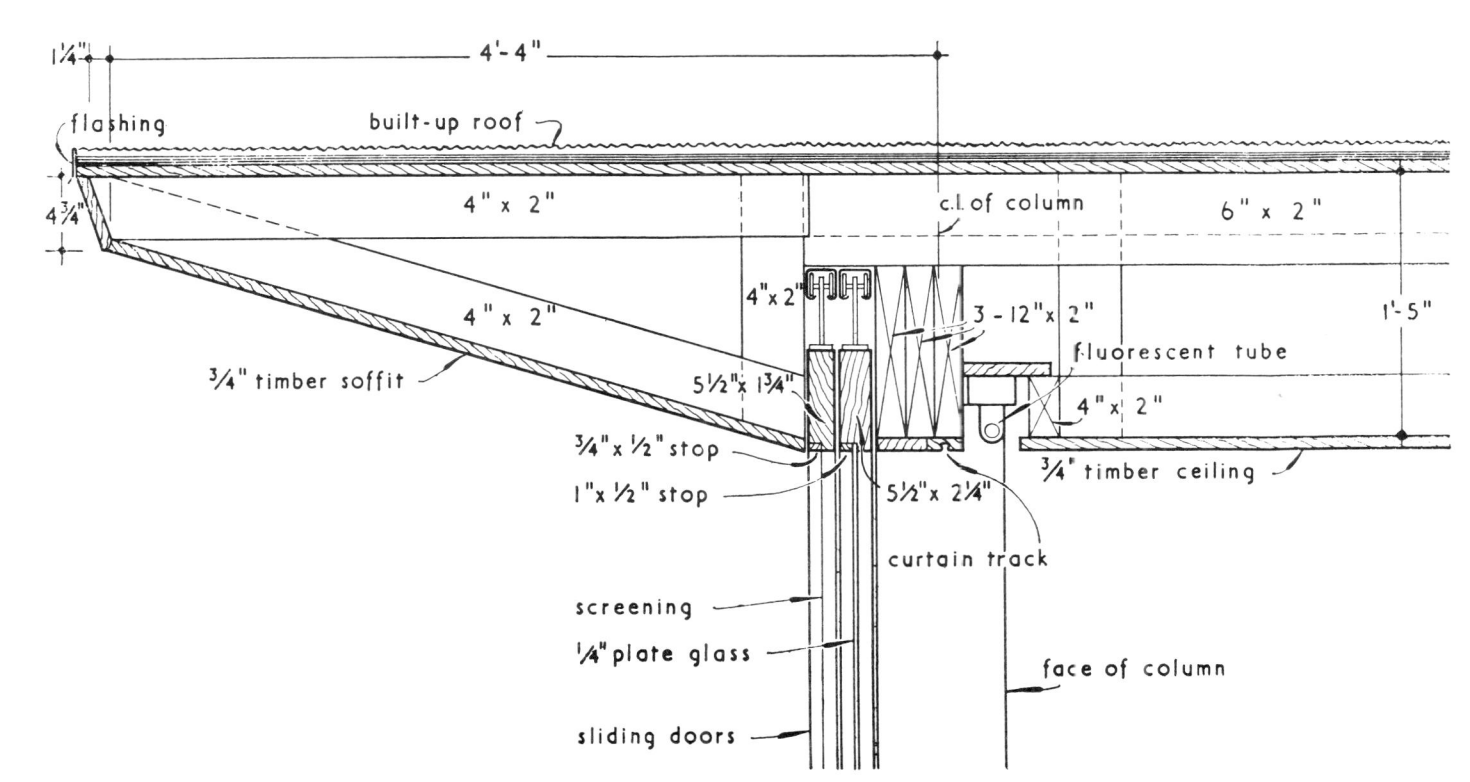

DETAIL SECTION THROUGH SUNROOM EAVES. scale 1"=1'-0"

194 DOORS

GLAZED SLIDING DOOR: HOUSE AT SANTA MONICA, CALIFORNIA
DESIGNED BY RICHARD J. NEUTRA

The wide sliding door is a single sheet of plate glass, framed in aluminium, and occupies the centre part of the window wall to the terrace.

DOORS 195

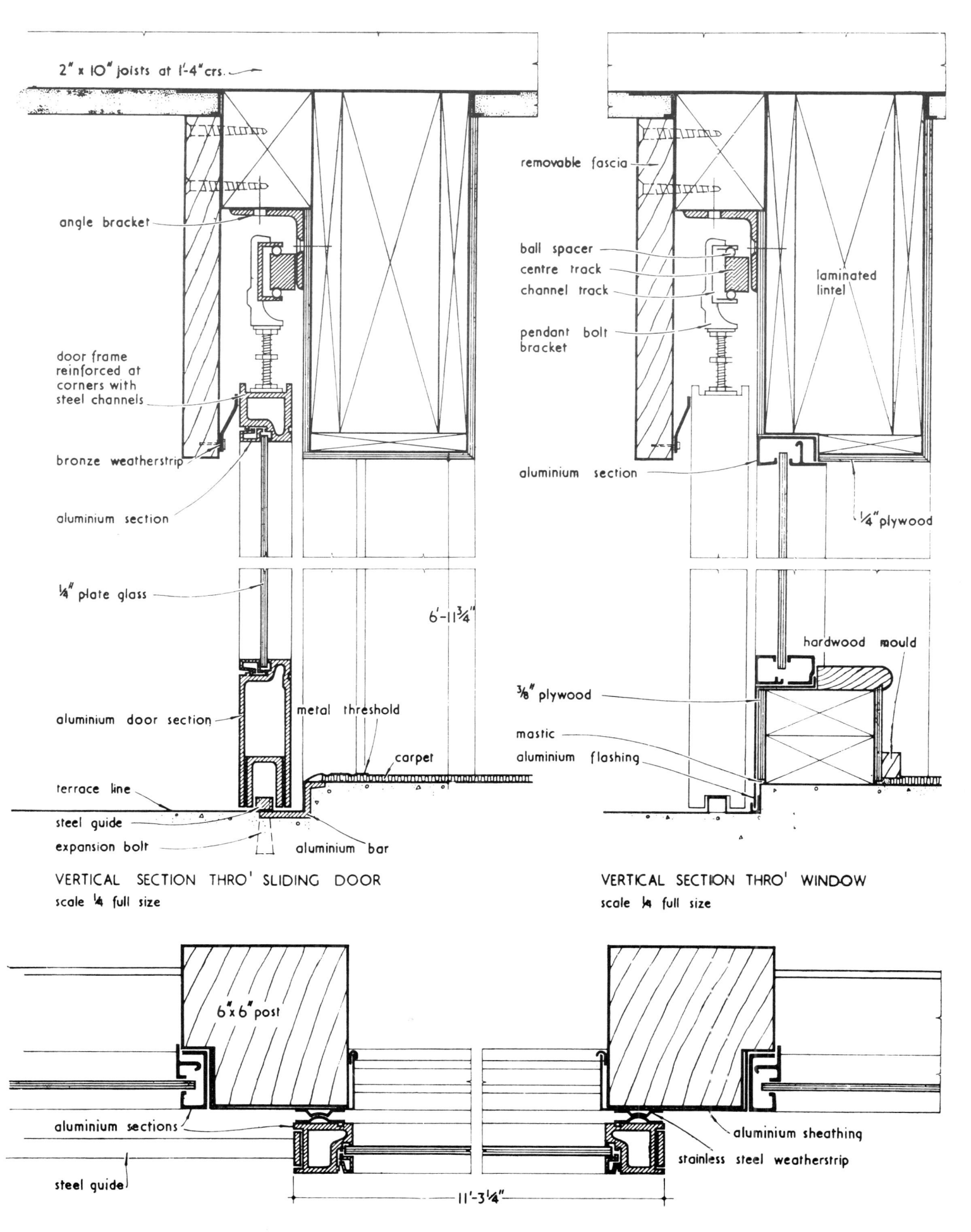

VERTICAL SECTION THRO' SLIDING DOOR
scale ¼ full size

VERTICAL SECTION THRO' WINDOW
scale ¼ full size

PLAN OF DOOR JAMBS   scale ¼ full size

196 COVERED WAYS AND CANOPIES

ORCHESTRA CANOPY: ROYAL FESTIVAL HALL
DESIGNED BY ROBERT H. MATTHEW AND J. L. MARTIN; EDWIN WILLIAMS (senior architect-in-charge);
PETER MORO (associated architect)

The photograph shows the arrangement of plywood box girders and transverse beams, the access gangways and the method of suspension from the superstructure

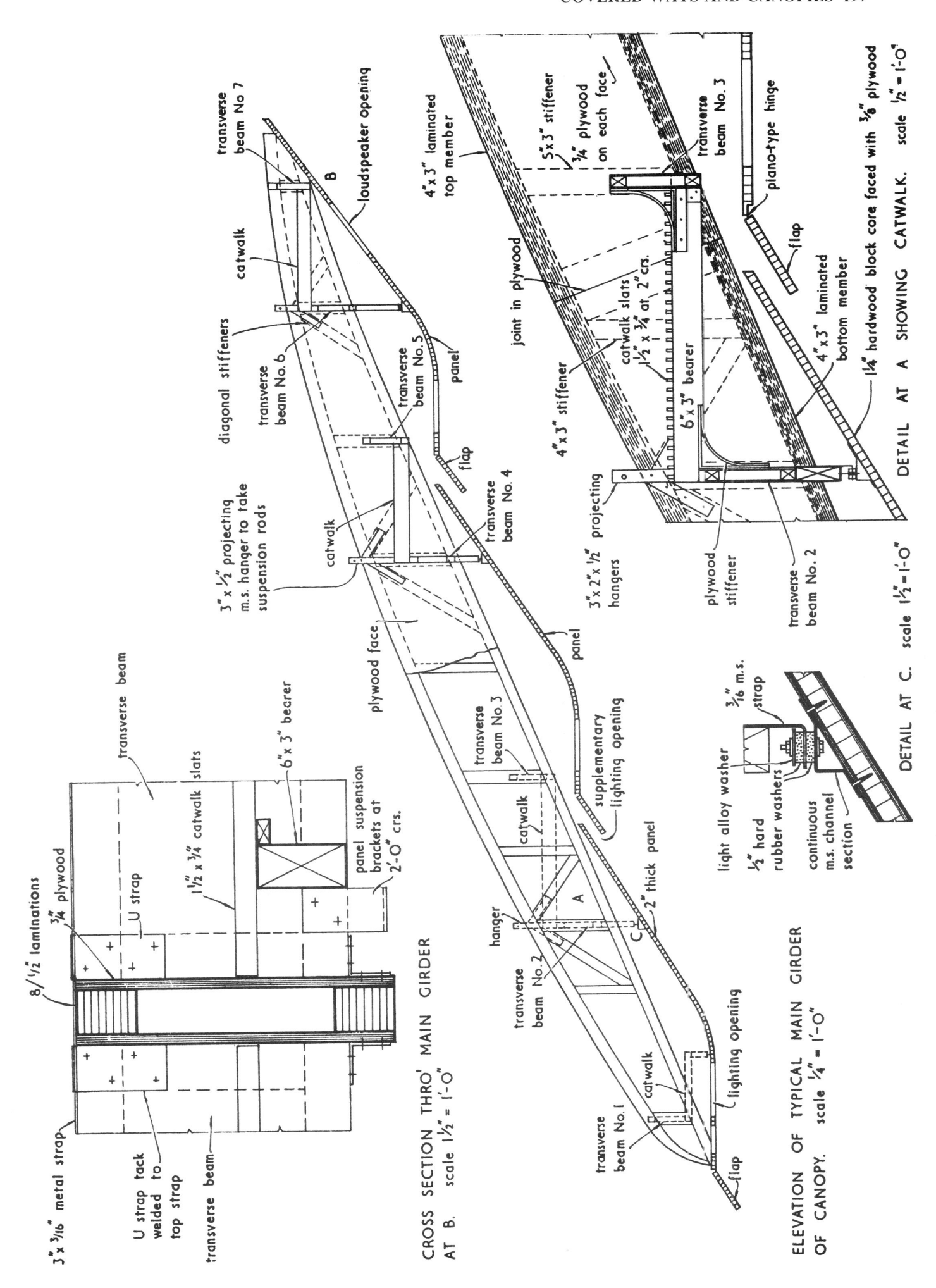

COVERED WAYS AND CANOPIES 197

198 COVERED WAYS AND CANOPIES

CANOPY: LONDON AIRPORT
DESIGNED BY FREDERICK GIBBERD

The canopy is supported on purpose-made r.s.j's which taper along their length and, passing over the top flange of one r.s. beam directly behind the wall face, are bolted to the web of another 6 ft. further back. The fascia is formed in aluminium-faced plywood clipped to a r.s. angle and the same material is used to box in the supporting r.s.j's.

COVERED WAYS AND CANOPIES 199

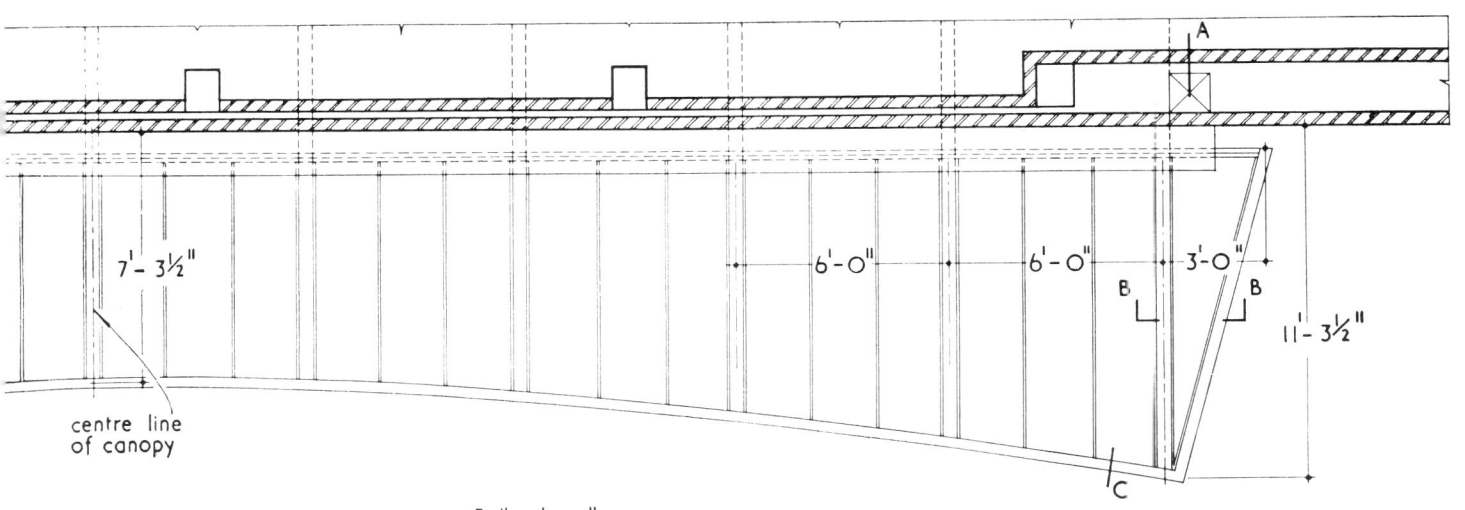

PART PLAN OF CANOPY. scale 3/16" = 1'-0"

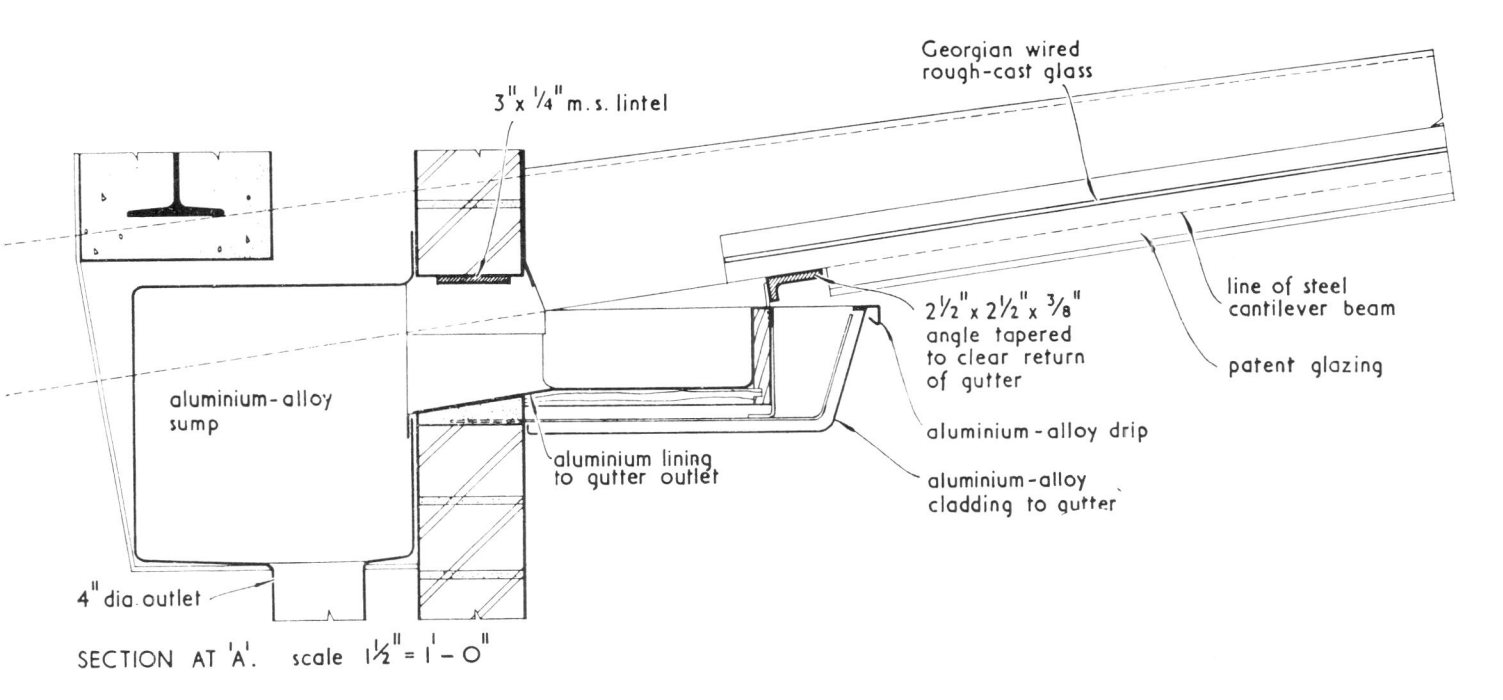

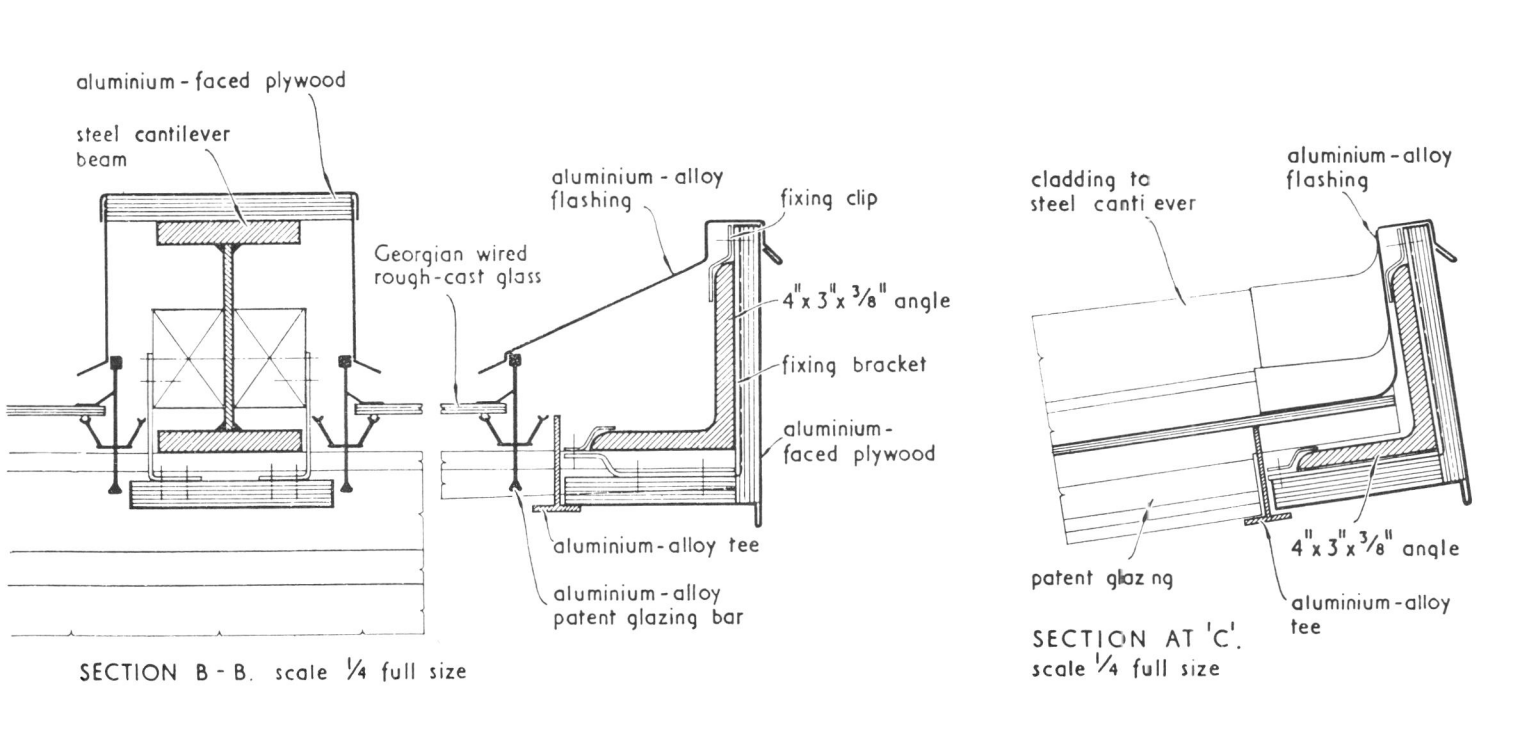

SECTION AT 'A'. scale 1½" = 1'-0"

- 3" x ¼" m.s. lintel
- Georgian wired rough-cast glass
- 2½" x 2½" x ⅜" angle tapered to clear return of gutter
- line of steel cantilever beam
- patent glazing
- aluminium-alloy drip
- aluminium-alloy cladding to gutter
- aluminium lining to gutter outlet
- aluminium-alloy sump
- 4" dia. outlet

centre line of canopy

7'-3½"   6'-0"   6'-0"   3'-0"   11'-3½"

SECTION B-B. scale ¼ full size

- aluminium-faced plywood
- steel cantilever beam
- aluminium-alloy flashing
- fixing clip
- Georgian wired rough-cast glass
- 4" x 3" x ⅜" angle
- fixing bracket
- aluminium-faced plywood
- aluminium-alloy tee
- aluminium-alloy patent glazing bar

SECTION AT 'C'. scale ¼ full size

- cladding to steel cantilever
- aluminium-alloy flashing
- patent glazing
- 4" x 3" x ⅜" angle
- aluminium-alloy tee

CANOPY: FACTORY AT AALBORG, DENMARK
DESIGNED BY PREBEN HANSEN

(*Material supplied by M. G. Andrews*)

The form of the canopy was dictated by three considerations: the desire to give a sufficient height at the front edge (actually 11 ft. 6 in.) to enable lorries to unload in the dry, to provide good daylight at the back of the loading bay, and to provide a neat method for disposing of rainwater.

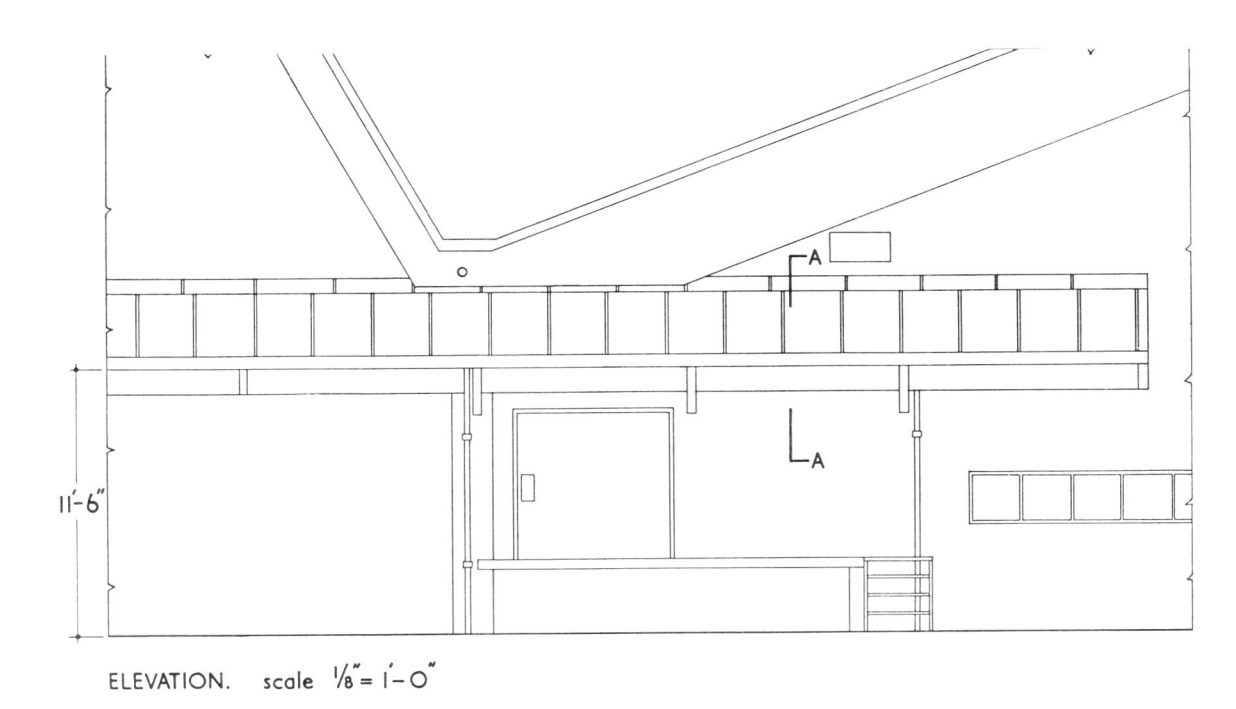

COVERED WAYS AND CANOPIES 201

ELEVATION. scale 1/8" = 1'-0"

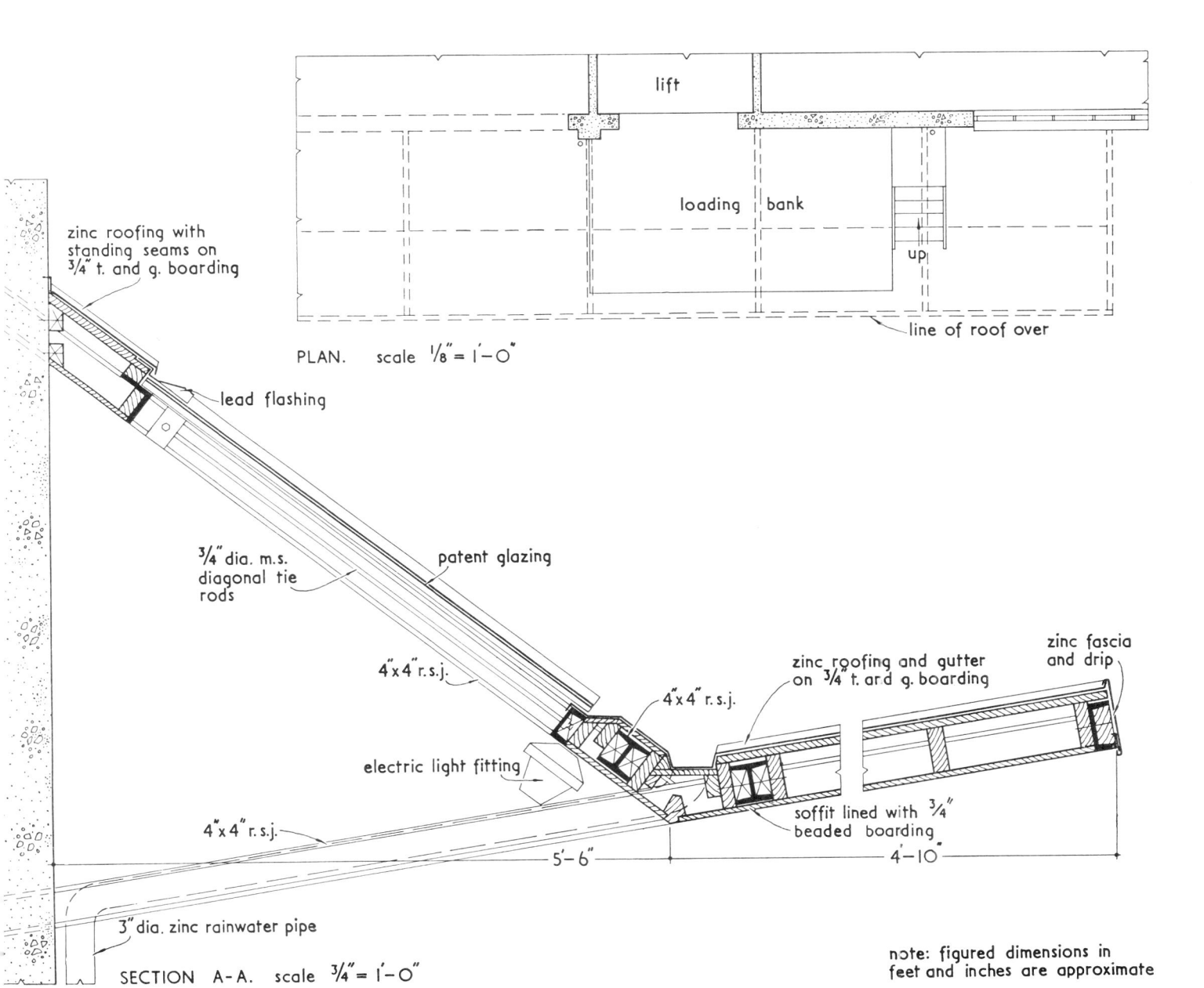

11'-6"

PLAN. scale 1/8" = 1'-0"

lift

loading bank

up

line of roof over

SECTION A-A. scale 3/4" = 1'-0"

- zinc roofing with standing seams on 3/4" t. and g. boarding
- lead flashing
- 3/4" dia. m.s. diagonal tie rods
- patent glazing
- 4"x4" r.s.j.
- 4"x4" r.s.j.
- zinc roofing and gutter on 3/4" t. and g. boarding
- zinc fascia and drip
- electric light fitting
- 4"x4" r.s.j.
- soffit lined with 3/4" beaded boarding
- 3" dia. zinc rainwater pipe
- 5'-6"
- 4'-10"

note: figured dimensions in feet and inches are approximate

202 COVERED WAYS AND CANOPIES

CANOPY OVER ENTRANCE: TOWN HALL AT RØDOVRE, DENMARK
DESIGNED BY ARNE JACOBSEN *(Material supplied by Michael Sadler)*

Both canopy and awning are framed in m.s. channels mitred and site-welded, and both are welded to r.s. sections. These sections are stopped off directly below the line of the aluminium flashing and are stiffened at the head by m.s. braces scribed between the flanges and welded. All steel is sand-blasted, zinc-sprayed and primed with zinc chromate before erection, and surface defects are painted over with pulverized zinc paint. The small projections below the front edge of the canopy near the corners are socket outlets for loud speakers.

COVERED WAYS AND CANOPIES 203

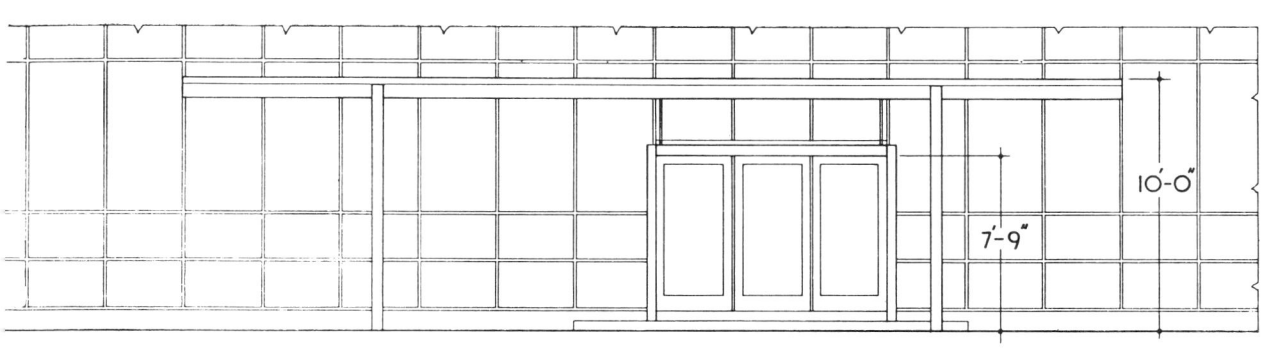

ELEVATION. scale ⅛" = 1'-0"

10'-0"
7'-9"

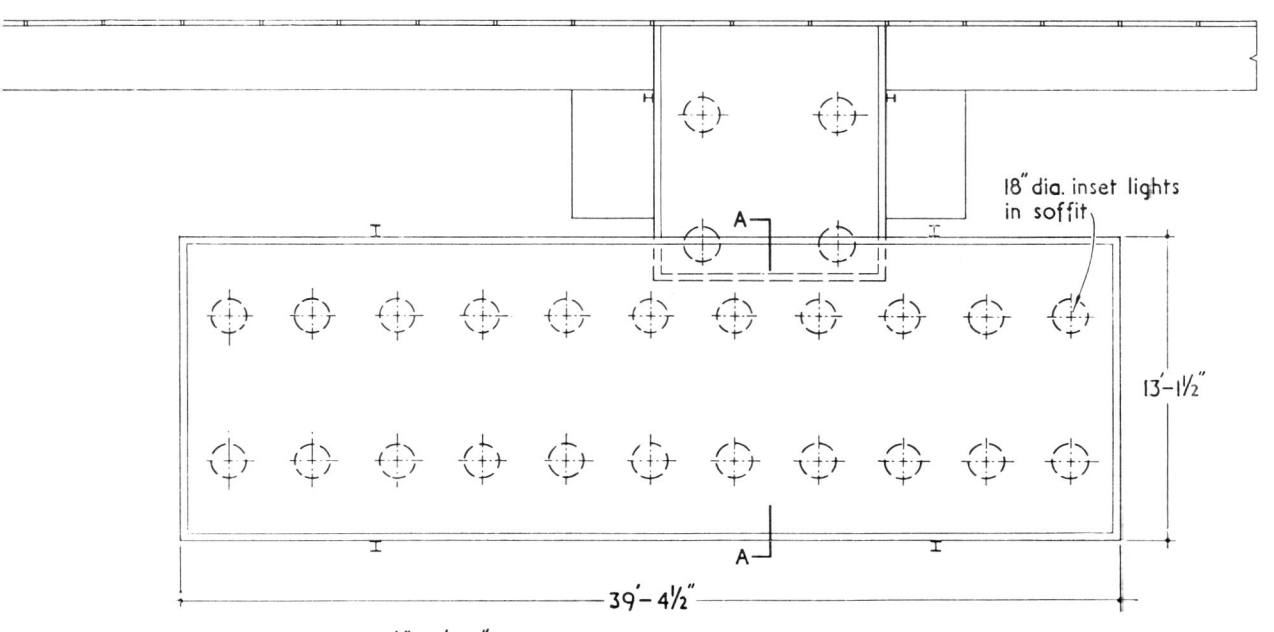

PLAN OF CANOPY. scale ⅛" = 1'-0"

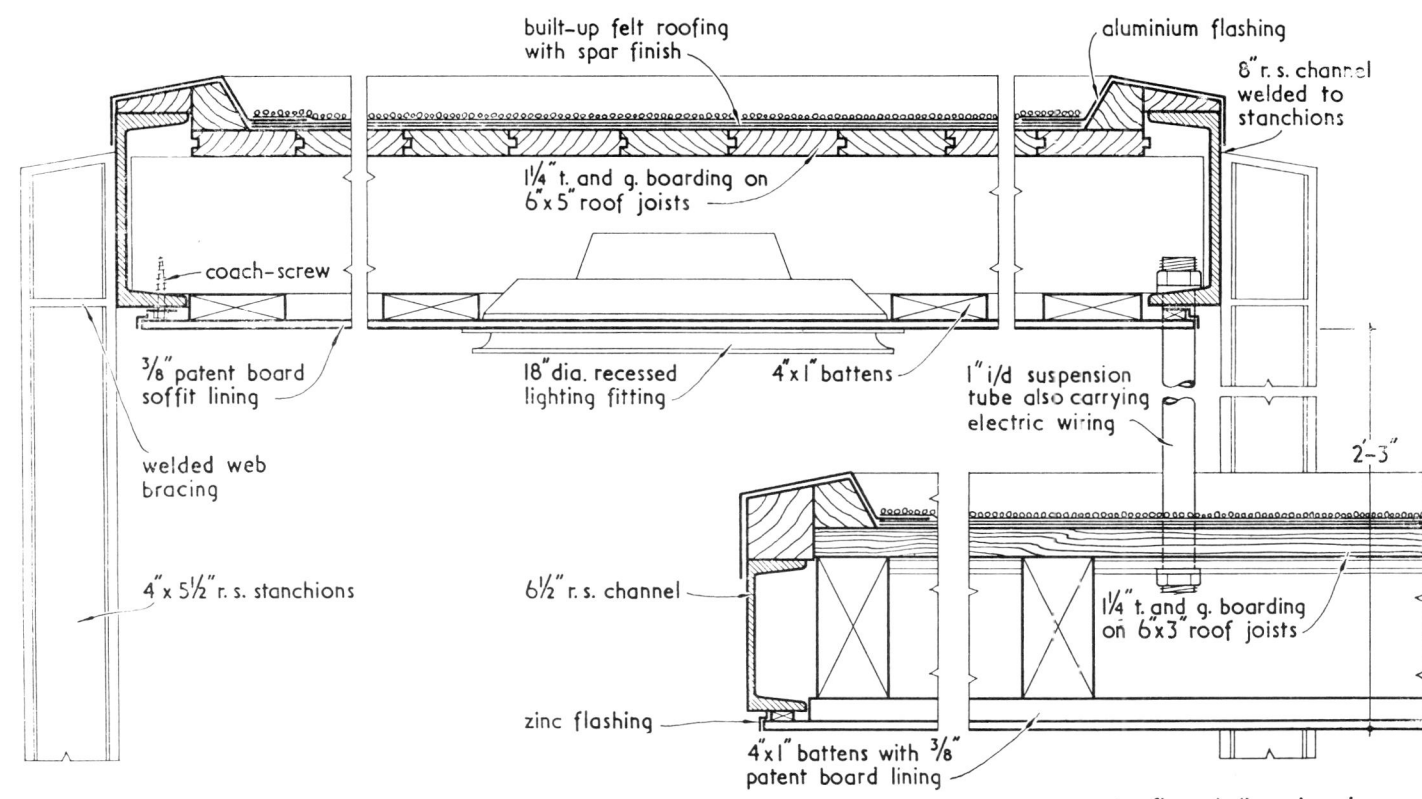

18" dia. inset lights in soffit
13'-1½"
39'-4½"

SECTION A-A. scale 1½" = 1'-0"

built-up felt roofing with spar finish
aluminium flashing
8" r.s. channel welded to stanchions
1¼" t. and g. boarding on 6"x5" roof joists
coach-screw
18" dia. recessed lighting fitting
4"x1" battens
1" i/d suspension tube also carrying electric wiring
⅜" patent board soffit lining
welded web bracing
4"x 5½" r.s. stanchions
6½" r.s. channel
zinc flashing
4"x1" battens with ⅜" patent board lining
1¼" t. and g. boarding on 6"x3" roof joists
2'-3"

note: figured dimensions in feet and inches are approximate

204 COVERED WAYS AND CANOPIES

CANOPY: OFFICE BLOCK IN VEVEY, SWITZERLAND
DESIGNED BY J. TSCHUMI

(*Material supplied by Dariush Borbor*)

This canopy is a tour de force in aluminium construction. The dramatic effect of the cantilever is heightened by the fact that the width at the extremity is slightly greater than that at the building face. Note (on the drawing) the ingenious manner of disposing of rainwater.

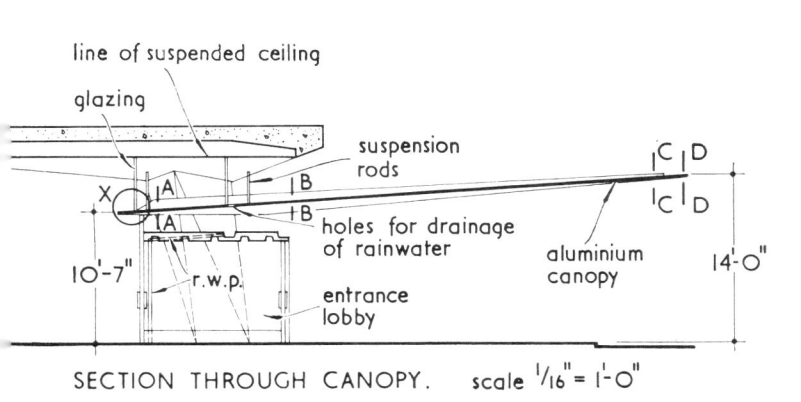

COVERED WAYS AND CANOPIES 205

SECTION THROUGH CANOPY. scale 1/16" = 1'-0"

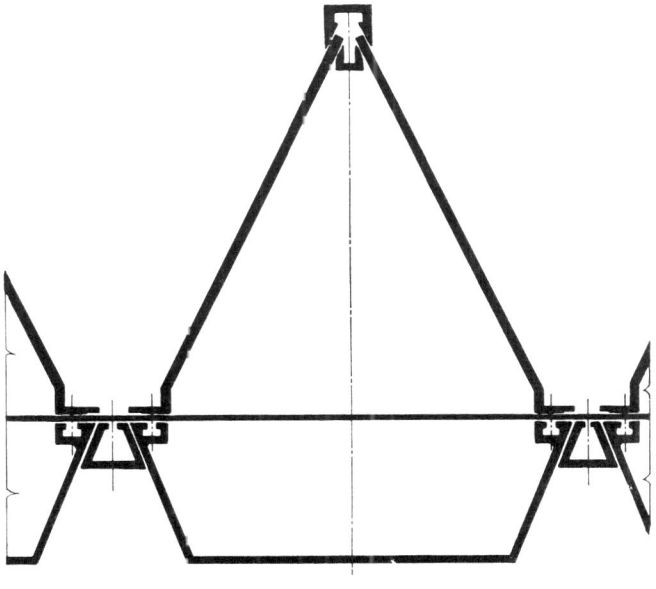

- line of suspended ceiling
- glazing
- suspension rods
- holes for drainage of rainwater
- aluminium canopy
- r.w.p.
- entrance lobby
- 10'-7"
- 14'-0"

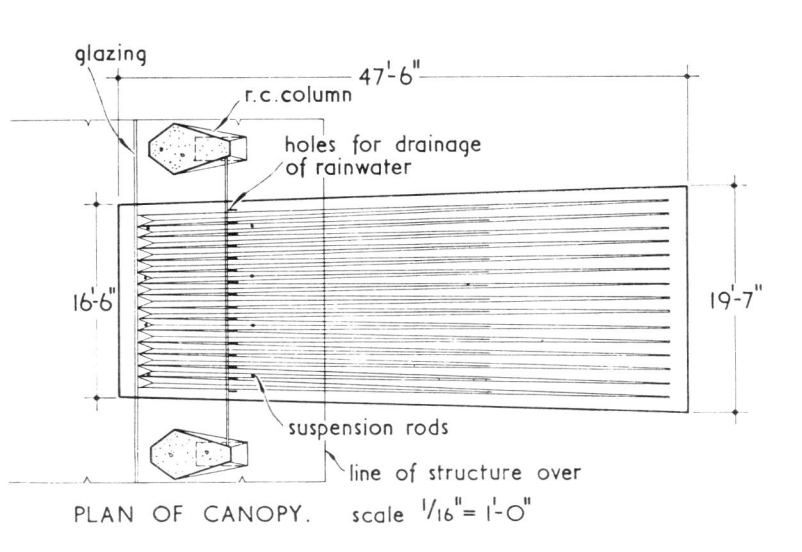

PLAN OF CANOPY. scale 1/16" = 1'-0"

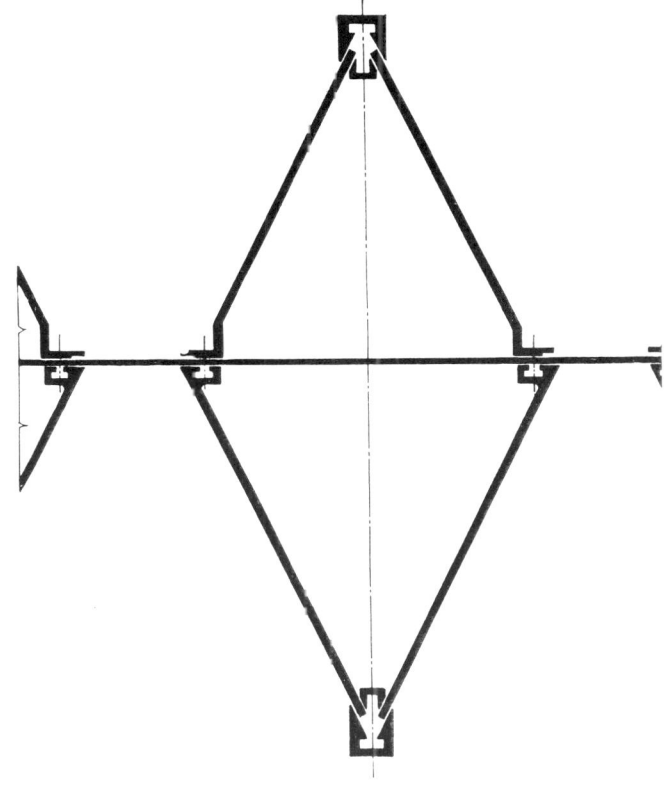

- glazing
- r.c. column
- holes for drainage of rainwater
- suspension rods
- line of structure over
- 47'-6"
- 16'-6"
- 19'-7"

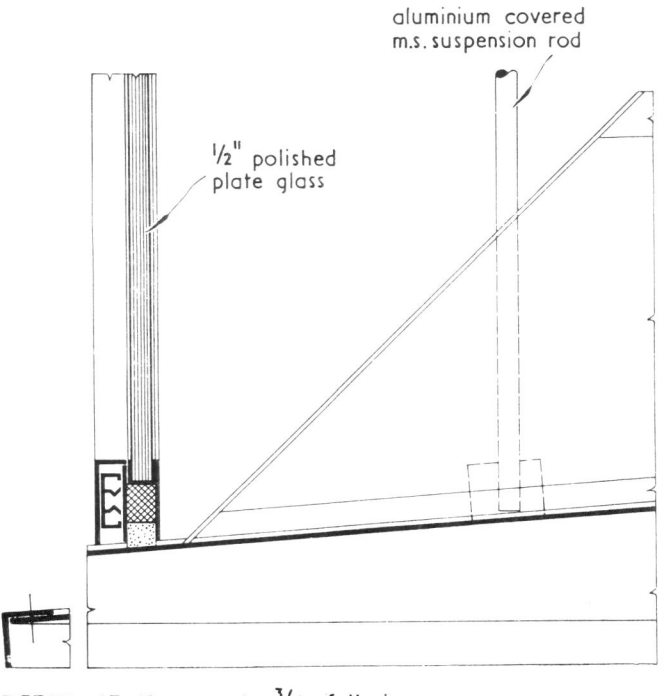

DETAIL AT X. scale 3/16 full size

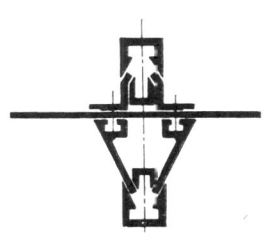

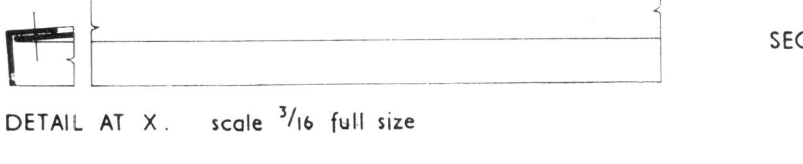

- 1/2" polished plate glass
- aluminium covered m.s. suspension rod

SECTION A-A. scale 3/16 full size

SECTION B-B.

SECTION C-C.

SECTION D-D.

note: figured dimensions in feet and inches are approximate

ENTRANCE CANOPY: EMBASSY IN ATHENS, GREECE
DESIGNED BY WALTER GROPIUS (*Material supplied by Garbis Urégian*)

The unusual thing about this canopy is that water splashes off the far edge instead of being guided into concealed downpipes on the inner edge. This is justified by the fact that the canopy projects beyond the far side of any waiting car. An advantage is that the canopy itself is horizontal and not canted in the usual way. To avoid in-situ staining at the edges, an aluminium fascia runs clear of the outer edge of the structural slab.

COVERED WAYS AND CANOPIES 207

PLAN. scale 1/16" = 1'-0"

SECTION. scale 1/16" = 1'-0"

SECTION A-A. scale 3/16 full size

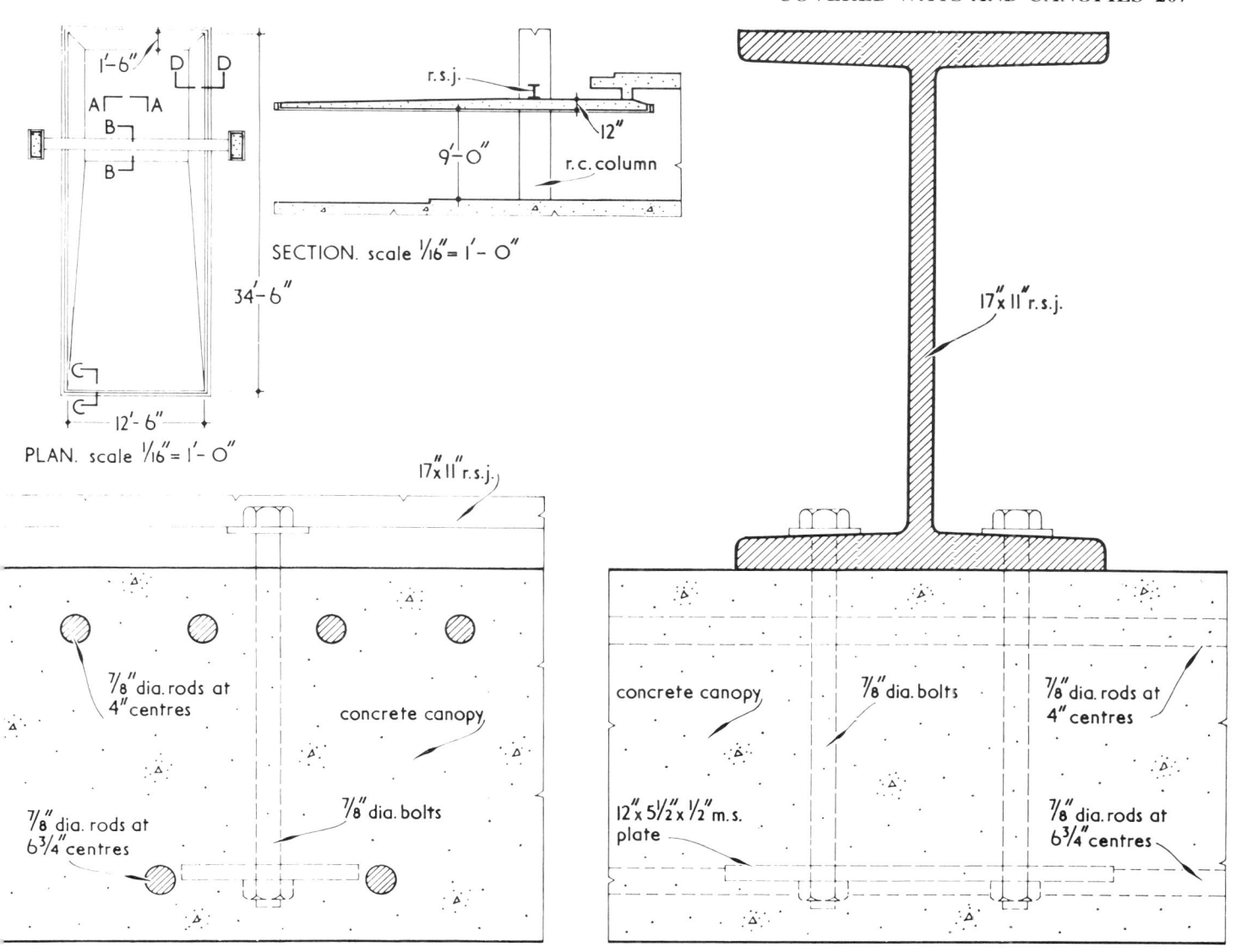

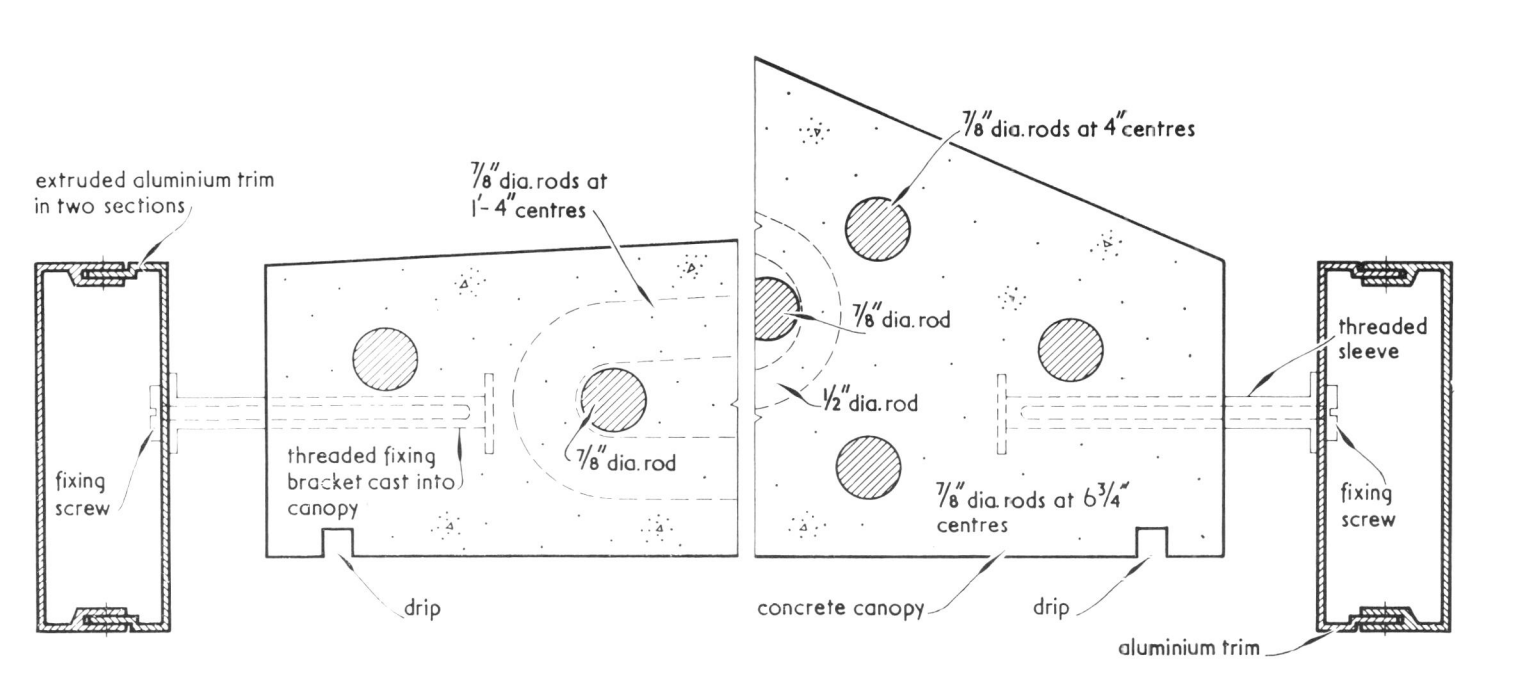

SECTION B-B. scale 3/16 full size

SECTION C-C. scale 3/8 full size

SECTION D-D.

note: figured dimensions in feet and inches are approximate

208 COVERED WAYS AND CANOPIES

ENTRANCE CANOPY: MUSEUM IN OSLO, NORWAY
DESIGNED BY ELIASSEN AND LAMBERTZ-NILSSEN (*Material supplied by J. C. Carlsen*)

This is a broad span canopy with a steel structure. It will be noticed that the supporting steel tubes are enclosed within bronze tubes and that the joists are also clad in bronze where they are open to the weather.

COVERED WAYS AND CANOPIES 209

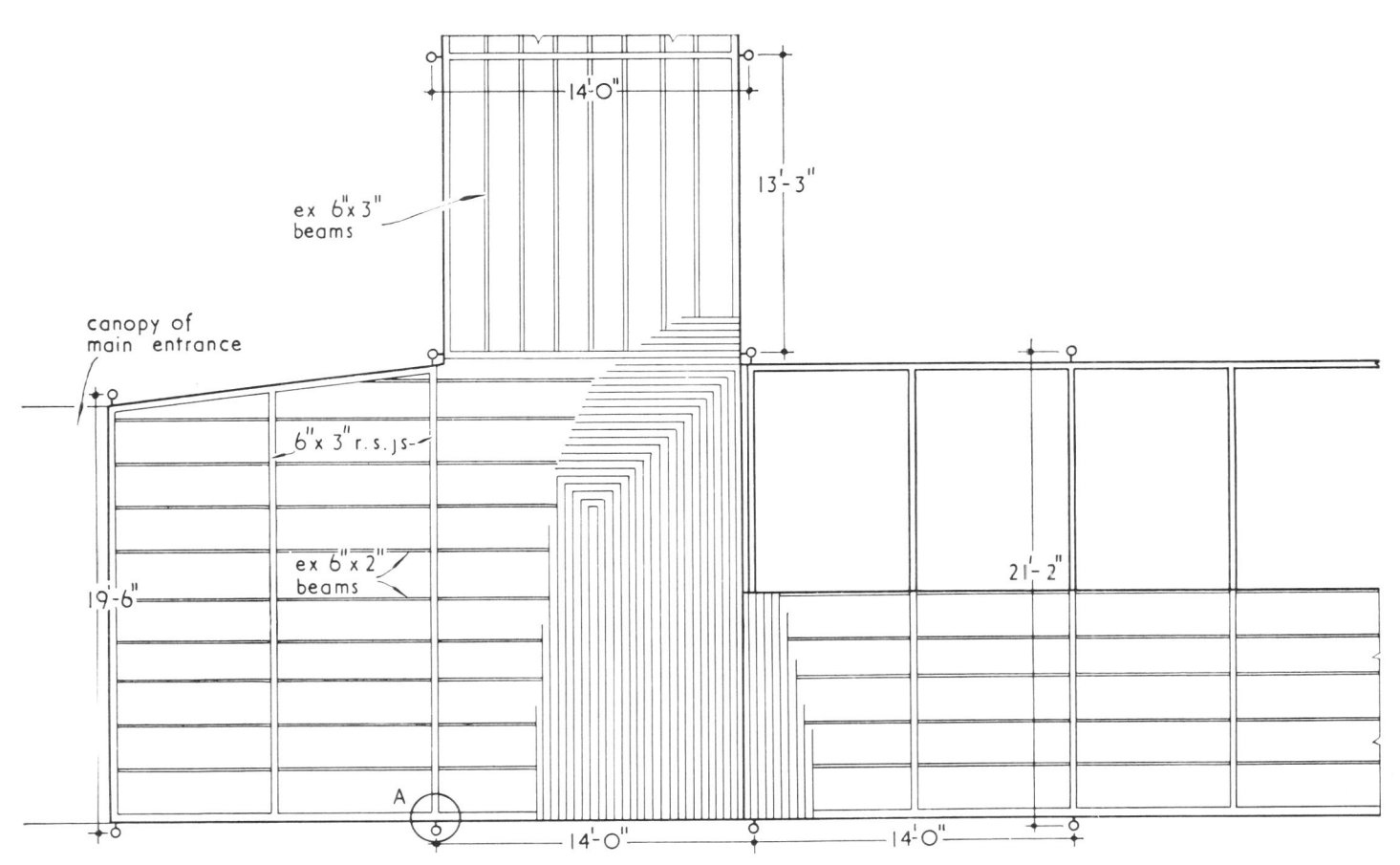

PART PLAN LOOKING UP SHOWING FRAMING. scale 1/8" = 1'-0"

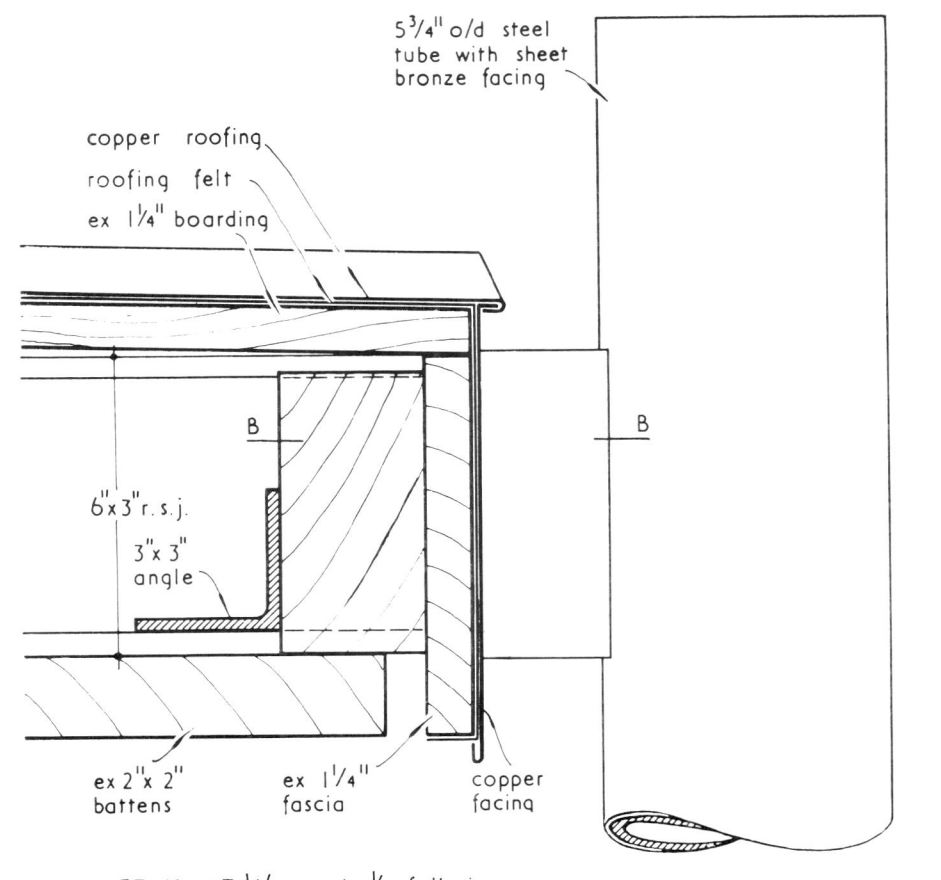

- canopy of main entrance
- ex 6"×3" beams
- 6"×3" r.s.js
- ex 6"×2" beams
- 14'-0"
- 13'-3"
- 19'-6"
- 21'-2"
- 14'-0"
- 14'-0"

DETAIL AT 'A'. scale 1/4 full size

- copper roofing
- roofing felt
- ex 1¼" boarding
- 5¾" o/d steel tube with sheet bronze facing
- 6"×3" r.s.j.
- 3"×3" angle
- ex 2"×2" battens
- ex 1¼" fascia
- copper facing

PLAN AT B-B scale 1/4 full size

- flanges of r.s.j. cut off
- web of r.s.j. with bronze facing

note: figured dimensions in feet and inches are approximate

210 COVERED WAYS AND CANOPIES

CANOPY: TOURIST INFORMATION PAVILION, OSLO, NORWAY
DESIGNED BY ODD BROCHMANNS   (*Material supplied by Tone Gengenbach*)

This light canopy employs timber in a form commonly found in concrete. All the structural members are timber and the unglazed section of the canopy itself is formed in laminated pine.

COVERED WAYS AND CANOPIES 211

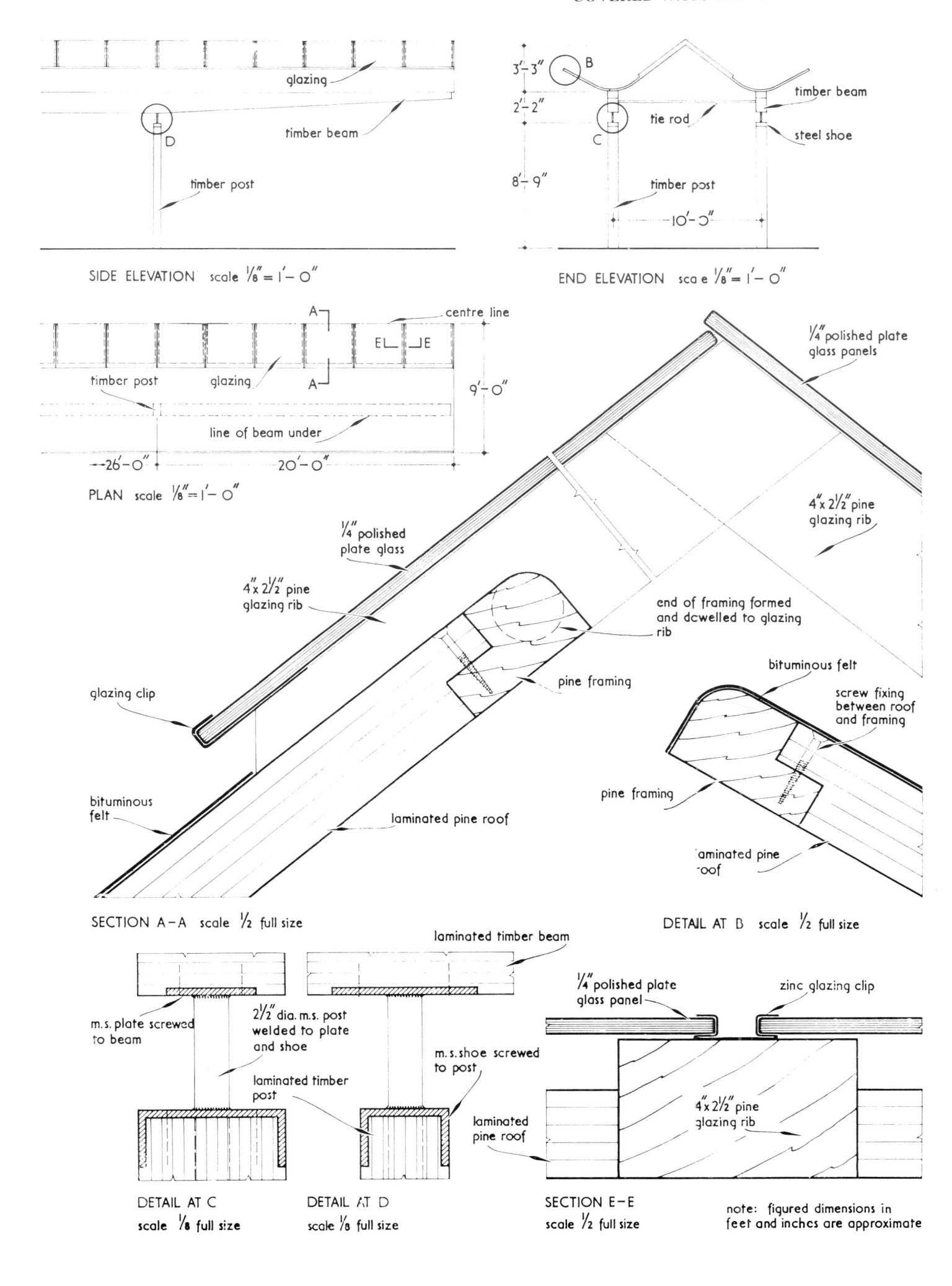

212 COVERED WAYS AND CANOPIES

CONNECTING BRIDGE: SCHOOL AT GREAT MISSENDEN, BUCKINGHAMSHIRE
DESIGNED BY FREDERICK B. POOLEY (architect to the Buckinghamshire County Council)

The bridge is supported at each end by two stanchions which are independent of either block so that the junction between bridge and main structure is an expansion joint. The tubular steel frames which form the side structures and the handrail brackets and core, and the 5 in. by 3 in. r.s.j. on which they rest, were shop-welded and were bolted to the stanchions. The roof structure comprises 4 in. by 3 in. r.s.j's. running crosswise and $\frac{20}{32}$ in. o.d. tubular diagonal bracing on which rest m.s. tee purlins and straw slabs: the floor structure comprises a grid of 5 in. by 3 in. r.s.j's. within which 5 in. by 2 in. joists have been scribed.

COVERED WAYS AND CANOPIES 213

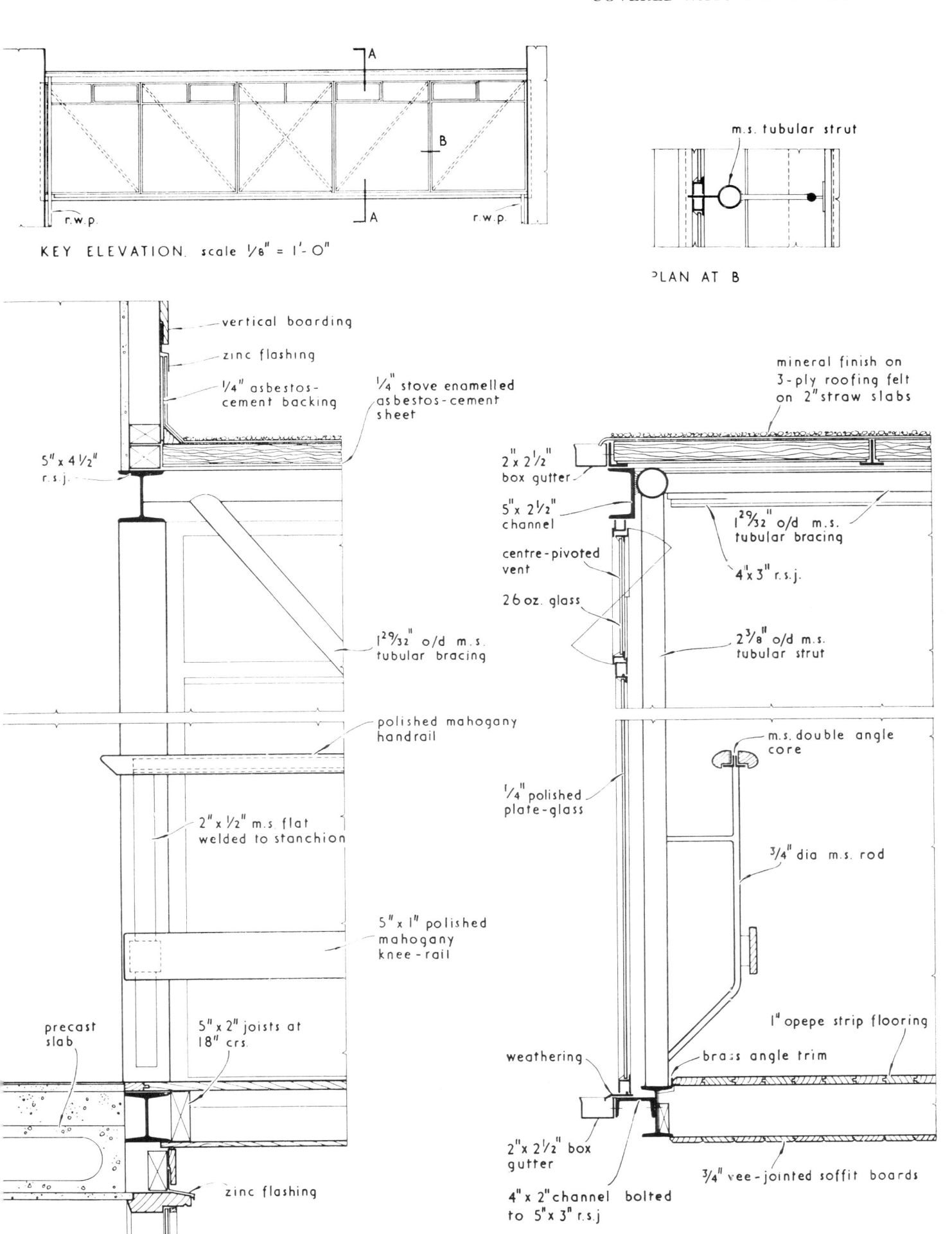

KEY ELEVATION. scale ⅛" = 1'-0"

PLAN AT B

m.s. tubular strut

SECTION AT JUNCTION WITH BUILDING.

- vertical boarding
- zinc flashing
- ¼" asbestos-cement backing
- 5" x 4½" r.s.j.
- ¼" stove enamelled asbestos-cement sheet
- 1²⁹⁄₃₂" o/d m.s. tubular bracing
- polished mahogany handrail
- 2" x ½" m.s. flat welded to stanchion
- 5" x 1" polished mahogany knee-rail
- precast slab
- 5" x 2" joists at 18" crs.
- zinc flashing

SECTION A-A. scale 1" = 1'-0"

- mineral finish on 3-ply roofing felt on 2" straw slabs
- 2" x 2½" box gutter
- 5" x 2½" channel
- centre-pivoted vent
- 26 oz. glass
- 1²⁹⁄₃₂" o/d m.s. tubular bracing
- 4" x 3" r.s.j.
- 2⅜" o/d m.s. tubular strut
- ¼" polished plate-glass
- m.s. double angle core
- ¾" dia m.s. rod
- 1" opepe strip flooring
- brass angle trim
- weathering
- 2" x 2½" box gutter
- ¾" vee-jointed soffit boards
- 4" x 2" channel bolted to 5" x 3" r.s.j

214 COVERED WAYS AND CANOPIES

LIGHT LOUVRES: SCHOOL IN FRESNO, CALIFORNIA
DESIGNED BY DAVID H. HORN AND MARSHALL D. MORTLAND

The ends of the steel roof beams, cased in timber, extend to form supports for the redwood louvres

Photograph: Julius Shulman

COVERED WAYS AND CANOPIES 215

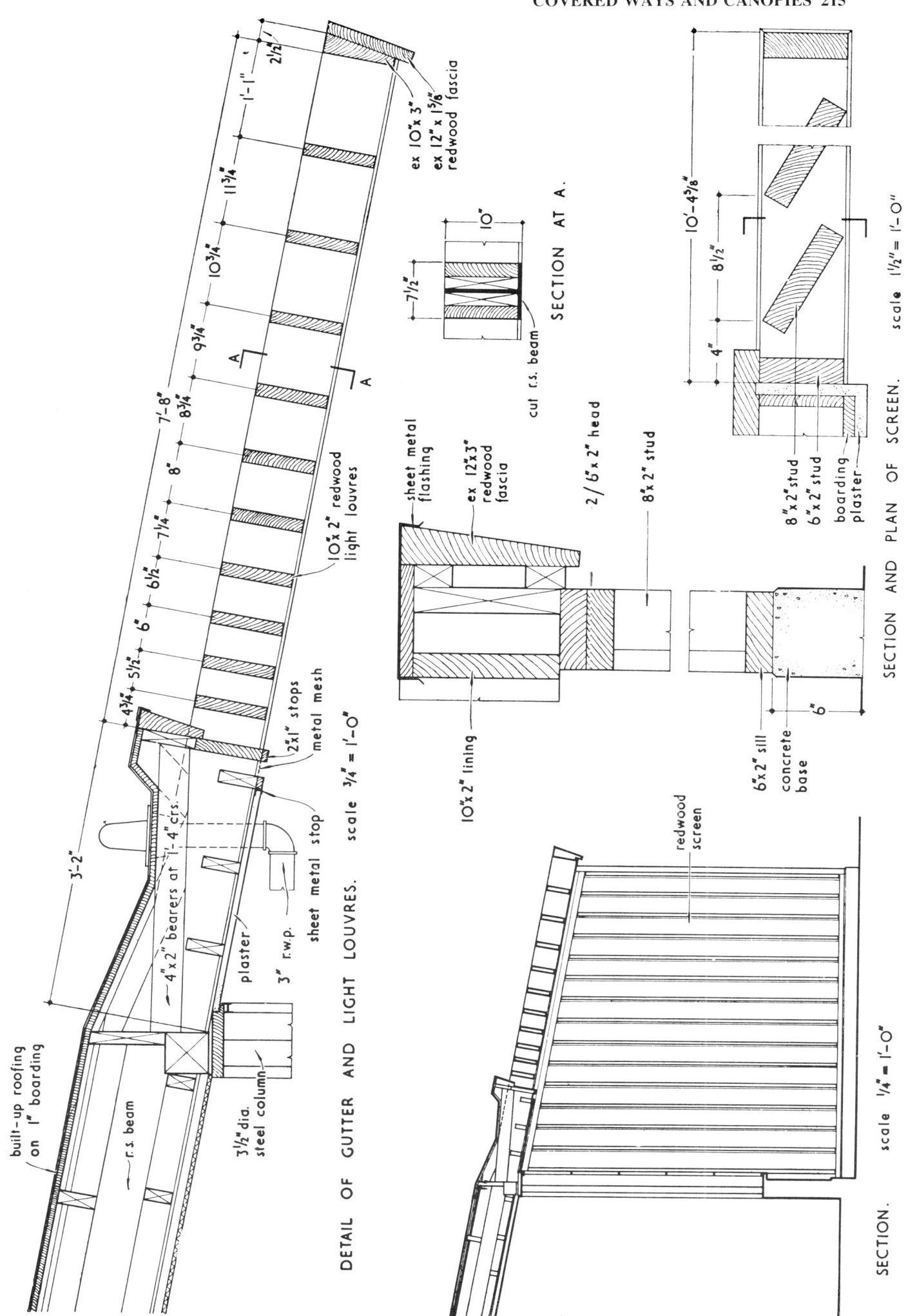

216 EXTERNAL FEATURES

DOUBLE-ACTION GATE: CATTLE MARKET AT GLOUCESTER
DESIGNED BY J. V. WALL (architect to the City of Gloucester)

This double-action gate was developed by the Gloucester City Architect's Department to close an opening giving on to a passage and to close the passage on either side of the opening. Hinges are provided on both sides of the opening and handles at both sides of the gate enable the operator to disengage the gate from either pair of hinges. In the course of development it was found necessary to add a special device which makes it impossible to lift the gate off both hinges at once.

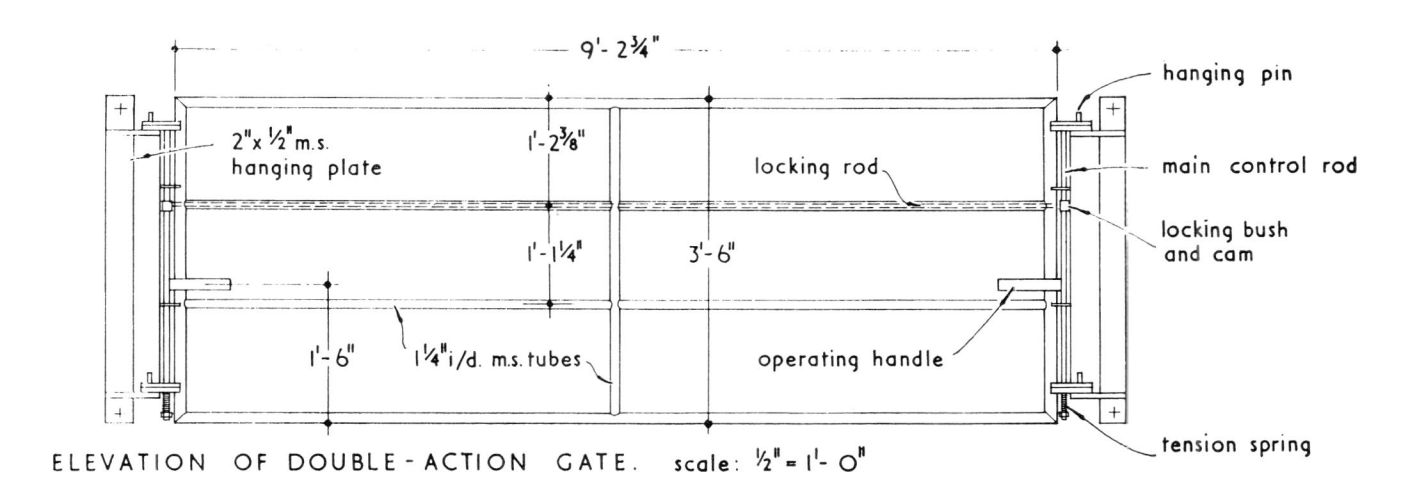

EXTERNAL FEATURES 217

ELEVATION OF DOUBLE-ACTION GATE. scale: ½" = 1'-0"

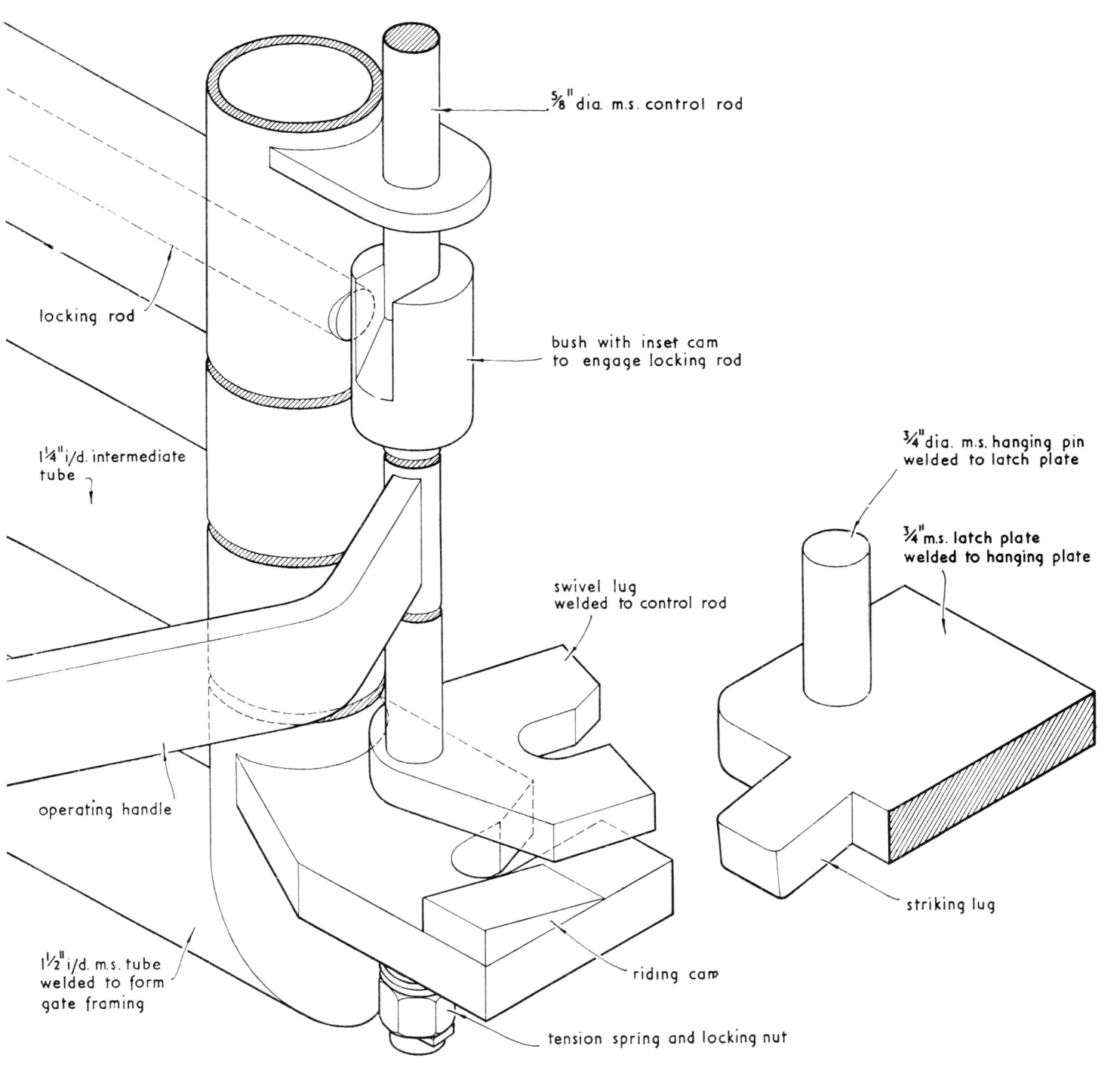

- hanging pin
- 2" x ½" m.s. hanging plate
- 1'-2⅜"
- locking rod
- main control rod
- locking bush and cam
- 1'-1¼"
- 3'-6"
- 9'-2¾"
- 1'-6"
- 1¼" i/d. m.s. tubes
- operating handle
- tension spring

ISOMETRIC VIEW OF HINGE MECHANISM scale: half full size.

- ⅝" dia. m.s. control rod
- locking rod
- bush with inset cam to engage locking rod
- 1¼" i/d. intermediate tube
- swivel lug welded to control rod
- ¾" dia. m.s. hanging pin welded to latch plate
- ¾" m.s. latch plate welded to hanging plate
- operating handle
- riding cam
- striking lug
- 1½" i/d. m.s. tube welded to form gate framing
- tension spring and locking nut

CONTROL GATES: OAKLAND COLISEUM ARENA, NIMITZ FREEWAY, OAKLAND, CALIFORNIA
DESIGNED BY SKIDMORE OWINGS AND MERRILL (*Material supplied by Duncan Macintosh*)

These crowd gates successfully incorporate standard panic exit devices. Matching panels adjacent to the gates lift out to allow quick exit of spectators after matches.

EXTERNAL FEATURES 219

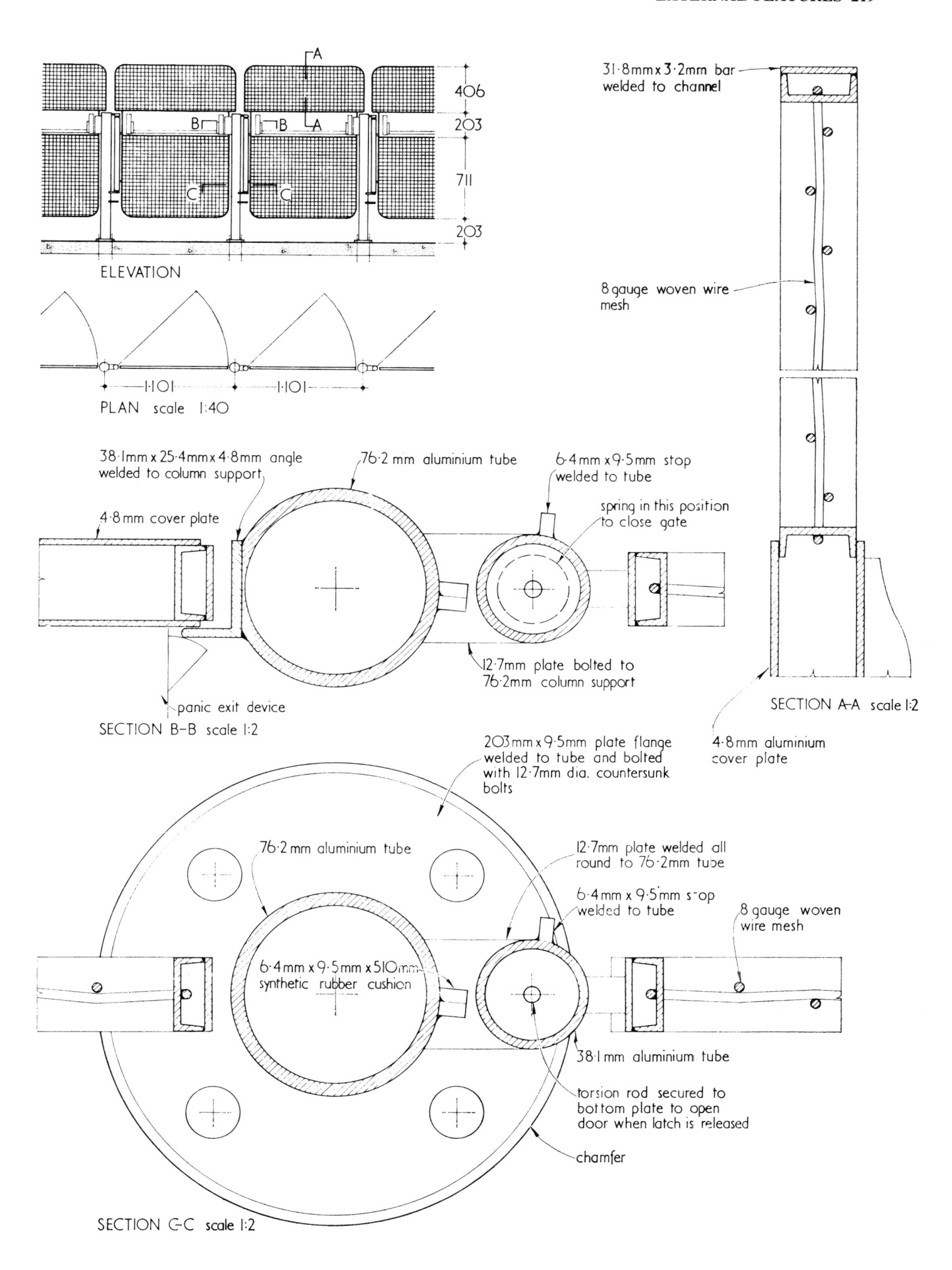

ELEVATION

PLAN scale 1:40

- 406
- 203
- 711
- 203
- 1·101
- 1·101

SECTION B-B scale 1:2

- 38·1mm x 25·4mm x 4·8mm angle welded to column support
- 4·8mm cover plate
- 76·2 mm aluminium tube
- 6·4mm x 9·5mm stop welded to tube
- spring in this position to close gate
- 12·7mm plate bolted to 76·2mm column support
- panic exit device

SECTION A-A scale 1:2

- 31·8mm x 3·2mm bar welded to channel
- 8 gauge woven wire mesh
- 4·8mm aluminium cover plate

SECTION C-C scale 1:2

- 203mm x 9·5mm plate flange welded to tube and bolted with 12·7mm dia. countersunk bolts
- 76·2mm aluminium tube
- 12·7mm plate welded all round to 76·2mm tube
- 6·4mm x 9·5mm stop welded to tube
- 8 gauge woven wire mesh
- 6·4mm x 9·5mm x 510mm synthetic rubber cushion
- 38·1mm aluminium tube
- torsion rod secured to bottom plate to open door when latch is released
- chamfer

220 EXTERNAL FEATURES

ASBESTOS-CEMENT GARDEN WALL: HOUSE IN BERLIN, GERMANY
DESIGNED BY EDUARD LUDWIG *(Material supplied by Ferenc Lantos)*

Standard 11 ft. 6 in. lengths of square-section corrugated sheeting, bolted together along their length and secured in in-situ concrete foundations, are used for the construction of this asbestos-cement garden wall.

EXTERNAL FEATURES 221

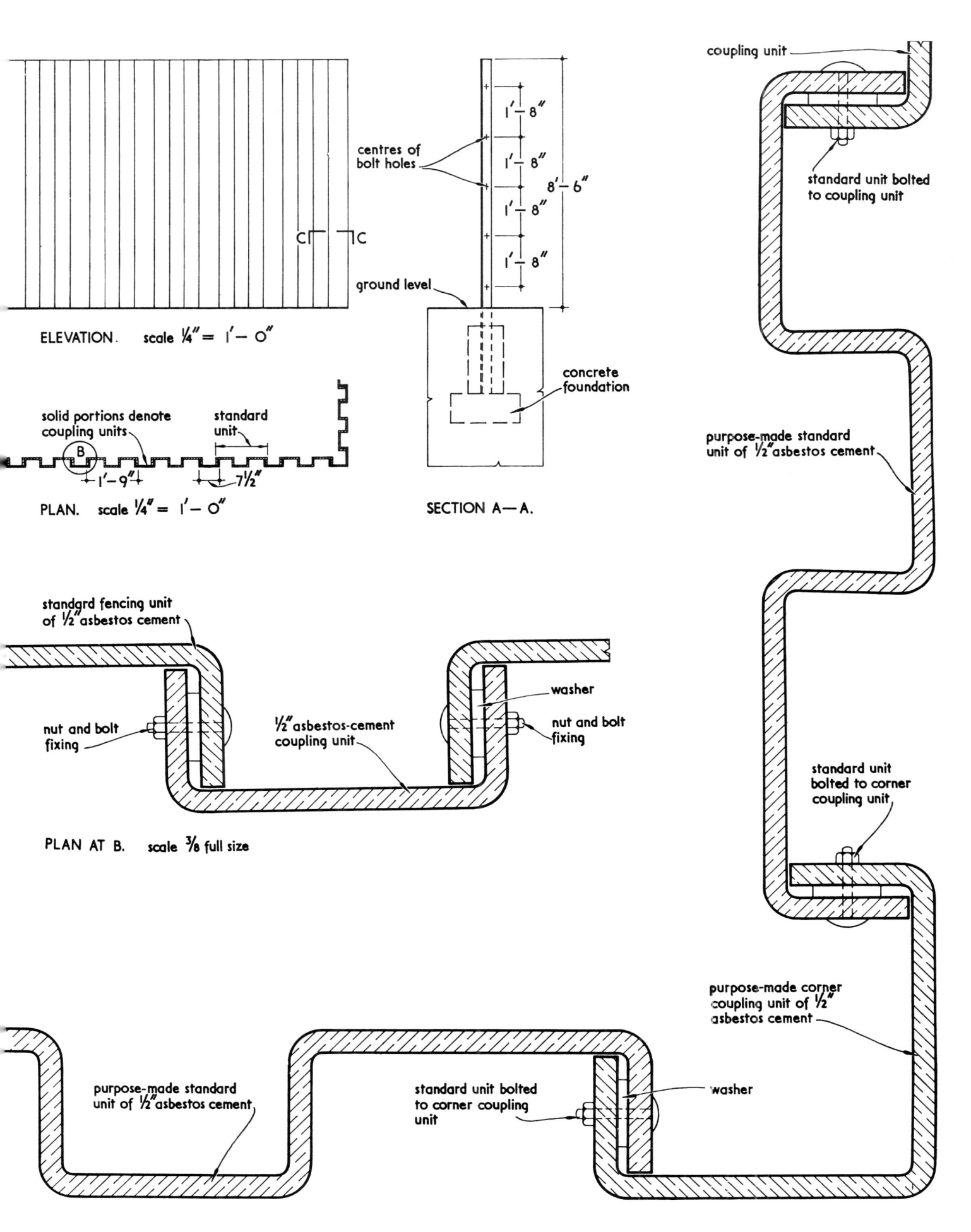

222 EXTERNAL FEATURES

CHIMNEY STACK AND WATER TANK: SCHOOL AT OLDBURY, WORCESTER
DESIGNED BY F. R. S. YORKE, E. ROSENBERG AND C. S. MARDALL
IN ASSOCIATION WITH F. W. B. YORKE AND H. M. BARKER

*The stack and tank are of concrete construction
and the outside of the latter is faced with 6 in. by 6 in.
frostproof tiles*

EXTERNAL FEATURES 223

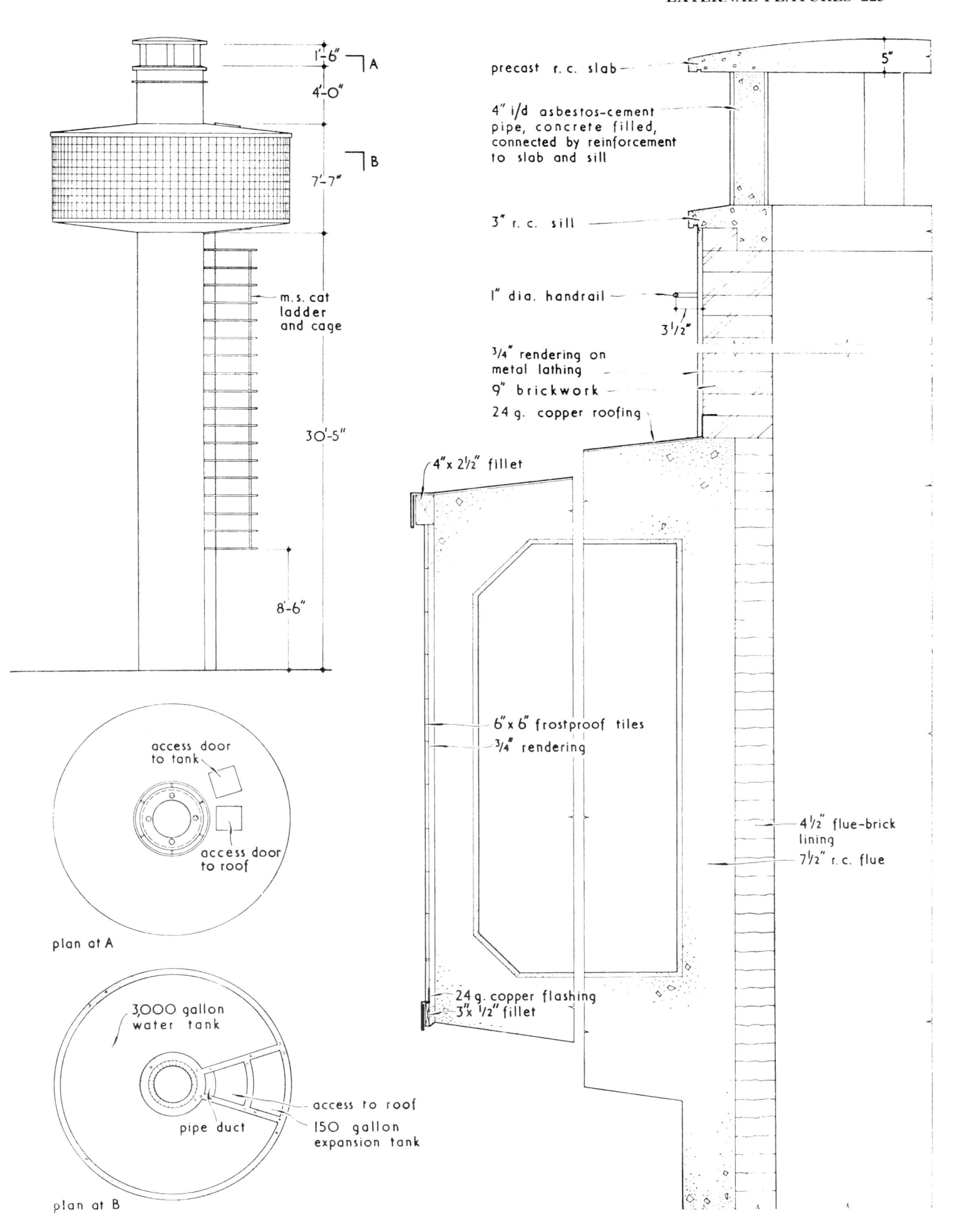

Labels on plans and elevation (left):

1'-6" A
4'-0"
B
7'-7"
m.s. cat ladder and cage
30'-5"
8'-6"

plan at A
access door to tank
access door to roof

plan at B
3,000 gallon water tank
pipe duct
access to roof
150 gallon expansion tank

PLANS AND ELEVATION. scale 1/8"=1'-0"

Labels on section (right):

precast r.c. slab
5"
4" i/d asbestos-cement pipe, concrete filled, connected by reinforcement to slab and sill
3" r.c. sill
1" dia. handrail
3½"
¾" rendering on metal lathing
9" brickwork
24 g. copper roofing
4" x 2½" fillet
6" x 6" frostproof tiles
¾" rendering
4½" flue-brick lining
7½" r.c. flue
24 g. copper flashing
3" x ½" fillet

SECTION THRO' TANK. scale ¾"=1'-0"

224 EXTERNAL FEATURES

TANK COVER AND SCREEN: SCHOOL IN LONDON, W.1
DESIGNED BY DRAKE AND LASDUN

The main tanks rest on r.s.j's. and are enclosed with 2-in. cork slab glued to the metal. Two layers of roofing felt were applied to the sides and top of the tanks, and the sides were further secured with chicken-wire netting. The aluminium glazing bars holding the tinted glass of the screen were screwed top and bottom to 2-in. by ½-in. m.s. hoops which were in turn cleated to a framework of 3-in. m.s. angles. The angles in the bottom framework were bolted to the r.s.j's. supporting the tanks; the top framework rests on pressure-creosoted deal pads laid on the felt-covered tank tops. L-shaped 'stabilisers' bolted to the framework and wedged to the sides of the tank further stops movement. Steelwork was painted with four coats of bituminous paint.

EXTERNAL FEATURES

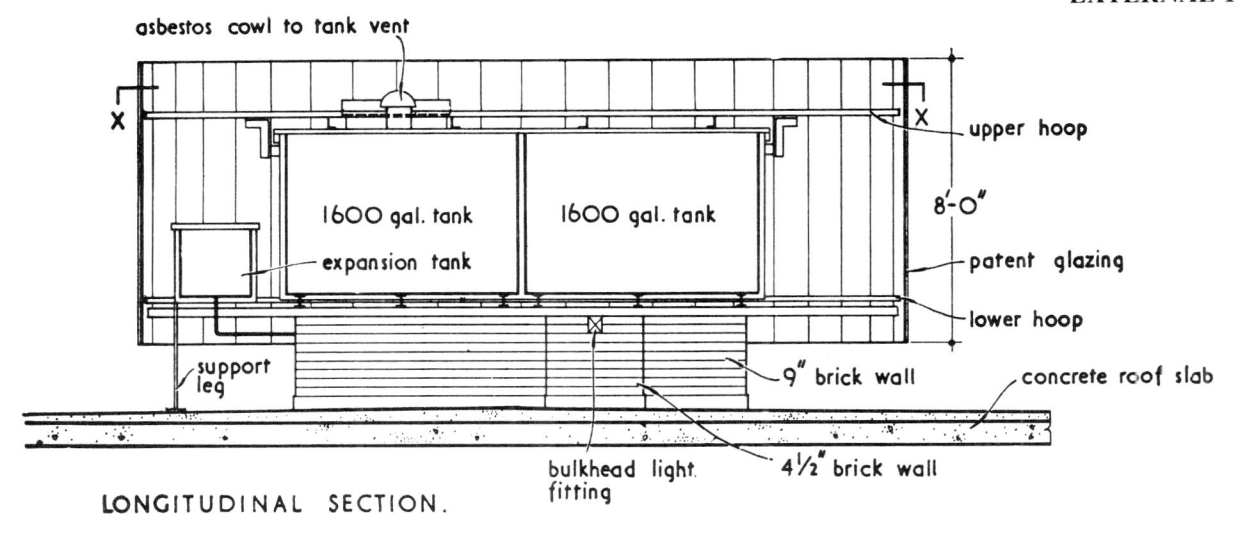

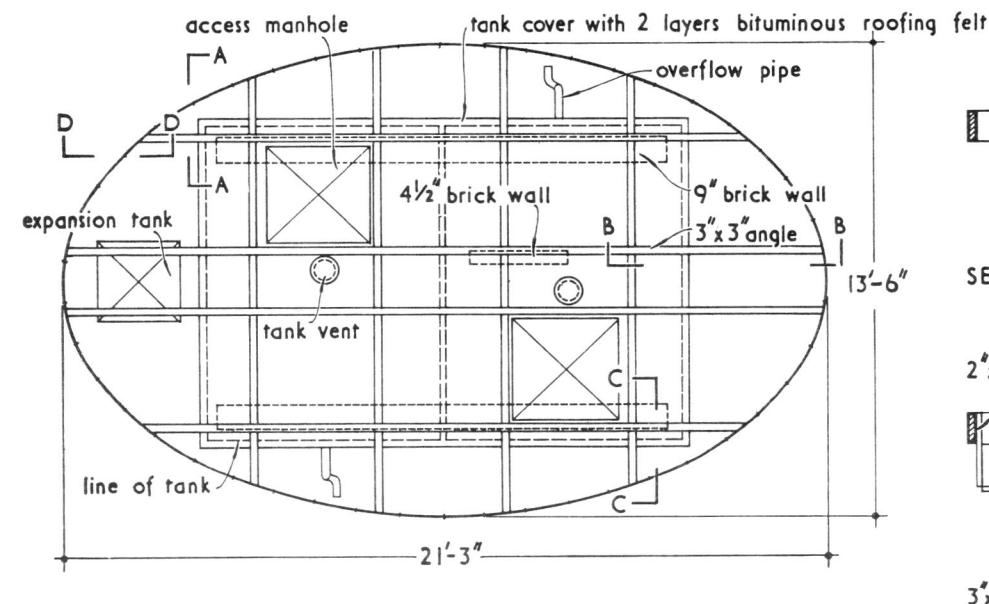

LONGITUDINAL SECTION.

Labels: asbestos cowl to tank vent; upper hoop; 1600 gal. tank; 1600 gal. tank; 8'-0"; expansion tank; patent glazing; lower hoop; support leg; 9" brick wall; concrete roof slab; bulkhead light fitting; 4½" brick wall

PLAN AT X-X. scale 3/16" = 1'-0"

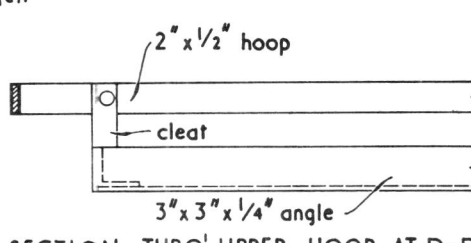

Labels: access manhole; tank cover with 2 layers bituminous roofing felt; overflow pipe; 4½" brick wall; 9" brick wall; 3"x3" angle; expansion tank; tank vent; line of tank; 13'-6"; 21'-3"

SECTION THRO' UPPER HOOP AT D-D.

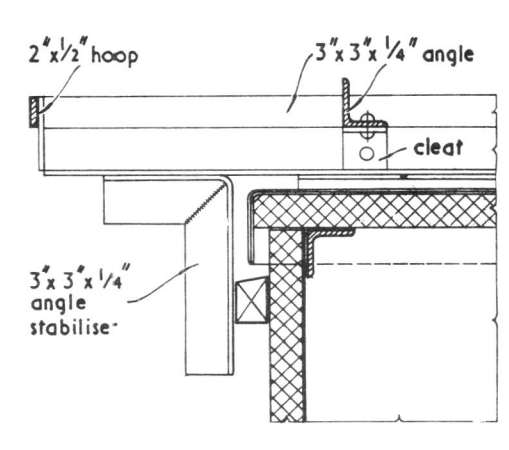

Labels: 2"x½" hoop; cleat; 3"x3"x¼" angle

SECTION THRO' UPPER HOOP AT C-C.

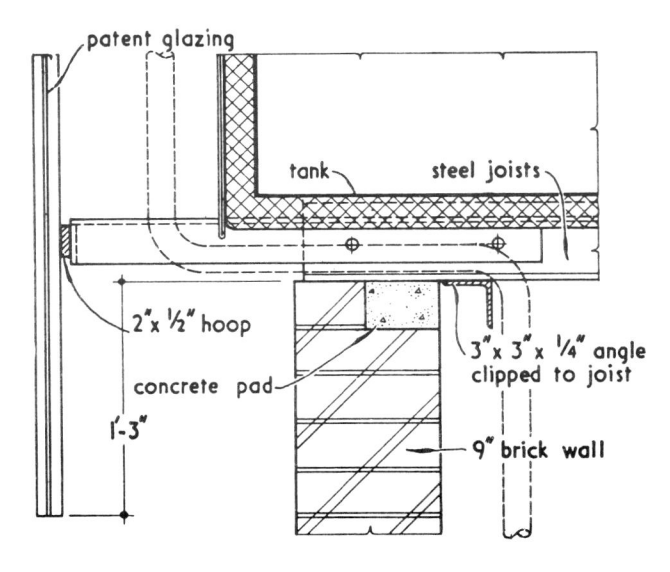

Labels: 2"x½" hoop; 3"x3"x¼" angle; cleat; 3"x3"x¼" angle stabiliser

SECTION THRO' LOWER HOOP AT A-A.

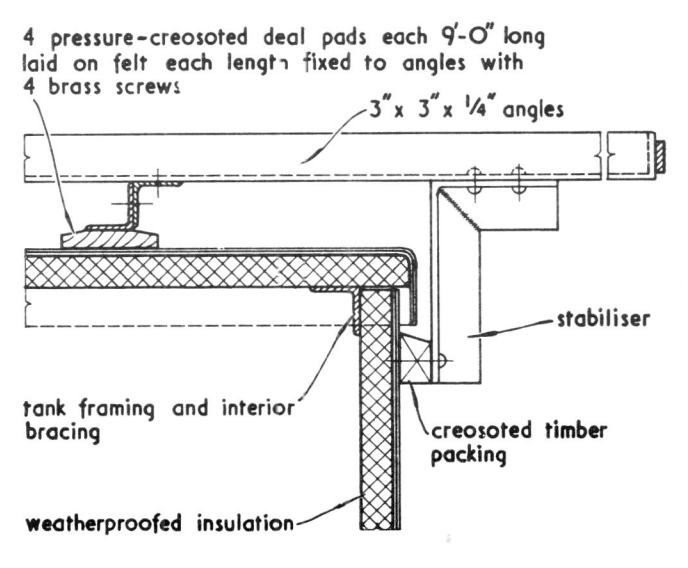

Labels: patent glazing; tank; steel joists; 2"x½" hoop; concrete pad; 3"x3"x¼" angle clipped to joist; 9" brick wall; 1'-3"

SECTION THRO' UPPER HOOP AT B-B. scale 1"=1'-0"

Labels: 4 pressure-creosoted deal pads each 9'-0" long laid on felt each length fixed to angles with 4 brass screws; 3"x3"x¼" angles; stabiliser; tank framing and interior bracing; creosoted timber packing; weatherproofed insulation

226 EXTERNAL FEATURES

SHELTER: STREET IN STOCKHOLM, SWEDEN
DESIGNED BY STOCKHOLM PARKS DEPARTMENT (*Material supplied by G. Dukes*)

The structural dissociation of the screens, the roofing and the structure enables each to be designed sensibly if not economically, and the use of rolled steel sections in the structure gives this shelter a good architectural character.

EXTERNAL FEATURES 227

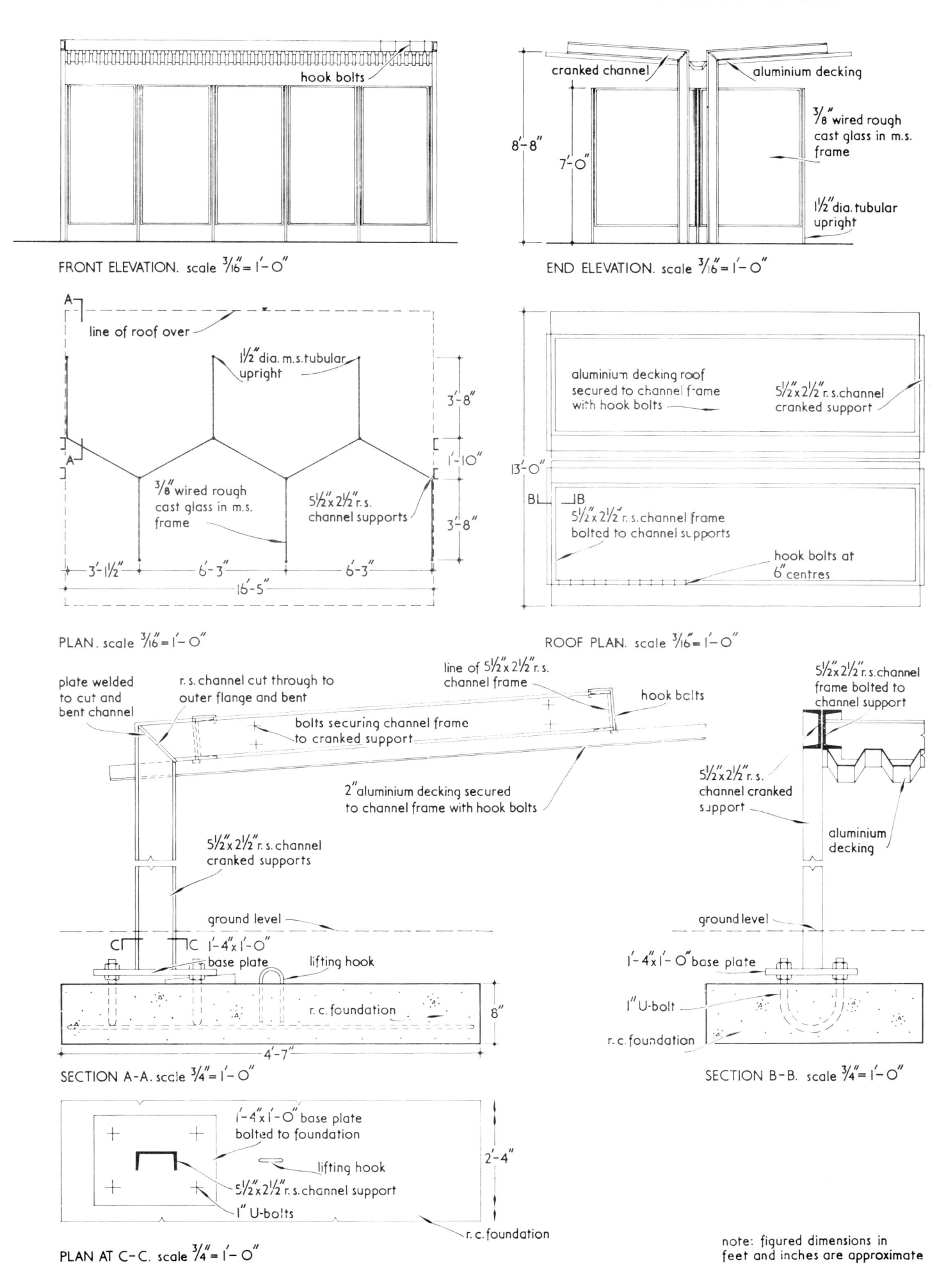

ENGLISH	FRENCH	GERMAN	SPANISH
Absorbent material	Matériau absorbant	Absorptionsmaterial	Material absorbente
Access	Accès	Zugang	Acceso, entrada
Acoustic tile	Dalle acoustique	akustische Fliese	Baldosa acustica
Acrylic sheeting	Feuillard acrylique	Akrylverkleidung	Plancha de plástico acrilico
Adjustable shelf	Étagère réglable	Verstellbares Gestell, Bort	Estante ajustable
Aggregate	Agrégat	Zuschlagstoff	Arido, (aglomerado)
Air-conditioning	Conditionnement de l'air	Klimaanlage	Aire-acondicionado
Air diffuser	Diffuseur d'air	Lufttrichter, Diffusor	Difusor
Air space	Couche d'air	Luftraum	Cavidad
Alloy	Alliage	Legierung	Aleación
Anchor	Ancrage	Anker	Ancla (enclaje)
Angle	Angle	Winkel, Ecke	Ángulo
Anodised metal	Métal anodisé	veredeltes Metall	Metal anodizado
Aperture	Ouverture	Öffnung	Avertura
Area	Surface	Fläche	Area
Arm	Bras	Arm, Querträger, Ausleger	Brazo
Arm rest	Accoudoir	Armlehne	Apoyo
Armour plate glass	Verre blindé	Verbundglas	Vidrio armada
Asbestos-cement	Amiante-ciment, fibrociment	Asbestzement	Fibrocemento
Ashtray	Cendrier	Aschenbecher	Cenicero
Assembly	Ensemble, montage	Aufbau, Aufstellung, Zusammenbau	Ensamble, montar
Attenuation box	Boitier d'étouffement, d'affaiblissement (des sons)	Schalltilgungskasten	Caja de atenuación
Back	Arrière	Rückseite	Parte posterior
Backing	Remplissage, renforcement, revêtement	Hintermauerung	Macizado
Backrest	Dossier	Rückenlehne	Respaldo
Balcony	Balcon	Balkon	Balcon
Ball	Bille, boule	Ball	Balón
Ballast	Ballast, blocaille	Ballast, Schotter,	Balastro
Baluster	Balustre	Geländerpfosten	Balaustre
Balustrade	Balustrade	Geländer	Balaustrada
Banister	Rampe (d'escalier)	Geländer	Estandarte, mastil
Bar, metal	Barre, métal	Metalleiste	Barra (redondo)
Barrier	Barrière	Schranke, Sperre,	Barrera
Basalt lava stone	Lave basaltique	Basalt, Lavastein	Piedra de basalto
Base	Base	Grundlage, Basis, Boden, Fundament, Fuss	Base
Basement	Cave, sous-sol	Kellergeschoss, Keller	Sótano
Basin	Bassin	Becken	Lavabo
Batten	Latte	Latte, Leiste,	Listón
Bead	Rebord	Flantsch	Bocel
Beam	Poutre	Balken,	Viga
Bearer	Sous-porte, poutre inférieure	Träger, Unterzug	Cabecera, soporte
Bed (garden bed)	Parterre (de jardin)	Beet (Gartenbeet)	Engravado, lecho de ...
Bed (layer or mortar)	Assise, lit (de béton, etc)	Schicht (Mörtelschicht)	Lecho, solado
Bench (laboratory)	Table de manipulations (laboratoire)	Bank (Werkbank)	Mesa de laboratorio
Bitumen	Bitume	Bitumen,	Betún
Bituminous	Bitumeux	bituminös	Bituminoso
Black	Noir	schwarz	Negro
Blade	Lame	Blatt, Klinge	Cuchilla
Blind (sunblind)	Store, jalousie	Markise, (Sonnenblende)	Celosia, persiana
Block	Bloc	Block, Klotz	Block
Blockboard	Panneau aggloméré	Spanholz	Chapeado de madera, contraplacado
Blocking	Blocage	Verschalung	Refuerzo
Board, boarding	Panneau, planchéiage	Brett, Diele, Verschalung,	Tabla, tablero, tablón
Bolt	Boulon	Bolzen, Riegel	Pestillo, cerrojo
Bolted	Support boulonné	verriegelt	Atornillado, asegurado
Booking office	Bureau de réservations	Fahrkartenschalter	Taquilla
Boot rack	Trémie, coffre, caisson	Schuhgestell	Vuelo, saliente para las botas
Bottom plate	Plaque inférieure	Bodenplatte, Sohlplatte, Fundament	Placa inferior

ENGLISH	FRENCH	GERMAN	SPANISH
Bottom-hung window	Fenêtre à suspension inferieure	an der Unterseite aufgehängtes Fenster	ventana con pernios en la base
Bowl	Godet, benne, caisse	Schale	Cuenco
Box	Boîte	Behälter, Kasten	Caja
Box Section	Section en caisson	Kastenprofil	Cuadrado de ...
Brace, bracing	Contre-fiche, renforcement	Strebe, Verstrebung	Abrazadera
Bracket	Support	Stütze, Träger	Soporte, palomilla
Brass	Laiton, cuivre jaune	Messing	Latón
Brazed metal	Métal brasé	verlotetes Metall	Metal soldado
Brick	Brique	Ziegel	Ladrillo
Brickwork	Maçonnerie	Backstein, Mauerwerk, Gemäuer	Fabrica
Bronze	Bronze	Bronze,	Bronce
Building	Bâtiment, édifice	Bauwerk	Edificio, construcción
Built-up roofing	Couverture multi-couche, étanchéite	Gestärktes Dachwerk	Techado compuesto
Bulb (lighting)	Ampoule (électrique)	Birne (elektrische)	Lampara, bombilla
Bush, bushing	Bague, coussinet, manchonnage	Buchse, Futter,	Collera
Cable	Câble	Kabel	Cable
Cafeteria	Cafétéria	Cafeteria	Cafeteria
Canopy	Auvent, marquise	Wetterdach	Marquesina
Cantilever	Porte-à-faux, encorbellement	Freiträger, freitragend	Cantiléver, voladizo
Capping	Chaperon, pierre de couverture (mur)	Bedeckung	Albardilla
Car Park	Parking	Autopark	Aparcamiento
Carpet	Tapis, moquette	Teppich	Alfombra
Case, casing	Boitier, encadrement	Gehäuse, Bekleidung, Verschalung	Casa, envasonado
Cast bronze	Bronze coulé	Gussbronze	Fundición en bronce
Cast iron (c.i.)	Fonte	Gusseisen	Fundición en hierro
Caulk	Entaillure, calfeutrement	Abdichtung, Einstemmen	Ramplón
Cavity	Creux	Höhlung, Vertiefung, Hohlraum	Cavidad
Cedar	Cèdre	Zeder	Cedro
Ceiling	Plafond	Decke	Techo
Cement	Ciment	Zement	Cemento
Centre line (c.l.)	Ligne médiane, axiale	Mittellinie	Linea central
Ceramic tile	Dalle de céramique	Keramische Fliese	Cerámica
Chamfer	Chanfrein	Schrägkante, Abschrägung	Chaflán
Channel	Caniveau, semi-caniveau	Kanal, Rinne, Ausflusskanal	Canal, mediacaña
Channel section	Profil en U	U-Querschnitt, Doppel-T-Profil, U-Profil	Sección acanalada, estriada
Changing room	Vestiaire	Umkleideraum	Vestuario
Chimney	Cheminée	Schornstein, Kamin	Chimenea, hogar
Chip, chipping	Gravillon, chippings	Splitter, Abfall	Granito desmenuzado, grava de granito
Chrome	Chrome	Chromium	Cromo
Chromium	Chromé	Chrom	Cromado -a
Chromium plated (c.p.)	Chromé	verchromt	Placa cromada (p.c.)
Church	Église	Kirche	Iglesia
Cladding	Revêtement, encapsulage	Verkleidung, Belag	Revestimiento
Clamp	Bride de serrage	Klammer	Pinza
Clayware	Produits de terre cuite	Steingut	Elemento de arcilla
Cleaning (window)	Nettoyage (fenêtre)	Fensterputzen	Limpieza de ventana
Cleat	Crampon	Klemmplatte	Zuncho
Clevis	Jumelle, anneau d'accouplement	Bügel, Haken	Horquilla
Clip	Attache, pince	Halter, Klammer, Klemmplatte	Grapa, brida
Clip-on tiles	Dalles ou carreaux à fixations métalliques	Versteckziegel, Versteckfliesen	Baldosas de mordaza
Closed door	Porte fermée	geschlossene Tür	Puerta cerrada
Closure strip	Bande de fermeture	Abschlusstreifen	Tapajuntas
Clothes rail	Portemanteau	Kleiderstange	Barra para la vestidura
Coat hanger	Cintre	Kleiderbügel	Percha
Coat hook	Patère	Mantelhaken	Gancho, escarpia
Coat of paint, etc.	Couche de peinture, etc	Schicht	Una mono de pintura
Collar	Col, collier	Kragen, Bund, Hals	Cuello
Coloured	De couleur	farbig, bunt	Coloreado
Column	Colonne	Säule, Pfeiler	Columna

GLOSSARY OF FOREIGN TERMS

ENGLISH	FRENCH	GERMAN	SPANISH
Concrete	Béton	Beton	Hormigón
Conduit	Conduit	Rohrleitung, Kanal	Conducto
Connection	Connexion	Anschluss	Conexión
Continuous	Type continu	fortlaufend, durchlaufend	Continuo
Control (s)	Commande (s)	Kontrolle, Leitung	Control (es)
Coping	Chape, dalle de recouvrement	Verdeckung, Abdeckung	Albardilla
Copper	Cuivre	Kupfer	Cobre
Core	Noyau, âme, mêche	Kern	Núcleo
Cork	Liège	Kork	Corcho
Corner	Coin	Ecke	Esquina
Corrugated	Ondulé	gewellt	Acanalado
Counter	Comptoir	Ladentisch, Schalter	Mostrardor
Countersunk (c.s.)	A tête noyée, fraisée	versenkt	Avellanado
Counter top	Surface de comptoir	Ladentischoberseite	Tablero mostrador
Cover	Couvercle, couverture	überdeckung, Schutzdeckel, Haube	Funda
Cover strip	Bande de couverture	Abschlusskappe	Listón, tapajunta
Crimped steel plate	Tôle d'acier sertie	Falzstahlplatte	Ribete de acero
Cross bracing	Entretoisement	Kreuzverband, Kreuzverspannung	Ensambladura en cruz
Cubicle	Cabine, alcôve, box	Zelle	Cabina
Cupboard	Placard	Schrank	Armario
Curtain	Rideau	Vorhang	Cortina
Curtain wall	Mur ou cloison d'extérieur	Fachwerkwand	Barra de cortina
Cushion	Coussin	Kissen	Cojin
Cut-out (electrical)	Disjonction (électrique)	Ausschalter (elektrisch)	Corte (eléctrico)
Damper	Amortisseur	Dämpfer, Dämpfungsvorrichtung, Klappe	Registro
Damp proof	Étanche	feuchtigkeitssicher	Capa aislante
Damp proof course (D.p.c.)	Couche hydrofuge	Bodensperrschicht	Hilada aislante
Decking	Tablier	Tragfläche, Rost	Paneles de cubierta
Demountable	Démontable	abnehmbar	Desmontable
Department Store	Grand magasin	Warenhaus	Almacén
Desk	Bureau (meuble)	Schreibtisch	Escritorio, mostrador
Dial (telephone)	Cadran d'appel (téléphone)	Wählscheibe (Telephon)	Marcar
Diameter (dia.)	Diamètre (dia.)	Durchmesser	Diametro
Diffuser	Diffuseur	Diffusor	Rejilla difusora de absorción
Dimension	Dimension	Abmessung	Dimensión
Dining cubicles	Alcôves de salle à manger (restaurant)	Esszellen	Cabina-comedor
Display board	Panneau d'affichage	Schaubrett	Tablero mostrario
Distribution (box)	Distribution (boîte)	Verteiler (-kasten)	Caja de distribución
Divider (division)	Séparation	Teiler, Verzweiger	Partición, división
Door	Porte	Tür	Puerta
Double-glazed	Double vitrage	doppelverglast	Cristal doble
Dowel	Goujon	Dübel	Espiga redonda
Drain	Égout	Abfluss	Tuberia
Drainage	Drainage, tout-à-l'égout	Abfluss	Drenaje
Drainpipe	Gouttière	Abflussrohr	Tubo de drenaje
Drawer	Tiroir	Schublade	Cajón
Drilled metal	Métal perforé	Bohrmetall	Metal taladrado
Drilling	Perforation, perçage, forage	Bohrung	Taladro
Drinking fountain	Fontaine publique, poste d'eau potable	Trinkbrunnen	Fuente
Drying cupboard	Séchoir	Trockenschrank	Tendedero
Duckboard	Passerelle	Lattenrost	Tablón de listónes clavados
Duct	Canalisation, Conduit	Kanal, Leitung, Durchführung	Condúcto
Earthenware	Poterie	Steingut	Elemento de arcilla
Edge	Bord	Rand, Bort, Kante	Arista, canto
Edging	Bordure	Umrandung, Vorstoss	Guarnición
Electric cables	Câbles électriques	elektrische Kabel	Cables electricos
Electrical	(Appareillage) électrique	elektrisch	Electrico
Element	Élément	Element, Glied, Teil	Elemento
Elevation	Élévation, façade	Vorderansicht, Fassade	Alzado
Embossed panel	Panneau travaillé en relief	Flachreliefplatte, Bückelplatte	Panel, embutido
Enamel	Émail	Emaille	Esmalte
End	Fin	Ende	Fin, final
End Wall	Mur d'extrémité	Endwand	Final de pared

232 GLOSSARY OF FOREIGN TERMS

ENGLISH	FRENCH	GERMAN	SPANISH
Entrance	Entrée	Eingang	Entrada
Epoxy resin	Résine époxy	Epoxydharz	Resina epoxídica
Exhibition	Exposition	Ausstellung	Exhibición
Expanded metal	Métal déployé	Streckmetall	Metal estirado, desplegado
Expansion bolt, joint	Boulon de scellement, joint de dilatation	Ausdehnungsfuge, Dehnfuge	Junta de dilatación
Exposed hardwood	Bois dur à découvert	freiliegendes Hartholz	Madera expuesta
External	Extérieur	aussenseitig, äusserlich	Externo, exterior
Extract fan	Ventilateur d'extraction	Lüftungsventilator	Extractor
Extruded aluminium, etc.	Aluminium extrudé, etc	stranggepresstes Aluminium	Aluminio extruido
Extrusion	Extrudage	Ausstossung	Repisa
Eye bolt	Boulon à oeil, anneau à piton	Augbolzen, Gewindeöse	Anilla
Fabric	Étoffe	Tuch	Fibra, tela
Face	Devant	Fläche	Cara
Facing	Revêtement, parement	Verkleidung	Revestimiento
Factory	Usine	Fabrik	Factoria, fabrica
Fairfaced	Lisse (chape)	Glattgemachter Grips	Yeso enrasado
False ceiling	Faux plafond	eingezogene Decke	Falso techo
Fan	Ventilateur	Ventilator	Ventilador
Fascia	Fasce	Stirnbrett, Traufbrett	Imposta
Fastener	Fermeture, attache	Verschluss	Grapa
Felt	Feutre	Filz	Fieltro
Fibre	Fibre	Faser	Fibra
Fibreboard	Panneau de matière fibreuse	Faserplatte	Tablero
Fibreglass	Fibre de verre	Faserglas	Fibra de vidrio
Filler piece	Pièce de remplissage, garnissage	Einlagestück, Stopfstück	Pieza de relleno
Fillet	Latte d'habillage	Leiste	Listón, chaflán
Filling	Remplissage, remblai	Füllung	Cubrejuntas
Fin	Ailette, bavure	Bart, Finne, Naht	Aleta
Finish	Fini, finition	Finish, Anstrichfilm	Acicalar
Fir	Sapin	Tanne	Abeto
Fire	Feu, incendie	Feuer	Fuego
Fire brick	Brique réfractaire	feuerfester Ziegel	Ladrillo refactario
Fireplace	Cheminée, âtre	Kamin	Hogar
Fireproofing	(Traitement) calorifuge	Feuerschutz	Protección contra incendios
First floor	Premier étage	erster Stock	Primer piso (Piso Primero)
Fitted	Monté, ajusté	ausgestattet	Aclopado, colocado
Fitting	Agencement, aménagement	Ausrüstung, Zusammenbau	Ajuste
Fix, fixing	Encastrement, ancrage, assujettissement	Einspannung, Zusammenstellen	Fijo
Fixed window	Fenêtre fixe	unbewegliches Fenster	Ventana fija
Flange	Flasque, bride	Flantsch	Collarin, brida
Flashing	Bavette, solin	Maueranschluss	Forrado
Flat (adjective)	Plat (adj.)	flach	Plana, liso
Flat (building)	Appartement (immeuble)	Appartment, Wohnung	Apartamento (piso)
Flat plate	Plaque plane	Flachplatte	Chapa plana
Flex	Câble flexible	Litze	Conducto electrico
Flexible	Souple, flexible	biegsam	Flexible
Floor	Plancher	Fussboden	Piso
Fluorescent lighting	Éclairage fluorescent	Leuchtrohre	Tubo fluorescente
Flyscreen	Écran contre les mouches	Sieb, Wurfsieb	Malla metalica
Foam rubber	Caoutchouc mousse	Schaumgummi	Goma-espuma
Foundation	Fondation	Fundament, Unterlage	Cimiento
Fountain	Fontaine	Brunnen	Fuente
Frame, framing	Cadre, encadrement	Rahmen, Umrahmung	Marco
Front	Avant, devant	Front, Stirn	Frente, alzado
Funnel	Entonnoir, trémie	Schornstein	Embudo
Furniture	Mobilier, ameublement	Möbel	Muebles
Galvanised iron (steel) (g.i.)	Tôle galvanisée	galvanisiertes Eisen (Stahl)	Metal galvanizado
Gasket	Joint d'étanchéité	Scheibe, Abdichtung	Empalme
Gate	Barrière	Tor	Verja
Gauge	Calibre, dimension	Masstab	Galga, calibre, dimensión
Gear	Engrenage, matériel	Getriebe	Aparejo
Girder	Poutre, solive	Balken, Träger	Viga (jácena)
Glare screen	Écran anti-éblouissant	Blendschirm	Superficie lisa
Glass	Verre	Glas	Cristal (luna)
Glass fibre	Fibre de verre	Glasfaser	Fibra de vidrio
Glass wool	Laine de verre	Glaswolle	Fibra de vidrio, vitrofibra

GLOSSARY OF FOREIGN TERMS

ENGLISH	FRENCH	GERMAN	SPANISH
Glazed wall	Séparation vitrée	glasierte Wand, verglaste Wand	Partieión de vidrio
Glazing	Vitrage	Verglasung	Cristal en posición
Globe (lighting)	Globe (éclairage)	Lampenglocke	Globo
Glove rack	Étagère à gants	Handschuhfach	Percha de guantes
Glue	Colle	Klebstoff	Cola
Gondola (for window cleaning)	Gondole (pour nettoyage des vitres)	Gondel (zum Fensterputzen)	Barquilla
Gravel	Gravier	Schotter	Grava
Grey	Gris	grau	Gris
Grid	Grillage	Gitter, Rost	Tela metalica, parrilla
Gridstone	Pierre à grille	Gitterstein, Schleifstein	Parrilla de adoquin
Grille	Grille	Gitter	Rejila
Groove	Virole, rainure	Kerb, Rille, Rinne	Ranura, rebajo
Ground floor	Rez-de-chaussée	Erdgeschoss	Planta baja
Grouting	Coulis, mortier clair	Zementierung	Embebido
Grummet	Rondelle	Unterlagsscheibe	Brida, boquilla
Guardrail	Garde-fou	Schutzschiene	Barandilla
Guide rail	Guide, barre d'appui	Laufschiene	Guia riel
Gutter	Gouttière	Dachrinne	Canalón
Gymnasium	Gymnase	Turnhalle	Gimnasio
Handle	Poignée	Griff, Halter	Mango, picaporte
Handrail	Main courante	Geländer	Padamano
Hanger	Cintre	Aufhänger	Estribo, herraje
Hardcore	Blocage	Trümmer, Steinschlag	Nucleo duro (endurecido)
Hardwood	Bois dur	Hartholz	Madera
Hat hook	Patère	Huthaken	Percha (para sombrero)
Haunching	Renfort, support	Feder	Espiga, refuerzo
Head	Supérieur, tête	Kopf, Dach, First	Cabeza
Heat	Chaleur	Hitze	Calor
Heater	Appareil de chauffage	Heizvorrichtung	Estufa
Heating	Chauffage	Heizung	Calefacción
Hermetically sealed	Scellé hermétiquement	luftdicht verschlossen	Hermeticamente cerrado
Hewn surface	Surface dégrossie, équarrie	behauene Fläche	Pulir, alisado
Hinge	Charnière	Türband	Bisagra, gonze
Hip	Arête (d'un comble)	Eckfirst, Grat, Hüfte	Caballete, lima tesa
Hip beam	Chevron d'arête	Grattäger	Cabio alto
Hole	Trou	Loch	Hueco
Hood	Hotte, capot	Abzugshaube, Kappe	Marquesina
Hook	Crochet	Haken	Gancho
House	Maison	Haus	Casa, edificio
Housing (structural)	Logement	Gehäuse, Nische (strukturell)	Bastidor
Ice house	Glacière	Eiskeller,	Fabrica de hielo (refrigerador)
Impregnated	Imprégné	impregniert	Impregnado
Induction unit	Unité d'induction	Induktionseinheit	Unidad de inducción
Inset	Pièce rapportée	Einsatz, Zwischenlage	Incrustación
Insitu concrete	Béton mélangé sur place	in situ Zement	Hormigón preparado
Installation	Installation	Einrichtung, Installation	Instalación
Insulation	Isolement thermique	Isolierung	Aislamiento
Intercom	Interphone	Rundspruchanlage	Teléfono interior
Internal	Intérieur	Innen	Interno
Intersection	Intersection	Schnittpunkt, Anschnitt, Kreuzungspunkt	Intersección
Inward-opening door	Porte ouvrant sur l'intérieur	sich nach innen öffnende Tür	Puerta, giro hacia dentro
Iron	Fer	Eisen	Hierro (metal)
Joint	Joint	Fuge, Naht	Junta
Joist	Poutre transversale	Balken	Tablón viga (vigueta)
Junction	Jonction, raccord	Stossfuge, Verbindungsstelle	Encuentro
Junction box	Boîte de raccordement	Anschlussdose, Kabelkasten, Anschlusskasten	Registro
Kerb	Bordure	Bordstein, Randstein	Bordillo
Kicking plate	Plinthe	Trittleiste	Zocalo de metal
Kneeling board	Panneau agenouilloir	Knieleiste	Elemento de madera para arrodillarse
Ladder	Échelle	Leiter	Escalera de tijera
Laminated wood	Bois stratifié	Schichtholz	Madera laminada
Lamp	Lampe	Lampe, Leuchte	Lampara
Larch	Mélèze	Lärche	Alerce

234 GLOSSARY OF FOREIGN TERMS

ENGLISH	FRENCH	GERMAN	SPANISH
Latch	Serrure de sûreté	Klinke	Seguro
Lavatory basin	Lavabo	Waschbecken	Lavabo
Law Courts	Cour de Justice	Gerichtsgebäude	Sala de justicia
Lawn, grass	Pelouse, herbe	Rasen (Gras)	Cesped
Layer	Couche	Schicht	Capa
Laylight	Fenêtre au plafond	Schichtlicht	Ventana de linterna
Lead	Plomb	Blei	Plomo
Leather	Cuir	Leder	Piel
Leg	pied, patte	Bein	Pata
Lens (glass)	Lentille, objectif (verre)	Linse (Glas)	Lentes
Lid	Couvercle	Deckel	Tapa
Light (lighting)	Lumière (éclairage)	Leuchte (Beleuchtung)	Iluminación
Light (window light)	Vitrage (carreau de fenêtre)	Verglasung	Ventana
Lighting	Éclairage	Beleuchtung	Electrico (punto)
Lightweight concrete	Béton léger	Leichtbeton	Cemento ligero
Limestone	Calcaire	Kalkstein	Piedra caliza
Lining	Garniture	Belag, Auskleidung, Ausfütterung	Forro
Link	Liaison, connexion	Gelenk	Conexión
Linoleum	Linoléum	Linoleum	Linoleo
Lip, lipping	Bord, rebord, lèvre	Ausguss, Ausgiessen	Borde
Lock	Serrure	Verschluss, Schloss	Cerradura
Locking device, nut, etc.	Dispositif (écrou etc.) de blocage	Verschlussvorrichtung, Gegenmutter, etc.	Caja de registros con seguro
Loop	Boucle	Öse, Schleife	Taladro, ojete
Louvre	Persienne	Jalousie mit unverstellbaren Platten	Respiradero, celosia
Lug	Oreille	Öse, Nase	Tetón, pivote
Magnet	Aimant	Magnet	Iman
Marble	Marbre	Marmor	Mármol
Mastic	Pâte à joints synthétique	Mastix	Masilla
Matt finish	Fini mat	mattes Finish	Terminación en mate
Mechanical	Mécanique	mechanisch	Instrumento mecanico
Member	Longeron, traverse	Glied	Miembro
Mesh	Treillis	Masche	Tela metálica
Mild Steel (m.s.)	Acier doux	weicher Stahl	Hierro laminado
Mineral wool	Laine minérale	Mineralwolle	Escoria
Mirror	Miroir, glace	Spiegel	Espejo
Monolithic	Monolithique	monolithisch	Monolitico
Mortar	Mortier	Mörtel	Mortero
Moulding	Moulure	Profil	Moldura
Mounting	Montage	Aufbau, Fassung, Futter	Montura
Mullion	Meneau	Fensterzwischenpfosten	Jamba, elemento de la vidriera
Multi-storey car park	Parking à plusieurs étages	Parkhochhaus	Edificio de aparcamiento
Museum	Musée	Museum	Museo
Natural finish	Fini naturel	natürliches Finish	Terminado al natural
Neoprene	Néoprène	Neopren	Goma sintetica
Non-ferreous metal	Métal non ferreux	nicht eisenhaltiges Metall	Metal anti-ferroso
Non-reflective glass	Verre non réflecteur (dépoli)	nicht reflektierendes Glas	Cristal sin reflexión
North	Nord	Norden	Norte
Nosing	Filet d'angle	Treppenstufennase	Guarda-cantos
Notched strip	Bande à encoches	gekerbter Spross	Entallado
Nursery	Nursery	Kinderzimmer, Kinderaufbewahrungsort	Emfermeria
Nut	Écrou	Mutter, Schraubenmutter	Tuerca
Oak	Chêne	Eiche	Roble
Obscured glass	Verre obscurci	Mattglas, mattes Glas	Vidrio opaco
O/d (outside diameter)	Diamètre ext.	Aussendurchmesser	Diametro exterior
Office building	Immeuble administratif	Bürogebäude	Edificio de Oficinas
Oil-rubbed bronze tube	Tube de bronze frotté à l'huile	ölpoliertes Bronzerohr	Tubo de bronce tratado con aceite
Open lid	Couvercle ouvert	offener Verschluss	Tapa Abierta
Opening light	Fenêtre ouvrante	zu öffnendes Licht	Hueco de ventilación
Oregon pine	Pin de l'Orégon	Oregonkiefer	Pseudotsuga taxifolia
Outlet	Sortie	Ausflussöffnung	Salida, escape
Outward-opening door	Porte ouvrant vers l'extérieur	sich nach aussen öffnende Tür	Puerta, giro hacia afuera

ENGLISH	FRENCH	GERMAN	SPANISH
Packing	Garniture, étoupe	Futter	Refuerzo, macizo
Pad	Tampon, plaquette	Polster	Apoyo para distribuir la carga
Painted	Peint	getüncht, bemalt	Pintado
Panel	Panneau	Platte, Tafel	Panel
Panic exit device	Dispositif de sortie d'urgence	Notöffnungsvorrichtung	Salida de emergencia
Parapet	Parapet	Balustrade	Parapeto
Particle board	Planchéiage de bois artificiel	gekörntes Holz	Contrachapado
Partition	Cloison	Zwischenwand	Partición, división
Patent glazing	Vitrage breveté	Patentverglasung	Luna asegurada
Path, pathway	Chemin, allée	Pfad	Senda, sendero
Pavers	Bétonnière motorisée	Plattenleger	Empedrado, adoquinado
Paving	Pavage, revêtement routier, pavé	Pflasterung	Pavimento
Pea gravel	Gravier fin	Kies von Erbsengrösse	Gravilla
Pebbles	Cailloux, galets	Kiesel	Cantos
Perforated metal	Métal perforé	perforiertes Metall, etc.	Metal perforado
Perimeter	Périmètre	Umfang	Perimetro
Piece	Pièce	Stück	Pieza
Pillar	Pillier	Pfeiler	Pilar
Pine	Pin	Kiefer	Pino
Pipe	Tuyau	Rohr	Tubo, tuberia
Pit	Fosse	Grube	Foso
Pitched roof	Toit en pente	Steildach	Cubierta de dos pendientes
Pivot	Pivot	Drehzapfen, Angel	Pivote
Pivot-hung (window)	Sur pivot (fenêtre)	Wendeflügelfenster	Ventana pivotante
Plan	Plan	Grundriss	Plano
Plank	Planche	Brett, Planke	Tablón
Plant bed (garden)	Parterre, planche (jardin)	Pflanzenbeet (Garten)	Area ajardinada
Plant (botanical) container	Conteneur pour plantes	Pflanzenbehälter	Caja para tener una planta
Plaster	Plâtre	Gips	Guarnecido
Plasterboard	Panneau plâtre	Gipsplatte	Yeso reforzado con cartón por ambos lados
Plastic	Plastique	Kunststoff	Plastico
Plate	Plaque	Platte	Placa
Plated finish	Fini plaqué	plattiertes Finish	Acabado de plancha
Plate glass	Glace de vitrage, verre laminé, cylindré	Spiegelglas	Cristal pulido
Platform	Plate-forme	Plattform	Plataforma
Play park	Parc de récréation	Spielpark	Jardin de recreo
Plinth	Plinthe	Sockel, Absatz	Zocalo
Plug	Obturateur, bouchon	Stecker	Tapón, taco
Plywood	Contreplaqué	Sperrholz	Contrachapado de madera
Polished	Poli	poliert	Lustre
Pool	Bassin (d'eau)	Schwimmbecken	Piscina
Portable unit	Unité portative, portable	transportable Einheit	Unidad portable
Post	Poteau, poste	Pfosten	Poste
Post-tensioned cable	Câble postcontraint	nachträglich gespanntes Kabel	Tirante (tensión)
Power outlet	Prise de courant	Stromanschluss	Toma de energia
Precast concrete (p.cc.)	Béton pré-coulé	Fabrikbeton	Hormigón prefabricado
Prefabricated	Préfabriqué	vorgefertigt	Prefabricado
Pressed steel	Acier embouti	Presstahl	Acero laminado
Pressure-formed metal	(Métal) formé sous pression	pressgeformtes Metall, etc.	Hierro forjado
Prestressed concrete	Béton précontraint	Spannbeton	Hormigón pretensado
Primary air supply	Alimentation d'air primaire	Erstluftzufuhr	Aire primario
Profile	Profil	Querschnitt, Seitenansicht	Perfil
Pull handle	Poignée	Ziehgriff	Tirador
P.V.C. (polyvinyl chloride)	P.V.C.	P.V.C.	Clorudo de polivinilo
Quarry tile	Dalle (tuile) de carrière	Bürgersteigplatte	Pizarra
Quilt	Matériel d'isolement	Steppdecke	Aislante termico
Rack	Cadre, rack	Gestell, Gerüst	Percha
Radiator	Radiateur	Heizkörper	Radiador
Rafter	Chevron	Sparren	Cabio
Rail, railing	Main courante, clôture, garde-fou	Geländer	Carril
Rainwater pipe (r.w.p.)	Gouttière	Abfallrohr	Bajante de pluviales
Rebate	Feuilleret (de rabot)	Rabatt	Rebajo
Receiver (telephone)	Combiné (téléphone)	Hörer (Telephon)	Auricular

236 GLOSSARY OF FOREIGN TERMS

ENGLISH	FRENCH	GERMAN	SPANISH
Recess	Renfoncement, niche	Nische	Retranqueo, mocheta
Red	Rouge	rot	Rojo
Redwood	Redwood, bois du Brésil	Rotholz	Pino silvestre
Reel of flex	Bobine de câble	Kabeltrage	Carrete de flex
Reinforced concrete (r.c.)	Béton armé	Stahlbeton	Hormigón armado
Reinforcement	Renforcement	Verstärkung	Refuerzo, armadura
Removable	Amovible	entfernbar	Movible
Rendering	Crépi, enduit	Putz, Verputz	Revocado
Resin	Résine	Harz	Resina
Return pipe	Tuyau de retour	Rückleitungsrohr	Tuberia de retorno
Reveal	Jouée, ébrasement	Leibung	Abierto
Reverse side	Envers (côté)	Rückseite	Lado opuesto
Rib	Arête	Rippe, gekrümmter Sparren	Costilla
River	Rivière	Fluss	Rio
Road	Route	Strasse	Carretera, calle
Rock wool	Laine minérale	Steinwolle	Mezcla de dolomita y arcilla silicea
Rod	Tige, barre	Stange, Stock	Barra, redondo
Rolled steel joist (r.s.j.)	Poutre d'acier laminé	Walzeisenträger	Viga perfil laminado
Rolled steel stanchion (r.s.s.)	Montant en acier laminé	Walzeisenrunge, – säule	Pilar perfil laminado
Roller blind	Store à rouleau	Rollblende	Persiana
Roll-up door	Porte escamotable sur cylindre supérieur	Rolltür	Puerta persiana
Roof	Toit	Dach	Tejado, cubierta
Rooflight	Lucarne, Lanterneau	Oberlicht	Traguluz
Room	Pièce (d'appartement)	Zimmer	Habitación, cuarto
Rope	Corde	Strick	Cordón, cuerda
Rough-sawn boarding	Planches grossièrement sciées	Blindboden	Tablón sin cepillar
Round-headed nut	Écrou à tête ronde	Rundkopf	Tuerca incrustada
Rubber	Caoutchouc	Gummi	Goma
Sand	Sable	Sand	Arena
Sash window	Fenêtre à guillotine	Aufziehfenster	Ventana de guillotina
Satin	Satin	Satin	Satinado
Scale	Échelle (de grandeurs)	Masstab	Escala
Scandinavian redwood	Redwood scandinave	Skandinavisches Rotholz	Pino silvestre escandinavo
School	École	Schule	Colegio
Screed	Couche de mortier ou béton	Putzleiste	Acabado de mortero
Screen	Écran	Schirm	Criba, arnero
Screw	Vis	Schraube	Tornillo
Sculpture, metal	Sculpture en métal	Skulptur, Metall	Escultura de metal
Seal, sealing, sealant	Scellement, étranchement	Verdichtung	Cierre hidraulico (hermetico)
Seat	Siège, assise	Sitz	Asiento
Seating	Assise	Sitzgelegenheit	Tipo de asiento
Section	Section, coupe	Teil	Sección
Securing bolt	Boulon de retenue, verrou, pêne, loqueteau	Befestigungsschraube	Cerroso con seguro
Security doors	Portes de sécurité	Sicherheitstür	Puertas de seguridad
Service panel	Panneau des services	Anschlusstafel	Registro de servicios
Services	Services	Versorgungsleitungen	Servicio
Sheet, sheeting	Feuille, tôle, flache	Verschalung, Einschalung	Plancha, piel
Sheet metal	Métal en plaques, tôles	Metallblatt	Plancha metálica
Shelf, shelves	Étagère	Bort, Ablage	Anaquel, anaqueles
Shingle	Gravier, bardeau	grober Kies	Grava de granito
Shoe	Chaussure	Schuh	Zapato
Shop	Boutique, magasin, atelier	Laden	Tienda
Shop-rivetted	Rivé à l'atelier	Werkstattgenietet	Remachado, remache
Showcase	Vitrine	Schaukasten	Escaparate, vitrina
Showroom	Salon d'exposition (d'un magasin)	Vorführraum	Escaparate
Shutter	Persienne	Laden	Contraventana
Side	Côté, latéral	Seite	Lado
Side-hung window	Fenêtre à charnières latérales	seitlich aufgehängtes Fenster	Ventana (con bisagras lateral)
Sill	Seuil, appui (de fenêtre)	Brett	Peana
Size (adhesive)	Apprêt, colle, détrempe	Leim, Kleister	Encoladura
Size (scale)	Dimensions (échelle)	Grösse, Mass	Medidas
Skin	Peau, recouvrement, superficiel	Haut	Terminado, mano
Skirting	Plinthes	Leiste	Rodapié, zócalo
Slab, slabbing	Dalle, dallage	Platte	Baldosa de pavimento
Sleeve	Manchon	Hülse	Arandela

GLOSSARY OF FOREIGN TERMS

ENGLISH	FRENCH	GERMAN	SPANISH
Sliding door, window	Porte, fenêtre coulissante	Schiebetür – fenster	Puerta, ventana corrediza
Sliding lid	couvercle coulissant	Gleitdeckel	Tapa corrediza
Slot, slotted	Fente, à fente(s)	Schlitz, geschlitzt	Ranura, ranurado
Snap-on ceiling	Plafond à fixation instantanée	einsetzbare Decke	Techo con corchete de sujeción
Snowguard	Pare-neige	Schneefang	Parapeto para nieve
Soffit	Douelle, intrados	Soffite	Sofito
Softwood	Bois résineux	Weichholz	Madera de coniferas
Soot door	Trappe à ramasser la suie	Reinigungstür	Registro de chimenea
Sound control	Contrôle acoustique	Schallkontrolle	Control de sonido
South	Sud	Süden	Sur
Spacer	Entretoise, pièce d'espacement	Abstandshalter	Anillo separador
Sphere	Sphère, globe	Kugel	Esfera
Spindle	Axe	Achse, Drehspindel	Polea
Splice plate	Couvre-joint	Verbindungsplatte	Capa de empalme
Split-pin	Goupille (fendue), clavette	Splint, Splinte	Pasador
Sponge	Éponge	Schwamm	Esponja
Spotlight	Projecteur convergent	Linsenscheinwerfer	Foco, lampara
Spout	Goulotte	Dachrinnenausguss	Caño
Spring	Ressort	Feder	Muelle, resorte
Spring-loaded	Monté sur ressort	gefedert	Muelle cargado
Sprinkler	Arroseuse	Sprenger	Extintores
Square section	Section carrée	Quadratprofil	Sección cuadrada
Stacked panels	Panneaux empilés	übereinandergestockte Platten, Tafeln	Paneles superpuestos
Stained finish	Fini mordancé (bois)	gebiztes, gesprenkeltes Finish	Teñido en ...
Stainless steel	Acier inoxydable	rostfreier Stahl	Acero anodizado
Stair	Marche, degré	Stufe	Escalera
Staircase	Escalier	Treppe	Escalera
Standard for lamp	Torchère	Ständer für Leuchte	Farola
Standard steel	(Acier) standard	Normalstahl	Acero (perfil normal)
Steel	Acier	Stahl	Acero
Step	Marche, gradin	Stufe	Peldaño
Stiffener	Renforcement	Aussteifung	Refuerzo
Stirrup	Étrier	Bügel	Anclaje
Stone	Pierre	Stein	Piedra
Stop (door-stop)	Arrêt, butée (de porte)	Türanschlag	Tope
Storage	Réserve, emmagasinage	Magazin, Lager, Ablage	Cuarto
Store	Magasin, réserve, entrepôt	Lager	Almacén
Stove-enamelled finish	Fini émaillé au four	Ofenlackfinish	Esmaltado al horno
Strainer	Filtre, crépine	Filter, Spanner	Filtro
Strap (connecting strap)	Courroie (de connexion)	Verbindungsband	Pletina
Strap hinge	Charnière-courroie	Bandscharnier	Pernio
Strip, stripping	Bande	Streifen	Listón, alistonado
Structural	Sturctural	Strukturell	Estructural
Structure	Structure, charpente	Struktur, Bau	Estructura
Stud wall	Mur de charpente	Pfostenfachwerkwand	Pared de entramado
Studding	Lattage, lattis, charpente, cloutage	Ausrahmen	Mainel
Sunblind	Store	Sonnenblende	Persiana
Sunbreaker	Brise soleil	Sonnenschutz	Protección solar
Sun visor	Pare-soleil	Sonnenschutz	Visera
Supply pipe	Tuyau d'amenée	Versorgungsrohr	Toma
Support	Support	Stütze	Soporte
Supporting rod	Tige (barre) de support	Stützpfosten	Soporte de barra
Suspended ceiling	Plafond suspendu	Hängedecke	Techo suspendido, falso techo
Suspension rod	Tige de suspension	Hängestange	Barra suspendida
Swimming pool	Piscine	Schwimmbad	Piscina
Synthetic rubber	Caoutchouc synthétique	Synthetischer Gummi	Goma sintetica
Table	Table	Tisch	Mesa
Tap	Robinet	Hahn	Grifo
Taper, to	Aller en s'amenuisant (de forme conique)	abschrägen	Remate en punta, pico
Teak	Teck	Teak	Teca
Tee section	Section en Té	T-Teil	Sección
Template	Plaque, semelle, sabarit	Platte, Tafel	Placa al temple
Thermoplastic tile	Dalle thermoplastique	Termoplastische Fliese	Azulejo termoplástico
Threaded rod	Tige filetée	Gewindestange	Barra en tensión

238 GLOSSARY OF FOREIGN TERMS

ENGLISH	FRENCH	GERMAN	SPANISH
Ticket window	Guichet	Fahrscheinschalter	Ventana de billetes
Tile	Dalle, tuile, carreau	Fliese	Baldosin
Tiled	Recouvert de dalles, tuiles ou carreaux	mit Fliesen belegt	Embaldosado
Timber	Bois de charpente	Holz	Madera
Tinted glass	Verre teinté	gefärbtes Glas	Cristal tratado
Tongue	Languette	Feder	Lengua
Tongued and grooved (t. and g.)	Embrevé, assemblage à rainure et languette	Nut und Feder	Ensamble a ranura y lengüeta
Top-hung door	Porte à charnières supérieures	Klapptür	Puerta de ventilación
Top member	Membrure supérieure	Deckglied	Cabio alto
Torsion rod	Barre de torsion	Drehstabfeder	Hierro torcido tetracero
Toughened (glass)	Verre trempé	Hartglas	Cristal endurecido
Track (curtain, lighting track)	Rail (rideau, rampe d'éclairage)	Schiene, (Vorhang, Leuchtschiene)	Carril
Training centre	Centre d'apprentissage	Schulungszentrum	Centro de ensenanza
Translucent panel	Panneau translucide	durchsichtige Tafel	Pavés, manpara transparente
Transom	Traverse, linteau, imposte, meneau horizontal	Oberlicht, Querbalken eines Skeletts	Montante
Tray	Plateau	Tablett	Bandeja
Tread	Giron (d'une marche d'escalier), échelon	Auftritt, Trittstufe	Huella
Treated wood	Bois traité	behandeltes Holz	Madera tratada
Triple glazing	Triple vitrage	Dreifachverglasung	Cristal triple
Trough	Auge, baquet	Abflussrinne, Rinne Wanne	Atresar
Trunk, trunking	Tronc	Verbindungsleitung	Conducto
Tube lighting	Éclairage au néon (tubes)	Leuchtröhr	Iluminación por tubo
Tube (metal)	Tube (métal)	Röhr (Metall)	Tubo metálico
Tungsten bulb	Ampoule au tungstène	Wolframbirne	Foco de volframio
Turnbuckle	Tendeur	Spannschloss, Spannmutter	Torniquete
Underside	Dessous, envers	Unterseite	Sofit
Unglazed clayware	Poterie non vernissée	unglasiertes Steingut	Gorgola de arcilla
Unit	Unité	Einheit	Unidad, elemento
Upright	Un montant	aufrecht, vertikal	De pie
Upstand	Vertical	Stütze	Resalto
Valve	Clapet, soupape	Ventil	Valvula
Vapour barrier	Barrière de vapeur	Dampfdichtung	Barrera de vapor
Varnish	Vernis	Lack	Barniz
Veneer	Plaqué	Furnier	Tablero
Venetian Blind	Store, jalousie (à lames mobiles)	Jalousie	Persiana veneciana
Vent	Évent, bouche d'aération	Entlüftungskanal	Tubo de ventilación
Ventilation	Ventilation, aération	Lüftung	Ventilación
Visor (sun vizor)	Pare-soleil	Blende (Sonnenblende)	Visera
Wall	Mur	Wand	Pared
Warm air	Air chaud	Warmluft	Aire caliente
Washer	Rondelle	Dichtung	Arandela
Waste-paper basket	Corbeille à papier	Papierkorb	Padelera
Water	Eau	Wasser	Agua
Water-bar	Barrière d'eau	Wasserbar	Cuadradillo
Waterproofing	Imperméabilisation	wasserdicht machen	Resistente humedo
Weep hole	Trou d'écoulement	Entwässerungsrohr	Agujero de desagüe
Weld	Soudure	Naht, Schweisstelle	Soldadura
Welded metal	Métal soudé	Schweissmetall	Metal soldado
Welfare centre	Dispensaire	Wohlfahrtszentrum	Asilo
West	Ouest	Westen	Oeste
White	Blanc	weiss	Blanco
Window	Fenêtre	Fenster	Ventana
Windowboard	Panneau de fenêtre	Fensterbrett	Repisa
Window cleaning	Lavage des vitres	Fensterputzen	Limpieza de ventana
Wire	Fil électrique ou métallique	Draht	Alambre
Wiring channel	Baguette électrique (pour câblage)	Schaltungskanal	Tubo berman
Wood	Bois	Holz	Madera
Woodwool	Laine, fibre de bois	Holzwolle	Aislante térmico
Wool	Laine	Wolle	Lana
Wrought-iron, steel, etc.	(Fer, acier, etc.) forgé.	Schweisstahl, etc	Hierro forjado

CONVERSION TABLES AND SCALES

Feet and inches to metres and millimetres (to nearest millimetre)

Feet	Inches 0	1	2	3	4	5	6	7	8	9	10	11
	Metres and millimetres											
0	—	25	51	76	102	127	152	178	203	229	254	279
1	305	330	356	381	406	432	457	483	508	533	559	584
2	610	635	660	686	711	737	762	787	813	838	864	889
3	914	940	965	991	1·016	1·041	1·067	1·092	1·118	1·143	1·168	1·194
4	1·219	1·245	1·270	1·295	1·321	1·346	1·372	1·397	1·422	1·448	1·473	1·499
5	1·524	1·549	1·575	1·600	1·626	1·651	1·676	1·702	1·727	1·753	1·778	1·803
6	1·829	1·854	1·880	1·905	1·930	1·956	1·981	2·007	2·032	2·057	2·083	2·108
7	2·134	2·159	2·184	2·210	2·235	2·261	2·286	2·311	2·337	2·332	2·388	2·413
8	2·438	2·464	2·489	2·515	2·540	2·565	2·591	2·616	2·642	2·637	2·692	2·718
9	2·743	2·769	2·794	2·819	2·845	2·870	2·896	2·921	2·946	2·972	2·997	3·023
10	3·048	3·073	3·099	3·124	3·150	3·175	3·200	3·226	3·251	3·277	3·302	3·327
11	3·353	3·378	3·404	3·429	3·454	3·480	3·505	3·531	3·556	3·581	3·607	3·632
12	3·658	3·683	3·708	3·734	3·759	3·785	3·810	3·835	3·861	3·886	3·912	3·937
13	3·962	3·988	4·013	4·039	4·064	4·089	4·115	4·140	4·166	4·191	4·216	4·242
14	4·267	4·293	4·318	4·343	4·369	4·394	4·420	4·445	4·470	4·496	4·521	4·547
15	4·572	4·597	4·623	4·648	4·674	4·699	4·724	4·750	4·775	4·801	4·826	4·851
16	4·877	4·902	4·928	4·953	4·978	5·004	5·029	5·055	5·080	5·105	5·131	5·156
17	5·182	5·207	5·232	5·258	5·283	5·309	5·334	5·359	5·385	5·410	5·436	5·461
18	5·486	5·512	5·537	5·563	5·588	5·613	5·639	5·664	5·690	5·715	5·740	5·766
19	5·791	5·817	5·842	5·867	5·893	5·918	5·944	5·969	5·994	6·020	6·045	6·071
20	6·096	6·121	6·147	6·172	6·198	6·223	6·248	6·274	6·299	6·325	6·350	6·375

Fractions of an inch to millimetres (to one place of decimals)

Inches	1/16	1/8	3/16	1/4	5/16	3/8	7/16	1/2	9/16	5/8	11/16	3/4	13/16	7/8	15/16
Millimetres	1·6	3·2	4·8	6·4	7·9	9·5	11·1	12·7	14·3	15·9	17·5	19·1	20·6	22·2	23·8

Additional Conversions

(Page 31): 23ft 0 in = 7·010 m   (Page 57): 24ft 1in = 7·341 m   (Page 93): 24ft 6in = 7·468 m
(Page 41): 30ft 0 in = 9·144 m   (Page 61): 29ft 6in = 8·992 m   (Page 113): 27ft 0in = 8·230 m
(Page 41): 55ft 4 in = 16·866 m   (Page 69): 24ft 9in = 7·544 m   (Page 151): 33ft 8in = 10·262 m
(Page 41): 87ft 4¾in = 26·638 m   (Page 91): 33ft 0in = 10·058 m   (Page 151): 63ft 10in = 19·456 m

Conversion Scales for Drawings

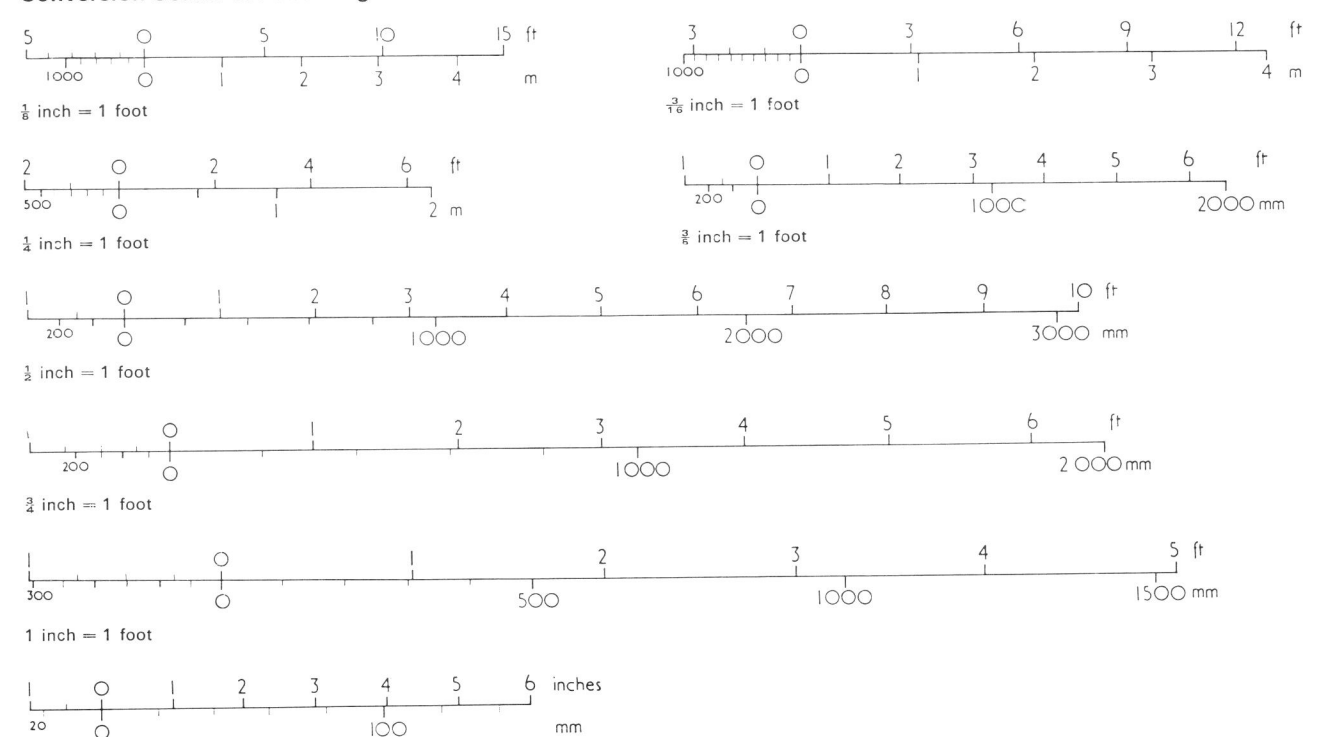

⅛ inch = 1 foot

3/16 inch = 1 foot

¼ inch = 1 foot

⅜ inch = 1 foot

½ inch = 1 foot

¾ inch = 1 foot

1 inch = 1 foot

⅜ full size